The Diversity of Irony

Cognitive Linguistics Research

Editors
Dirk Geeraerts
Dagmar Divjak

Honorary editors
René Dirven
Ronald W. Langacker

Volume 65

The Diversity of Irony

Edited by
Angeliki Athanasiadou
Herbert L. Colston

DE GRUYTER
MOUTON

ISBN 978-3-11-077751-2
e-ISBN (PDF) 978-3-11-065224-6
e-ISBN (EPUB) 978-3-11-064866-9
ISSN 1861-4132

Library of Congress Control Number: 2019955042

Bibliographic information published by the Deutsche Nationalbibliothek
The Deutsche Nationalbibliothek lists this publication in the Deutsche Nationalbibliografie;
detailed bibliographic data are available on the Internet at http://dnb.dnb.de.

© 2021 Walter de Gruyter GmbH, Berlin/Boston
This volume is text- and page-identical with the hardback published in 2020.
Typesetting: Integra Software Services Pvt. Ltd.
Printing and binding: CPI books GmbH, Leck

www.degruyter.com

Preface

Irony as a broad phenomenon has been addressed by modern language and communication sciences as one of two primary things: verbal irony, involving irony in a person's spoken, written or other kinds of expression, and situational irony, pertaining to irony in situations in the world. As such, irony has already been treated by language scholars as a thing extending significantly beyond language. This breadth suggests that irony is a much more deeply seated capacity in people, penetrating beyond a mere communication technique. It also entails that irony must be broadly connected to multiple other important facets of human functioning extending widely beyond people interacting. Irony might thus be rightly argued to require a diverse array of approaches, perspectives, explanatory frames and even disciplines to fully capture its complexity, even for the modest goal of understanding how it works in language.

The chapters in this volume arose from a theme session at the 2017 International Cognitive Linguistics Conference specifically organized to grapple with this "Diversity of Irony". The works bring a variety of disciplines to bear on questions about irony for communication, including: Linguistics, Psychology, Philosophy, Cognitive Science, Computer Science and Human Physiology. The chapters address questions on topics such as, irony and multimodality, new forms of expression of and influence on irony, irony and empathy, irony in diverse human populations and irony as a fundamentally embodied phenomenon. But this diverse treatment also intertwines to a degree in that overlappings can be observed among many pairs and other sets of these approaches and questions. The book is presented thusly as a treatment of irony as a form of thought and communication both broad and inter-connected among its important and necessary facets.

Herbert L. Colston and Angeliki Athanasiadou

University of Alberta, Canada
Aristotle University of Thessaloniki, Greece

February 2019

Contents

Preface —— V

Angeliki Athanasiadou and Herbert L. Colston
Introduction. On the diversity of irony —— 1

Part I: Diversity across figures

John Barnden
Uniting irony, hyperbole and metaphor in an affect-centred, pretence-based framework —— 15

Rachel Giora, Shir Givoni and Israela Becker
How defaultness affects text production: Resonating with default interpretations of negative sarcasm —— 66

Angeliki Athanasiadou
Irony in constructions —— 78

Mihaela Popa-Wyatt
Hyperbolic Figures —— 91

Graham Watling
Denying the salient contrast. Speaker's attitude in hyperbole —— 107

Part II: Diversity across languages

Patrawat Samermit and Apinan Samermit
Thai irony as an indirect relational tool to save face in social interactions —— 133

Andreas Musolff and Sing Tsun Derek Wong
England is an appendix; Corrupt officials are like hairs on a nation's arm:
Sarcasm, irony and self-irony in figurative political discourse —— 162

Victoria Escandell-Vidal and Manuel Leonetti
Grammatical emphasis and irony in Spanish —— 183

Part III: Diversity across media

Herbert L. Colston
Eye-rolling, irony and embodiment —— 211

Vera Tobin
Experimental investigations of irony as a viewpoint phenomenon —— 236

Sabina Tabacaru
Faces of sarcasm. Exploring raised eyebrows with sarcasm in French political debates —— 256

Hannah Leykum
A pilot study on the diversity in irony production and irony perception —— 278

Index —— 305

Angeliki Athanasiadou and Herbert L. Colston
Introduction
On the diversity of irony

The present volume includes contributions both theoretical and descriptive on irony in at least some of its broad diversity. The general aim of these works is to continue exploration of irony in its multiple forms. But the collection sought particularly to highlight irony's multifaceted character and to delve more deeply into its potential underpinnings which may have repercussions on the study of figuration in general.

A quick search of the literature on irony reveals diversity as to its types (verbal irony, situational irony, irony of fate, dramatic irony, Socratic irony, etc.); the theories of verbal irony, the echoic interpretation theory (Sperber 1984; Sperber and Wilson 1986/1995; Wilson and Sperber 1992; 1993), the pretense theory (Clark 1996; Clark and Gerrig 1983; 1984, Kumon-Nakamura et al. 1995/2007), and other pragmatic theories; the issue of its deliberateness (Gibbs 2012); the distinction between irony and non-irony. Diversity is also observed as to the communication factors of ironic production and the range of irony's influences along the continuum from processing, through comprehension, to interpretation. Irony has even been treated as a matter of folk psychology (Pálinkás 2014) by means of the special cognitive tool of conceptual integration. Context, salience-based effects, and especially irony and negation are devices broadly discussed by Giora and collaborators (2005; 2013; 2015). Irony has arisen in issues of the semantics/pragmatics distinction (Popa 2014). Irony also often combines with humor, jocularity, banter and teasing. It has also been approached as a viewpoint phenomenon (Tobin and Israel 2012).

One might note how parallel issues of diversity also hold for other figures, such as metaphor and metonymy. But something about irony might be noteworthy – it having necessitated two recent conference theme sessions (ICLC 2015 Newcastle and ICLC 2017 Tartu), a recent edited volume (Athanasiadou and Colston 2017), and now the present collection concerning irony's diversity.

The call for papers initially addressed to participants for the latter theme session (ICLC 2017), and later to other specialists for this volume, invited contributions from scholars working on irony in its full diversity including diversity vis a vis irony types (situational and verbal irony); in gestural or other non-verbal usage media; in processing (comprehension, interpretation, etc.); on irony in constructions and in broader discourses; on multimodal irony, and via potential

---

Angeliki Athanasiadou, Aristotle University of Thessaloniki, Greece
Herbert L. Colston, University of Alberta, Canada

https://doi.org/10.1515/9783110652246-001

linkages among the various types of irony. And all the above topics as they might specifically pertain to different languages and cultures as well as within a single particular language/culture, were also encouraged.

1 Why irony diversity?

Let us pull back for a moment and note briefly what attracted us to hosting this consideration of the diversity of irony – the origin story, as it were, detailing the historical beginnings and modern range of irony's diversity. One initial incarnation of irony was as a learning-leveraging tool employed by Socrates – it marked his method of pretending to be ignorant in order to reveal someone else's ignorance (or their knowledge) on an issue. Another incarnation involved Eiron, a stock character in Ancient Greek drama (comedy or tragedy) – a witty character who may have come across as selfless – hiding words and thoughts, but by means of humor could ridicule and scorn the weaknesses of others. So Eiron established an initial link between irony and performance.

The cognitive and conceptual mechanisms of irony have developed and proliferated since these recorded historical sources. So one question arising now is how we might view all these various conceptions of "irony"? Are they part of a family, or are they instead perhaps similar, but fundamentally separable phenomena (i.e., looking alike, but not related)? Or, put more fundamentally, is irony a diverse range of phenomena with some usefully uniting characteristics, or is it instead a set of similar but different phenomena united only by a common moniker?

Irony in its modern manifestations does seem to bear a special characteristic of perhaps not being just a figure – it could be, if only from the proliferation of the term "irony", that irony is just such a broad category, being present in, or overlapping with, other closely related phenomena like sarcasm, rhetorical questions, humor, parody, pastiche, satire, self-deprecating humor, etc., to name a few. One might see an analogy perhaps with an ecological system – these modern forms of irony occupying an "ecological niche", with intricate interconnections and interactions among fellow species residing within the niche.

Moreover, the meanings assigned to "irony" today can be defined relative to neighboring meanings (diachronically and synchronically). But the introduction of new, extended functional and cognitive descriptions of irony, may have also affected some older meanings. Recent definitions of irony, for instance, involving the notions of oppositeness or reversibility/negation, or that of pretense and echoing might now be viewed as subsumed by broader notions from the cognitive realm such as contrariness, juxtaposition of oppositionality or something similar.

Another question presupposed by this changing, more encompassing modern view of the "members of the irony family" would also be whether the foundational dramatic irony and Socratic irony, encompassing the expositional and portrayal aspects above from antiquity, are themselves separate phenomena. Might there be cognitive underpinnings derivable from modern and evolving conceptualizations of irony which justify the common lexical item *all* these terms share?

The discussion above involves diversity as to the definition of and/or scope of irony. From the point of view of irony interpretation we also have diversity concerning the meta-representations involved as well as the interpretation speeds of simple ironies relative to ironies combined with other figures. How are speakers led to interpreting an ironic utterance, an ironic metaphor or a metaphoric irony? Diversity also avails in gestural or other generally non-verbal ironic usage accompanied by speech.

As to cultural diversity, it is expected that the mechanism of irony draws at least to a degree from the source diachronic meaning it has had within a culture. Cultural groups employ irony in order to criticize, rebuke, ridicule, save face, complain with plausible deniability, etc., among many other different purposes. This implies that irony usage is not a unified mechanism, and irony might be employed and/or understood differently by speakers of different cultures.

Finally, in addition to philosophical, psychological and cultural aspects of irony, there is also diversity as to the constructional markers employed within a language or across languages for irony evocation. Differing language typologies may afford ways of being ironic in one or some languages that just aren't available in other languages. The diversity of such constructional parameters may also be investigated with different cognitive mechanisms (frames, mental spaces, etc.).

So our interest in the diversity of irony arose from these myriad of sources – irony's diversity across its forms (i.e., in situations, in language, in performance, in images, etc.), across its purposes (i.e., for education, for entertainment, for expression, for nuance, for negativity management, etc.), across its human expressional media (e.g., talk, gesture, facial expression, other nonverbal components, etc.) and how all this varies cross-linguistically and cross-culturally. Indeed a diversity of diversity.

2 The contributions

The chapters in the volume are organized into three parts. The first part provides a treatment of constructional parameters utilized to convey verbal irony. This section also provides a detailed cognitive processing model of irony, hyperbole and metaphor. It discusses how default sarcastic interpretations of negative constructions are reflected by their neighboring utterances significantly more often than their non-default literal counterparts. This section also investigates how hyperbole works when formed into compounds with metaphor, and also when blended with irony.

2.1 Part I: Diversity across figures

John Barnden. *Uniting Irony, Hyperbole and Metaphor in an Affect-Centred, Pretence-Based Framework*
Rachel Giora, Shir Givoni and Israela Becker. *How Defaultness Affects Text Production: Resonating with Default Interpretations of Negative Sarcasm*
Angeliki Athanasiadou. *Irony in Constructions*
Mihaela Popa-Wyatt. *Hyperbolic Figures*
Graham Watling. *Denying the Salient Contrast. Speaker's Attitude in Hyperbole*

Barnden's chapter develops a cognitive or computational processing model combining irony, hyperbole and metaphor. The framework he uses is pretense (a variety of fiction in his view), following the author's pretense-based account of metaphor, and his recent account of ironic pretense. In this chapter, he attempts a pretense-based account of hyperbole. Since this framework had been proposed for irony and metaphor and only partially for hyperbole, he now suggests a model of processing of all three figures within a pretense-based approach treating them in a consistent way and handling combinations of them. A key additional feature of the model is that it gives the communication of affect (emotion, evaluation, etc.) an unusually central role, notably in helping to drive the derivation of meaning that has traditionally been accounted for in non-affect-based ways. The work is presented not specifically as a model for how human processing necessarily would handle irony, metaphor and hyperbole. But, in consideration of how one might construct a theoretical computational model of processing irony, metaphor and hyperbole, perhaps for use by a computer, the author demonstrates aspects of mapping and problem-solving which would likely have to be implicitly handled by a human processor. In this way, this work can inform and enlighten our conceptualizations of human figurative comprehension.

In a corpus-based study, **Giora et al.**, examine utterances, involving strong attenuation of highly positive concepts, which further meet the conditions for default, (unconditional) interpretations. Items included 151 negative Hebrew constructions, of four types, embedded in naturally occurring contexts: *s/he is not the most X; s/he is not particularly X/s/he is not X in particular; s/he is not extremely X; s/he is not really X*. When in isolation, these negative, attenuated constructions are rated as sarcastic rather than literal, thus indicating their defaultness. Hence, when in context, their neighboring utterances resonate with their default sarcastic interpretations more often than with their nondefault literal alternatives. Default interpretations of such negative constructions prevail, and get prompted directly, irrespective of parameters such as negation, novelty, or supportive context. They further affect text production, via resonating with default interpretation. Such results lend support to the acclaimed superiority of default interpretations over nondefault (here literal) counterparts.

Athanasiadou's chapter investigates the constructional devices that can be responsible for the emergence of verbal irony. This work starts from the assumption that conceptual frames play an important role in mediating between constructions and figuration. All three issues, frames, constructions and irony, allow us to trace ironic intentions. The particular constructions that are discussed belong to discourse conditionals of the metacommunicative subtype: *if any, if anything, if anywhere, if at all, if a little + adjective* or *adverb, if ever, if I may*. Such elliptical, parenthetical or idiomatic *if*-clauses motivate intense instances of verbal irony. The speaker, using these forms, does not express something positive about something negative, nor something negative about something positive, but instead balances between accepting and rejecting a particular frame. Such constructional devices allow the speaker to present alternatives that either enrich, or question/violate frames. The chapter recognizes the role of constructions on irony evocation and gives prominence to the particular constructions motivating it.

Popa's chapter deals with hyperbole, but predominantly with different ways in which hyperbole mixes with metaphor and irony. Popa's aim is to discuss that hyperbole's main role when used in figurative blends, is to form hyperbolic figures. In the blend that arises from the mixing of hyperbole with these other figures, Popa argues that only one figure fulfills the speakers' goal(s). The other figure simply supports the prominent one. This differs from other kinds of figurative blending, such as in blends of irony and metaphor, where more preserved individual functioning of the different figures can be observed. The role of hyperbole when used in other-figure *supportive* instances, though, is to intensify the other figure, be it metaphor, irony, or whatever hyperbole mixes with. According to Popa, hyperbolic metaphor and hyperbolic irony are still *metaphor* and *irony* respectively but with more emphasis provided by the hyperbolic rendering. Hyperbole, the chapter argues, thus modulates the effects of the figures with which it blends.

Watling's chapter investigates the way speakers produce hyperbolic speech, namely overstating and understating the magnitude of something. He employs the term "salient contrast" by Walton and applies it to hyperbolic quantities (*more, less, tiny*), qualities and frequencies (*never, always, ever, forever,…*). He claims that hyperbolic meanings depend on salient contrast together with the attitude of the speaker and his/her subjective evaluation. The motivation that makes a speaker use hyperbole is to establish a salient contrast. This tool is very useful in that it gives a further dimension to the figure of hyperbole – the speaker's concern to deny and contrast forcefully towards the direction of the scale that is chosen to be intensified. Through denials we are informed on how exaggerated speech is employed in hyperbole but at the same time we are informed on the speakers' attitudes and emotional states. It should be noted that the exaggerated denial may also involve irony.

The second part investigates the use of irony cross-linguistically. This section discusses how irony functions differently within different cultural and language contexts, including Thai, Mandarin, British English and Spanish.

2.2 Part II: Diversity across languages

Patrawat Samermit and Apinan Samermit. *Thai Irony as an Indirect Relational Tool to Save Face in Social Interactions*

Andreas Musolff and Derek Wong. *England is an Appendix; Corrupt Officials are like Hairs on a Nation's Arm: Sarcasm, Irony and Self-irony in Figurative Political Discourse*

Victoria Escandell-Vidal and Manuel Leonetti. *Grammatical Emphasis and Irony in Spanish*

Samermit P. and **Samermit** A. describe the way irony is used in Thai. In this particular cultural context, irony is often humorous and through this use of humor speakers and hearers can be indirectly polite with one another. In the ways that Thai people interact and socially negotiate, they often exhibit being ironic together with hyperbole, jocularity, rhetorical questions, sarcasm and understatement. The authors argue that this inclusion of a wide array of different ironical forms, namely a combination of irony with all the afore-mentioned figures, is primarily due to the humor by the forms and their combinations, allowing interlocutors to successfully navigate face issues. The use of irony in Thai works as an indirect criticism which is nonetheless able to maintain politeness, avoid direct confrontation and manage face issues by both speaker and hearer.

Musolff and **Wong** discuss instances of metaphors using source domains of the BODY which are then ironically or sarcastically criticized. The frameworks they employ are both the echoic mention and the pretense models of irony, which enable the authors to evaluate these metaphorical utterances when ironically or sarcastically contradicted. The metaphorical scenarios analyzed in their corpus material were instances of the target domain NATION being discussed as parts of the human BODY, under the consideration of the *UK ending its EU membership*. For instance, one such metaphor which received a number of ironic renderings was the slogan, "Britain at the heart of Europe". Ironic twists on this core frame, for instance, "...if Mr. Major wanted to be at the heart of Europe, it was, presumably, *as a blood clot*", were analysed eliciting interpretations by English-L1 and Mandarin-L1 speakers. It was revealed that English speakers more frequently tended towards employing sarcastic criticism of the nation in their interpretations, and moreover, with concepts of *lowly* and *disgusting* statuses. This latter issue does not hold as much for Mandarin speakers.

Escandell-Vidal and **Leonetti** claim that ironic interpretations are facilitated by intensification and emphasis. Intensification, they argue, involves the use of grammatical means in order to express a high degree of a property, while emphasis is a form of intensification used to reject or cancel an assumption. In an attempt to examine how sentences in Spanish can get an ironic interpretation, the authors investigated the syntactic forms the utterances have. Their prediction is that sentences with emphatic syntax and marked word order tend to be ironically interpreted compared to neutral sentences and sentences with intensification. To this end, they carry out a survey to evaluate which sentences tend towards ironic interpretations when no contextual background is provided. The results of the survey confirm the prediction that the grammatical expression of intensification and emphasis facilitate irony.

The third Part contains three chapters which investigate the diversity of irony through particular types of gestures, postures and facial expressions in normal adults. One other chapter in this section investigates nonverbal cues' role in irony comprehension among normal-hearing participants versus people with cochlear implants.

2.3 Part III: Diversity across media

Herbert Colston. *Eye-rolling, irony and embodiment*
Vera Tobin. *Experimental Investigations of Irony as a Viewpoint Phenomenon*
Sabina Tabacaru. *Faces of Sarcasm. Exploring Raised Eyebrows with Sarcasm in French Political Debates*
Hannah Leykum. *A Pilot Study on the Diversity in Irony Production and Irony Perception*

Colston's chapter concerns the human nonverbal behavior of eye-rolling and ways in which it may be a deeply embodied, expressive symptom, as well as marker, of irony. Together with eye-rolls, other forms of nonverbal behavior such as facial expressions, head and body movements, and hand/body gestures, all accompanied by speech, serve to affect the nuance of ironic expression. Eye-rolling is thus a complex phenomenon often motivated by irony but which need not necessarily be accompanied by other forms of speech or behavior. Eye-rolling can indicate disapproval with or without verbal irony, manifested in terms of five possible embodied underpinnings (detachment, appeal, physical experiences, lack of control and embodied irony). These appear to operate together with two other characteristics – experience yoked with demonstrativeness and optimality. The chapter presents an empirical study of eye-rolling and verbal irony usage – showing how perceived disapproval conveyed by eye-roll direction (i.e., upward eye-rolling is particularly strong at displaying disapproval) supports claims of embodied underpinnings, experience yoked with demonstrativeness and optimality.

Tobin's chapter discusses irony as a figure of viewpoint. The viewpoint theory of irony holds that people take a complex, "view of a viewpoint", which may unite different types of irony. According to this approach, irony is, "a special kind of stance on the part of the interpreter". The author's framework for irony is situated in Mental Spaces Theory. On the basis that irony involves taking a perspective, people interpret a statement as sarcastic when they are primed with viewpoint arrangements. This idea was tested with evaluative statements which can be sarcastic or sincere, being accompanied by images where people shown to participants either are or are not looking at others when speaking. Versions with just the speaker, with one other person or with two other people were shown. Participants interpreted utterances as sarcastic when the utterances occurred in scenes of multiple embodied viewpoints. This effect was strongest in scenes containing only two people (speaker and hearer), though, not three. Tobin's chapter thus provides empirical support that irony processing does involve considerations of viewpoint.

Tabacaru's chapter draws attention to multimodality in sarcasm (i.e., sarcasm residing not only in language but also in facial expressions, tone of voice and body position, among many other modes of expression). Tabacaru is particularly interested in how eyebrow movement plays a role in the production and interpretation of sarcastic utterances. Sarcastic multimodality is investigated in images from television debates in French in order to show how speakers spontaneously make their sarcastic intentions known to at least a portion of their audience(s) – with several audiences being available (the debate moderators, interlocutors, other debaters present, the local audience, the broader viewing audience). The examples, Tabacaru discussed, show that sarcastic implications are triggered by subtly raised eyebrows which here mark a shift to a pretense space.

Leykum's chapter reports a pilot study in Standard Austrian German of people's ability to detect irony using audio, video or both cues. The study involved audio and video recordings of a speaker producing utterances both ironically and literally. Detailed analysis of the produced utterances revealed reliable differences between ironically and non-ironically realized productions (ironies had, for instance, longer durations, lower pitch, lower word intensity, etc.) and Leykum's perception experiment compared how irony recognition proceeded in 6 normal-hearing and 2 cochlear-implant listeners. The results of the study (one speaker and eight listeners, two of the listeners being CI individuals) showed that one of the CI listeners detected verbal irony similarly to normal-hearing individuals. But the other CI listener had an overall lower detection accuracy of irony and relied more upon visual cues relative to all the other listeners. The author contends that although the experiment was conducted on a small scale, its findings are valuable as a proof-of-concept in that it seems likely that at least a portion of CI listeners rely on a different suite of cues in order to detect and interpret verbal irony.

3 Conclusion

The present volume set out to explore and obtain evidence for either potential commonalities or deviances in what constitutes "irony" across multiple areas of diversity, with a specific aim toward an increased understanding of irony as a potentially fundamental mode of thought and communication. The research goal in this collection of works on the diversity of irony seems to have been accomplished. The contributions explore strands of irony performance and cognition, they evaluate potential underlying causes, motivations, fundamentals and other parent phenomena of irony, be they embodied, cognitive, linguistic, social or other, and the contributions expand our exploration of irony into new languages, new constructions, new blends, new media and new processes.

As to the motivating question concerning the unitary nature of the varieties of "ironies", we leave it for readers to decide ultimately on their own. Our view is that this volume's highly interesting collection of chapters, dealing both with theoretical investigations as well as with descriptive applications, reveal a central figure whose underlying nature(s) also pervade(s) human thought and language. Akin to a kitchen utensil (i.e., a knife) whose central function, dividing something into segments, serves a wide variety of applications (e.g., peeling, slicing, chopping, carving, mincing, crushing (in the case of a broad knife and garlic), etching, nicking, puncturing, shaving, hacking, splitting, lopping, slashing, etc.), the core function of irony also has many applications. Irony serves a variety of functions and can appear in many guises. But its core family resemblance of means of juxtaposing oppositionality for a variety of uses provides a powerful multi-tasking tool – useful in our thinking and in our communicating.

But clearly much more remains to be done to delve into the details and thoroughly evaluate such a claim. If indeed irony is a fundamental and ultimately embodied mode of thought, then one might expect to see possible forms of transfer between types of irony. For instance, if a person observes or contemplates a situational irony, might they be facilitated if then dealing in verbal irony?

(e.g., more apt to produce it, producing stronger or more complex versions of it when producing it, more likely to perceive others' use of it, faster comprehension of others' use of it, etc.). If a person experiences Socratic irony, would they be more sensitive to witnessing a portrayal of dramatic irony? Would a contemplation of cosmic irony prime people to seeing a subtle ironic delivery in a nonverbal mode?

And beyond these big questions about irony as a cognitive and/or embodied fundamental, many questions remain unanswered about the more fine-grained venues of irony and their interactions, i.e., which has more influence, the constructions in which an ironic utterance is made or blends of that ironic utterance with other figures? Are there cultural cross-over effects of irony in the same way we see linguistic cross-over effects when learning an L2, e.g., if a person grows up in a culture where irony is mainly used to save face, what happens when this person moves to a culture where irony is often used for aggression? How do subtle non-verbal aspects of irony interact, e.g., viewpoint priming and eye-rolling?

In our previous edited volume on irony, we concluded the introduction by pointing out an irony of irony – that people often experience verbal or situational forms of irony as something exceptional (e.g., when events go badly awry and a speaker exclaims, "Utterly stupendous, I could *not* be happier!", or when the world famous mountain climber, who had summited each of the fourteen peaks in the world over 8,000 meters tall, died while climbing a short step-ladder). Yet, it appears irony is actually quite prevalent, common and widely used in our thinking and communicating. We'll conclude this introduction with another irony of irony: Our general conclusion of this introduction seems to claim we've reached a summit or plateau or sorts in irony research – our now seeing it as the potentially central, cognitive and embodied process it might be. Yet, given the array of bigger and smaller questions remaining to be answered of irony, we may have just barely scratched its surface.

References

Athanasiadou, Angeliki & Herbert L. Colston (eds.). 2017. *Irony in Language Use and Communication*. Amsterdam & Philadelphia: J. Benjamins Publishing Company.
Clark H. Herbert. 1996. *Using language*. Cambridge: Cambridge University Press.
Clark H. Herbert & Richard J. Gerrig. 1983. Understanding old words with new meanings. *Journal of Verbal Learning and Verbal Behavior* 22. 591–608.
Clark H. Herbert & Richard J. Gerrig. 1984. On the pretense theory of irony. *Journal of Experimental Psychology: General* 113. 121–126.
Gibbs, W. Raymond, Jr. 2012. Are ironic acts deliberate? *Journal of Pragmatics* 44. 104–115.

Giora, Rachel, Ofer Fein, Jonathan Ganzi, Natalie Alkeslassy Levi & Hadas Sabah. 2005. On negation as mitigation: The case of negative irony. *Discourse Processes* 39(1). 81–100.

Giora, Rachel, Shir Givoni & Ofer Fein. 2015. Defaultness reigns: The case of sarcasm. *Metaphor and Symbol* 30/4. 290–313.

Giora, Rachel, Elad Livnat, Ofer Fein, Anat Barnea, Rakefet Zeiman & Iddo Berger. 2013. Negation generates nonliteral interpretations by default. *Metaphor and Symbol* 28(2). 89–115.

Kumon-Nakamura, Sachi, Sam Glucksberg & Mary Brown. [1995] 2007. How about another piece of pie: The allusional pretense theory of discourse irony. In Raymond W. Gibbs & Herbert L. Colston (eds.), *Irony in Language and Thought*, 57–95. Lawrence Erlbaum Associates. Taylor & Francis Group. New York, London.

Pálinkás, István. 2014. Blending and folk theory in an explanation of irony. *RCL* 12:1. 64–98. doi: 10.1075/rcl.12.1.03pal

Popa-Wyatt, Mihaela. 2014. Pretence and echo: Towards an integrated account of verbal irony. *International Review of Pragmatics* 6(1). 127–168.

Sperber, Dan. 1984. Verbal Irony: Pretense or Echoic Mention? *Journal of Experimental Psychology: General* 113(1). 130–136.

Sperber, Dan & Deirdre Wilson. 1986/1995. *Relevance: Communication and Cognition*. Oxford: Blackwell.

Tobin, Vera & Michael Israel. 2012. Irony as a viewpoint phenomenon. In Barbara Dancygier & Eve Sweetser (eds.), *Viewpoint in Language*, 25–46. Cambridge: Cambridge University Press. doi: 10.1017/CBO9781139084727.004

Wilson, Deirdre & Dan Sperber. 1992. On verbal irony. *Lingua* 87. 53–76.

Wilson, Deirdre & Dan Sperber. 1993. Linguistic form and relevance. *Lingua* 90. 1–25.

Part I: **Diversity across figures**

John Barnden
Uniting irony, hyperbole and metaphor in an affect-centred, pretence-based framework

Abstract: This article makes steps towards a detailed cognitive processing model of irony, hyperbole and metaphor. The intent is not just to deal with irony, hyperbole and metaphor in a consistent way, but also to deal with intimate combinations of these types of figurative language. The model is being developed by uniting some existing models: the author's own ATT-Meta model of metaphor, his separate, recently developing model of irony, and the hyperbole model of Peña & Ruiz de Mendoza. The irony and metaphor models are overtly of the "pretence" based style that various authors have followed. The hyperbole model can also be regarded as being in this style. The melding of the models proceeds largely by extending, into the models of hyperbole and irony, a certain major provision in the metaphor model. This is a provision for the transformation and exportation of aspects of pretended scenarios into the actual situations being addressed by the speaker. Another salient feature of the overall model is its strong affect-centredness. The model does not only pay much attention to the affective (i.e., evaluative or emotional) connotations of hyperbole, irony and metaphor. It goes yet further by often giving affect the *driving* role in deriving a contrasting value in irony (e.g., the degree of badness of the weather conveyed by an ironic *"Sure, great weather!"*) or a scaled-down value in hyperbole (the actual rough weight of the suitcase in a hyperbolic *"This suitcase weighs a ton!"*). This approach was partly inspired by Peña & Ruiz de Mendoza's work, and opposes the traditional assumption that the central issue in irony and hyperbole is the derivation of such contrasting and scaled-down values that are not dependent on the details of the affective connotations.

Keywords: Irony, hyperbole, metaphor, pretence, cognitive processing, affective processing

---

Acknowledgments: The research in this article was initially supported in part by Research Project Grant F/00 094/BE from the Leverhulme Trust in the UK. I am grateful to editors and reviewers for comments that have led to important improvements to the article.

John Barnden, School of Computer Science, University of Birmingham, UK

https://doi.org/10.1515/9783110652246-002

1 Introduction

This article works towards a combined cognitive processing model of irony, hyperbole and metaphor within a pretence framework. According to such a framework, the speaker is non-deceptively pretending something. For instance, with an ironic *"Sure, such great weather"* she is pretending to be someone who believes that the weather is great; with a hyperbolic *"This suitcase weighs a ton"* she is pretending the suitcase weighs a ton and that's why it's frustratingly difficult to lift; with a metaphoric *"John's exam marking overflowed into the weekend"* she is pretending among other things that the marking is a liquid (or something else that can physically flow, such as loose powder). Various authors (see below) have proposed pretence approaches for irony and metaphor, over many years now, and recently there has been a pretence proposal for hyperbole as well. However, pretence been applied to the three types of figuration largely separately, and not using detailed mechanisms that are consistent across all three. My aim is instead to cope with all three completely consistently, and furthermore to handle combinations of them (hyperbole-with-metaphor, hyperbole-with-irony, metaphor-with-irony, or all three together). Combinations have been much discussed at a high theoretical level and addressed to an extent in psychological and corpus-based work, but the detailed processing involved has only been addressed sketchily.

As for further, related types of figurative language such as understatement and oxymoron, I consign them to further development of the approach here. On the other hand, the remaining main type of figurative language in current research – namely metonymy – would not appear to *benefit* strongly from a pretence framework (though see Fauconnier 2009 on handling metonymy in "blending" theory, noting that that theory's blend spaces can be seen as pretended scenarios in the sense of this article). Nevertheless, it will be important in the future to add a treatment of metonymy that somehow fits smoothly with this article's approach.

Hyperbole is often present in irony and metaphor (Athanasiadou 2017, Brdar-Szabó & Brdar 2010, Burgers, Konijn & Stein 2016, Carston & Wearing 2015, Claridge 2011, Colston & Keller 1998, Dynel 2016, Kreuz & Roberts 1995, McCarthy & Carter 2004, Musolff 2017, Norrick 2004, Peña & Ruiz de Mendoza 2017, Popa-Wyatt [this volume], Sperber & Wilson 1995). Indeed, irony tends to be exemplified in research papers by ironic sentences that have hyperbolic qualities. For example, as a reaction to a claim that someone is *"clever,"* ironic responses such as hyperbolic *"Yeah, he's a genius"* are likely to be considered rather than non-hyperbolic counterparts like *"Yeah, he's a clever person."* The word *"genius"* ridicules not what was actually claimed but an exaggeration of it. By this means it heightens the ridicule, in a way to be explicated below. In saying metaphorically that someone is an *"angel"* the speaker is likely not to be attributing a degree of goodness, protectiveness, helpfulness, etc. as high as a traditional angel's, so the statement is a hyperbolic metaphor, not just a metaphor.

The combination of irony with metaphor or simile (Camp 2006, Dynel 2016, Grice 1989, Katz & Lee 1993, Popa 2009, Popa-Wyatt 2017, Musolff 2017, Ritchie 2006, Stern 2000, Veale 2012) is illustrated by *"Yeah, he's just a sloth"* used to praise an energetic person, using a stereotype of sloths as being non-energetic.

My strategy is to meld three previously separate accounts, one each for metaphor, irony and hyperbole. These are: an existing pretence-based account of metaphor understanding that I have developed (and called *ATT-Meta:* Barnden 2001, 2006a,b, 2015a, 2016, Barnden & Lee 2002; with "ATT" deriving from "attitudes"); an account of ironic pretence that I have also been developing but much more recently (Barnden 2017; to be called *ATT-Iro* here); and a recent account of hyperbole by others (Peña & Ruiz de Mendoza 2017; see also Ruiz de Mendoza 2014, 2017). This last account can be described as pretence-based with respect to the light notion of "pretence" used in this article.

The three models all involve *correspondences (mappings)* between aspects of a pretence and aspects of the actual situation the speaker is talking about. In all three models, such correspondences support the ability to *export* (or *transfer*) some aspects of the pretended scenario to apply, though in possibly changed forms, to the real situation. The melding of the three models is mainly a straightforward matter of extending certain export provisions of ATT-Meta (the metaphor model) to hyperbolic pretence and ironic pretence. The only significant change needed is to introduce a comprehensive sort of *potential attenuation* of the degrees to which circumstances apply in the pretence – such as the suitcase-lifter's degree of frustration in the pretence – when they are exported to become degrees of holding of corresponding circumstances in reality – such as the lifter's real degree of frustration. I argue that this attenuation not only serves hyperbole well but also works for irony and metaphor across the board.

Our reaching towards a consistent, combined model parallels the aim of Peña and Ruiz de Mendoza (2017), who take steps towards consistently bringing together the processing of various forms of figurative language, including irony, hyperbole and metaphor. Indeed, there are specific similarities in the efforts; for instance, the export provision in our approach is paralleled in their work by an Extended Invariance Hypothesis originally proposed largely for metaphor, and they suggest extending this to hyperbole and irony. However, there are major differences, including our more detailed and constrained approach to mappings and our addition of a focus on how degrees (see above) are managed.

A major, long-standing concern in research on irony, hyperbole and metaphor has been the *affective* connotations that these phenomena have. An ironic *"Sure, great weather"* in response to someone, Alan, who thinks the weather is good, may come with considerable criticism, mockery, ridicule, etc. of Alan, although there are other, milder possibilities. (For a variety of work on attitudes in irony, see Colston 1997, Colston & Keller 1998, Gibbs [2000] 2007, Kumon-Nakamura et al. [1995] 2007, Sperber & Wilson 1995, and Watling [this volume]) I will refer generically to negative attitudes by the term *criticism* for brevity. Importantly, as Dynel (2018) argues, there is some criticism even in "positive" (or "praising") irony, as when someone says *"Sure, she's [or: you're] totally stupid"* about a very clever person P, in reaction to a claim by a claimant C that P is stupid. The irony is certainly praising P, but is of course still at least mildly criticizing the claimant C for being misguided. This holds even when P and C are one and the same.

As for hyperbole, an utterance of *"This suitcase weighs a ton"* is arguably not just communicating the exceptional weight of the suitcase but also, say, frustration at the difficulty of manipulating it. (See Peña & Ruiz de Mendoza 2017 on this example. For other types of affect in hyperbole, see Brdar-Szabó & Brdar 2010, Carston & Wearing 2015, Colston & Keller 1998, McCarthy & Carter 2004, Musolff 2017, Ruiz de Mendoza 2017.) Finally, in metaphor, affective connotations are often important (Deignan 2008, Eubanks 2005, Fainsilber & Ortony 1987, Hampe 2005, Littlemore & Low 2006, McMullen & Conway 2002, Musolff 2004, Schön, 1993, Vervaeke & Kennedy 2004). For instance, saying metaphorically that someone is Hitler is likely to communicate strong negative affect about the person.

Hence, much of this article is centred on affect. In fact, the article makes this centrality even more intense by giving affect a driving role in the derivation of types of meaning that are normally assumed to arise by other means. Examples are the derivation of a contrasting value in irony (e.g., the degree of badness of the weather conveyed by an ironic *"Sure, great weather!"*) or a scaled-down value in hyperbole (the actual rough weight of the suitcase in a hyperbolic *"This suitcase weighs a ton!"*). Such contrasting and scaled-down values are almost always assumed to be derived by some process that is not itself dependent on considerations of affect, while the affective connotations are assumed to be partly dependent on what the contrasting and scale-down values are. Thus, the approach in this article, which owes some of its inspiration to the involvement of affect in the work of Peña & Ruiz de Mendoza (2017) turns some usual assumptions on their head.

The article cannot give anything like a full account of what either the speaker or hearer does in using figurative language. The model concentrates on the detailed structure and manipulation of possible pretences and how information about the real situation can be extracted by the hearer, but does not offer mechanisms whereby the hearer can use intonation, facial expressions, wording etc. as clues to ironic effect, or can conjecture that an utterance is hyperbolic or metaphorical. The model is therefore only a highly incomplete one when compared to the whole landscape of irony, hyperbole and metaphor.

The article is structured as follows. Section 2 outlines the ATT-Iro irony model, largely following but slightly updating the model in Barnden (2017). Section 3 outlines the Peña & Ruiz de Mendoza (2017) model of hyperbole, proposes significant modifications, and unites the result with ATT-Iro. Section 4 outlines some relevant aspects of the ATT-Meta metaphor model. Section 5 melds that model with the approach to irony and hyperbole resulting from Section 3, and culminates in making a start on the question of irony/metaphor combinations. Section 6 concludes.

A presentation-simplifying assumption that I make throughout is that the ironic, metaphorical and hyperbolic sentences considered are all uttered about real-world situations, rather than being embedded in stories, jokes, accounts of what some third party believes, etc. This follows common practice in most writing on figurative language. However, the treatments below are appropriate for coping with such embedding. That this is so will hopefully seem plausible to the reader but will need to be substantiated in detail in further work.

2 ATT-Iro: The existing model of (possibly hyperbolic) irony

This section outlines and updates the irony model presented in Barnden (2017), with significant changes to some of the fine detail. The model covers various alternative purposes of verbal irony, and notably that of (a) criticizing someone who seems to have an incorrect belief about a situation, or instead that of merely (b) expressing disappointment that a situation has not measured up to what the speaker hoped for. This article will concentrate on purpose (a) for brevity and will refer to it as *critical irony*. The article will not explicitly deal with positive irony (irony that praises, expresses gladness, etc.) but the approach extends straightforwardly to it.

Cutting across the distinction between (a) and (b) is the dimension of hyperbole. Although, as hinted in the Introduction, non-hyperbolic cases of irony may be less typical and idiomatic than hyperbolic ones, we will start with a non-hyperbolic example in order to separate certain issues from each other. When we get to hyperbole, we will illustrate both *scalar* hyperbole (e.g., using "great weather" instead of "good weather" in an irony) and *fictively-elaborating* hyperbole. The term "fictively elaborating" was introduced in Barnden (2017) and covers cases where invented qualitative details are added by the speaker, as in ironically saying that *"Sure, such good weather, what with the hot sun and balmy breeze"* in criticizing someone who has claimed that the weather is good but who has *not* claimed that the sun is hot or that there's a balmy breeze. Many examples of this phenomenon have appeared in the literature (Athanasiadou 2017, Herrero Ruiz 2009, Kapogianni 2017, McCarthy & Carter 2004, Musolff 2017), even if not necessarily singled out and dwelt upon, and there are extreme examples of the phenomenon in the form of lengthy satires, but the phenomenon deserves much more detailed analytic attention than it has been given.

Pretence is the basis of one of the main approaches to irony. (For versions and discussion of the approach see Clark & Gerrig [1995] 2007, Currie 2006, 2010, Kumon-Nakamura, Glucksberg & Brown [1995] 2007, Popa-Wyatt 2014, See also Coulson 2005, Kihara 2005, and see Tobin & Israel 2012 for a similar approach based on mental spaces.) When Beth ironically says *"Sure, it's great weather"* in response to someone, Alan, who seems to think the weather is good when it should be evident to him that the weather is bad, she is *only pretending* to be someone who claims and thinks that the weather is great. The various pretence accounts differ significantly in regard to what is pretended and also with regard to what pretence itself amounts to. The latter consideration is especially significant when the approach is compared and contrasted to others such as echoing-based approaches (Wilson 2006, Wilson & Sperber 2012, Ruiz de Mendoza 2017; for further comparison of the approaches, see also papers cited above on the pretence approach). Across all pretence approaches, however, the pretence is not of the deceptive sort as when someone pretends to be a police officer in order to kidnap someone. Rather, the hearer is meant to realize that the ironic speaker does not believe what she appears to be saying, much as when a joker pretends to be telling a real story or an actor is pretending to be a character in a play.

And indeed, pretending can be thought of as putting on an act or *[micro-]drama*. ATT-Iro develops an ironic-pretence-as-drama approach, loosely following previous suggestions in the field: Clark & Gerrig ([1984] 2007) talk of the ironist acting a role, and see Carston & Wearing (2015) and Popa-Wyatt (2014) for further references and commentary. The dramatic worlds in the present article are reminiscent of the contexts in the pretence-based approach of Récanati (2007: 224–226) but serve a different purpose. However, ATT-Iro develops the pretence-as-drama idea in a more thorough-going and consistent way than previously.

Notice that neither the idea of pretence in general nor of acting in particular requires speakers to exhibit the same tone of voice or overall behaviour that people who were sincerely uttering the sentence would. A speaker can do things like put on a special facial expression or tone of voice to signal ironicity, much as actors on stage can make sidelong glances at the audience or make verbal asides to the audience to poke fun at dramatic scenarios. In fact I will shortly propose that an ironic speaker's sentence is often if not typically like an aside.

A theory of irony couched in terms of drama does not require the speaker or hearer themselves to be thinking about the communication in terms of drama. The drama view is just a heuristic for use by us as theoreticians.

2.1 Critical irony: A non-hyperbolic example

Consider the following conversation segment, when the weather is bad. Moreover, Beth thinks that Alan should have noticed that the weather is bad, and so she engages in critical irony:

(1) Alan: *"It's good weather today."*
     Beth: *"Yeah, good weather."*

Beth may, but need not, say this with a sarcastic tone, or while rolling her eyes, and so forth.

ATT-Iro casts Beth's momentary pretending as her being engaged in acting a dramatic character who thinks that the weather is good. This character is part of a (micro) drama. See Figure 1, which depicts the drama and its relation to the real world as far as Beth is concerned. In the world of the drama, the weather is bad, just as it is in the real world according to Beth. The acted character is one that corresponds to Alan, and we might intuitively say that the drama therefore features Alan. But, to keep the distinction between the dramatic character and the real-life person clear, I will give the dramatic character a different name in explaining what is going on. In Alan's case I will use "Palan," short for "Pretend-Alan."

A variant, slightly more complex treatment could have it that the acted character is not meant to be a depiction of Alan, but just of someone or other who believes that the weather is good, though still we some weaker notion of correspondence to or similarity to Alan. The rest of this article could go through on this basis, but there does not seem to be any pressing reason to adopt it.

Note also that, in the type of example under consideration, where Beth is not commenting on anything to do with herself, she Beth does not place herself as *a character in* the drama. She is merely the actor of the Palan character. (Barnden 2017 gives examples of cases where Beth herself does appear in the drama as a character Peth, while also acting some character, which in some circumstances is Peth but in others is a different character such as Palan.) There is no need for Beth to include herself in the drama as someone, a character Peth, who endorses Palan's views – there's no need for the drama to contain two characters with the same view. Rather, the drama is presented to the intended "audience" (Alan) for contemplation, with an implied criticism by Beth (the real person) of the character Palan.

Another caveat is that the words Beth utters are not always or even typically to be considered as words uttered by the acted character to some other character in the drama. Instead, they are often if not typically best thought of as asides to the audience. The words show what propositions, etc. are being *mentally* entertained by the acted character, not what the character is saying to other characters. This point is important in view of the common phenomenon of ironic statements being uttered with special intonation etc. or starting with expressions such as *"Yeah"* or *"Great"*. But the point gains added importance in a variant case such as where Alan has claimed to be clever and Beth says, *"Yeah, sure, you're a genius."* In the drama, it is not that Palan is addressing a character (himself?) and telling him he is a genius. Rather, *"you're a genius"* tells Alan, who is the "audience" of the drama that the proposition being ascribed to Palan is that he Alan (in the guise of Palan) is a genius. So Palan thinks he himself is a genius. It is a drama where the only (or main) audience member is depicted as a character in the drama, so an aside to the audience can be effectively about that character even though not addressed within the drama to that character.[1]

A final caveat is that the ironic utterance in (1) only explicitly specifies what Palan thinks, and does not specify the nature of the drama's world (= world of the drama). This implicitness is akin to what happens when an actor is improvising away from any stage, for instance in an acting workshop, or when a radio drama is conveyed entirely by the characters' utterances.

Beth is implicitly criticizing Palan for having *failed to notice* that the weather is bad. By failure to notice I do not mean merely not-noticing, but rather not-noticing-something-one-should-have-noticed. The reason that, in the first place, Beth does insert a failure to notice into the drama, and criticizes Palan for it, is that she feels critical of Alan for this in the real world. So in constructing the drama setup, she first *imports* the Alan failure and her criticism of him into the drama. Note carefully here the difference between what Beth as speaker does and what a hearer needs to do. A hearer (whether Alan or an overhearer) might not know in advance of the utterance that Beth is critical of Alan, so has to somehow work this out from the utterance. But, of course, Beth herself is making her ironic utterance precisely because she already is critical – she doesn't have to work this out from inspecting her own drama! Rather, she inserts criticism into the drama as

---

[1] I am grateful to an anonymous reviewer for raising the need to discuss this type of example.

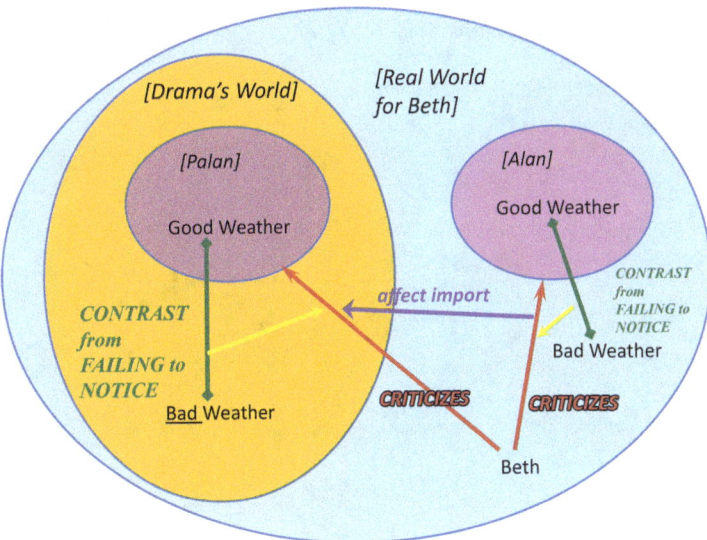

Figure 1: A drama set-up for the speaker's (i.e. Beth's) view of irony example (1).[2]

she constructs it in her mind,[3] based on her real-world critical stance towards Alan. Figure 1 shows reality and its relationship to the drama from Beth's point of view.

Of course, Alan has a different perception of the weather in reality, so from his point of view the setup is captured by Figure 2, if he manages accurately to conjecture what Beth is doing. This Figure shows Alan's reality and Beth's reality (as construed by Alan) as different spaces. In Alan's reality space, the weather is good; in Beth's it isn't. At some point, Alan *may* (or may not) become persuaded by Beth's view of things, but for the moment at least he still believes that the weather is good.

---

[2] The label "drama's world" in this and other Figures should not be regarded as reflecting a use (at least, not a conscious one) of the concept of drama within the speaker or hearer's own mind. The drama's world is depicted by the large oval on the left. It includes an inner oval depicting Palan. A person-oval such as this includes wording showing some of the person's mental contents, or alternatively, what the world is like according to them. (The diagram shows affect import as opposed to the export shown in comparable diagrams in Barnden, 2017. The latter's export links depicted what the speaker expected the hearer to do, whereas the present diagram shows only what the speaker does. The matter of export is shown in succeeding Figures, which are from the hearer's point of view.)

[3] Such construction is not necessarily conscious. This article does not try to separate conscious from unconscious acts in the course of producing or understanding figurative language, and thus follows a general trend of work in the field, for good or ill.

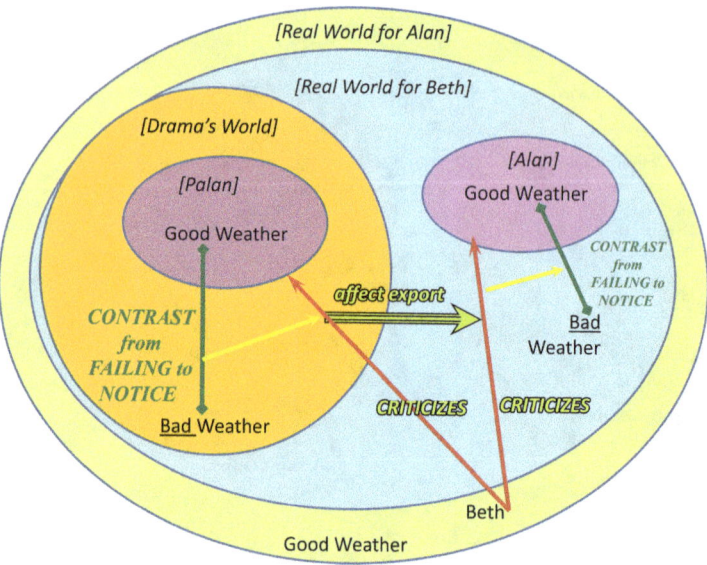

Figure 2: The drama setup, from Alan the hearer's point of view, for irony example (1).[4]

The model proposes a particular course of events on Alan's side, on the assumption that he first realizes that (or is at least exploring the possibility that) Beth is engaging in irony that is critical of him. He might assume (or explore) the ironic possibility because of clues such as: the mere fact that what Beth says echoes what he himself claimed; her tone of voice, which may be dry or sarcastic; her facial expression; her use of *"Yeah"*; her prior established nature as a sarcastic person; etc. Furthermore, let us assume that Alan presumes that, if Beth is being critical of him, her criticism is indeed prompted by the claim he has just made that the weather is good (not by someone else's claim, for instance). The model does not yet cover mechanisms for these acts of realization or presumption. It has been aimed at what happens after this point.

Given those assumptions, Alan entertains the idea there is a drama in which he features, as a character we are calling Palan, and where Beth is criticizing *Palan* for thinking that the weather is good. Since Palan is being criticized for believing the weather to be good, it is reasonable for Alan to infer that, within the drama, the weather is bad but that Palan has failed to notice this (otherwise

---

[4] The affect export is a mental action by Alan (not an action by Beth as considered by Alan) aimed at conjecturing Beth's attitude to Alan. The criticism arrows show criticism that Alan conjectures that Beth feels.

it would be strange for Beth to be criticizing him). Alan now e*xports* the criticism of Palan in the drama to become criticism that applies now to Alan within (his construal of) Beth's real world. See the export arrow in Figure 2. Hence, Alan now infers that Beth is criticizing *him*, the real Alan, for failing to notice bad weather. From this he infers that, in Beth's world, the weather is bad and he, Alan, has failed to notice this. The export of the criticism is analogous to the fact that when a staged drama leads us to feel critical of a character in it, we tend to feel critical also of comparable or corresponding people in the real world.[5]

A drama's world can be arbitrarily much like the real world, or arbitrarily much unlike it. In the current example it is identical to it, apart from Alan being replaced by Palan, but this is a very special case. Differences can arise in other circumstances, including hyperbolic irony, to which we now turn.

2.2 Critical irony: A hyperbolic case

Consider now:

(2) Alan: *"It's good weather today."*
 Beth: *"Sure, such great weather, what with singing birds, warm sun and balmy breeze!"*

The drama setup is essentially the same as before, except that Palan now believes that the weather is *"great"* rather than just *"good"* and furthermore involves singing birds, warm sun and a balmy breeze. (This example is inspired by an overstatement example in Herrero Ruiz 2009 and work on elaborated pretences in Currie 2006.) See Figure 3. Thus, the contrast of Palan's belief with the weather in the surrounding drama's world is greater than before, so he merits more criticism than before.

The example involves both scalar hyperbole in virtue of the *"great"* (as opposed to *"good"*) and fictively-elaborating hyperbole in virtue of the singing birds, etc. The latter additional elements are not things that Beth thinks that Alan actually believes in. They're entirely imaginary extras on her part. Barnden (2017) gives various examples from real discourse that contain fictively elabo-

---

[5] In detailing this process of understanding, I've considered the hearer to be the addressee Alan, not some other hearer. The process another hearer would go through would be similar, except that he may not have any prior views about what the weather is like. The distinction between what such overhearers versus addressees do is nevertheless very important in irony, or indeed in language understanding in general, and is insufficiently attended to in the field, in my view.

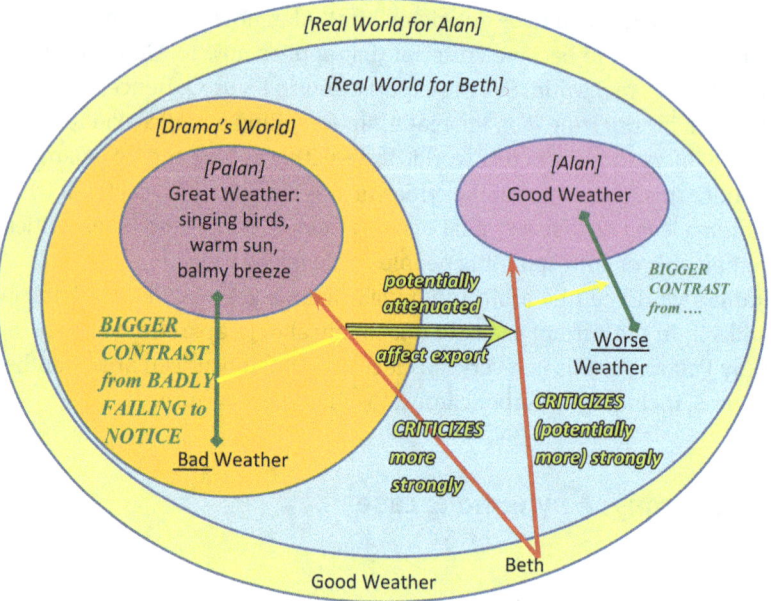

Figure 3: A drama setup (from Alan the hearer's point of view) for hyperbolic-irony example (2).[6]

rating hyperbole. We combine scalar and fictively-elaborating hyperbole in one example here for brevity, but they can be treated separately but otherwise on the same lines as below.

Given that only Palan, and not Alan himself, is claimed to believe that the weather is *great* and to have those fictive extras, there is a need for the strength of exported criticism to be *potentially attenuated*, as shown in the Figure. The level of criticism that Beth feels and intends to convey, and the level that Alan understands she feels, may be higher than in the original example in section 2.1, but this does not mean it is as high as it would have been had Alan actually said *"great weather, what with singing birds, …"*

This point is similar to one we will make below at greater length as regards a non-ironic hyperbolic sentence such as *"This suitcase weighs a ton."* The frustration the speaker of this sentence intends to convey may be greater than if she had just given a reasonable estimate of the suitcase's great weight, but this does

---

[6] The words "more" and "worse" are used in labels in the diagram to suggest that Alan is conjecturing levels of criticism, contrast and weather badness greater than in the example of Figure 2: the words should not be read as depicting a use by Alan of comparative terms in his own thinking.

not mean it is as high as it would have been had the suitcase really weighed a ton. Now, the hearer cannot necessarily come to a specific idea about how frustrated she is, so all we can say in general is that the hearer understands a level or (possibly wide) range of levels that is somewhere between high and the level suitable for a suitcase that weighs a ton.

Similarly, in our irony example, we will assume that Alan understands a level or range of levels of criticism to apply to him that is between what would be appropriate to direct at someone who thought merely that the weather was good and a level that would be appropriate for someone who thinks the weather is great and involves singing birds, etc. It could be as high as the latter level but need not be.

It is also possible that he perceives intensification of criticism if Beth has a sharper tone of voice, rolls her eyes more, etc., but it is important to account for the fact that the hyperbole by itself can provide the potential intensification, while simultaneously allowing freedom to Alan, using whatever evidence he finds appropriate, to conjecture a level or range of levels of criticism.

2.3 Critical irony with another type of fictively elaborating hyperbole

Other types of fictively-elaborating hyperbole in critical irony arise not from exaggerating and elaborating the goodness of the weather in Palan's view, but rather (A) introducing a yet more criticizable relationship than failure-to-notice between Palan and the rest of the drama's world and/or (B) exaggerating the badness of the weather in the drama's world and/or (C) being fictively elaborative in detailing imaginary effects of the bad weather. All three arise in the following interchange:

(3) Alan: *"Good day for a picnic."*
    Beth: *"Sure, it's fun to sit in the pouring rain eating soggy sandwiches!"*

See Figure 4 (where we continue to assume that Alan does correctly perceive what Beth is pretending). Palan here is not being criticized for failing to notice the bad weather and its effects on the sandwiches but, on the contrary, for noticing these things and yet, bizarrely or ridiculously, finding them *fun*. This illustrates (A). (For other examples of absurdity introduced into irony, see especially Kapogianni 2011.) We get (B) if the bad weather in Beth's view doesn't actually go so far as to involve pouring rain. We get (C) if the soggy sandwiches are an invented detail included to heap more ridicule on Palan and therefore (potentially) onto Alan

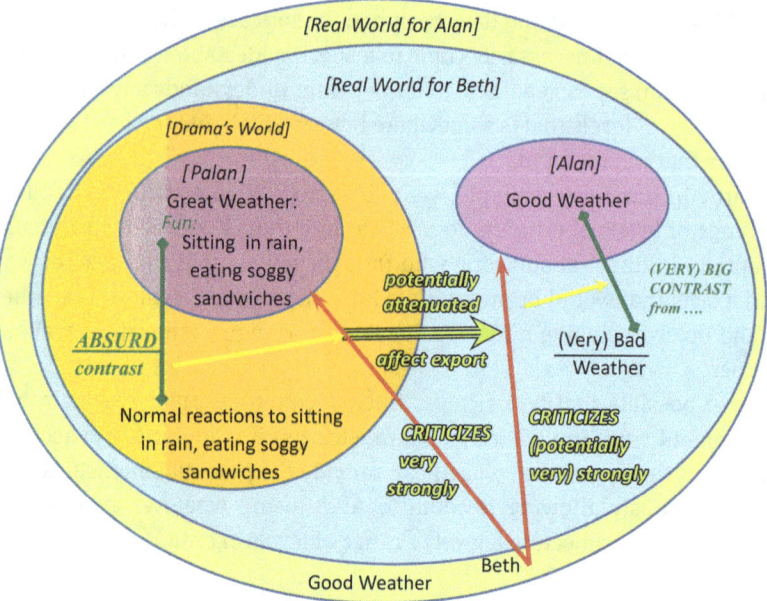

Figure 4: A drama setup for hyperbolic-irony example (3).[7]

himself. The bizarre and ridiculous elements in the drama further intensify Beth's criticism of Palan and hence, at least potentially of Alan.

2.4 Just how bad is Beth's weather? – affect-drivenness

I will assume that hyperbole as above, whether as in section 2.2 or section 2.3, and whether of the scalar or fictively-elaborating type, has the effect of (i) intensifying the badness of the weather that Alan takes Beth to believe, as opposed to just (ii) intensifying the criticism he perceives Beth to be making of him. That effect (i) happens appears to be a general assumption across discussions of irony. But just how does the hyperbole achieve (i)?

It is tempting, and common, to think that intensification as in (i) arises from the use of some sort of opposition operator (see for instance Athanasiadou 2017, for discussion), and indeed this notion is easily prompted by the common description of irony as a matter of the speaker saying the opposite of what she

---

[7] In that the drama's world, Palan is sitting in the rain eating soggy sandwiches, but this is not shown in the diagram for reasons of space.

wishes to convey. According to this idea, the intensification arises because an opposition operator flips positive scale points to negative points (or vice versa) in a systematic way, so that for instance *good* is mapped to *bad*, *great* is mapped to some worse point such as *very bad, wonderful* is mapped to something like *terrible,* and so forth (where these italicized terms denote internal meanings for the corresponding English words). However, while this might superficially sound plausible, there is difficulty in providing a principled basis for such an operator. For example, what does *"wonderful"* mean, and why should that meaning map to the meaning of *"terrible"* rather than the meaning of *"nasty"*, say? In fact, many researchers recognize that on the one hand there's often/usually no well-defined opposite for a given value, but that on the other hand if we depart from oppositeness then we have the problem of what more loosely contrasting values to consider (Burgers & Steen 2017, Colston 2017, Partington 2007).

ATT-Iro has the virtue of removing the necessity for such an opposition operator, or indeed any operator that purports to convert scale values systematically. It provides instead for (i) in an *affect-driven* way, namely that *(i) is a side-effect of (ii)*. All that we required above about good and bad was that Alan presume that, if it's wrong to think something (e.g., the weather) is good, then that something is bad *to some extent*. But this does not require any systematic mapping of specific scale points to opposite, specific scale points. Rather, effect (i) drops out naturally from the way degrees of (e.g.) criticism arise and are exported. We saw that using *"great"* rather than *"good"* naturally intensifies the criticism of Palan, because it's all the more ridiculous that Palan should think the bad weather to be great than to think that it should merely be good. This intensified criticism is exported by Alan to become (potentially) intensified criticism of Alan himself. Recall here that criticism is potentially attenuated, where the extent of attenuation, if any, depends on many factors that Alan might bring to bear. Hence, there is a tendency (but merely a tendency) for stronger criticism of Plan to suggest stronger criticism of Alan. If Alan does infer intensified criticism in the hyperbolic case, he then infers a bigger contrast between his own belief about the weather and Beth's belief than he does in the non-hyperbolic case – bigger criticism means presumably that there must be a bigger contrast. This implies he takes the weather to be worse in Beth's view than he does in the non-hyperbolic case. The more extreme the hyperbole, whether through words like *"great"* or though fictive elaborations, the bigger the criticism he tends to perceive, and so the worse he tends to assume the weather-according-to-Beth is, other things being equal. Where these various points are on the weather badness scale cannot, and indeed should not, be provided by a theory of irony or hyperbole as such, but depends on the particular discourse context, including other clues that Beth might give about how bad she thinks the weather is.

Note that by this argument the weather badness will also have a tendency to be intensified if Beth just seems more critical because of a more marked sarcastic tone, eye-rolling, etc., irrespective of any hyperbolic wording. This intuitively seems to be a reasonable prediction of the theory, and renders the indirect, weather-badness intensification effect as a seamless combination of hyperbolic wording and other signals such as intonation, etc.

3 A hyperbole model, some modifications, and melding with ATT-Iro

3.1 The model (PRM)

Peña & Ruiz de Mendoza (2017: Fig.1 and preceding text) present a model of hyperbole,[8] which I will here call the PRM model. They do so largely by means of the following example:

(4) *"This suitcase weighs a ton."*

The suitcase is one that the speaker herself (let's say Beth) is trying to lift and carry. Peña & Ruiz de Mendoza seek to explain not only how the sentence conveys that the suitcase is exceptionally heavy but also how the sentence conveys Beth's emotional reaction, for example frustration, arising from her attempts to handle the suitcase. The authors go far as to say that the meaning implications of the example are centred on such emotion. (See also Ruiz de Mendoza 2017, and Watling, this volume.)

PRM involves a mapping between an imaginary situation in which the suitcase really does weigh a ton and is therefore impossible to lift, so that Beth is (for example) frustrated in that imaginary situation, and the real situation of the suitcase being merely very heavy but still too heavy to lift, so that Beth is also frustrated in the real situation. See Figure 5.

---

8 For a sample of other work on hyperbole, see Brdar-Szabó & Brdar (2010), Carston & Wearing (2011, 2015), Claridge (2011), Herrero Ruiz (2009), McCarthy & Carter (2004), Norrick (2004), Popa-Wyatt (this volume), Walton (2017) and Watling (this volume). Also see Barnden (2018) for a development of hyperbole in an unusual direction. Peña & Ruiz de Mendoza (2017) provide rich discussion of hyperbole aside from their presentation of the model that I am reporting.

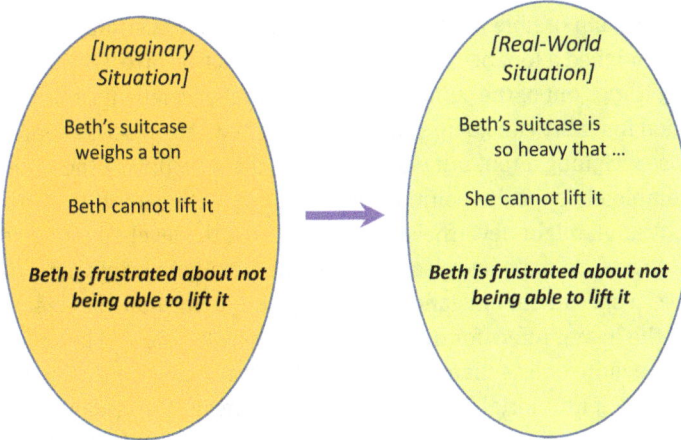

Figure 5: A treatment of hyperbole example (4) following Peña & Ruiz de Mendoza (2017).[9]

This account is broadly appealing, but it is beneficial to make some significant initial adjustments to it and clarifications of it, as follows.

3.2 Some adjustments and clarifications to PRM

One adjustment is to modify the assumption that Beth is, in the real situation, completely unable to lift the suitcase. It could be simply that the suitcase's weight makes it difficult enough to lift for Beth to be frustrated, amazed, or whatever. Of course, in a specific context, it might be that Beth cannot lift the suitcase at all, and the hearer may, moreover, be able to see that she can't. But in other contexts the hearer may just get the message that the suitcase is at least very difficult to lift.

Another, related, adjustment is that we should allow for the degree of frustration to be attenuated in the move from the imaginary situation to reality. For one thing, if she merely finds it very difficult to lift rather than impossible to lift, her real frustration may well be less than with an impossible-to-lift suitcase. But also,

---

9 The diagram is adapted from Figure 1 in Peña & Ruiz de Mendoza (2017). The single mapping arrow is borrowed from their Figure, but their text implies that the arrow summarizes the mapping of the various individual aspects of the imaginary situation to the pretence situation – the suitcase itself, what it weighs, the difficulty of lifting it, Beth's frustration. The content of the imaginary situation has been slightly adapted for presentational reasons: Peña and Ruiz de Mendoza say that in that situation the suitcase "weighs too much for [the speaker] to lift" it.

even if she does find it impossible to lift, she still may not be as frustrated as she might be if it really weighed a ton, because she could more easily correct the situation by, say, taking things out of the suitcase than if it actually weighed a ton. The degree of frustration in reality can go up some way towards what would be appropriate for a suitcase weighing a ton, but need not go all the way. But, at the same time, there is a completely opposite point: even if in reality Beth can lift the suitcase a bit, her frustration might nevertheless be nearer or at the level appropriate to a ton-weight suitcase, perhaps because she is an abnormally irascible person. This would be a very special circumstance, but makes the point that the degree of frustration that the hearer infers for the real situation may be affected by many factors, and could be more or less than, or equal to, the level arising in the imaginary situation, but that if no special evidence is available, the degree is some high value up to that appropriate to the ton-weight suitcase in the imaginary situation.

As a clarification of PRM, it is useful in this article to place more explicit focus on other emotions Beth may have. She could be amazed or amused at the weight of the suitcase, for instance. Such emotions will play significant role below. It is also useful for us to be more explicit about some causal links in the situations. In the imaginary situation, Beth's inability to lift the suitcase is caused by its weighing a ton, and her frustration is presumably caused by her inability to lift it and not just by its weighing a ton. Analogous causal links hold in the real situation.

3.3 Some further modification of PRM, and melding with ATT-Iro

I draw inspiration from PRM because we can re-label the imaginary situation as a pretended situation, indeed a drama much like those arising in irony, and because PRM's use of mappings chimes well with ATT-Meta and ATT-Iro. Also, I borrow, adjust and extend a major insight in PRM, namely that what the hearer mainly infers about the weight of the suitcase in the real situation is that the suitcase is too heavy to lift. This is in marked contrast to the idea, which otherwise seems to be uncritically assumed in the hyperbole literature, that the hearer's main task in our example is to infer some value for the weight – whether a numerical value, range of numerical values, or a qualitative value (or range) such as *very heavy* or *exceptionally heavy* – by in some way attenuating the overt value, here "*a ton*", by going down the weight scale from it.[10]

---

10 For presentational reasons the instances of hyperbole in this article are all "from above," where the hearer is invited to go down a scale from an overt value such as "*a ton*", though still

Before proceeding further, we need to distinguish certain issues that are bundled together or left implicit in Peña & Ruiz de Mendoza (2017).

3.3.1 Separating out some issues

Certain matters are obscured by the implicit first-person nature of (4), because Beth is both the speaker and the person who is seeking to handle the suitcase. We should also consider a third-person example where the speaker, Beth, is observing someone else, Bertie, trying to lift a suitcase:

(5) *"Bertie's suitcase weighs a ton."*

Any frustration may now just be Bertie's, not Beth's, although there are circumstances in which Beth could be frustrated by the situation (e.g., if Bertie is travelling with Beth and delaying her). However, and extremely importantly, I will assume that Beth may have other affect about the weight of the suitcase, for instance amazement at it, or finding the weight ridiculous or at least remarkable.

But even (5) still conflates some issues by having a person involved in the depicted situation. It is analytically salutary to make another step, and move to a more basic, impersonal example of hyperbole, such as

(6) *"That suitcase on the carousel is about a mile long!"*

I call this impersonal on the assumption that it is clear in context that the comment is merely about the length as such, not about any practical effect that it might have on someone, such as handling difficulty, or consequent emotional effect on someone other than the speaker. Rather, the affect the speaker is conveying is her own surprise, wonder, amusement, etc. Of course, turning back now to (5), we see that Beth's affect there should be treated much as that of the speaker of (6) is; and then turning back to (4) we see that, as it is now the speaker who is herself in the situation being hyperbolically commented on, her affect should in part be treated like the *speaker* affect in (5) and (6) and partly like *Bertie's* affect in (5).

Now, so as to be as general as possible across affect types and degrees, I have found it convenient and productive to couch hyperbole as conveying that

---

to some high value, rather than "from below" as in *"My piece of cake is infinitesimal!,"* where the hearer is invited to go up a scale from the *"infinitesimal"* overt value, though still to some very low value. Note that such from-below hyperbole should be distinguished from ironic understatement, as in the use of *"My infinitesimal piece of cake"* to convey that the piece is actually very large.

the value in explicit question (weight of a suitcase, or whatever) is *notably* high (or low).[11] The notability always implies affect, but it might merely be a weak interestingness appropriate to an exceptionally high (or low) value. In example (6), the speaker may find the suitcase length extremely notable to the extent of being ridiculous, say. Furthermore (and here I go beyond my previous work) I unpack the notability as a relationship between speaker and situation feature, for instance as Beth's finding the suitcase's length extremely notable, or Beth's finding the suitcase's length ridiculous. The precise unpacking depends on the utterance details and context.

Because of the sparseness and impersonality of the pretended scenario in (6), we have here an extreme, degenerate form of drama, of course. There would be little reason to propose a drama based analysis for (6) if it weren't for the fact that drama is an appropriate notion for richer, personal examples of hyperbole such as (4, 5), and the fact that hyperbole can be combined with irony that is usefully given a dramatic analysis. Without such considerations, it would be enough to use more neutral notions such as pretence, fiction or imaginary situation.

Before detailing drama setups for our examples, there are some further claims and proposals, as follows.

3.3.2 The nature of values derived, why derive a value, and affect-drivenness

We need to guard against the highly implausible idea that a hearer of a hyperbolic utterance, especially one that mentions a specific value as in *"a ton"*, chooses some numerical value on a scale, such as some particular large weight less than a ton. Rather, the hearer of a hyperbolic statement may only be able to, or may only be inclined to, commit to a range of values, and possibly quite a wide one. Moreover, it may often be reasonable to suppose that the hearer just has some vague, qualitative, mental representations, analogous to linguistic phrases such as *"very heavy"* or *"very heavy up to extremely heavy,"* without having any idea of what these representations amount to in terms of numerical values. Or, the hearer may just have an embodied sense of what a very heavy suitcase feels like. These points apply not only to overtly addressed issues such as the weight of a suitcase but also analogously to implicit issues such as an attendant level of frustration.

We saw that ATT-Iro has an *affect-driven* account of the derivation of a value such as the badness of the weather, proceeding via the strength of the exported

---

11 I have used notability in recent discussion of hyperbole elsewhere, e.g. in Barnden (2018). It is a development of the view of hyperbole in Barnden (2017).

criticism. I make a similar proposal for hyperbole. While it may be that the suitcase weight, the degree of inability to lift, the level of the lifter frustration etc., and the level of the speaker's amazement etc. may be separately exported (with potential attenuation) into the real situation (and I say more on this in section 5), I claim that one important – and in many cases the most important – route to representing a weight for the suitcase is via an estimate of lifter's and/or speaker's intensity of affect. To the extent that Alan as hearer can sense that Beth as speaker of (4) is frustrated, whether from the wording of the utterance – especially in a variant example such as *"This effing suitcase weighs a ton!"* – or from Beth's tone of voice, etc., or from other surrounding discourse, he can surmise reasons for her frustration; and given that she mentions the weight of the suitcase, it is not difficult for him to infer that she is frustrated because she finds the suitcase difficult to lift, and that it is difficult to lift because it is suitably heavy. Thus, he has an opportunity to estimate the weight (in the sense of deriving a possibly-qualitative value range, or embodied sense) on the basis of an estimate of how difficult it is to lift it, and to derive this estimate in turn from the level of frustration. Somewhat analogous reasoning applies when Beth says (5): Alan might estimate the weight directly from the level of amazement (etc.) he senses that Beth is experiencing, possibly in concert with any information he might have about how frustrated Bertie is.

The affect-drivenness in this approach raises a further, radical, suggestion: that the hearer's only, or main, mental representation of (say) the length of the suitcase in (6) may itself be explicitly *affectively framed*, by which I mean something on the lines of *long enough to amaze the speaker*, which explicitly describes the value in terms of the affect. Such a representation is possibly all the hearer needs to derive. Accordingly, I propose that such a value description is the main (perhaps only) one that a hyperbole theory needs to provide. Nevertheless, a hearer could have reasons to work out non-affectively framed values or value ranges (at least of the qualitative or embodied sorts above). What value or value range is arrived at is, however, not necessarily a matter for a theory of *hyperbole* as such. The most that a hyperbole theory might say in general is that hearers pick some high values or ranges of levels no higher than the imaginary, hyperbolic values (for, e.g. the suitcase weight and for the attendant affect). What "high" amounts to, or, alternatively, what "high enough to amaze the speaker" amounts to, is a matter of the hearer's knowledge about the type of situation in question, and any knowledge he may have about the particular situation and people involved, whether from the surrounding discourse, his own perception of the situation, or general knowledge. All this is a matter of general-purpose inferencing independent of hyperbole itself.

The affect-drivenness (whether the resulting values are affectively framed or not) is very much in the spirit of the insight that PRM offers, that the weight of the suitcase in (4) is inferred to be so high as to make it difficult for Beth to lift it. The affect-drivenness lies in the fact that the lifting difficulty can be inferred from the frustration, as noted above. But, bearing in mind our comment above that the weight itself may influence the frustration by a route other than lifting difficulty, a better suggestion would be that the hearer infers that *the suitcase is so heavy that it is very and frustratingly difficult for Beth to lift it*, which is, in part, explicitly based on affect.

This inference about the weight is consistent with direct, attenuated export of the ton value. Suppose that such export by itself suggests a value such as *extremely heavy* or a value range such as *unusually heavy up to extremely heavy*. The affect-driven route gives a more usefully constrained value, but the directly exported one does no harm.

3.3.3 Inclusion of the overt value

Barnden (2015b) introduced the notion that a potentially hyperbolic utterance can often be given a *liberal* interpretation, in that the overtly stated value is itself included in the value range inferred by the hearer. In effect, the literal value is kept as an option. This could for instance apply to *"Mary has hundreds of living relatives"* with the hearer deriving the meaning that *Mary has many living relatives and possibly even hundreds*. Or, bearing in mind our proposal of affectively framed values, the hearer might derive something like *Mary has amazingly many relatives and perhaps even hundreds*. It's perfectly possible for someone to have hundreds of relatives.[12] It's just that many contexts may happen to suggest that Mary has fewer than this, or it may be immediately obvious from the wording that the overt value is to be excluded (e.g., with *"trillions"* in place of *"hundreds"*). But in other circumstances there is no reason for a hearer to have to make a decision as to whether the overt value is included or not, let alone to have to view the utterance as ambiguous between two alternative interpretations, one literal and one narrowly hyperbolic. The hearer would just need to adopt a value range that extends up to the overt value.

This chimes well also with a point made above about the level of frustration in suitcase examples: the real level experienced by the lifter *might* be as much as he would experience for a suitcase that really weighed a ton, especially if it was so heavy that he couldn't lift it at all. There's no reason in principle for a theory of hyperbole, itself, to exclude this possibility from consideration, although particular contexts may point to its exclusion on general practical or logical grounds.

---

12 E.g., a person I met who claimed 200 cousins, let alone other relatives!

To my knowledge, liberal interpretations of (potential) hyperboles have not been discussed in the literature on hyperbole, but for this article they are central, and fit well with the nature of merely-potential attenuation of degrees in pretence-to-reality exportation in the overall model of this article, as further discussed below.

Taking everything in section 3 so far on board, we are now ready to present a drama-based treatment of the examples that is consistent with ATT-Iro.

3.3.4 Treatment of the examples

We will look at (6), (5) and (4) in that order. For (6), with Beth as speaker and Alan as hearer, see Figure 6.

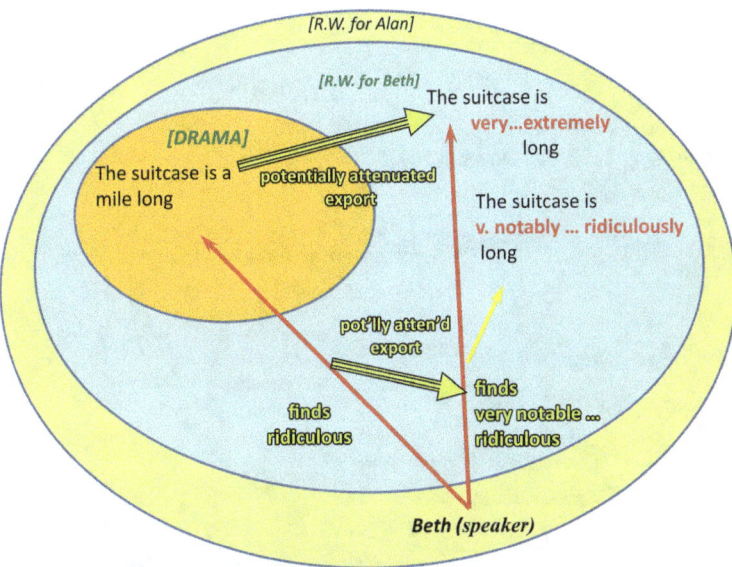

Figure 6: A drama setup for hyperbole example (6).[13]

---

13 "R.W." is short for "real world." As before, the oval marked as Beth's real world is actually what Alan conjectures her real world to be. The value ranges within the overall are not entertained by Beth herself, but indicate Alan's uncertainty about how things are from Beth's point of view. The yellow arrow on the right shows affect-driven inference by Alan. As in irony examples, the roughly horizontal arrows show export actions by Alan (not by Beth).

For the sake of example, I have taken Beth to find the *pretended* suitcase length ridiculous (a way of finding it to be extremely notable). In the export of this ridicule, its intensity is attenuated to some range that stretches up to ridicule, generating the inference that Beth finds the *real* length at least very notable and perhaps even ridiculous. This may then lead to an affectively framed value for the real length, such as *so long as to strike Beth as ridiculous*. This is all parallel to the export of criticism in our irony examples and the resulting driving Alan's view of how bad Beth thinks the weather is. The Figure also shows an independent attenuated export of the pretended length itself.

Turning to example (5), we have inferences and exports like those in Figure 6, especially to handle Beth's finding the weight of the suitcase to be very notable if not ridiculous; but we now need also to take care of the suitcase lifters' levels of frustration (those of Pertie in the drama and Bertie in Beth's real world). See Figure 7.

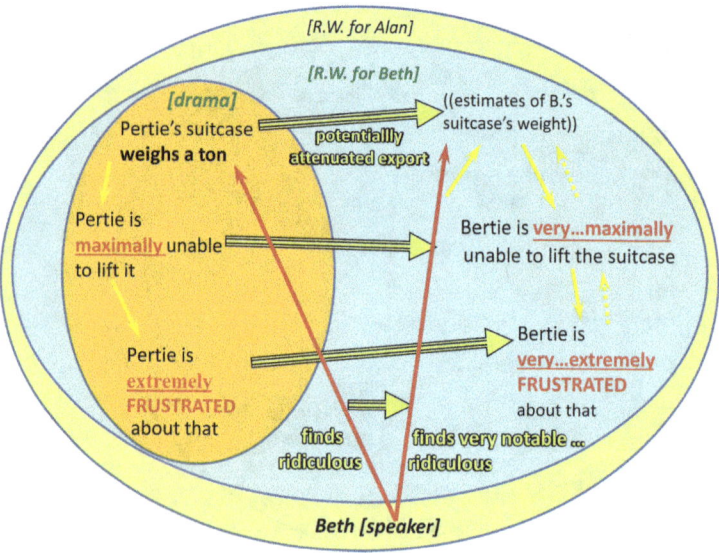

Figure 7: A drama setup for hyperbole example (5).[14]

---

14 Structure that is directly analogous to all that in Figure 6 is to be considered to be included here, but is compressed at the top right of the diagram for reasons of space. The suitcase is replaced by Bertie's suitcase, length is replaced by weight and a mile is replaced by a ton. There is additional structure because there is now a person interacting with the suitcase. Some arrows are dotted for reasons explained in the text. All the roughly-horizontal lines continue to depict potentially attenuated exportation.

Pertie's frustration is exported by Alan to become Bertie's. Previously, for our examples of irony, and for hyperbole example (6), we just had export of the affect of a person (Beth) outside the drama. Now we are allowing exportation of the affect of within-drama characters.

There is an important difference from the type of drama we had for our particular examples of irony. Beth is presenting a drama in which there is a character corresponding to Bertie. But there is no reason to think of her as acting that character. If we wished to proceed by strict analogy with our irony treatment, we could take (5) to be analogous to *"The weather's great"* in that treatment, where there was a dramatic character Palan (defectively) observing the weather, and thus take Beth to be acting a dramatic character who is observing Pertie grappling with his suitcase. So the drama would be like that in Figure 7 but would additionally include such an observer. This would appear not to add any benefit as to what is communicated about Bertie and his suitcase, or about Beth's own attitudes. Therefore, we propose that the simpler analysis of Figure 7 is appropriate. The extra simplicity is possible because we do not have the complication that the drama needs to contain a criticizable observer such as Palan (observer of the weather, in our irony examples).

The Figure shows an affect-driven route (to the suitcase weight) that uses Beth's affect, and another one using Bertie's. However, the arrows on the Bertie route are dotted, to indicate that it is only tentatively and provisionally proposed. Although the route could be included, it is more likely that Alan can get a clear impression of Beth's type and strength of affect than of Bertie's, unless there is extra information from context. For instance, Beth's intonation and facial expressions would help Alan to estimate her affect, but would not (or not as directly) help him to estimate Bertie's.

Finally, for example (4), see Figure 8. Here, in effect, Beth becomes one with Bertie. We have almost the same setup as for example (5), but now Beth herself appears in the drama as Peth, we moreover regard Beth as acting the role of Peth, and all her affect – her frustration as well as her finding-ridiculous – may now contribute to Alan's affect-driven view of the suitcase weight.

3.3.5 More on consistency with ATT-Iro

Section 2, on irony, made no mention of "notability," despite the discussion of hyperbole there. Nevertheless, the critical stances taken by the speaker in section 2 amount to her finding a dramatic character notably defective in some way, e.g. in failing to notice bad weather in the drama. The critical affect in section 2 just a special way of finding something notable, just as finding something to be ridic-

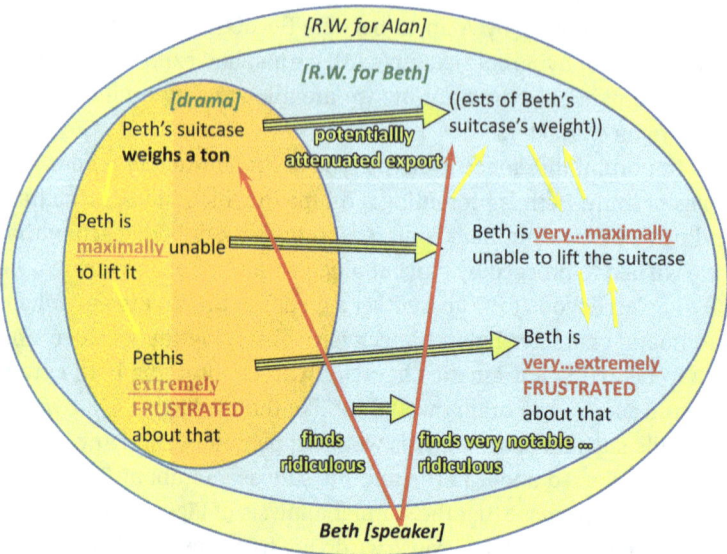

Figure 8: A drama setup for hyperbole example (4).[15]

ulous, amazing, etc. in the current section has been. The export of criticism in section 2 is the parallel of the export of notability in the current section.

Importantly, the way hyperbole works within irony in section 2 does not involve plugging in the current section's treatment in any simple way. For instance, if Beth's utterance *"Sure, the weather's wonderful"* is criticizing Alan for thinking the weather is (merely) good, then dramatic character Palan thinks that the weather is wonderful. This is not treated as some sort of hyperbole within the drama, and would not be even if the drama went to the lengths of having Palan say *"the weather is wonderful"* rather than just thinking it. Palan in the drama really does think the weather is wonderful, not merely good. Rather, this inflated thought increases Beth's criticism, leading to effects such as increasing the badness of the weather than Beth communicates to Alan. So, while *"the weather is wonderful"* in Beth's utterance can felicitously be said to bear a hyperbolic relationship to Alan's claim that *"the weather is good,"* the hyperbolic quality works in an indirect way, one that is thoroughly intertwined with the rest of the working of the irony. This is very much in line with the claim by Popa-Wyatt (this volume) that hyperbolic irony is "a single figure coloured with hyperbolic tinges," and should not be taken to be a compounding of figures in any normal sense.

---

15 The setup is almost exactly like the one in Figure 7, but with Bertie replaced by Beth herself, and the dotted inference route in Figure 7 replaced by a more definite route.

4 The existing metaphor model [ATT-Meta]

The author's ATT-Meta approach is based on pretences or fictions (see Section 5 for commentary on the term used). In this respect, it has some similarity to fiction/pretence-based work on metaphor in philosophy (Egan 2008, Hills 2017, Walton 2004/1993) and a proposed addition of meta-representations to a Relevance Theory account of metaphor (Carston & Wearing 2011). Consider the following metaphorical sentence:

(7) *"John's exam marking overflowed into the weekend."*

Assume that John had been marking during the traditional working week of Monday to Friday. Now, as is the case with many metaphorical terms, the phrase *"to overflow into"* applied to an activity and a time period might have an entrenched metaphorical meaning that is coded – stored in the hearer's memory and ready for immediate use – and delivers a plausible meaning of (7). The stored meaning might be on the lines of *to continue undesirably and inadvertently at times that are later than an expected ending time and are during the mentioned time period*. Any full account of metaphor must take account of such stored meanings. However, the ATT-Meta model is, instead, more focussed on how a hearer is to proceed in the absence of suitable stored metaphorical meanings. So, for the sake of illustration, I will assume that neither *"overflow into"* nor *"overflow"* and *"into"* separately have suitable stored meanings for a particular hearer. If it did, we could change the example to use some other more creative term such as *"splashed out into."*

Then, according to the ATT-Meta approach, the speaker and hearer of (7) momentarily pretend that (=imagine that, = construct a fiction that) John's exam marking was something that literally physically overflowed from the working week into the weekend. (That the literal meaning is quickly activated in cases of metaphors with – at least, but not exclusively – non-stored meaning has considerable experimental support: see, e.g., Giora 1997 and Giora, Fein, Kotler & Shuval 2015.) Henceforth, I will concentrate on what the hearer needs to do with the pretence: i.e., conducting inference within the pretence to elaborate it, and drawing information out of the pretence to say something about the real world. The hearer can infer that, in the pretended scenario, John's marking is a body of something that can physically flow. For brevity, I will assume that he infers that it is presumably a liquid.[16] Then again, since overflowing of a liquid must be from a

---

[16] But the treatment can be adjusted to include other possibilities, such as a powder, or just some unspecified physical substance capable of flowing.

suitable physical container into a spatial region outside it, the working week must be such a physical container and the weekend must be such a spatial region. The pretended scenario can be further elaborated by inference, based on the hearer's common-sense knowledge about liquids, overflowing, containers, etc. It can be inferred that the marking-liquid was originally all in the working-week-container and then some of it was instead in the weekend-region.

But, importantly, the overflowing of a liquid is typically unexpected and unintended, and its results negatively valued by relevant agents. Let us assume that the hearer presumes (i.e., infers as a default) that, in the pretence, John moderately dislikes the situation of some of the marking-liquid being in the weekend-region. All these inferences are of a type that an ordinary hearer can quickly and easily make when physical overflowing occurs. With these inferences performed, the nature of the pretence (pretended scenario) is as depicted in Figure 9.

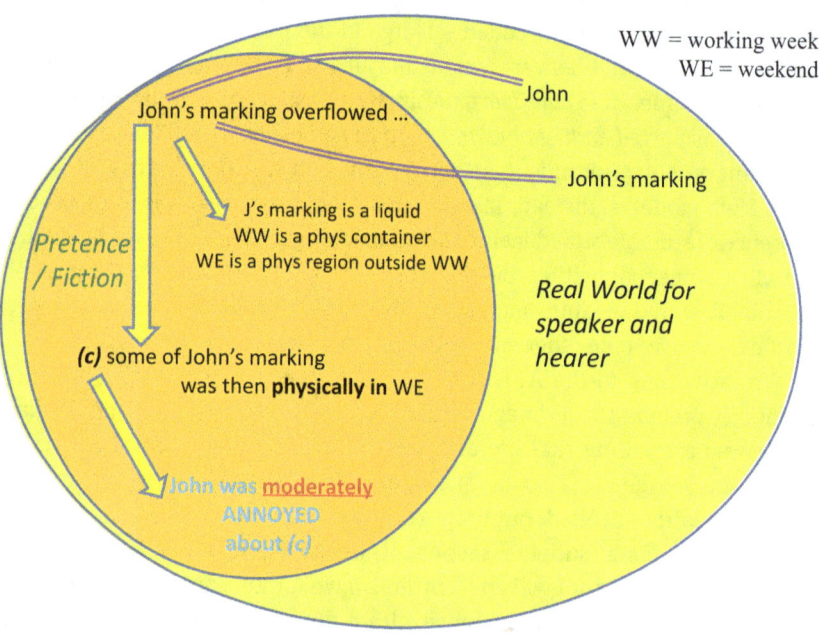

Figure 9: Some initial aspects of a pretence or fiction setup in ATT-Meta, for metaphor example (7).[17]

The work on ATT-Meta has largely made the simplifying assumption that the speaker and hearer do not disagree on what the real world is like, at least as

---

[17] The correspondences shown by double lines are ones that the hearer assumes the speaker stipulates on starting to engage in the pretence.

regards the current local interests of the discourse, so the real world in the Figure is the real world for both for the speaker and hearer. Cases of disagreement will be touched on below.

The hearer needs to export and modify information from the pretence to become information about the real-world situation of John's marking. For this purpose two types of mapping construct are used: *view specific mapping rules* and *view-neutral mapping adjuncts* (VNMAs). Both are assumed to be a pre-existing part of the long-term knowledge of a typical hearer. The only view-specific mapping rule needed in the case of (7) is one that, for a process P and a time interval T, makes P-*physically-located-within*-T in a pretence correspond to P-*temporally-occurs-during*-T in reality, in suitable circumstances. It can be expressed informally as follows:

IF
in reality: P is a process AND T is a time interval
AND
in the pretended scenario: P is a physical object AND T is a physical location

THEN
P being physically located within T in the pretended scenario
      CORRESPONDS TO
P occurring in (a subinterval of) T in reality.

If we wish, this can be theoretically regarded as reflecting both the view of A TIME PERIOD AS A SPATIAL REGION and a view of A PROCESS AS A PHYSICAL OBJECT. This is because of the conditions in the IF part of the rule. The presence of such conditions explains the designation of the rule as "view-specific." There may in principle be other mapping rules with similar conditions, in which case they also reflect one or both of those two views. However, these views are not reified as entities in their own right – in ATT-Meta there is no explicit bundling of view-specific mapping rules into constructs such as conceptual metaphors. Two rules that both reflect a given view, say, A PROCESS AS A PHYSICAL OBJECT, by virtue of their IF parts are not thereby formally connected. It is just that they may both be activated when a pretence contains something that is a physical object in the pretence but is a process in reality.

The above rule can be used to infer that the following correspondence exists:

a portion of John's marking-liquid in the pretence being physically located in the weekend-region

CORRESPONDS TO

that marking portion occurring within the weekend in reality.

This is merely a correspondence between two conceivable situations, which may or may not occur. But some of the marking-liquid *is* actually in the weekend-region in the pretence, and this actuality is carried over to reality, so that it is inferred that some of John's marking does occur during the weekend in reality. Figure 10 shows where the hearer has got to now.

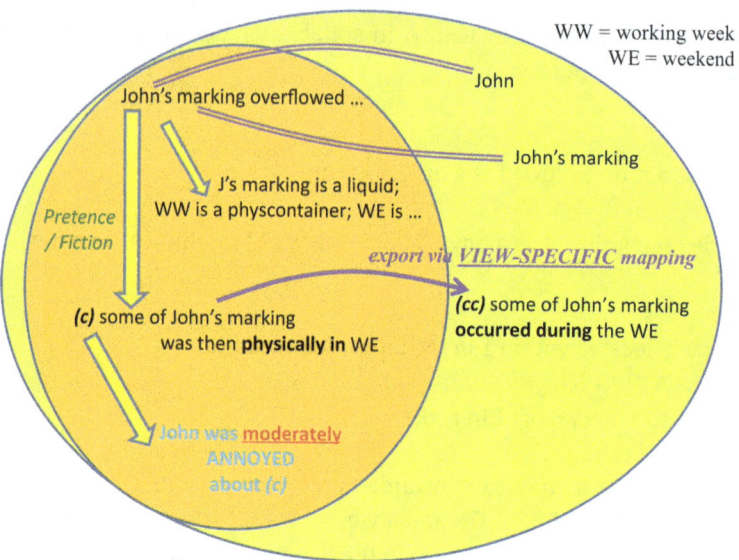

Figure 10: Example (7) continued, now also showing the export of an aspect of the pretence by view-specific mapping.

Turning to view-neutral mapping adjuncts (VNMAs), they are mapping rules that deal with certain broad types of information that strongly tend to be exported in metaphor *whatever* specific metaphorical views are in play. These types include matters such as temporal relationships, temporal qualities of processes such as intermittency and termination, causation/enablement/prevention relationships, ability, easiness/difficulty, logical operations/relations such as disjunction and implication, modal aspects such as necessity and obligation, mental qualities, mental states, affective states and degrees of holding of circumstances. VNMAs play a role somewhat similar to that played by the Extended Invariance Hypothesis of Peña & Ruiz de Mendoza (2017) and by the systematicity and the transfer of higher-order relations in Structure Matching Theory (Gentner & Bowdle 2008)

Importantly for example (7), and for this article as a whole, there is a VNMA that I will call here the *Within-Scenario Affect VNMA*. This leads to the export of affect that within-pretence agents have about within-pretence matters to become corresponding affect in the real situation. This VNMA can be expressed as:

IF
cognitive agent P in a pretended scenario CORRESPONDS TO cognitive agent Q in reality AND
thing or circumstance X in the pretended scenario CORRESPONDS TO Y in reality

THEN
P having affective attitude of type A towards X in the pretended scenario
      CORRESPONDS TO
Q having affective attitude of type A towards Y in reality.

In our example, we can take both P and Q to be John, A to be dislike, X to be the circumstance of some portion of marking-liquid being physically located in the weekend-region and Y to be the circumstance of that marking portion occurring during the weekend. P and Q then correspond because of being identical, and the action of the above view-specific mapping rule makes X and Y correspond. So the VNMA rule provides the inference that John's dislike of X in the pretence corresponds to his dislike of Y in reality. Again, this is merely the establishment of a correspondence, not yet an inference about an actual circumstance. But, putting aside the question of degree of dislike for a moment, we see that since John, in the pretence, does actually dislike the location of the marking, he also, in reality, dislikes the marking occurring during the weekend, if, as before, we let actuality be carried across a correspondence.

In ATT-Meta as it currently stands, there is also a *Degree VNMA* that just makes the degree of holding of a circumstance in the pretence corresponds to the same degree of holding of a corresponding real circumstance if there is one. The effect is that the degree of John's dislike in reality is inferred (initially at least) to be moderately high, because the degree of the corresponding dislike in the pretence is moderately high. With this included, the hearer derives the setup shown in Figure 11.

Another, closely related, VNMA is one I call here the *External-Affect VNMA*. This leads to the export of affective attitudes that the speaker or hearer, rather than a within-pretence agent such as John, has towards within-pretence matters, to become affective attitudes by the speaker or hearer towards corresponding aspects of the real situation. This VNMA can be expressed as:

IF

thing or circumstance X in the pretended scenario CORRESPONDS TO Y in reality

THEN

the speaker or hearer having affective attitude of type A towards X in the pretended scenario

    CORRESPONDS TO

the speaker or hearer (resp.) having affective attitude of type A towards Y in reality.

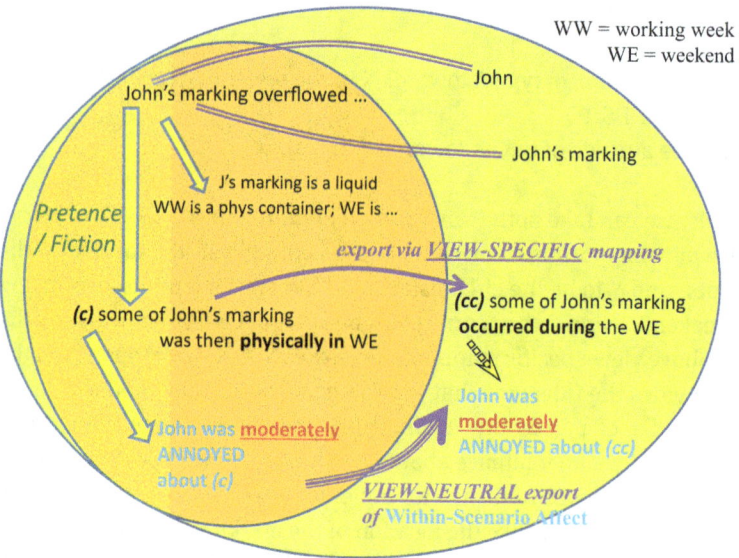

Figure 11: Example (7) continued, now also showing the export of affect by the Within Scenario VNMA.

There are further long-standing VNMAs in ATT-Meta that will be significant below. There is a *Value-Judgment VNMA*, concerning judgments as to whether something is good, important, etc. There is also the *Mental-States VNMA*. This is very similar to the Within-Scenario Affect VNMA but handles any other sort of non-affective mental state, including perceptual relationships. If for instance an agent in the pretence believes something X, and Y in the real situation corresponds to X (i.e., it is X as translated by mappings that have been applied), then the VNMA leads to the default inference that a corresponding agent in reality (if there is one) believes Y. So, in example (6), if the hearer inferred within the pretence that John notices that some of his marking has come to be physically located in the weekend-region, then it will be inferred by default that in reality he notices that some of his marking occurs during the weekend. Also, from commonsense knowledge about situations where liquids overflow, the overflowing in the pretence can be inferred to be, by default, inadvertent – i.e., unintended by John – even though an action of John's might have been a contributing cause. This likely inadvertence (lack of intention) gets carried over by the Mental-State VNMA, in conjunction with a Logical VNMA that carries over logical operations such as negation, to become likely inadvertence of what happened in reality. This is major connotation of the sentence, although it could perhaps be defeated in a specific context.

In ATT-Meta, most inference is of a default nature. For instance, an inference that someone is annoyed about the overflow of some liquid is merely a default, and can be defeated by other sufficiently strong evidence. Equally, mapping rules, whether view-specific or view-neutral, are defaults, and actuality is only carried by default from pretence to reality across a correspondence between events. These features lend the approach a great deal of necessary flexibility. Notably, it allows the effect of attempted exports to be defeated by sufficiently well-established countervailing information about the real situation, while at the same time allowing exports to defeat sufficiently uncertain information about the real situation.

A major feature of ATT-Meta is that many aspects of metaphorical pretences have no correspondent (no parallel) in reality, or, more precisely, there is no attempt to find correspondents for them. The liquidity of the exam marking in the pretence is not made to correspond to any constitution of the marking in reality. The overflowing event itself is not made to correspond to any event in the real situation. The ATT-Meta philosophy here is that it would be a waste of time to seek such correspondences, especially as the search could well fail. There was some complex series of circumstances, no doubt, that in reality led to John not finishing his marking during the working week, but it is likely to be difficult and pointless, as regards understanding (7), to isolate a specific event that caused him to mark at the weekend. What is important is simply that it did come to be that he did some marking at the weekend, that this was probably inadvertent, and that he probably disliked doing so. In short, ATT-Meta seeks as far as possible to find metaphorical meaning just by using already known mappings, in the form of the existing view specific and view-neutral mapping rules, in concert with performing within-pretence and within-reality inferences.. There are certainly cases where new mappings need to be found, for instance by analogy invention on the lines of Structure-Matching Theory (Gentner & Bowdle 2008). Analogy invention could be added to ATT-Meta to get a more complete approach, but this has not yet been done.

Finally, ATT-Meta can cope with speaker-reality being different from hearer-reality, and can place a pretence within any type of space. The main case of this so far in ATT-Meta work has been the nesting of pretences within other pretences as a treatment of chained metaphor (Barnden 2016). But a different possibility, to be exploited in section 5.4, is sketched in Figure 12. This setup would be appropriate when the hearer does not wish to adopt, or is not in a position to adopt, what the speaker thinks is real, and furthermore, the nature of speaker's reality affects the details of what is put into the pretence or how it is elaborated. In effect, the Figure shows the hearer simulating the speaker engaging in a pretence although the hearer does not himself adopt that pretence. The mapping actions are now ones that Alan conjectures Beth intends. The resulting setup is clearly very similar to those in previous Figures for hyperbole and irony.

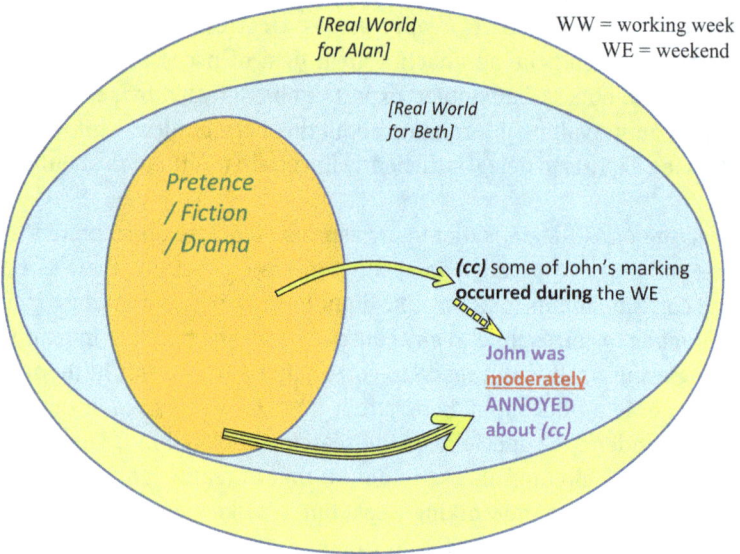

Figure 12: Example (7) continued. An outline of the setup when Alan the hearer explicitly represents Beth's real world.

5 Melding ATT-Meta with the extended ATT-Iro

A central, shared feature of ATT-Meta, ATT-Iro and the above hyperbole model is the exportation of affect, sometimes within-scenario and sometimes external. Clearly, for this purpose we could augment the hyperbole model and ATT-Iro with ATT-Meta's VNMAs concerning affect. But in fact I propose that the models be more thoroughly melded by the simple expedient of letting all of ATT-Meta's VNMAs – not just the affect ones – be used in hyperbole and irony as well, though with one adjustment. This adjustment is that the Degree VNMA needs to be modified, as it does not allow for the attenuation of degrees that was a central feature of the above treatments of hyperbole and irony. This modification will be addressed in section 5.1. In the resulting overall model, pretences are variously ones for pure hyperbole, pure irony or pure metaphor, or for combinations of these as already illustrated for hyperbolic irony, and as will be illustrated below for hyperbolic metaphor and ironic metaphor. The proposal is that the VNMAs would apply uniformly in all cases, and the discussion below supports the validity of doing this. Note straightaway that the descriptions of the VNMAs in section 4 do not require the pretences to be *metaphorical* ones. All that they rely on is that certain things within pretences be deemed to "correspond" to certain entities outside the pretences.

There is no danger of spreading of the view-*specific* mappings from the treatment of metaphor into the treatment of irony and hyperbole. The conditions demanded by the IF parts of view-specific mapping rules will simply not apply in pretences that are not metaphorical. So the rules can simply "sit around" in the whole model, and will automatically come into play to act upon metaphorical pretences, but not upon non-metaphorical hyperbolic or ironic pretences.

The fact that we talked in sections 2 and 3 of ironic and hyperbolic pretences as *dramas*, but did not use this term in the case of metaphor in section 4, need not detain us. The use of the notion of drama is just a theoretical heuristic, and it is not proposed that within the pretence setups of sections 2 and 3 there is any information, usable by speaker or hearer, that the pretences are dramas. Equally, the term "pretence" as used in the ATT-Meta approach means just an imaginary situation, but the term has been adopted in preference to "imaginary situation" as it has a more dynamic feel, and more intuitively suggests that the consequences of what is pretended are to be considered: the pretence is to elaborated as much as necessary for the communicative purposes at hand. So, the spirit of the term is: let's pretend that such and such is the case and see where it leads.

However, an alternative term I have increasingly used in discussing ATT-Meta is that the pretences are (small) "fictions," and of course drama is a type of fiction. Fiction could be a good term for all the different types of pretence across hyperbole, irony and metaphor. The way the pretences work with respect to real life is quite similar to the way fictional stories work, and the fiction label avoids connotations raised, for some commentators, of a richer sort of pretending than I mean. The word fiction also stresses a commonality with fiction-based work on metaphor in philosophy, although the notion of "make-believe" (Walton 2004/1993,

Hills 2017), which has some prominence in that discipline, might chime better with the term "pretence" or "drama". Camp (2009), Camp (forthcoming) and Wearing (2012) argue against casting metaphor in terms of fiction or pretence, but I cannot present my case against their claims here. Instead, see Hills (2017) for a rebuttal.

Some of the pretences needed in pure hyperbole and pure metaphor are quite "dramatic", in involving characters who have thoughts and feelings and (try to) do things. In these cases the pretences/fictions can easily be called dramas. So, it is convenient also to view the suitcase examples in section 3 as exercises in drama. We could regard the mile-long suitcase example of hyperbole as an exercise in non-dramatic fiction, the metaphorical marking-overflow example (7) as an exercise in dramatic fiction (though with the speaker not acting any character), but a more impersonal metaphor example such as *"All the money has leaked out of the country"* as again an exercise in non-dramatic fiction, unless there are relevant agents other than the speaker whose view of what has happened is important in the discourse.

Although this article cannot hope to present a full explanation and vindication of the proposed way of melding the models, the following subsections suggest the idea is promising. Section 5.1 discusses hyperbolic metaphor and, as a result, makes the mentioned adjustment to ATT-Meta's Degree VNMA. This modified version is then to be used across the whole breadth of the overall model, to help handle irony and hyperbole as well as metaphor. That this works out well will be argued in section 5.3, but section 5.2 first addresses the validity of letting all the rest of ATT-Meta's VNMAs be used for hyperbole and irony. Section 5.4 proposes an initial, partial treatment of utterances that combine metaphor and irony.

5.1 Hyperbole and attenuation in metaphor

An important feature of much metaphor is that it is inherently hyperbolic. In saying

(8) *"Albert is an archangel"*[18]

---

[18] This is adapted from an example in Peña & Ruiz de Mendoza (2017). In particular I have replaced "angel" by "archangel" to ensure that a relatively unconventional metaphor is in play, so that understanding is not a matter of simple meaning retrieval. For another novel hyperbolic metaphor, we can take *"Her eyes are an endless flame,"* which Peña & Ruiz de Mendoza (2017) analyse as being hyperbolic in conveying the strong feelings of awe one would have in looking at an endless flame.

where Albert is a human being whom the speaker considers to be exceptionally good morally, or exceptionally helpful or protective, the speaker would, presumably, rarely intend to convey that Albert is as morally good, helpful or protective as a traditional archangel. Thus the metaphor is also hyperbolic.

What we need for (8), in a pretence-based approach such as ATT-Meta, is an analysis on the lines of Figure 13.

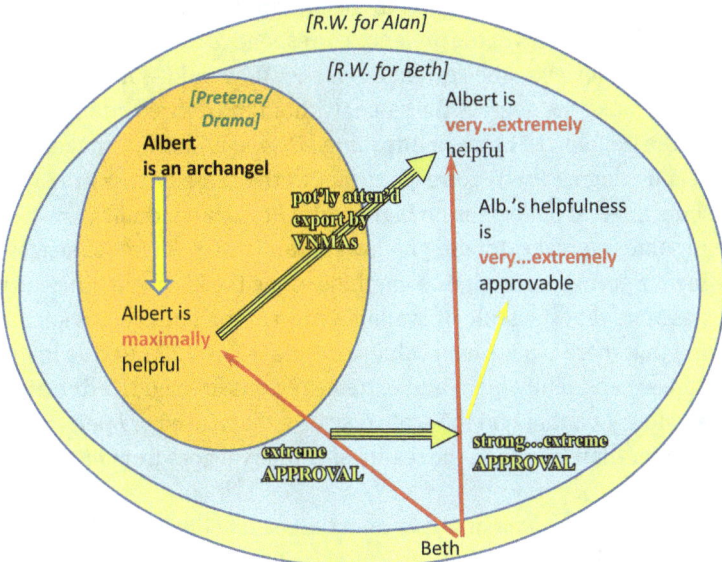

Figure 13: The setup for hyperbolic-metaphor example (8).

Here, for simplicity, I take archangels to be maximally helpful, so there is an inference within the pretence that Albert is maximally helpful. (The setup could alternatively or additionally involve qualities of archangels other than helpfulness.) Then we need a potentially-attenuated export of the maximal-helpfulness to become something looser or lesser in reality. The attenuation proposed in the Figure is that *maximally* is loosened to the degree-interval going from *highly* up to *maximally,* in line with the comments on attenuation in section 3.2.

The Figure also shows speaker affect and its export, and consequent affect-driven influence on the strength of helpfulness ascribed to Albert, possibly leading to the affectively framed value on the lines of *so helpful as to merit the speaker's strong-to-extreme approval.*

Beth's extreme approval of the pretend Albert is, again, implicitly a matter of *notability:* she finds archangel Albert's helpfulness extremely notable in a positive way. Interestingly, discussions of examples such as (8) concentrate on features conveyed about the mentioned entity, Albert here, missing the point that (presumably) in (8) the speaker thinks it's (very) good that Albert is good in the contextually appropriate sense. This speaker approval is inferred from the point that in our culture an archangel is to be approved of, not regarded as an annoying goody-two-shoes or a "helicoptering" parent.

The export of Albert's helpfulness is provided by a VNMA that deals with matters of helping, enabling, causing, etc. In the present case it would make the issue of the Albert's helpfulness in the pretence correspond to the issue of Albert's helpfulness in reality. However, the current *Degree VNMA* would – albeit only as a default anyway – make the degrees the same, without the desired attenuation. Hence, I replace the Degree VNMA by an *Attenuated Degree VNMA* that makes any (high) pretence-side degree PretD correspond not to the same degree in reality but rather to some interval of degrees no higher than PretD (and, dually, any low degree PretD to some interval extending no lower than PretD). An initial suggestion, to be refined in future research, is something along the following lines. For definiteness, I assume that the scale of available degrees includes values such a *low* and *high* and that there is a *medium* value; extreme regions of the scale in the high direction are exceptionally high, and extreme regions in the other direction are exceptionally low. At either end the scale may be either closed or open.

(a) If PretD is higher than *high* then the reality-side interval goes from *high* up to PretD;
(b) otherwise, if PretD is *medium* or above then the reality-side interval goes up from *medium* up to PretD.
(c) Analogously, if PretD is lower than *low* then the reality-side interval goes from *low* down to PretD, and
(d) otherwise, if PretD is *medium* or below then the interval goes up from *medium* down to PretD.

Clause (a) then copes with the above attenuation of maximal helpfulness to an interval going from highly helpful up to maximally helpful. It is then a matter of common-sense inference about the particular real situation, using whatever clues are available from the discourse context, whether to hone in on a smaller interval of degrees or pick a position within the interval. If no such clues are available, then the interval is left as it is. However, if the hearer deploys knowledge that no human being can be maximally helpful, the interval can be suitably curtailed, perhaps to something like *very helpful up to extremely helpful*.

Importantly, the proposal is that the *Attenuated Degree VNMA* be used across the board for export of graded circumstances in metaphor, not just when the hearer surmises that an utterance is hyperbolic. So, even in the case of example

(7) about exam marking the export process would result in the degree of John's annoyance in the real situation being in the interval *medium* to *moderately high*. The hearer could refine the interval if there is further evidence.

This throwing of responsibility onto reality-side inference in all cases of graded export in metaphor, not just in clearly hyperbolic metaphor, is actually no big leap from the current ATT-Meta, which already has degrees as mere default inferences anyway, subject to possible further adjustment and to replacement by a degree derived from other evidence. All in all, the adoption of the Attenuated Degree VNMA just further consolidates a policy that a degree interval that results from export is just a guide, to be considered along with other evidence. Clear cases of hyperbolic metaphor are merely ones where it happens that there is an exceptionally high degree within the pretence and the hearer ultimately infers a degree or degree interval within the real situation that is markedly lower than that degree. If, on the other hand, he happens ultimately to infer the same degree as that which arises in the pretence, the metaphor is, in this respect, not hyperbolic at all. In line with section 3.3.3, there can also be "liberal" hyperbolic interpretations of metaphor where there a degree range is inferred and includes the extreme value in the pretence.

5.2 VNMAs in irony and hyperbole

The External Affect VNMA is appropriate for the type of export discussed in Section 2, namely, export of Beth's criticism. This is external criticism of the dramatic character (Palan), and this within-fiction agent corresponds to the real agent Alan. Hence, Beth's criticizing Palan is made by the VNMA to correspond to her criticizing Alan. We address the question of the potential attenuation of the degree of criticism in Section 5.3.

But we need to analyse the situation more closely to check whether the VNMAs have the right effect across different examples. In (1) he is criticized because (a) he does not notice the weather's-being-bad in the drama and indeed thinks it's good, but (b) he should indeed have noticed its being bad. Now, the weather's-being-bad in the drama does correspond to the weather's-being-bad in reality, so by means of VNMAs (notably the Mental-State VNMA) we get a correspondence between Palan's not noticing the weather is bad in the drama, and instead thinking it's good, to Alan's not noticing the weather's bad in reality and instead thinking it's good. This correspondence then enables, by the External Affect VNMA, the inference of a correspondence between the criticism of Palan for not noticing the weather's bad and thinking it's good to the criticism of Alan for the same thing. Since the former criticism actually exists, the latter's actuality is inferred as well. Also, separately, the Mental-States and Logical VNMAs lead to Alan inferring that, in Beth's world, he has indeed not noticed the bad weather.

This argument does not yet deal with element (b) above, that Palan should notice the bad weather. This proposition is, of course, a crucial part of what Beth is criticizing. Now, if Beth thinks Alan himself should have noticed the bad weather, as we have presumed all along in discussing the example, then this obligation on Alan corresponds to the obligation on Palan because of the Modality VNMA briefly mentioned in section 4. The effect is that Alan ends up being criticized for exactly the same thing Palan is criticized for.

There is a considerably different story to tell about criticism when we shift to the picnic example, (3), where Palan does notice actual features or consequences of the weather in the drama (his getting wet, the sandwiches being soggy, etc.). Here the criticism is of his thinking, nevertheless, that the weather is great. It is a criticism of his bizarre way of thinking, not of a failure to notice as it was in example (1). The theoretical issue for us, though, is that the idea that Palan does notice the weather features is just a fictive elaboration: Beth does not think Alan himself notices them (and anyway they don't exist at all in reality), let alone that he thinks that they are fun. Because of this it turns out that there will be no inference by means of our VNMAs that the particular ways of thinking in drama and reality correspond to each other. Hence, the External Affect VNMA is powerless to export criticism of Palan's particular case of bizarre thinking. Thus, we need to enrich the analysis slightly by supposing that there is a consequent, more generic criticism of him, on the lines of his having defective cognition for thinking that the weather is good. The Mental-State VNMA deals with mental qualities as well as occurrent states, so it leads to a default inference that Alan is cognitively defective in thinking the weather is good. External affect export then delivers a criticism of Alan for that defective cognition.

The extensive non-parallelism between pretence and reality that we discussed in section 4 according to ATT-Meta is helpful. The non-parallelism tendency allows an element of the pretence to be exported into reality even though its inferential supports within the pretence are not exported. So the degree of criticism of a dramatic character can be exported to apply to the real character even though the support for that degree is not exported. Palan's enjoyment of soggy sandwiches can serve to intensify Beth's criticism of his cognitive powers and hence (potentially) her criticism in reality, even though that enjoyment itself is not transferrable.

A further point to note is that there is no VNMA-based problem with the fact that Palan notices entirely fictive elements of the drama such as soggy sandwiches. These elements do not correspond to anything in reality, so there is no question of the Mental States VNMA leading to a conclusion that Alan notices soggy sandwiches. The soggy sandwiches are there purely as an excuse to intensify the criticism of Palan's cognitive deficiencies. The more this criticism is, the more scope there is for the exported criticism to be higher. This observation about the role of the soggy sandwiches is very much of a piece with the ATT-Meta approach to metaphor, where there can be a rich body of information and inferencing in the pretence that simply has no correspondence to anything in reality and exists purely to support inferencing whose conclusions do get exported.

As for the VNMAs other than those already discussed in this subsection, I propose that the correspondences they establish are just as appropriate in hyperbole and irony as they are in metaphor. A VNMA that is commonly needed for metaphor is one that handles abilities, and it seems reasonable that if an agent and an action in a pretence of any sort correspond to an agent and an action, respectively, in reality, then the matter of the agent's ability to do the pretend action corresponds to the real agent's ability to do the real action, unless there is strong countervailing evidence in a particular case. Thus the ability VNMA, combined with one that handles logical operations (such as negation) provides for the export of Pertie's and Peth's inabilities to lift the suitcase in Figures 7 and 8. Also, as to the VNMAs handling causal and temporal links, it seems reasonable that if some entities in a pretence correspond to some entities in reality, then causal and temporal links between them should also correspond, unless there is strong countervailing evidence. For example, a tacit assumption about the suitcase examples in section 3 is surely that, in both pretence and reality, the difficulty of lifting is caused by the weight, and the frustration is caused by the difficulty.

5.3 Degree attenuation revisited

As the *Attenuated Degree VNMA* was devised in the first place to handle hyperbolic aspects of metaphor, it can also suitably handle pure hyperbole. Here we note that a ton is an exceptionally high weight for a suitcase, a mile is an exceptionally large value of height of a tree, and hundreds is an exceptionally high number of pets to have. So, the VNMA makes these degrees correspond to degree-intervals going from high up to exceptionally high. This happens provided that it is stipulated, when the pretence is set up, that the circumstance of the suitcase having a weight in the pretence corresponds to that circumstance in the real situation (similarly for tree height and pet number). This correspondence is set up by stipulation as part of the creation of the pretence in the first place.

We need also to consider the affect inferred within the pretence, e.g., the suitcase owner's frustration, and about aspects of the pretence, e.g., the speaker's amazement. Here, it is reasonable to suppose that both of these affective states have an exceptionally high degree, and then the Attenuated Degree VNMA provides a reasonable result that the degree of actual affect in/about the real situation is at least very high and perhaps extremely high.

As for mild hyperbole, let's look at *"Bob has dozens of pets,"* when in fact he only has, say, eight. The overtly stated number of pets (dozens) is only moderately high, and the amazement on the pretence side may only be moderately high. Thus, again by the Attenuated Degree VNMA, we get the result that the real number of pets is in an interval from a medium number up to dozens, and the amazement is from medium up to moderately high.

As for irony, consider the use of, say, *"great"* instead of *"good"* in relation to weather, as in (2). Palan believes that the weather is great. But if we assume it is evident to Alan that Beth realizes that *he* thinks the weather is merely good, not great, there is no problem about what degree of goodness might result from VNMA- based export of features of Palan's mental states to features of Alan's mental states. The information that, in Alan's beliefs according to Beth, the weather is merely good will override higher values that export would offer. What is important is the export of Beth's criticism. The degree of criticism of the dramatic character (such as Palan in our examples in Section 2) can be anything from medium in, say, (1), up to exceptionally high, as in (3), where Beth ironically attributes to Palan a liking of sitting in the rain eating soggy sandwiches. The more moderate degrees get transferred with relatively little or no attenuation by the Attenuated Degree VNMA, whereas the exceptionally high degree is expanded to an interval going up from high. This seems a reasonable outcome of the theory, given that, as always, the hearer can come to a more specific judgment about the speaker's intensity of criticism on the basis of other clues such as her demeanour in uttering the sentence or other things she has said.

5.4 Irony/Metaphor combination

Let us turn now to a type of utterance that is illustrated by Beth's ironic response in the following conversation:

(9) Alan: *"This train is going fast."*
     Beth: *"Yeah, it's a real rocket."*

Beth's utterance in (9) is a metaphorical sentence that could be used straightforwardly to claim that a train is fast, but is here being used ironically because Beth considers the train to be slow. Thus, there is an intimate combination of metaphor and irony. Notice also in passing that there is hyperbole in the metaphor in Beth's utterance, in that rockets are stereotypically much faster than any present-day train could possibly be.

In the following, I will ignore any intensifying effect the "real" in Beth's utterance may have, and assume, for the sake of argument, that *"rocket"* does not have a simple stored metaphorical meaning, such as *something that goes very fast*.

Combinations of irony and metaphor have been discussed in the figurative-language literature from a number of points of view (Camp 2006, Dynel 2016, Grice 1989, Katz & Lee 1993, Popa 2009, Popa-Wyatt 2017, Musolff 2017, Ritchie 2006, Stern 2000, Veale 2012). A natural suggestion (Camp 2006, Popa 2009) is that the hearer first extracts a metaphorical meaning ignoring the irony (i.e., temporarily treating the sentence as *non*-ironically stated) and then treats this resulting meaning as something to be ironically reversed. For instance, it can be readily envisaged that Alan can first interpret Beth's utterance metaphorically (and hyperbolically) to mean that the train is very fast, and then base an ironic interpretation on this, just as if Beth had ironically but non-metaphorically said *"Yeah, it's so fast."*

But note that it is crucial in this process that, precisely because Alan does think the train is fast, he can pursue metaphorical interpretation as he standardly would, i.e., as if the sentence were a sincere comment on reality. But things are more difficult on Beth's side. Beth cannot construct the metaphor of the train being a rocket as she would if she wasn't being ironic, precisely because *she* thinks the train is slow. Setting up a comparison between the actual train and a rocket would give a misleading and irrelevant metaphorical meaning, such as that the train makes a loud roaring sound or can fly. She must set up the metaphor either in a context where the train is not yet considered either slow or fast or a context where it is considered to be fast. Here our ATT-Iro/ATT-Meta melding suggests a natural possibility, shown in Figure 14.

In the Figure 14 setup, Alan regards Beth as taking someone else to be engaging in the metaphorical pretence that the train is a rocket, rather than herself engaging in it for her own purposes. Moreover, that someone-else is Palan, a character in a drama. So the metaphorical fiction apparatus is deployed within the mind of Palan within the drama. A metaphorical meaning is extracted, within his mind, to the effect that the train is at least very fast. In the real world outside Alan's mind, and in the drama's world outside Palan's mind, the train is slow; but Palan fails to notice that the train is slow. The example thus works analogously to our criticism-irony examples about weather. The only difference is that Beth ascribes to Palan some metaphorical-fiction based reasoning about the speed of the train. If Alan successfully grasps what drama Beth is constructing, he gets the ironic metaphorical meaning of her utterance.

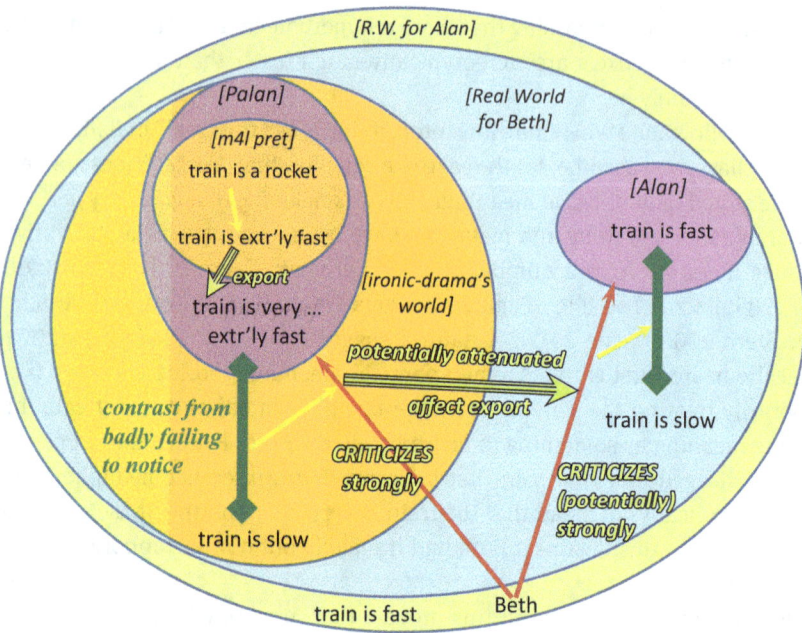

Figure 14: The setup for ironic-hyperbolic-metaphor example (9).

The Mental-State and other VNMAs operating between the drama and Beth's real world will lead to a default inference that Alan himself, in Beth's real world according to Alan, is engaging in a metaphorical fiction that the train is a rocket. This may be a harmless if incorrect inference, but in any case could (if necessary) be blocked by Alan, if he reasons that Beth is unlikely to think that he is engaging in such a fiction given that he himself doesn't use the rocket metaphor in his sentence.

6 Conclusion

This article has suggested a way of devising a partial model of consistent, combined processing of irony, hyperbole and metaphor, within a fiction-based (pretence-based, imaginary-situation-based) approach. The metaphorical aspect of the model comes from the author's long-standing ATT-Meta approach, the irony aspect from the author's recent further elaboration of the well-known, long-standing pretence approach to irony developed by others, and the hyperbolic aspect partially from a recent approach by others based on imaginary situations. It is not just that the model handles cases of pure irony, pure hyperbole and pure metaphor along similar lines, but rather that it copes in a seamless way with hyperbolic aspects of irony and of metaphor and with at least one type of combination of irony and metaphor.

The model is (the start of) a "unified" approach to metaphor, irony and hyperbole, though of course these three figures have their own peculiarities that the model does not currently address (e.g., lexical, prosodic and contextual clues as to whether the speaker is using metaphor, irony and/or hyperbole). Moreover, the figures are not unified in the model in the sense of all being cast as variants of the same phenomenon. Their purposes remain different; relations of contrast play a special and key role in irony as opposed to pure hyperbole or metaphor; and metaphorical-view-specific mappings are used for metaphor but naturally not for non-metaphorical irony or hyperbole. However, at the level of the mechanisms presented, there is extensive unification. There is no difference, mechanically, between the three figures as to the way mappings work (though the precise nature of and motivations for the mappings used may be different) and pretences are elaborated by just the same processes of inference. Affect transfer (export) is handled in the same way across the figures, and the same affect-drivenness is available.

The melding of models was performed largely by extending, to the case of irony and hyperbole, ATT-Meta's extensive metaphorical-view-neutral mapping provision (VNMAs) and that model's tendency towards allowing extensive non-parallelism between pretence and reality. The non-parallelism allows for fictive elaborations in irony and, as a closely related point, the ability to export intensified criticism even though the basis for the intensification is not itself exported.

The developments have led to a significant but localized change to ATT-Meta, notably to its provision for the export from the pretence to reality of degrees to which circumstances hold. This provision originally kept degrees constant, but the new version of the provision allows for attenuation of degrees. This change to ATT-Meta was essentially prompted by the need to cover hyperbole, and, in particular, a hyperbolic quality that metaphor tends inherently to have, so the improvement to the approach was of pressing importance aside from any considerations about irony. A profound effect of the change is that degrees to which circumstances hold are potentially subject to attenuation across the board in metaphor and irony, not just when there is any clear hyperbolic element. However, the attenuation is always only potential, and it is up to the hearer to use the broad "suggestions" about degrees that come from utterances in combination with other evidence from discourse context and long-term knowledge to arrive at a final degree or range of degrees.

Quite apart from putting hyperbole, irony and metaphor into consistent, combined processing model, the approach taken has recognized affect as a central concern in all three types of figuration, with processing of affect fully integrated with the rest if the model. Indeed, so central is it in the approach to irony and hyperbole that we have turned normal notions about irony and hyperbole on their head in proposing affect-drivenness. This is about how the hearer estimates, for instance, a value (range) for the badness of weather in our irony examples or a value (range) for the suitcase weight in some of hyperbole examples. In both cases, export of speaker affect (her criticalness in ironic cases, her frustration/amazement in the non-ironic hyperbolic cases) serves to provide an important route – and for irony the main or only route – to estimating the value. (This does not prevent the converse flow of influence happening as well, to the extent that there are other clues as to what the value is.) According to the proposal, it is not the case that the values are estimated by going from the overt point on some scale of values directly to a different point/region on general principles that are usually left as being rather mysterious and are in any case not dependent the hearer's sense of the speaker's affect. The affect-centred proposal provides a powerful, well-founded guide to value estimation, and systematically takes care of hyperbole within irony.

Affect-drivenness also leads to the even more radical suggestion that the only value a hearer might derive could be itself based on affect, i.e., affectively framed. We made this point in the case of hyperbole, where the value for the suitcase weight might be *heavy enough for it to be frustratingly difficult for Beth to lift*, but it applies just as much to irony, where the hearer might merely derive that the weather is *bad and noticeable enough for Beth to criticize me*. It is rarely asked in the irony and hyperbole literatures *why* we should imagine that a hearer comes up with any more specific estimates than these; and it is not emphasized that if he does do so, it's on the basis of further reasoning that has nothing particularly to do with irony or hyperbole as such.

Affect-drivenness also applies to metaphor when there is an important affective component. For instance, in the marking-overflow example, John is inferred to experience some amount of annoyance that in the pretence, on the basis of how annoying it is in general when liquid overflows from its intended container. The amount of annoyance is exported, with potential attenuation, to reality, and this can then affect an estimate of how *much* marking had to be done during the weekend. Indeed, in line with the idea of affectively framed values, perhaps the hearer just comes up with *annoyingly much marking*. However, considerable further research is needed on these matters as well as on validating the accuracy and effectiveness of the overall model.

Finally, a word on the location of contrast relationships in the model. As the Figures show, the ones of most interest for the types of example in this article are not between the drama's world and the real world or between a pretended character's mental state and the real world – even though there is of often such contrast, not explicitly marked in the Figures – but rather between the mental state of some pretended character and the drama's world and analogously between the mental state of the corresponding real person and the real world. On the other hand, in some examples in Barnden (2017) where the irony conveys the speaker's disappointment or regret about a situation rather than criticism of someone, the main contrast of interest is between the drama's world and the real world. This variegation of the location of contrast is allowed by the fact that the model does not portray irony merely as interplay between the overt meaning of an utterance and the real world, but rather as interplay between that meaning, a drama's world and the real world. The variegation of contrast location is what gives the model much of its power to address different types of irony effectively.

References

Athanasiadou, Angeliki. 2017. Irony has a metonymic basis. In Angeliki Athanasiadou & Herbert L. Colston (eds.), *Irony in language, thought and culture,* 201–216. Amsterdam: John Benjamins.

Barnden, John A. 2001. Uncertainty and conflict handling in the ATT-Meta context-based system for metaphorical reasoning. In Varol Akman, Paolo Bouquet, Richmond Thomason & Roger A. Young (eds.), *Modeling and Using Context: Third International and Interdisciplinary Conference* (CONTEXT 2001). Lecture Notes in Artificial Intelligence, Vol. 2116, 15–29. Berlin: Springer.

Barnden, John A. 2006a. Artificial intelligence, figurative language and cognitive linguistics. In Gitte Kristiansen, Michel Achard, René Dirven & Francisco J. Ruiz de Mendoza (eds.), *Cognitive Linguistics: Current Applications and Future Perspectives*, 431–459. Berlin: Mouton de Gruyter.

Barnden, John A. 2006b. Consequences for language learning of an AI approach to metaphor. In Joana. Salazar, Marian Amengual & Maria Juan (eds.), *Usos Sociales del Lenguaje y Aspectos Psicolingüísticos: Perspectivas Aplicadas,* 15–57. Palma,Mallorca: Universitat de les Illes Baleares.

Barnden, John A. 2015a. Open-ended elaborations in creative metaphor. In Tarek R. Besold, Marco Schorlemmer & Alan Smaill (eds.,) *Computational Creativity Research: Towards Creative Machines,* 217–242. Berlin: Atlantis Press (Springer).

Barnden, John A. 2015b. Metaphor, simile, and the exaggeration of likeness. *Metaphor and Symbol* 30 (1), 41–62.

Barnden, John A. 2016. Mixed metaphor: Its depth, its breadth, and a pretence-based approach. In Ray W. Gibbs, Jr. (ed.), *Mixing Metaphor,* 75–111. Amsterdam: John Benjamins.

Barnden, John A. 2017. Irony, pretence and fictively-elaborating hyperbole. In Angeliki Athanasiadou & Herbert L. Colston (eds.), *Irony in Language Use and Communication,* 145–177. Amsterdam: John Benjamins.

Barnden, John A. 2018. Broadly reflexive relationships, a special type of hyperbole, and implications for metaphor and metonymy. *Metaphor and Symbol* 33 (3). 218–234.

Barnden, John A. & Mark G. Lee. 2002. An artificial intelligence approach to metaphor understanding. *Theoria et Historia Scientiarum* 6 (1). 399–412.

Brdar-Szabó, Rita & Mario Brdar. 2010. "Mummy, I love you like a thousand ladybirds": Reflections on the emergence of hyperbolic effects and the truth of hyperboles. In Armin Burkhardt & Brigitte Nerlich (eds.), *Tropical Truth(s): The Epistemology of Metaphor and Other Tropes,* 383–427. Berlin / New York: De Gruyter.

Burgers, Christian, Elly A. Konijn & Gerard J. Steen. 2016. Figurative framing: shaping public discourse through metaphor, hyperbole, and irony. *Communication Theory* 26. 410–430.

Burgers, Christian & Gerard J. Steen. 2017. Introducing a three-dimensional model of verbal irony: irony in language, in thought, and in communication. In Angeliki Athanasiadou & Herbert L. Colston (eds.), *Irony in Language Use and Communication,* 87–108. Amsterdam: John Benjamins.

Camp, Elizabeth. 2006. Contextualism, metaphor, and what is said. *Mind and Language* 21 (3). 280–309.

Camp, Elizabeth. 2009. Two varieties of literary imagination: Metaphor, fiction, and thought experiments. *Midwest Studies in Philosophy* 33. 107–130.

Camp, Elizabeth (forthcoming). Imaginative frames for scientific inquiry: metaphors, telling facts, and just-so stories. In Arnon Levy & Peter Godfrey-Smith (eds.), *The Scientific Imagination: Philosophical and Psychological Perspectives.* Oxford: Oxford University Press.

Carston, Robyn & Catherine Wearing. 2011. Metaphor, hyperbole and simile: A pragmatic approach. *Language and Cognition* 3 (2). 283–312.

Carston, Robyn & Catherine Wearing. 2015. Hyperbolic language and its relation to metaphor and irony. *Journal of Pragmatics* 79. 79–92.

Claridge, Claudia. 2011. *Hyperbole in English: A corpus-based study of exaggeration.* Cambridge: Cambridge University Press.

Clark, Herbert H. & Richard J. Gerrig [1984] 2007. On the pretense theory of irony. In Ray W. Gibbs, Jr. & Herbert L. Colston (eds.), *Irony in Language and Thought: A Cognitive Science Reader,* 25–33. New York: Lawrence Erlbaum Associates. Reprinted from *J. Experimental Psychology: General* 113, 121–126 (1984).

Colston, Herbert L. 1997. Salting a wound or sugaring a pill: The pragmatic functions of ironic criticism. *Discourse Processes* 23 (1). 25–45.

Colston, Herbert L. 2017. Irony performance and perception: What underlies verbal, situational and other ironies?. In Angeliki Athanasiadou & Herbert L. Colston (eds.), *Irony in Language Use and Communication,* 19–41. Amsterdam: John Benjamins.

Colston, Herbert L. & Shauna B. Keller. 1998. You'll never believe this: irony and hyperbole in expressing surprise. *J. Psycholinguistic Research* 27 (4). 499–513.

Coulson, Seana. 2005. Sarcasm and the space structuring model. In Seana Coulson & B. Lewandowska-Tomaszczyk (eds.), *The Literal and Nonliteral in Language and Thought,* 129–44. New York: Peter Lang.

Currie, Gregory. 2006. Why irony is pretence. In Stephen Nichols (ed.), *The Architecture of the Imagination,* 111–133. Oxford: Oxford University Press.

Currie, Gregory. 2010. Echo et feintise: quelle est la difference et qui a raison? *Philosophiques.* 35 (1). 12–23.

Deignan, Alice. 2008. Corpus linguistics and metaphor. In Ray W. Gibbs, Jr. (ed.), *The Cambridge Handbook of Metaphor and Thought,* 280–294. Cambridge, U.K.: Cambridge University Press.

Dynel, Marta. 2016. Two layers of overt untruthfulness: When irony meets metaphor, hyperbole or meiosis. *Pragmatics & Cognition* 23 (2), 259–283.

Dynel, Marta. 2018. Deconstructing the myth of positively evaluative irony. In Manuel Jobert & Sandrine Sorlin (eds.), *The Pragmatics of Irony and Banter*, 41–57. Amsterdam: John Benjamins.

Egan, Andy. 2008. Pretense for the complete idiom. *Noûs* 42 (3). 381–409.

Eubanks, Philip. 2005. Globalization, "corporate rule," and blended worlds: A conceptual-rhetorical analysis of metaphor, metonymy, and conceptual blending. *Metaphor and Symbol* 20 (3). 173–197.

Fainsilber, Lynn & Andrew Ortony. 1987. Metaphorical uses of language in the expression of emotions. *Metaphor and Symbolic Activity* 2 (4). 239–250.

Fauconnier, Gilles. 2009. Generalized integration networks. In Vyvyan Evans & Stéphanie Pourcel (eds.), *New Directions in Cognitive Linguistics*, 147–160. Amsterdam: John Benjamins.

Gentner, Dedre & Brian Bowdle. 2008. Metaphor as structure-mapping. In Ray W. Gibbs, Jr. (ed.), *The Cambridge Handbook of Metaphor and Thought*, 109–128. Cambridge, U.K.: Cambridge University Press.

Gibbs, Ray W., Jr. [2000] 2007. Irony in talks among friends. In Ray W. Gibbs, Jr. & Herbert L. Colston (eds.), *Irony in Language and Thought: A Cognitive Science Reader*, 339–360. New York: Lawrence Erlbaum Associates. Reprinted from *Metaphor and Symbol* 15, 5–27 (2000).

Giora, Rachel. 1997. Understanding figurative and literal language: The graded salience hypothesis. *Cognitive Linguistics* 8 (3). 183–206.

Giora, Rachel, Ofer Fein, Nurit Kotler & Noa Shuval. 2015. *Know Hope*: Metaphor, optimal innovation, and pleasure. In: Geert Brône, Kurt Feyaerts & Tony Veale (eds.), *Cognitive Linguistics and Humor Research. Current Trends and New Developments*, 129–146. Berlin/New York: Mouton de Gruyter.

Grice, H. Paul. 1989. Logic and conversation. In *Studies in the Way of Words*, 22–40. Cambridge, Mass.: Harvard University Press.

Hampe, Beate. 2005. When *down* is not bad, and *up* is not good enough: A usage-based assessment of the plus-minus parameter in image-schema theory. *Cognitive Linguistics* 16 (1). 81–112.

Herrero Ruiz, Javier. 2009. *Understanding tropes: At the crossroads between pragmatics and cognition*. Frankfurt am Mein: Peter Lang.

Hills, David. 2017. The what and the how of metaphorical imagining, Part One. *Philosophical Studies* 174 (1). 13–31.

Kapogianni, Eleni. 2011. Irony via "surrealism". In Marta Dynel (ed.), *The Pragmatics of Humour across Discourse Domains*, 51–68. Amsterdam/Philadelphia: John Benjamins.

Katz, Albert N. & Christopher J. Lee. 1993. The role of authorial intent in determining verbal irony and metaphor. *Metaphor and Symbolic Activity* 8 (4). 257–279.

Kihara, Yoshihiko. 2005. The mental space structure of verbal irony. *Cognitive Linguistics* 16 (3). 513–530.

Kreuz, Roger J. & Roberts, Richard M. 1995. Two cues for verbal irony: Hyperbole and the ironic tone of voice. *Metaphor & Symbol* 10 (1). 21–31.

Kumon-Nakamura, Sachi, Sam Glucksberg & Mary Brown. [1995] 2007. How about another piece of pie: The allusional pretense theory of irony. In Ray W. Gibbs, Jr. & Herbert L. Colston (eds.), *Irony in Language and Thought: A Cognitive Science Reader*, 57–95. New York: Lawrence Erlbaum Associates. Reprinted from *J. Experimental Psychology: General* 124, 3–21 (1995).

Littlemore, Jeannette & Graham D. Low. 2006. *Figurative thinking and foreign language learning*. Basingstoke, UK: Palgrave, Macmillan.

McCarthy, Michael & Ronald Carter. 2004. "There's millions of them": hyperbole in everyday conversation. *Journal of Pragmatics* 36 (2). 149–184.

McMullen, Linda M. & John B. Conway. 2002. Conventional metaphors for depression. In Susan R. Fussell (ed.), *The Verbal Communication of Emotions: Interdisciplinary Perspectives*, 167–181. Mahwah, NJ: Lawrence Erlbaum.

Musolff, Andreas. 2004. *Metaphor and political discourse: Analogical reasoning in debates about Europe*. Basingstoke, UK: Palgrave Macmillan.

Musolff, Andreas. 2017. Irony and sarcasm in follow-ups of metaphorical slogans. In Angeliki Athanasiadou & Herbert L. Colston (eds.), *Irony in language, thought and culture*, 127–141. Amsterdam: John Benjamins.

Norrick, Neal R. 2004. Hyperbole, extreme case formulation. *J. Pragmatics, 36*, 1727–1739.

Partington, Alan. 2007. Irony and reversal of evaluation. *J. Pragmatics* 39. 1547–1569.

Peña, M. Sandra & Francisco J. Ruiz de Mendoza. 2017. Construing and constructing hyperbole. In Angeliki Athanasiadou (ed.), *Studies in Figurative Thought and Language*, 42–73. Amsterdam: John Benjamins.

Popa, Mihaela. 2009. Is semantics really psychologically real? In Jesus Larrazabal & Larraitz Zubeldia (eds), *Meaning, Content and Argument*, 497–514. University of the Basque Country Press.

Popa-Wyatt, Mihaela. 2014. Pretence and echo: Towards an integrated account of verbal irony *International Review of Pragmatics* 6 (1), 127–168.

Popa-Wyatt, Mihaela. 2017. Compound figures: priority and speech-act structure. *Philosophical Studies* 174 (1). 141–161.

Popa-Wyatt, Mihaela. (this volume). Hyperbolic Figures.

Récanati, François. 2007. Indexicality, context and pretence: A speech-act theoretic account. In Noel Burton-Roberts (ed.), *Advances in Pragmatics*, 213–229. Palgrave-Macmillan.

Ritchie, L. David. 2006. *Context and connection in metaphor*. Basingstoke, U.K and New York: Palgrave Macmillan.

Ruiz de Mendoza, Francisco J. 2014. Mapping concepts. Understanding figurative thought from a cognitive-linguistic perspective. *Revista Española de Lingüística Aplicada* 27 (1). 187–207.

Ruiz de Mendoza, Francisco J. 2017. Cognitive modeling and irony. In Angeliki Athanasiadou & Herbert L. Colston (eds.), *Irony in language, thought and culture*, 179–200. Amsterdam: John Benjamins.

Schön, Donald A. 1993. Generative metaphor: A perspective on problem-setting in social policy. In Andrew Ortony (ed.), *Metaphor and Thought*, 2nd edn., 137–163.

Sperber, Daniel & Deirdre Wilson. 1995. *Relevance: Communication and Cognition*. Oxford: Blackwell.

Stern, Josef. 2000. *Metaphor in context*. Cambridge, MA: Bradford Books, MIT Press.

Tobin, Vera & Michael Israel. 2012. Irony as a viewpoint phenomenon. In Barbara Dancygier & Eve Sweetser (eds.), *Viewpoint in Language: A Multimodal Perspective*, 25–46. Cambridge, UK: Cambridge University Press.

Veale, Tony. 2012. *Exploding the creativity myth: The computational foundations of linguistic creativity*. London, New Delhi, New York, Sydney: Bloomsbury.

Vervaeke, John & John M. Kennedy. 2004. Conceptual metaphor and abstract thought. *Metaphor and Symbol* 19 (3). 213–231.

Walton, Kenneth [1993] 2004. Metaphor and prop oriented make-believe. In Eileen John & Dominic M. Lopes (eds.), *Philosophy of Literature – Contemporary and Classic Readings: An Anthology*, 239–247. Oxford: Blackwell 2004. Reprinted from *European J. of Philosophy* 1, 39–57.
Walton, Kenneth. 2017. Meiosis, hyperbole, irony. *Philosophical Studies* 174 (1). 105–120.
Watling, Graham (this volume). Denying the salient contrast – Speaker's attitude in hyperbole.
Wearing, Catherine. 2012. Metaphor, idiom, and pretense. *Noûs* 46. 499–524.
Wilson, Deirdre. 2006. The pragmatics of verbal irony: Echo or pretence? *Lingua* 116. 1722–1743.
Wilson, Deirdre & Daniel Sperber. 2012. Explaining irony. In Deirdre Wilson & Dan Sperber (eds.), *Meaning and Relevance,* 123–145. Cambridge: Cambridge University Press.

Rachel Giora, Shir Givoni and Israela Becker
How defaultness affects text production: Resonating with default interpretations of negative sarcasm

Abstract: According to the Defaultness Hypothesis, interpretations of constructions, involving strong attenuation (e.g., by means of negation) of highly positive concepts, such as *S/he is not the most mesmerizing person around; S/he is not particularly smart; S/he is not extremely friendly*; and *S/he is not really the ideal teacher*, will spring to mind by default, immediately and directly. Hence, when in natural discourse, such constructions will be echoed by their environment via their default, here, sarcastic interpretation (e.g., *S/he is dull; S/he is stupid; S/he is reserved; S/he is the worst teacher*). Results show that, in natural discourse, default rather than nondefault interpretations prevail; indeed, the contexts of the negative constructions studied here evolve and unfold via resonating with their default interpretations.

Keywords: The Defaultness Hypothesis, default/nondefault interpretations, contextual resonance, negative sarcasm

1 The defaultness hypothesis

According to the Defaultness Hypothesis (Giora, Givoni, and Fein 2015b), **default** responses crucially affect our language comprehension and production. For a response (here, a constructed interpretation) to be considered a default, it has to be activated automatically, immediately and directly, regardless of other factors assumed to affect processing, such as degree of negation/affirmation (e.g., Clark and Clark 1977; Horn 1989), non/literalness (Grice 1975), novelty (nonsalience

---

Acknowledgments: We are very grateful to John Barnden and to Mihaela Popa for their illuminating comments. This research was supported by an Israel Science Foundation grant (no. 540/19) awarded to Rachel Giora. Shir Givoni was awarded a scholarship for outstanding graduate students funded by the Rector of Tel-Aviv University and matched by her supervisor – Rachel Giora. Israela Becker was awarded a scholarship for outstanding graduate students, funded by the Rector of Tel-Aviv University and by an Israel Science Foundation grant (no. 431/15) awarded to her supervisor – Mira Ariel.

Rachel Giora, Shir Givoni and Israela Becker, Tel Aviv University

https://doi.org/10.1515/9783110652246-003

vs. salience-based; see Giora 2003), or strength of contextual support (strong vs. weak; see e.g., Gibbs 1986, 1994, 2002).

When tested experimentally, an automatic response will be considered a default, if its stimulus, whether literal or nonliteral, is

(i) novel, so that the response, activated automatically, will be noncoded (non-salient or salience-based), i.e., constructed, rather than accessed directly from the mental lexicon;
(ii) free of internal cues such as semantic anomaly or internal incongruity, prompting nonliteralness (see, Beardsley 1958; Partington 2011); and
(iii) free of explicit contextual information, including cues, so that a preference (among various responses) is allowed (for more details, see Giora et al. 2015b).

1.1 The defaultness hypothesis: Predictions

According to the Defaultness Hypothesis (Giora et al. 2015b), utterances, meeting the conditions for default interpretations (i-iii above), further involving strong attenuation (*not*) of highly positive concepts (*most candid*) as in, *S/he is not the most candid person I know* (see Giora et al. 2005; Giora et al. 2018), will be interpreted sarcastically by default.[1] Their non-attenuated (e.g., affirmative) counterparts will be interpreted compositionally (often literally) by default. Specifically,

(a) when presented in isolation, utterances, involving strong attenuation (*not*) of highly positive concepts (e.g., *S/he is not the most candid person I know*), will be interpreted sarcastically (meaning 'S/he is dishonest') and rated as more sarcastic compared to their literal interpretation (meaning 'S/he is candid but others are more candid than her/him'); their non-attenuated affirmative counterparts (*S/he is the most candid person I know*) will be interpreted compositionally (here, literally) by default (meaning 'S/he is very honest'; see Giora et al. 2015b Exp. 1).
(b) Hence, when in equally strong contexts, such utterances will be processed faster when embedded in contexts, biasing them towards their default nonsalient sarcastic interpretation than towards their **nondefault** (equally strongly biased) salience-based (literal) interpretation. Furthermore, when in equally strong contexts, supportive of their sarcastic interpretation, they will also be processed faster than their nondefault non-attenuated (e.g., affirmative)

---

[1] Sarcasm refers here to verbal irony. Verbal irony can also be classified as an understatement. For example, Gibbs (2000), who investigated five main forms of irony, found that understatements, the category to which the negative constructions studied here belong, is the least frequent one — ~0.2%.

counterparts, biased towards the same, equally strongly supported sarcastic interpretation (Giora et al. 2015b Exp. 2).

(c) Therefore, when in natural discourse, (i) these negative constructions will be rated as sarcastic rather than literal; their non-attenuated affirmative counterparts will be rated as (salience-based, often) literal (as shown by Becker and Giora 2018). Hence (ii) the neighboring utterances of these attenuated (e.g., negative) items will echo or resonate with their highly accessible default interpretations more often than with their nondefault literal interpretations, low on accessibility. Along the same line, their nondefault, non-attenuated, contextually compatible affirmative sarcastic counterparts will also be echoed via their default, contextually incompatible, salience-based (often literal) interpretation (as shown for similar constructions by Giora, Drucker, and Fein 2014a; Giora et al. 2014b).

(d) Furthermore, when in natural discourse, it is nondefault interpretations (not high on speakers' and addresses' mind) that rely on cues, rejecting utterances default automatic interpretations (e.g., the sarcastic interpretation of specific negative constructions, such as those studied here, and the compositional often literal interpretation of their affirmative counterparts). Indeed, prompting contextually appropriate yet *nondefault interpretations* by cues, rejecting default counterparts, while inviting nondefault alternatives, has been attested to by Becker and Giora (2018) for both nondefault negative literalness and nondefault affirmative sarcasm, and by Givoni, Giora, and Bergerbest (2013) for nondefault *meanings*.

Here we test predictions (1.1ci-cii) with regard to strongly attenuated highly positive concepts, such as *S/he is **not** the **most** candid person I know*, which, according to Giora et al. (2005, 2015b, 2018), are interpreted sarcastically by default (1.1ci). Hence, as predicted by the Defaultness Hypothesis, they will affect both the prevalence of their sarcastic interpretations (1.1ci) and their effect on discourse production (1.1cii).

Note that the defaultness of such constructions has been established earlier, both experimentally and via corpus-based studies. When tested experimentally, constructions, negatively attenuating highly positive concepts (e.g., *Candidness is not her/his forte/best attribute*; *Candid s/he is not*; *S/he is not the most candid person I know*) were shown to be interpreted sarcastically when in isolation ('S/he is dishonest'). They were therefore processed faster in contexts biasing them towards their default sarcastic interpretation ('S/he is dishonest') than towards their equally strongly biased nondefault literal counterpart ('S/he has other strong attributes'/'S/he is honest but others are more honest than her/him'; see Giora et al. 2015a; Giora et al. 2013). They were also shown to be processed faster than nondefault affirmative sarcasm, as in *S/he is the most candid person I know* (Giora et al. 2015b).

Usage-wise, stimuli such as *Candidness is not her/his forte/best attribute; Candid s/he is not*, extracted from Hebrew corpora, were further shown to be interpreted by 3 external expert judges as sarcastic and to be echoed by their natural context via their default sarcastic interpretation (Giora et al. 2013, 2014a). Additionally, stimuli, such as the negative constructions studied here (*S/he is not the most candid person I know,*) were also shown to be rated as sarcastic when in natural use. For instance, Becker and Giora (2018) conducted a corpus-based study by compiling a list of 171 instances of such negative constructions, preceded by a metalinguistic comment *to put it mildly*, which acts as an additional attenuator, mitigating a harsh message. These 171 items accommodated adjectival phrases, noun phrases, or verb phrases. The vast majority of these items (167/171=97%) were rated as sarcastic by at least 2 out of the 3 expert judges, versed in the field of non/literal language. In addition, the judges were asked to indicate the polarity of the concept in the scope of these constructions, whether it is positive, neutral, or negative. Results show that 146 items of these 167 sarcastic items were rated as positive (by 2 or more judges), whereas only 21 items were rated as non-positive (by 2 or more judges). Namely, there are significantly more positively-oriented concepts (146/167=87%) in the scope of these negative constructions than non-positive concepts (21/167=13%), binomial test, $p=2.68\times10^{-24}$ (highly more significant than $p<0.001$).[2]

These recent results provide converging corpus-based evidence to our online findings, attesting to the close association between the sarcastic interpretation of attenuated constructions and the polarity of the concepts which they host. Put differently, the default sarcastic interpretation of these negative constructions is induced by the strong attenuation of the highly positive polarity of the concept it scopes over.

Having shown that constructions, strongly attenuating highly positive concepts, such as *S/he is not the most candid person I know*, are rated as sarcastic, both in natural context and out of context (see predictions (1.1a) & (1.1ci)), and are processed faster than nondefault counterparts (see prediction (1.1b)), here we will look for converging evidence showing that these items' default interpretation further affects discourse production via resonating with default interpretations. Based on items from the Hebrew *HeTenTen* web-corpus (see Appendix A below), we will test here prediction (1.1cii) of the Defaultness Hypothesis, related to resonating with default sarcastic interpretations.

---

[2] Note that in Becker and Giora (2018), the authors also provided evidence supportive of prediction (d), regarding cueing.

2 Resonating with default interpretations

In this section, we test predictions (1.1cii) of the Defaultness Hypothesis, related to discourse resonance with default interpretations.

2.1 What is resonance?

Resonance is defined as "the catalytic activation of affinities across utterances" (Du Bois 2014: 359; Du Bois and Giora 2014: 351), involving given and new information, uttered within and between speakers, in both prior and subsequent context (Du Bois, 2007, 2014; Du Bois and Giora 2014; Giora 2007). Resonance is, therefore, a property of the relation between elements in discourse. The affinities activated may be based on similarity (e.g., 'smart' and 'bright') or difference (e.g., 'smart' and 'stupid'), and resonance can be perceived whenever a suitable structural parallelism, supporting the affinity, occurs. Resonance can arise from parallelism in pairs across meanings (e.g., 'not the smartest' and 'stupid') as well as structures or constructions (e.g., 'not the brightest' and 'not exactly bright'). Whenever language users reproduce some aspect of a prior or subsequent utterance, they create parallelisms and resonances. These, in turn, result in an environment that aligns with utterances' interpretations (Du Bois 2004, 2014). As such, resonance can reflect the interpretation of a given ambiguous (i.e., sarcastic or literal) utterance.

Previous research, attesting experimentally to the defaultness of sarcastic interpretations of various negative constructions (e.g., *Candidness is not her/his forte/best attribute*; see Giora, et al. 2014a; or *Candid s/he is not*; see Giora et al. 2013), further attests to contextual resonance with these default sarcastic interpretations, rather than their nondefault literal interpretation. For instance, in Giora et al. (2014a), findings from 2 corpus-based studies of (Hebrew and English) negative constructions lend usage-based support to the Defaultness Hypothesis (see also Giora et al. 2010, 2013, 2014b). They show that, when in natural discourse, such utterances are interpreted sarcastically and rated as more sarcastic than their affirmative alternatives. Hence, their neighboring utterances further reflect their default nonsalient sarcastic interpretation rather than their nondefault salience-based often literal counterpart. In contrast, affirmative sarcasm, whose default interpretation is a salience-based often literal interpretation (see Giora et al. 2015a,b), is echoed by its contextual environment via that literal interpretation, even if contextually inappropriate (Giora et al. 2014b).

2.2 A corpus–based experiment

In order to test predictions (1.1ci-cii), we conducted an experiment in which 3 judges, versed in the field of sarcasm, were presented with 151 negative constructions of the following 4 variants – *s/he is not the most X; s/he is not particularly X / s/he is not X in particular*[3]; *s/he is not extremely X;* and *s/he is not really X* – embedded in their natural context. The judges' tasks were to decide (1) whether these constructions are sarcastically or literally interpreted and (2) whether the context, in which they are embedded, resonates with their sarcastic (here, default) or literal (here, nondefault) interpretation.[4]

2.2.1 Materials

We exhaustively extracted from *HeTenTen* web-corpus (see Appendix A) all instances of *not really X (what we learnt at school [...] is not really accurate)* (14159 instances); *not extremely X (Their food is not extremely tasty)* (8126 instances); *not the most X (on the face of it, not the most respectable profession)* (4000 instances); *not particularly X/not X in particular (It was probably not particularly successful; the leadership was not creative in particular)* (761 instances), hosting an adjective in the *X* slot. From each of the 4 lists, we then pseudo-randomly sampled 300 instances. Based on the authors' judgements, we further narrowed down the resulting list of 1200 results into a preliminary list of 1140 instances, hosting potentially positively-oriented (rather than non-positively-oriented) adjectives in the *X* slot of the negative constructions listed above. Then, following a strict selection procedure, we further filtered out instances hosting adjectives that were (a) semantically ambiguous (e.g., *gay*) (b) or positively-oriented only when in context (such as *ambitious, relevant,* or *quiet*). We ended up with 516 instances, following this filtering procedure.

Striving to produce as diverse as possible a list of highly-positive adjectives (embedded in the 4 negative constructions listed above), while minimizing repetition of adjectives but keeping the list as balanced as possible construction-wise, we compiled a set of 151 items — *not the most X* (47); *not particularly X/not X in particular* (40); *not extremely X* (34); *not really X* (30), comprising 103 diverse positive adjectives — comprising 73 unique adjectives, 13 adjectives repeated twice, 16 adjectives repeated 3 times, and 1 adjective repeated 4 times. Note that

---
3 This ordering of the construction (*s/he is not X in particular*) is equivalent to its Hebrew ordering.
4 The 3 external expert judges were, at the time, MA students. They rated the items individually without consulting each other or any of the authors.

adjectives repeated more than once were not repeated within the same constructions and were different from each other with regard to the grammatical gender and number, since in Hebrew the grammatical gender and number are explicitly marked on adjectives.

Instances of resonance are shown in (1–2), translated from our Hebrew items. Target sentences are underlined and in bold, as presented to the judges. For resonance with *default* sarcastic interpretation of sarcastic targets (in bold here, for convenience), see example (1); for resonance with *nondefault* literal interpretation of literal targets (in italics here, for convenience) see example (2):

(1) A year ago Ha'aretz[5] disclosed that some of Kafka's manuscripts were held in a small flat [...] in Tel Aviv. Max Brod, Kafka's friend, is the person who held the originals [...] some of which he later shared with the appropriate authorities but still kept many of the manuscripts. He left his property, including the manuscripts, to his secretary, Ilse Esther Hoffe. Hoffe dealt with the inheritance the way she felt like, which probably **wasn't particularly successful**. Apart from this hidden treasure being inaccessible to the public, she probably **wasn't particular about its preservation**. In 2006, Ha'aretz reports that Hoffe's neighbors complained about **bad smell coming up from her flat. The municipality's inspectors found out that the flat was populated by tens of cats and some dogs...**[6]

(2) I saw in your response to the question on the origin of the Ashkenazim,[7] that what we learnt in school about the expulsion of the Jewish people by the Romans **isn't really accurate.** As we get nearer to Tisha Be-Av[8] (even though the massive deportation was after the Bar Kokhba revolt, according to what I have learnt), perhaps tell us *what **is** accurate. When did the exile begin? Why? Where were the Jewish people exiled to in the beginning? What happened with the Jewish people who did stay in the land of Israel?*[9]

2.2.2 Procedure

Our 3 expert judges were presented with the above list of 151 pseudo-randomly ordered items. Each item comprised one of the 4 negative constructions, embedded in their natural context, namely, 2–5 sentences, both preceding and following

---

[5] *Ha'arets* is an Israeli daily newspaper.
[6] http://mitzidlaw.blogspot.co.il/2009/09/blog-post_08.html
[7] *Ashkenazim* refers to Jewish people descending from (Eastern) European countries.
[8] *Tisha B'Av* refers to an annual fast day in Judaism.
[9] http://news.nana10.co.il/Article/?ArticleID=502067

the target construction, as in examples (1) and (2) above.[10] Note that the target construction was marked in bold and was further underlined for the judges' convenience.

Apart from being asked to decide (1) whether these constructions are sarcastically or literally interpreted and (2) whether the embedding context resonates with any of the two optional interpretations (i.e., sarcastic or literal), the judges were also asked (3) to mark the resonance (if found) either in red, when sarcastic, or in blue, when literal; in addition, (4) they were further asked to state explicitly whether the resonance is content-related or structure-related, that is whether one of the 4 kinds of negative constructions is also structurally replicated. Note that our focus here is on the results of the first two assignments (1–2). However, the other two assignments (3–4) aimed at making the judges reflect upon their answers to their second (2) assignment, the one in which they were asked to check for any potential resonance with content.

2.2.3 Results

(a) Rating degree of non/literalness

Rating degree of non/literalness reveals that, as predicted (see 1.1ci), the list of 151 items comprises significantly more sarcastically-oriented constructions than literally-oriented constructions. Specifically, 2 or more judges rated 118 items of the 151 cases as sarcastic (118/151=78%), whereas 2 or more judges rated the remaining 33 items as literal (33/151=22%), binomial test, $p=1.96\times10^{-12}$ (highly more significant than $p<0.001$). Such results provide support for the prediction that the negative constructions of the kind studied here convey their default sarcastic interpretation more often than their nondefault literal interpretations, when hosting positive concepts.

(b) Resonance with non/literalness

Deciding whether the neighboring utterances resonate with any of the two optional interpretations (i.e., sarcastic or literal), reveals that, as predicted (see 1.1cii), 2 or more judges indicated that the environment of 109 out of 118 sarcastic cases, resonated with any of their interpretations. (In the remaining 9 items, no

---

[10] Our predictions don't distinguish between resonance with targets by an early context as opposed to resonance with targets by a late context; still it makes more sense to expand on targets by late context rather than by early context. Indeed, generally speaking, less resonating segments were found before as opposed to after targets, but that doesn't seem to make a difference.

resonance was detected). Specifically, there were significantly more items whose environment echoed their default sarcastic interpretation (77/109=71%) than their nondefault literal interpretation (32/109=29%), binomial test, $p=1.94 \times 10^{-5}$ (more significant than $p<0.001$).

In all, these results support the Defaultness Hypothesis. They show that, as predicted, these negative constructions (a) convey their default sarcastic interpretation more often than their nondefault literal interpretation; namely, significantly more such negative items are interpreted sarcastically than literally. They further show that, as predicted, when interpreted sarcastically, (b) their environment resonates with their default sarcastic interpretation rather than their nondefault literal interpretation, when hosting positively-oriented adjectives.

3 Discussion and conclusion

According to the Defaultness Hypothesis (Giora, et al. 2015b, 2018), default interpretations of some negative constructions will spring to mind unconditionally, initially and directly, irrespective of negation, novelty, nonliteralness, or contextual support. A case in point is the sarcastic interpretation of e.g., *not particularly successful* in *Hoffe dealt with the inheritance the way she felt like, which probably* **wasn't particularly successful** (rated here as sarcastic, meaning 'unsuccessful', see example (1) above). Indeed, rating degree of non/literalness of such naturally occurring instances of the form *not the most X; not particularly X; not X in particular; not extremely X;* and *not really X*, involving strong attenuation (e.g., by negation) of highly positive concepts (e.g., *particularly successful*) reveals that their vast majority are judged as sarcastic, as predicted by the Defaultness Hypothesis (see ci, section 1.1 above).

Prediction (1.1b), when first tested experimentally in Giora et al. (2015b Exp. 2), was supported by results attesting to the speed superiority of default interpretations over nondefault counterparts. Here, as per predictions (1.1ci-cii), it has gained further corpus-based support. Findings adduced here indicate superior prevalence of default negative sarcasm (see example (1) above) over nondefault negative literalness (see example (2) above, and as shown in subsection (a) of the Results, in subsection 2.2.3).

The Defaultness Hypothesis further predicts (see cii, section 1.1) that, as a result of their speed superiority (attested to by Giora et al. 2015b), the negative constructions' neighboring utterances will resonate with their default sarcastic interpretation (in bold, in example (1) above) rather than with nondefault literal alternatives (in italics, in example (2) above). Being so prominent on our mind, these interpretations will affect discourse production, which will evolve while reflecting these utterances' default interpretations. As predicted by the Defaultness Hypothesis, resonating with default interpretations will supersede resonating with nondefault counterparts. Investigating these constructions' effect on prior and ongoing natural discourse, we show here that default rather than nondefault interpretations prevail. Specifically, the default sarcastic interpretations of the negative constructions studied here are reflected by their neighboring utterances significantly more often than their nondefault literal counterparts (see subsection (b) of Results, in subsection 2.2.3).

In sum, results in this corpus-based study provide converging usage-based evidence supportive of the Defaultness Hypothesis, both in terms of the prevalence of their sarcastic interpretations and their effect on the discourse production.

References

Adler, Meni. 2007. *Hebrew morphological disambiguation: An unsupervised stochastic word-based approach.* Beer-Sheva, Israel: Ben-Gurion University of the Negev dissertation.
Baroni, Marco, Silvia Bernardini, Adriano Ferraresi & Eros Zanchetta. 2009. The WaCky wide web: A collection of very large linguistically processed web-crawled corpora. *Language Resources and Evaluation* 43 (3). 209–226.
Beardsley, Monroe C. 1958. *Aesthetics.* New York, NY: Harcourt, Brace and World.
Becker, Israela, & Rachel Giora. 2018. The Defaultness Hypothesis: A quantitative corpus-based study of non/default sarcasm and literalness production. *Journal of pragmatics* 138. 149–164.
Clark, Herbert H. & Eve V. Clark. 1977. *Psychology and Language.* New York, NY: Harcourt Brace Janovich, Inc.
Du Bois, John W. 2004. Searching for intersubjectivity: 'Too' and 'either' in stance alignment. Paper presented at the the 25th Conference of the International Computer Archive of Modern and Medieval English (ICAME). University of Verona, 19–23 May .
Du Bois, John W. 2007. The stance triangle. In Robert Englebretson (ed.), *Stancetaking in discourse: Subjectivity, evaluation, interaction,* 139–182. Amsterdam: John Benjamins.
Du Bois, John W. 2014. Towards a dialogic syntax. *Cognitive Linguistics* 25 (3). 359–410.
Du Bois, John W. & Rachel Giora. 2014. From cognitive-functional linguistics to dialogic syntax. *Cognitive Linguistics* 25 (3). 351–357.
Gibbs, Raymond W. 1986. On the psycholinguistics of sarcasm. *Journal of Experimental Psychology: General* 115 (1). 3–15.
Gibbs, Raymond W. 1994. *The Poetics of Mind: Figurative Thought, Language, and Understanding.* New York, NY: Cambridge University Press.
Gibbs, Raymond W. 2000. Irony in talk among friends. *Metaphor and Symbol* 15 (1–2). 5–27.
Gibbs, Raymond W. 2002. A new look at literal meaning in understanding what is said and implicated. *Journal of Pragmatics* 34 (4). 457–486.

Giora, Rachel. 2003. *On our Mind: Salience, Context, and Figurative Language*. New York, NY: Oxford University Press.

Giora, Rachel. 2007. "A good Arab is not a dead Arab – a racist incitement": On the accessibility of negated concepts. In Istvan Kecskes & Laurence. R. Horn (eds.), *Explorations in Pragmatics: Linguistic, Cognitive and Intercultural Aspects*, 129–162. Berlin: Mouton de Gruyter.

Giora, Rachel, Ari Drucker & Ofer Fein. 2014a. Resonating with default nonsalient interpretations: A corpus-based study of negative sarcasm. *Belgian Journal of Linguistics* 28. 3–18.

Giora, Rachel, Ari Drucker, Ofer Fein & Itamar Mendelson. 2015a. Default sarcastic interpretations: On the priority of nonsalient interpretations. *Discourse Processes* 52 (3). 173–200.

Giora, Rachel, Ofer Fein, Jonathan Ganzi, Natalie Alkeslassy Levi & Hadas Sabah. 2005. On negation as mitigation: The case of negative irony. *Discourse Processes* 39 (1). 81–100.

Giora, Rachel, Ofer Fein, Nili Metuki & Pnina Stern. 2010. Negation as a metaphor-inducing operator. In Laurence R. Horn (ed.), *The Expression of Negation*, 225–256. Berlin: Mouton de Gruyter.

Giora, Rachel, Shir Givoni & Ofer Fein. 2015b. Defaultness reigns: The case of sarcasm. *Metaphor and Symbol* 30 (4). 290–313.

Giora, Rachel, Inbal Jaffe, Israela Becker & Ofer Fein. 2018. Strongly mitigating a highly positive concept: The case of default sarcastic interpretations. *Review of Cognitive Linguistics* 6 (1). 19–47.

Giora, Rachel, Elad Livnat, Ofer Fein, Anat Barnea, Rakefet Zeiman & Iddo Berger. 2013. Negation generates nonliteral interpretations by default. *Metaphor and Symbol* 28 (2). 89–115.

Giora, Rachel, Moshe Raphaely, Ofer Fein & Elad Livnat. 2014b. Resonating with contextually inappropriate interpretations in production: The case of irony. *Cognitive Linguistics* 25 (3). 443–455.

Givoni, Shir, Rachel Giora & Dafna Bergerbest. 2013. How speakers alert addressees to multiple meanings. *Journal of Pragmatics* 48 (1). 29–40.

Grice, Herbert Paul. 1975. Logic and conversation. In Peter Cole & Jerry L. Morgan (eds.), *Syntax and Semantics: Speech Acts* (Vol. 3), pp. 41–58. New York, NY: Academic Press.

Horn, Laurence R. 1989. *A Natural History of Negation*. Chicago, IL: University of Chicago Press.

Kilgarriff, Adam, Vít Baisa, Jan Bušta, Miloš Jakubíček, Vojtěch Kovář, Jan Michelfeit, Pavel Rychlý & Vít Suchomel. 2014. The Sketch Engine: Ten years on. *Lexicography* 1 (1). 7–36.

Partington, Alan. 2011. Phrasal irony: Its form, function and exploitation. *Journal of Pragmatics* 43 (6). 1786–1800.

Appendix A

The corpus

As a consequence of the strict criteria we followed compiling the list of negative constructions, which are practically rare,[11] and given the need to compile a fair number of items for the sake of reliable statistics, we used the largest corpus of Modern Hebrew available, *HeTenTen*,[12] a web-corpus which comprises about 1×10^9 tokens.

HeTenTen was compiled using a web-crawler. It contains approximately 1.2×10^6 web documents which were mined, filtered, and processed using a generic algorithm suggested by Baroni et al. (2009). Crucially, the corpus was crawled in a way that would not allow it to be biased by topic while still covering a wide range of language varieties as represented over the web, including semi-spoken languages.

Each word of HeTenTen (i.e., 'surface form') was Part-of-Speech-tagged and morphologically annotated for additional morphological features (see Adler 2007), such as gender, number, affixes, etc.[13] The corpus can be queried by using an extended version of a Corpus Querying Language (CQL)[14] (Kilgarriff et al. 2014), which enables users to retrieve lines whose patterns are defined by specifying sequences of token and sub-token-level features. Due to the morphological annotation (Adler 2007), the queries can be defined over many features which address the rich morphology of Hebrew. Additionally, upon request, a wider context can be suggested beyond the line/sentence level, and there is always a pointer to the URL from which the web page was crawled.

---

11 Only few instances of the 4 negative constructions (e.g., *not the most X*) are found in the Corpus of Spoken Israeli Hebrew (a free-access popular corpus of spoken Israeli Hebrew, which includes ~40,000 tokens, in contrast to several tens of the affirmative counterparts (e.g., *the most X*). For instance, only a single case of *not the most X* is found, whereas 34 cases of *the most X* are detected, binomial test, $p=1.2 \times 10^{-14}$ (highly more significant than $p<0.001$). http://cosih.com/
12 http://www.sketchengine.co.uk
13 https://www.sketchengine.co.uk/hetenten-corpus/#Tokenattributes
14 http://cwb.sourceforge.net/temp/CQPTutorial.pdf

Angeliki Athanasiadou
Irony in constructions

Abstract: The chapter investigates the constructional parameters utilized to convey verbal irony. It is suggested that there may be particular constructional properties and devices that facilitate irony. Constructions like *if any, if anything, if anywhere, if at all, if a little* + adjective or adverb, *if ever, if I may*, occur systematically and frequently. They appear in the beginning, in the middle or at the end of the utterance and are highly responsible for intense irony evocation. It will be claimed that these grammatical constructions enhance a special ironic effect. In fact, their elliptic character gives rise to even more intense irony. What will be discussed is how the grammatical form is employed to convey figurative meaning although its primary meaning is not figurative.

Keywords: constructions, frames, *if*-clauses, verbal irony

1 Introduction

Studies on the cognitive process of metaphor have primarily focused on the way it is conveyed. We clearly have metaphoric words as, for instance, *jail* which, in addition to its literal meaning 'the place for the confinement of people accused or convicted of a crime', namely 'prison', can also acquire suffocating attributes as in *My job is a jail*. From this latter example it appears that words are not enough for the emergence of metaphor and that grammatical constructions are highly relevant to this end. There have been studies that recognize the importance of constructions in metaphor evocation like Turner (1987; 1991) for the *XYZ* construction, Dancygier and Sweetser (2014) for nominal modification, for genitives, for the *XYZ* construction, Langacker (2009) on metonymic grammar, Panther and Thornburg (2009) for figuration in grammar, among many others. Sullivan (2013) has largely refined how grammatical constructions contribute to metaphoric language. She has investigated their role in adjectival constructions (domain and predicating adjective constructions), in argument structure constructions

---

Acknowledgments: Special thanks are due to J. Barnden, R. Giora and M. Popa as well as the anonymous reviewer who provided suggestions and commented on an early version. All remaining errors are my responsibility.

Angeliki Athanasiadou, Aristotle University of Thessaloniki

https://doi.org/10.1515/9783110652246-004

(resultatives, ditransitives); she has also examined Turner's *XYZ* construction, as well as relative clauses and conditional constructions.

The studies above clearly recognize the role of constructions in metaphor and metonymy evocation. In the case of verbal irony, however, rather few studies discuss the linguistic forms irony appears in, such as Kreuz et al. (1999) on tag questions, Fraenkel and Schul (2008) on adjectival phrases and recently Colston (2018). And there are even fewer studies, to the best of my knowledge, (Giora, Givoni, and Fein (2015) with regard to negative sarcastic constructions – in this paper sarcasm pertains to verbal irony, and also Camp and Hawthorne (2008) on the use of *like/as if* as a vehicle of sarcasm) that primarily focus on whether or how irony emerges constructionally.

I start from the assumption that verbal irony, especially affirmative irony, almost always relies on a broader context to ensure it is communicated (Giora 2016; Giora, Givoni, and Fein 2015) and that the development and the diversity of the figurative process of irony are necessarily based on the way it is produced. We deal with two possibilities expressed by different types of constructions: an utterance can ironically (a) reject something previously said, or (b) accept it. The speaker, in (1), (informal conversation among academics) may seemingly assert or agree with something although she does not honestly accept or acknowledge it:

(1) A: *The world-famous professor was not elected to the post by the members of the board.*
    B: *Yeah, right. Their CV was a lot better than his.*

The speaker in the form of a question performs an act of offering although she may actually reject and criticize the hearer who has drunk the whole bottle all by himself[1]:

(2) *Would you like to have another glass?*

Different constructions, then, are available to the speaker employing irony with the intended meaning of carrying various pragmatic functions like ridiculing, criticizing severely, rebuking. The ironic patterns very systematically seem to fall into two types: (a) either being positive about negative issues or being negative about positive issues. The ironic functions reveal a variety of speakers' intentions such as to criticize harshly or lightly, or anywhere in between, or, though rarely, a speaker may even use irony to praise (Pexman and Olineck 2002).

---

[1] This is one of the examples provided by scholars supporting the Allusional Pretense Theory of Discourse Irony, such as Kumon-Nakamura, Glucksberg, and Brown [1995], 2007.

Constructionally, these two patterns are expressed via a variety of utterance forms. The incongruity and the reversal of values between positive and negative issues arouse the interest of the audience, to say the least. This also, no doubt, gives rise to the overemphasis of the operation of contrast in the literature of verbal irony, also referred to as contrary, contradictory.

There is, however, a third pattern in which there is a kind of balance between accepting and rejecting. The speaker may evaluate and assess between these two, offering alternatives or simply leaving it to the hearer to decide which interpretation is to be taken. This is expressed via a group of short clauses embedded within the construction or attached to it. This is a very deliberate process on the part of the speaker in which the hearer is intentionally puzzled and confused by the speaker and thus is confronted with alternatives from which she needs to draw inferences and comment on them. This pattern is facilitated by a group of elliptical *if*-clauses, like *if any, if anything, if anywhere, if at all, if a little* + adjective or adverb, *if ever, if I may*. It needs to be pointed out in advance, that these *if*-clauses do not always evoke irony as can be seen in the COCA corpus as well as in articles in the internet. They may form part of different sorts of constructions. For instance, in (3), *if any* + noun, *if any evidence,* is a direct object of the verb *assess*:

(3)   The second objective of the study was to assess if any evidence existed that associated alcohol consumption in first-year students with retention into second year.[2]

If anything goes wrong in (4) is the antecedent of the conditional construction:

(4)   We live on a high-risk margin and if anything goes wrong, we are forced to be highly indebted.
      https://www.iol.co.za/business-report/opinion/business-unusual-9334285

In the way *if any-* or *if anything*-constructions are used, as in (3) and (4), it follows that, no ironic purposes are derived.

The elliptical *if*-clauses that are of interest here belong to the discourse conditional type and have been termed "metacommunicative" (Athanasiadou and Dirven 2000: 17–22); they exhibit a variety of uses:

---

[2] Example met in COCA taken from an article by Liguori, G. and Lonbaken, B. "Alcohol consumption and academic retention in first-year college students". ACAD: *College Student Journal.* Spring 2015, Vol 49 Issue 1: 69–77.

(5) (a) *Splendid! Now ladies, if you'll excuse us, we have a lot to do.* (Metapragmatic)
   (b) *I've come to offer my congratulations, if that's the right word.* (Metalinguistic)
   (c) *The change, if any, in foreign policy will consist rather of a freshness of approach.* (Restrictive)

Metacommunicatives constitute a subtype of pragmatic conditionals: "these *if*-clauses can be seen as comments on various aspects of the communicative act and are therefore metacommunicative in nature" (Athanasiadou and Dirven 2000: 17).

My focus is on cases like (5) and especially like (5c) where the speaker asserts there is a change and at the same time questions it. Depending on broader context this can or cannot be ironic. In case it is, the ironic intent is evoked by this third constructional pattern. This internal incongruity, known as the essence of irony, has become distinct via a set of such elliptic *if*-constructions which motivate and implement this internal clash, eventually resulting in affecting irony (see also Partington 2011). It is worth mentioning that in the first two patterns, positive about negative and vice versa, the particular group of *if*-clauses can be omitted, i.e. the ironic effect holds and is intense even without them. However, the aim of the chapter is to give prominence to constructions, of the third pattern, that highly motivate the expression of irony.

2 Frames, constructions, and irony

The chapter has benefited from insights from Construction Grammar and Frame Semantics. These are two of the tools employed by Sullivan 2013 for metaphoric language. Construction Grammar and Frame Semantics will be employed and applied here to ironic language. Following Goldberg (2006: 5), constructions are "learned pairings of form with semantic or discourse function, including morphemes or words, idioms, partially lexically filled and fully general phrasal patterns". The *if*-clauses to be discussed here are constructions that contribute with their form and meaning to irony evocation. Semantic frames comprising components like elements, participants, roles, relations, frame structure in general, in the sense of Fillmore 1982, are appropriate for assigning verbal irony. They are thought to be very useful devices as they comprise both conceptual and linguistic knowledge about things and relations and their slightly or maximally modified or reversed values. The discussion on frames, constructions and irony can be illustrated by the example that follows, taken from Twitter, although Speaker's B utterance does not include an instance of the *if any, if anything, ...* list of constructions.

(6) A: *Did you go to the gym today to get some exercise?*
    B: *Yeah, sure, I took the garbage to the bin.*

An act of exercising involves certain standard elements in the exercise frame, like the exerciser, his/her body or body parts, effortful movements like going to a special place, the gym, in order to carry out programs like spinning, cross training, power bars as well as high intensity aerobic programs, among many other activities. Taking the garbage to the bin is ironically used as an effortful movement which is said to belong to the exercising frame but only in order to ridicule it. Semantic frames appear to be an appropriate tool for irony evocation as the speaker may employ elements and roles that restrict, question, negate it or reverse its values. The question is which parts of the frame structure will be employed to intensely evoke irony, in other words, which elements are selected, and used by the speakers, in order to express themselves ironically. In the afore-mentioned example (6), it is the element of effort which yields inferences against the established frame of exercise. Speaker B seemingly agrees she went to the gym but only to ridicule the frame by highlighting the least effort. Even though Speaker B addresses Speaker A, the irony as such is addressed towards B herself; it is criticizing B, not A. This ironic construction, which is actually an instance of self-sarcasm, self-ridicules the ironist. It has also a variety of functions to be revealed by broader contexts.

As for conceptual frames, the speaker may comment on an entity or a concept that either belongs to the frame or contradicts it as long as the issues involved are included in the same domain of experience in spite of their contrariness. Frame structure can be preserved even when it is questioned or negated. The intuitive vicinity of even antonymous entities or concepts is one of the ways speakers employ when they decide to be ironic by offering alternative options to their addressees which can also cancel the standard expectations, to say the least. It has been argued (Athanasiadou 2017) that the metonymic basis of irony lies on the contiguity of opposite entities which form part of a single domain. In this chapter, this view is further developed foregrounding the contribution of conceptual frames which reflect shared world knowledge and comprise entities and concepts which cross cut with domains of experience. Irony is evoked due to the alleged incongruity between the source domain of the "literal world" and the target domain of the speakers' intended world, which may of course involve multiple frames.

Concerning the particular patterns of *if*-constructions: as is known, conditionals allow us to oscillate along a continuum ranging from close to factuality to hypotheticality till counterfactuality. Dancygier and Sweetser contend they "allow one to consider alternative possibilities in the metaphoric mapping world, as well as in other worlds". Conditionals are "constructions whose semantics is inherently alternative[3]" (2014: 150). This applies to conditional constructions in general. The question is how do such elliptical *if*-clauses work? Do they follow the same pattern with other types of conditional constructions or do they exhibit different properties to ensure the irony which eventually runs along with other types of mechanisms like metaphor or metonymy? In the analysis that follows, the particular pattern of metacommunicative *if*-clauses will be discussed in terms of how it leads to irony evocation.

3 Analysis

My observations focus on examples from various sources but mainly from the COCA corpus. From a collection of approximately 400 instances of contexts in which the *if any, if anything, if anywhere, if at all, if a little* + adjective or adverb, *if ever, if I may* constructions appear, I have isolated around 60 cases of metacommunicative *if*-clauses as it was found they follow an identical pattern. Such cases seem to be systematically and recurrently used in COCA and, in my opinion, deserve attention. Internet has also been a precious source for some of my examples, as well as informal conversations in which I was one of the participants. The corpus search revealed that most of the metacommunicative cases are employed with an ironic and/or sarcastic effect.[4] Each one of the examples discussed below exhibits a somehow different way of irony evocation.

---

3 Dancygier and Sweetser (2005: 132–136) provide an example where bridges can be thought of as different kinds of horses: *If the beautiful Golden Gate is the thoroughbred of bridges, the Bay Bridge is the workhouse.* They call this type of conditional constructions meta-metaphorical. This type builds "alternative relationships between metaphoric construals of a domain" (also discussed in Dancygier and Sweetser 2014: 150). Conditional constructions like these "build or evoke alternative metaphoric construals". However, such conditional constructions can be highly ironic as well.
4 This observation additionally strengthens our decision (Athanasiadou and Dirven 2000) to include this subtype of conditional constructions within the discourse type.

(7) A: *Have you noticed I have lost weight lately? I'm preparing myself for my graduation.*
B: *When was the last time, if ever, that you tried to lose weight for an event?*[5]

In (7), irony arises even in the absence of the *if ever*-construction. Speaker B, by asking *When was the last time*, seems to presuppose that there was at least one time, when Speaker A did try to lose weight for an event. However, speaker B believes that A has never tried to. Moreover, Speaker B avoids/dodges a straightforward, though offensive, ironic reply like: *you have? I haven't noticed it*. Instead, by means of the *if ever*-clause, she reorients the discussion and scorns or makes fun of speaker A indirectly by focusing on the fact that there was no such time in the past when she ever tried such a thing. Speaker A is faced by alternative situations in order to cope with the interpretation of speaker's B ironic utterance: she didn't lose weight on account of an event and she never attempted to lose weight. The *if ever* is broadening the attack to encompass even any attempts whatsoever to lose weight (before going to events). The latter alternative is due to the *if ever*-clause. The *if ever*-clause builds on even a stronger ironic effect: Speaker A never in fact tried to lose weight for an event. It is in this sense that the *if ever*-construction clarifies and intensifies the irony. Not only does it undermine the presupposition that she lost weight but rather questions whether she even ever tried to. Speaker B questions the frame of being fit and thin by highlighting the temporal frame which is also questioned. It is worth mentioning that the ironic effect is further intensified by means of speaker's B interrogative construction, but I will only focus on the parenthetical *if ever*-construction here.

(8) *She is very emotional. Her feelings, if any, were not shown.*

The speaker, in (8) (informal conversation among friends), ironically believes she is very emotional and questions whether in case she has feelings, she doesn't show them. The *if any*-clause focuses on a particular lexical entity, namely, *feelings*. Instead of saying something like *yeah right, she is unemotional*, which would also be ironic when marked by a particular tone of voice, the speaker selects an entity from the frame of emotionality which involves entities and roles like having a human face, having feelings… and, seemingly, indirectly, is being very intense. The alternatives here suggest that she doesn't show her feelings; this would still be ironic even without the *if any*-clause. But the *if any*-clause

---

5 # When was the last time, if ever, that you tried lose weight for an event? # Natalie Eilbert: I4617-05-21 USSan Francisco ExaminerABC be where they're at right now.

intensifies even more strongly the unemotionality, conveying that she is totally emotionless, perhaps not human, (i.e., she doesn't have any feelings at all). In this example, the reversal of values (she is emotional/she is not emotional), an issue on which the typical definition of verbal irony lies, is not enough. An entity from the frame of emotionality is being highlighted in order to sarcastically cancel it. *If any* is here used to straightforwardly intensify irony. Without it, the speaker would merely be implying a lack of feelings since they are not shown; but by means of the *if any* the possibility of a complete lack of feelings is explicitly suggested. So we have a fairly intensified expression of irony in the overt meaning of the utterance, enhancing the contrast to what the speaker really believes (i.e. the person is very emotional). The intensity of the ironic effect is, in this example, further enhanced by the negative construction, but again this won't be discussed here.

(9) *Now that you've grown up, (even) if a little late, you'll show a bit of respect.*
 (Athanasiadou and Dirven 2000: 21, adapted)

In this example, the addressee is an adult but (still) not as grown-up as she might be. Showing respect is not a necessary condition linked to age; it might either be or not be something that one would expect from a grown-up. Without the *if a little late*-construction, irony arises from the canceling of the link between being grown-up and being respectful.

In (9), the speaker, first, asserts and seemingly accepts that she has grown up. The irony here lies in the violation of the growing up frame. Being grown up involves being independent, making your own decisions ... but not necessarily showing respect. In other words, age is not necessarily linked to showing respect. This ironic comment arises even without the parenthetical *if a little late*-clause. But the embedded *if a little late*-clause intensifies irony furthermore; the speaker is being very offensive towards the hearer and questions not only whether she has grown up but that it also took her long to grow up. This additional meaning is due to the particular embedded clause, which restricts the validity of one's maturity. In fact, by means of it, a concession is expressed in order to maximize the offence; the elliptic clause actually is *even if a little late*. The alternatives the hearer faces are if she has grown up and, even if she has, it has taken her long. The *if a little late*-clause contributes to the intensified ironic comment.

In the cases above, the frame structure is restricted, invalidated, or violated.

The example that follows is an idiomatic construction, most frequently used in American English. The definition provided by dictionaries for the *if a little late to the dance* expression is either something that has come up too late than is relevant or appropriate or even, as in this case, a stupid apology:

(10) *I do believe his apology is genuine if a little late to the dance.*

In (10), one faces a highly contradictory and ambiguous situation. This case is of those instances of irony that make scholars suggest that irony may refer to something totally irrelevant. We need to be based on the additional context in order to attempt to figure out the ironic intent of the speaker.[6] On the one hand, she is projecting understanding; she acknowledges the seriousness of the event and emphatically states, by means of *do*, that she takes the apology at face value; this is drawn from the first part of the construction. On the other hand, she is suspicious and critically comments on the lateness of the apology. The *if*-clause seems to be in total contrast with the main clause. The speaker could have literally said: *I accept the apology but I don't appreciate his attitude*. Again, here, as in (9), concession is expressed: *even if a little late to the dance*. The speaker is not absolutely certain about this conduct but still does not want to argue on it, as it is really a rather delicate matter, thus she pretends to accept it. However, by means of the concessive idiomatic construction, the speaker reduces the strength of her belief; it is as if saying: 'I do not really believe this; he hasn't shown restraint or maturity on the situation'. The incongruity of this ironic example leaves the hearer speechless and confused as to what to take into account. Here the frame of apologizing is canceled.

The example that follows is a constructed example but there are many instances of this pattern in COCA[7]:

(11) *What, if any, are the requirements of success?*

The context is: 'Although she's very sharp, she failed the exam and didn't get the job. So what, if any, are the requirements of success?'

In (11), we have the violation of the frame of succeeding in an exam, which demands entities like intelligence, hard work, discipline, or even luck. By means of the rhetorical question *what are the requirements of success*, the speaker questions the link between requirements and success. It is as if saying: 'there are no

---

6 The context is: Although Justin Trudeau obviously should've shown some kind of restraint, not to mention a tad bit of maturity and leadership with respect to his shenanigans, I do believe his apology is genuine if a little late to the dance. In BC Local News. Mitchell's Musings: Splashing into summer. https://www.bclocalnews.com/.../mitchells-musings-splas...
7 For instance:

| 53 | 2017 | ACAD | Stanford Law Review | A | B | C | N.W.2d 456, 466–67 (Iowa 2016). It is unclear what, if any, effect the decision will have on child support cases. # 118. E-mail |

requirements for success, she may be sharp but the director supported/promoted someone they knew'. This alternative emerges even without the *if any*-clause. The speaker ridicules the one who thinks there are requirements for success by canceling the link between requirements and success. It also reveals the speaker's suspicion that there were not any success requirements employed. The embedded *if any*-clause focuses on *requirements* and serves to intensify the ironicity of the rest of the sentence. Using the *if any*-clause, the speaker seemingly accepts the frame of requirements for success and makes one wonder which they are: 'if being sharp isn't a requirement then what is? Why has she failed if she's sharp? Has she studied hard enough? Then she's not sharp enough'. This makes the ironic example even more intense. The hearer, with an ironic tone of voice, could say *yeah, she studied hard, yeah, she is sharp*. Instead, the speaker offensively questions the requirements frame of success while simultaneously violating it.[8]

4 Discussion

This paper has drawn attention to constructions that motivate highly ironic expressions. In this small set of examples, irony works at more than one level, where two very important conceptual mechanisms seem to be operating: conceptual frames and constructions. These two mechanisms have been taken into account for metaphor and metonymy (Sullivan 2013) and, as it was shown, they seem to work for the figure of irony as well.

Frames can be restricted, invalidated, violated, or canceled. In such cases, the speaker balances alternatives by doing both, accepting and rejecting a particular frame. This contributes enormously to the ironic effect. The alternatives can range between rejections of concepts, or events, or situations, using entities that restrict or challenge conceptual frames. They seem to involve the juxtaposition of incompatible issues and if the standard definition of irony is to be followed, one could say that the incompatibility lies in that the issues do not match. Their function, though, is to highlight, comment, relativise, or restrict the presuppositions being made. In any case, though distant and seemingly irrelevant, the alternative options are expressed with entities within the conceptual frame. In this way the ironic effect is rendered very intense. Superficially, a contradiction is involved, but only seemingly so.

---

[8] One might wonder if the examples discussed can be instances of understatement. Gibbs (2007) actually takes understatement (and overstatement) as varieties of irony. However, understatement, though close to irony, has different roles in conversation (see also Walton 2017).

Elliptical, parenthetical, concessive, or idiomatic *if*-clauses work somehow differently when compared with conditional constructions in general. In terms of form, they either highlight particular entities, *feelings* in (8), or *requirements* in (11); they may highlight clauses, the *now-that* clause in (9), or they may express an attitude toward the content of the construction as a whole, as in (10). In terms of the functions they perform, they ironically comment rather harshly, and, as it has been indicated, they first puzzle or surprise the addressee by making a statement, which they then deny or invalidate (as in the elliptic, concessive *even if,* which has an inherent restrictive use), thus forcing the hearer to recognize one of the options offered and take a stance following some further thought. These properties make them absolutely indispensable for a powerful ironic effect.

We seem to be somehow distanced from definitions of verbal irony like pretense or echoing accounts. These two approaches to the study of irony are based on the way it is expressed: positive for something negative and negative for something positive. The speaker then expects the hearer to understand her pretense (e.g., Clark 1996; Clark and Gerrig 1983; 1984) or in terms of echoing accounts she echoes what has been said before (e.g., Sperber 1984; Sperber and Wilson 1986/1995; Wilson and Sperber 1992; 1993). Instead, and on the basis of the particular constructional properties, we are faced with alternatives that either enrich, or question, or seemingly violate particular frames. This is facilitated by means of the elliptical *if*-clauses. These elliptical metacommunicative *if*-clauses are responsible for the blend or even the difficulty in the interpretation of the ironic utterances. It is particularly true of examples (10) and (11), which, at first sight, seem to be irrelevant, ambiguous or unordered. However, they are not; such elliptical clauses contribute to the expression of irony with a double scope: the description of a situation (feelings (8) or requirements (11)) together with the expression of skepticism as to whether there are really any feelings or requirements. The hearer now faces alternatives: the focus may not be on whether the feelings were shown but primarily on whether they exist (in order to be shown). Similarly, the focus may not be on which requirements are needed for success but on whether there are any. In fact, it has been claimed that such constructions contribute to the highlighting of intense ironic instances. Now the operation of opposition and the conflict between values become secondary parameters. The choice between alternatives or the highlighting of extra aspects of the conceptual frame by means of such elliptical clauses used in context further enhances the ironic effect. This can be seen if we add the *if anything*-clause in the beginning of example (1) *If anything, their CV was a lot better than his.*

Thus, the metacommunicative *if*-constructions may either heighten the irony or they may trigger it (irony wouldn't be evoked without them). This point could be related to Popa's observation (this volume). She discusses the distinction between metaphoric irony and hyperbolic irony. In the former case, the irony relies on the metaphor while in the latter the hyperbole strengthens the irony. Metacommunicative *if*-constructions seem to work in a rather similar way.

Accounting for the mechanism of conceptual frames with their elements, roles, and relations, as a step in-between constructions and figuration, it has been suggested here that we are in a better position to trace the ironic intentions. Although the examples discussed are limited, they, however, recur rather frequently in the corpus. These particular *if*-constructions seem to be indicative of yielding intense irony with a variety of pragmatic functions.

References

Athanasiadou, Angeliki. 2017. Irony has a metonymic basis. In Angeliki Athanasiadou & Herbert L. Colston (eds.), *Irony in Language Use and Communication*, 201–216. Amsterdam & Philadelphia: J. Benjamins Publishing Company.

Athanasiadou, Angeliki & René Dirven. 2000. Pragmatic Conditionals. In Ad Foolen & Frederike van der Leek (eds.), *Constructions in Cognitive Linguistics*, 1–26. Amsterdam & Philadelphia: J. Benjamins Publishing Company.

Camp, Elisabeth & John Hawthorne. 2008. Sarcastic 'like': A case study in the interface of syntax and semantics. *Philosophical Perspectives* 22. 1–21.

Clark H. Herbert. 1996. *Using language*. Cambridge: Cambridge University Press.

Clark H. Herbert & Richard J. Gerrig. 1983. Understanding old words with new meanings. *Journal of Verbal Learning and Verbal Behavior* 22. 591–608.

Clark H. Herbert & Richard J. Gerrig. 1984. On the pretense theory of irony. *Journal of Experimental Psychology: General* 113. 121–126.

Colston L. Herbert. 2018. Irony as indirectness cross-linguistically: On the scope of generic mechanisms. In Alessandro Capone (ed.), *Indirect Reports and Pragmatics in the World Languages: Perspectives in Pragmatics, Philosophy & Psychology* (Vol. 19), 109–131. Switzerland: Springer.

Dancygier, Barbara & Eve Sweetser. 2005. *Mental spaces in grammar: conditional constructions*. Cambridge: Cambridge University Press.

Dancygier, Barbara & Eve Sweetser. 2014. *Figurative Language*. Cambridge: Cambridge University Press.

Fillmore J. Charles. 1982. Frame Semantics. In The Linguistic Society of Korea (ed.), *Linguistics in the morning calm*, 111–137. Seoul: Hanshin Publishing Co.

Fraenkel, Tamar & Yaacov Schul. 2008. The meaning of negated adjectives. *Intercultural Pragmatics* 5–4. 517–540.

Gibbs, W. Raymond, Jr. 2007. Irony in talk among friends. In Raymond W. Gibbs & Herbert L. Colston (eds.), *Irony in language and thought: A cognitive science reader*, 339–360. New York: Lawrence Erlbaum Associates.

Giora, Rachel, Shir Givoni & Ofer Fein. 2015. Defaultness reigns: The case of sarcasm. *Metaphor and Symbol* 30/4. 290–313.

Giora, Rachel. 2016. When negatives are easier to understand than affirmatives: The case of negative sarcasm. In Pierre Larrivée & Chungmin Lee (eds.), *Negation and polarity: Experimental perspectives*, 127–143. Cham: Springer.
Goldberg, Adele. 2006. *Constructions at Work*. Oxford: Oxford University Press.
Kreuz, J. Roger, Max A. Kassler, Lori Coppenrath & Bonnie McLain Allen. 1999. Tag questions and common ground effects in the perception of verbal irony. *Journal of Pragmatics* 31. 1685–1700.
Kumon-Nakamura, Sachi, Sam Glucksberg & Mary Brown. [1995] 2007. How about another piece of pie: The allusional pretense theory of discourse irony. In Raymond W. Gibbs & Herbert L. Colston (eds.), *Irony in Language and Thought*, 57–95. Lawrence Erlbaum Associates. Taylor & Francis Group. New York, London.
Langacker, W. Ronald. 2009. Metonymic grammar. In Klaus-Uwe Panther, Linda L. Thornburg & Antonio Barcelona (eds.), *Metonymy and Metaphor in Grammar*, 45–71. Amsterdam & Philadelphia: J. Benjamins Publishing Company.
Panther, Klaus-Uwe & Linda L. Thornburg. 2009. Introduction: On figuration in grammar. In Klaus-Uwe Panther, Linda L. Thornburg & Antonio Barcelona (eds.), *Metonymy and Metaphor in Grammar*, 1–44. Amsterdam & Philadelphia: J. Benjamins Publishing Company.
Partington, Alan. 2011. Phrasal irony: Its form, function and exploitation. *Journal of Pragmatics* 43. 1786–1800.
Pexman, M. Penny & Kara M. Olineck. 2002. Does sarcasm always sting? Investigating the impact of ironic insults and ironic compliments. *Discourse Processes* 33. 199–217.
Sperber, Dan. 1984. Verbal Irony: Pretense or Echoic Mention? *Journal of Experimental Psychology: General* 113(1). 130–136.
Sperber, Dan & Deirdre Wilson. 1986/1995. *Relevance: Communication and Cognition*. Oxford: Blackwell.
Sullivan, Karen. 2013. *Frames and Constructions in Metaphoric Language*. Amsterdam & Philadelphia: J. Benjamins Publishing Company.
Turner, Mark. 1987. *Death is the mother of beauty: Mind, metaphor, criticism*. Chicago: University of Chicago Press.
Turner, Mark. 1991. *Reading minds: The study of English in the age of Cognitive Science*. Princeton, New Jersey: Princeton University Press.
Walton, L. Kendall. 2017. Meiosis, hyperbole, irony. *Philosophical Studies* 174(1). 105–120.
Wilson, Deirdre & Dan Sperber. 1992. On verbal irony. *Lingua* 87. 53–76.
Wilson, Deirdre & Dan Sperber. 1993. Linguistic form and relevance. *Lingua* 90. 1–25.

Mihaela Popa-Wyatt
Hyperbolic Figures

Abstract: It's natural for hyperbole to mix with metaphor and irony, and other figures of speech. How do they mix together and what kind of compound, if any, arises out of the mixing? In tackling this question, I shall argue that thinking of hyperbolic figures along the lines familiar from ironic metaphor compounds is a temptation we should resist. Looking in particular at hyperbolic metaphor and hyperbolic irony, I argue, they don't yield a new encompassing compound figure with one figure building on another. Instead, what we have is one dominant figure – metaphor and irony, respectively – that is coloured with hyperbolic tinges. So, what does hyperbole bring to the mixing pot? I suggest we should think of hyperbole in hyperbolic figures as being an interpretive effect, modulating the working of the figure it mixes with, and thereby rendering it more emphatic.

Keywords: hyperbole, metaphor, irony, hyperbolic metaphor, hyperbolic irony, ironic metaphor, order of interpretation

1 Introduction

Hyperbole is the neglected sister of metaphor and irony. As Carston & Wearing (2005: 79) put it, "it's a less interesting, substantial or effective use of language, perhaps even facile or trivial" compared to other figures. It's not uncommon to hear people making utterances such as "the best thing ever", "the greatest", "unbelievable", "jaw-droppingly great", "tremendous", "triumphant", "formidable". These promote something as being better than it is. Conversely, someone may present things in a more negative light than justifiable, saying that it is "all terrible", "absolutely horrendous", "a real killer", "the end of the world", and so forth. Clearly, what one says is more than what one means, whether good or bad. So, what's the communicative function hyperbole fulfils? I argue that the point of hyperbole is *emphasis*. We do so by drawing attention that a certain order of

---

Acknowledgements: The research in this article was initially supported in part by Research Project Grant F/00 094/BE from the Leverhulme Trust, UK, and finalised with funds from the Research Project Grant "HaLO" (841443) from the Marie-Skłodowska Curie.

Mihaela Popa-Wyatt, Leibniz-Zentrum Allgemeine Sprachwissenschaft (ZAS), Berlin

https://doi.org/10.1515/9783110652246-005

things turned out to be *greater*, or *lesser*, than we expected or desired, and thus convey a degree of *greater*, or *lesser*, surprise, excitement, or frustration, disappointment, had things been otherwise.

This idea builds on recent work (Popa-Wyatt forth), where I've argued that the essence of hyperbole is to increase the salience of the target property. Key to this is overstating the gap between what one says and how one would have expected things to normally turn out. This thus increases the gap between how things actually are and how they were expected to be in order to show how much the former exceeded the latter. As a result, the target property that the speaker aims to put forward becomes much more salient than if it were expressed literally. Correlatively, by increasing the gap between reality and expectation, the speaker is also able to express a range of more intense and colourful affective responses that are typically associated with surpassed, or thwarted, expectations.

Here I want to extend this idea by looking at cases where hyperbole co-occurs with other figures of speech to form *hyperbolic figures*. This question has been recently pursued by Carston & Wearing (2015) who discuss hyperbolic compounds such as hyperbolic metaphor and hyperbolic irony as working on a similar pattern to a more familiar compound such as ironic metaphor (see Stern 2000, Bezuidenhout 2001, 2015, Camp 2006, 2012, Popa-Wyatt 2009, 2010, 2017, ms.). While I agree with Carston & Wearing that hyperbole is a "distinctive figure in its own right", I disagree with the suggestion that hyperbolic figures are anything like a figurative compound in the way ironic metaphor is.

By figurative compounds I mean cases where two figures mesh together to form a more encompassing figure, which contains elements of both, but where only one figure fulfils the speaker's primary communicative goal, while the other is merely subservient to achieving this goal. For example, when someone utters (1) about a messy piece of handwriting, illegible and covered in ink blotches:

(1) What delicate lacework! (from Stern 2000)

what the speaker means is that the handwriting is illegible. The utterance is intended both metaphorically and ironically, but the speaker's main communicative point is ironic, not metaphorical. The metaphor merely serves as input to achieve ironic purposes.

This raises a familiar question of the order in which two figures in a compound are to be interpreted. This is important because it is telling of the kind of constraints they put on the interpretation of each other, and ultimately the kind of compound they yield. In cases of ironic metaphor, the ironic content is conditioned on the metaphorical content, which thus functions as the object of ironic ridicule (Popa-Wyatt 2017; see Stern 2000, Bezuidenhout 2001). This suggests that the compound is primarily ironic in that irony corresponds to the overarching intention, whereas metaphor is subsumed to making an ironic point.

Can we explain hyperbole mixing with other figures along similar lines? I argue this is a temptation we should resist. This is because in such hyperbolic mixing, the hyperbole is neither an overarching figure subsuming the other figure in its service, nor does it function as a vehicle in the service of the other figure. In both hyperbolic metaphor and hyperbolic irony, the speaker is concerned primarily to make a metaphoric and ironic point, respectively, not a hyperbolic one. This means that hyperbole doesn't lend a substantive content to the mixture in the way metaphor does in ironic metaphor. Instead, the hyperbole modulates the working of the figure it mixes with, so that it intensifies its effects. Thus, we can think of the contribution made by hyperbole as an interpretive effect that infuses hyperbolic tinges into the figure it mixes with.

2 Hyperbolic figures

It is very common for hyperbole to mix with other figures of speech within a single utterance. Carston and Wearing (2015: 81) list some examples:

(2) That child is the devil incarnate. (*hyperbole and metaphor*)

(3) They go about together like Siamese twins. (*hyperbole and simile*)

(4) The gargantuan paunch over there is my step-father. (*hyperbole and metonymy*)

(5) It's the end of the world. (*hyperbole and irony*)
[describing someone's angry reaction when he finds he's got a parking fine]

(6) Those tickets cost an arm and a leg. (*hyperbole and idiom*)

(7) Money is the root of all evil. (*hyperbole and proverb*)
[in response to a situation in which someone has claimed a little more on their expenses than they were strictly entitled to].

What makes hyperbole so flexible in mixing with all sorts of figurative uses, as well as stock phrases like idioms and proverbs? In this paper I will focus on hyperbolic metaphor and hyperbolic irony as two paradigmatic cases of hyperbole mixing with other figures of speech.

To understand what goes on in such hyperbolic figures, we can ask which figure is conditioned upon the other? In other words, what is the *logical order of interpretation*?[1] Second, how do hearers interpret such combinations? In other words, what is the *temporal order of interpretation*? Applied to hyperbolic figures the question becomes: do we first interpret the utterance hyperbolically and only then determine the other figurative interpretation, or the other way round?

I will approach these questions by looking at parallel arguments deployed in relation to ironic metaphor. There, the order of interpretation has been *the* driving argument to establish the distinctiveness of metaphor and irony (see Stern 2000, Bezuidenhout 2001, Popa-Wyatt 2010, 2017). The distinctiveness uncovered has taken the form of distinct *types of content or speech-acts* – where metaphorical content is asserted; ironic content is implicated. A more general way to uncover the distinctiveness is to say that metaphor is in the business of putting forward a *representation* of the world, while irony is in the business of *evaluating* or *expressing* attitudes of the speaker towards the thoughts or actions of others (Popa 2009, Carston & Wearing 2015). Such differences are indicative of a certain complementarity between metaphor and irony, so when they combine together it is natural for a metaphorical description of a situation to serve as object of critical ironic attitudes. Can we conclude a similar kind of distinctiveness between hyperbole and metaphor on the one hand, and hyperbole and irony on the other, by looking at their respective mixing?

This is a question that Carston & Wearing (2015) take seriously, especially given that the status of hyperbole is less clear. Assuming that we can divide, following Stern (2000: 236), figurative uses in two distinct families of figures – *M*-type and *I*-type (with *M*-type family including figures that work roughly on the pattern of metaphor, such as simile, metonymy, synecdoche, oxymoron; and *I*-type family including figures that work roughly on the pattern of irony and understatement) – where shall we group hyperbole? Stern lumps it in the *I*-type family. On the other hand, Sperber & Wilson (2008), Wilson & Carston (2007), lump hyperbole with metaphor. Elsewhere I've argued that hyperbole is more of a mixed figure in that it has characteristics of both *M*-family and *I*-family: it is descriptive like metaphor, and evaluative like irony (Popa 2009: 270).

Carston & Wearing (2015) go further in refining this distinction. They argue that hyperbole is a figure in its own right: it is neither like metaphor nor like irony,

---

[1] Stern 2000, Bezuidenhout 2001, 2015, Camp 2006, 2012, Popa-Wyatt 2009, 2010, 2017, ms.

though it has features in common with each. It is like metaphor in that it describes the world as experienced by the speaker, though by appeal to "a shift of magnitude along a dimension which is intrinsic to the encoded meaning of the hyperbole vehicle" (2015: 88). It is like irony in that it expresses an evaluation, though it's an evaluation of the state of affairs in the world, and not of other people's thoughts and expectations. As Carston & Wearing note, a hyperbolic speaker is expressing that she finds the situation she is describing to "have (much) more of some property than she expected or wanted" (2015: 90). This is something that transpires in typical paraphrases of hyperboles along the lines that there is "more or less of [some property] *F* than the speaker expected (or wanted).[...] the paraphrase of what the speaker meant doesn't merely capture a quantity or degree which is more factually accurate than the encoded quantity; it also expresses an element of evaluation of the state of affairs described" (2015: 85). This is very much on the right line; however Carston and Wearing are not explicit about how this evaluation comes about.

Walton (2017) provides precisely such a mechanism to account for this evaluative component. He argues that in overstating, the speaker is representing, by what she says, a quantity as being larger than what she asserts it to be. To measure how much larger, he introduces a notion of "salient contrast" to characterise what the speaker is especially concerned to indicate is not the case in a context. Thus, an utterance counts as hyperbole if the distance between what the speaker says and the salient contrast is bigger than the distance between what she actually means and the salient contrast. In Popa-Wyatt (forth) I propose to think of the salient contrast as a *normative point* on the relevant scale, which captures the range of expectations, hopes and desires that are raised to salience only to convey that they have been either surpassed or thwarted. This is useful because it helps locating what is meant on the relevant scale, as a point in between what is said and what is expected, hoped or desired. What matters is that even though what is meant is *more* (or *less*) than what is said, it's still *less* (or *more*) than what would normally be expected.

Thus, the point of hyperbole is *emphasis*. By overstating that things are *greater* (*lesser*) than expected, hoped, or desired, we shift the salience of the target property, thus making it more salient. This is, after all, the whole point in exaggerating: presenting reality in a more emphatic light. In addition, the speaker is expressing surprise or other relevant affect in reaction to how much, or how little, our expectations have been either exceeded or thwarted. The bigger the gap between what the speaker says and how she expects things to be, the bigger the contrast between expectations and reality is, thus eliciting a greater sense of surprise. Conversely, the smaller the gap is (i.e. the closer to the literal meaning we get), the less surprising it is.

The gist of hyperbole thus resides in conveying that things have turned out way better, or way worse, than what one might have expected, hoped or desired in the circumstances. This comparison is possible precisely because of the anchoring in the normative point, which enables to compare how things have turned out to be relative to how they were expected to be in the circumstances. In this way we are able to appreciate how much more the former exceeded, or conversely fell short of, the latter. Thus, the driving force in making a hyperbolic point is to shift the salience of the target property to make a more emphatic point, and in so doing express how one feels about the gap between how things are and how they were expected to be.

Having sketched the main features of hyperbole in pure uses, I now consider what happens when hyperbole mixes with other figures. I start with hyperbolic metaphor, and then turn to hyperbolic irony.

3 Hyperbolic metaphor

Hyperbole often co-occurs with metaphor. We often say of someone that she's a "saint", "angel", "star", "Maria Teresa"; that he's a "giant", "rocket", "dynamite", "towering figure", "devil", "genius", "Spartan", etc. Admittedly, these are worn-out metaphors. Nevertheless, they are indicative of the sense in which they count as hyperbolic. This is because the vehicle for the metaphor is also a vehicle for hyperbole in the sense that the property that it literally encodes is both a property that exploits a qualitative difference between the subject and how they are characterised, and a property that is quantifiable along a relevant scale. For example, saying of Mary

(8) She's such an angel. Always there for you; I can't imagine my life without her.

conveys that she's extremely kind and good, ready to help, perhaps more than anyone else, but she is not really as good as an angel. What happens here is that because the property of goodness associated with "angel" is very high on a scale of human kindness, then the metaphorical properties selected as what the speaker seeks to convey will be much more intense than what a counterpart literal expression of "*she's very kind*" would be able to express.

How does mixing metaphor and hyperbole work here? Which figure is input for the other? Do we first derive metaphorical properties, and then interpret them hyperbolically? Or do we first derive the hyperbole, and then use it as input to the metaphor?

Carston and Wearing don't address this question full on, though they make useful suggestions about the distinct mechanisms involved in understanding metaphor and hyperbole, respectively. Metaphor, they say, is about a *qualitative shift*, whereas hyperbole is about a *quantitative shift*. This results in different kinds of content which bear a different relation to the literal meaning of the word used as vehicle: "hyperbolic uses involve a shift of magnitude along a dimension which is intrinsic to the encoded meaning of the hyperbole vehicle, while metaphor involves a multi-dimensional qualitative shift away from the encoded meaning of the metaphor vehicle" (2015: 86). This means that different operations are applied to adjust the meaning of words along different dimensions: metaphor involves broadening the literal meaning of the vehicle in search of similarities between distinct conceptual domains; while hyperbole involves a weakening of the stated claim. For example, saying of Mary that *"she is a saint"*, they argue that "the property of being canonised is given up altogether at the same time that those literal saints who are known for their 'saintly' behaviour are excluded from the denotation on the figurative interpretation. And there's also something to the idea that these utterances have a hyperbolic quality, that in each case one has moved to a more extreme point on a *quantitative* scale (she may be virtuous but not to that extremely high degree)" (2015: 87).

What does this tell us about what goes on when metaphor and hyperbole mix? Carston and Wearing are non-specific about the order of interpretation and the kind of compound that arises. They do mention a difference in purpose: "metaphor is a bid to give precise expression to a thought or experience for which there is no literal linguistic encoding, while what is fundamental to hyperbole is the expression of an evaluation (positive or negative) of a state of affairs" (2015: 89). This suggests that we might expect hyperbole to be conditioned on metaphor, such that the hyperbolic evaluation concerns the metaphorical, and not the literal, content. This seems correct as far as it goes.[2] But this also suggests, if we take ironic metaphor as a paradigmatic compound, that hyperbole is the overarching figure subsuming metaphor in its scope. This doesn't seem right. Instead, I shall argue, what we get is metaphor tinged with hyperbolic effects, rather than a hyperbolic compound in the way ironic metaphor is. This is because there is no hyperbolic content feeding into a metaphorical interpretation, nor vice versa.

I shall start by noting that the relationship between metaphor and hyperbole is in practice much more intimate than Carston and Wearing take it to be. Going back to our example in (8) of Mary being an "angel", it is important to note that the utterance cannot but be interpreted metaphorically first. This is because there

---

[2] This bears on the logical order of interpretation.

is no sensible literal reading of the utterance such that hyperbole could operate first, by weakening the property that is literally associated with "angel". If anything, "angel" taken literally might invoke a scale of worthiness or importance of supernatural beings, ranking them along their powers to help, say, including elves, fairies, oracles, angels, culminating perhaps with God. Surely, trying to find a point on this scale that is lower than the point corresponding to "angel" would be putting the cart before the horses. Instead, it would be much more natural if hyperbole operates on the metaphorical features of "angel", so that metaphor and hyperbole work in tandem.

This provides us with a hypothesis about what the temporal order of interpretation might look like. The starting point, I assume, is for the hearer to grasp the speaker's metaphorical intent. This need not require working out the full-blown metaphorical content. The same holds for grasping the speaker's hyperbolic intent. In this way, the hearer can pull out interpretive characteristic resources of both metaphor and hyperbole until the computation of content is stabilised. One possibility is to work out the metaphorical interpretation under the guidance of a prospective hyperbolic interpretation. In other words, whatever metaphorical dimension and properties are chosen as relevant in context – say, in the case of "angel", goodness, kindness, helpfulness – these are the very properties which will further undergo a hyperbolic operation of downscaling in order to convey properties of human-like goodness, allowing faults and failings. Thus, an utterance of (8) conveys that Mary is a good-hearted person with a natural propensity to help others, but not at any time, and without fail.

In addition to making processing more efficient, this interleaved interpretation presents a further advantage of setting clear constraints on the metaphorical interpretation. Instead of undergoing an open-ended metaphorical search of similarities, as when metaphor is used for its own sake, we can expect that in hyperbolic metaphor the metaphorical search can be narrowed down to only those features which can be further weakened via a hyperbolic operation of scaling down the target property. Thus, metaphor and hyperbole undergo an interleaved processing.

Now, what kind of figure do we get out of this mix? Is hyperbolic metaphor anything like an ironic metaphor compound? I argue we should resist this temptation. In ironic metaphor like (1), the speaker is not committed to being metaphorical. Rather, she exploits the communicative power of metaphor to achieve ironic purposes. In contrast, in hyperbolic metaphor like (8), the speaker aims primarily to make a metaphoric point. The hyperbole is neither an overarching figure, in the way irony is in ironic metaphor, nor is it subsumed to the metaphorical content. Thus, there is no parallel structure to that of the compound that we find in ironic metaphor. Instead, the metaphor is conveyed as the primary figure, whereas the hyperbole serves to render the metaphorical effects even more colourful and forceful than they would have otherwise been. This suggests that hyperbole is more like an interpretive effect, modulating the metaphor with *hyperbolic tinges*, rather than as a full-blown hyperbolic content as when used for its own sake.

Having considered simple cases of hyperbolic metaphor, I argue that the analysis extends straightforwardly to more creative uses as below:

(9)   She's the Empire State Building.

(10) Writing a PhD thesis may sometimes be a painful marathon.

(11) After winning the English cup Manchester United fans reached the Everest of optimism for winning the European cup. (BBC-radio 4)

(12) Sara's bedroom is the size of Cornwall (Carston & Wearing 2015; from Wilson)

(13) Here I am, brain the size of a planet, and ask me to take you to the bridge. Call that job satisfaction, 'cause I don't. (Adam Douglas, *Hitchhikers' Guide to the Galaxy*)

What stands out in these examples is that the characteristic metaphorical effects are rendered more intense and colourful precisely by the choice of a vehicle that is also a vehicle for hyperbolic exaggeration. For example, what we exaggerate in (9) is the impressive stature of a woman; in (10) the sustained effort that writing a thesis requires; in (11) that Manchester United fans were extremely optimistic about winning the European cup; in (12) that Sara's living arrangements were very spacious and comfortable; and finally in (13) that Marvin is a highly intelligent robot.

These are colourful metaphors not only because of the multi-dimensionality of the vehicle used, but also precisely because these are vehicles that can invoke a surprising scale for measuring the target property. Thus, by choosing a metaphoric vehicle that is at one extreme end of the relevant scale, the speaker is able to convey more emphatic metaphorical effects than had she chosen a less evocative vehicle.

4 Hyperbolic irony

Irony and hyperbole function very differently in conversation. We use irony typically to criticise or complain about something or other which hasn't lived up to our expectations. We do so by pretending to do one thing in order to draw attention to something else we aim to complain about. It's dramatising something, in a ridiculing way, with a view to mocking, disparaging, expressing contempt, and thereby conveying some inverted content. Hyperbole, on the other hand, is typically used to draw attention to how much something has exceeded our expectations, whether they have been surpassed or thwarted. By presenting something as larger, or smaller, than expected, hoped or desired, we make the target property salient, thereby making a more emphatic point.

So, both hyperbole and irony are evaluative: they are both in the business of expressing how the speaker feels about how things turn out compared to how they were expected, hoped or desired. They differ however in their object of evaluation: hyperbole involves an evaluation of some state of affairs in the world, whereas irony involves evaluating someone's thoughts, hopes and expectations, with a view to ridiculing them. Now, if both hyperbole and irony are evaluative, which one is the driving figure when they mix together?

Let us consider some examples:

(14) *(after a boring movie)* I was on the edge of my seat. (Wilson 2017)

(15) *(about a dump of a house advertised as perfect for a romantic weekend)* This is absolutely the most amazing spot for a quiet weekend. That's all we dreamt about.

(16) *(to a lousy friend)* Wow, that was the most brilliant piece of advice I've ever had in my entire life. The best friend ever, that's what you are.

Clearly, these are intended ironically, but there is also an element of exaggeration. However, in contrast to cases of hyperbolic metaphor (see §3), where the vehicle for hyperbole is the same as the vehicle for metaphor, in (14)-(16) the vehicle for hyperbole need not be the same as the vehicle for irony. Hyperbole might be identified locally at the level of words and expressions which encode properties that can located on a relevant scale. Irony, in contrast, is not necessarily lodged in words, but it's a matter of contextual contrast between what the speaker presents herself to be saying and known/manifest facts about how the world really is.

That irony is global in this sense, whereas hyperbole is local, might suggest an order of interpretation where hyperbole is derived first, so that irony can build on it. This doesn't seem right, though. This is because if hyperbole were interpreted first, then the utterance would convey that a weaker description in fact holds. This weaker description, however, would provide less of an incentive to grasp the contrast between what the speaker says and how things are in reality, compared to what one would have expected, hoped or desired them to be. To see this, compare the non-hyperbolic utterance in (17) to the hyperbolic one in (18):

(17)   Sure, he's very clever.

(18)   He's a genius.

(18) is clearly stronger in effect than (17), but this would get lost if "genius" were taken to mean merely "very clever".

So, what's the role of hyperbole in the mix? Various people have noted that hyperbole works to facilitate the perception of irony (Kreuz and Roberts 1995). Wilson (2017) notes that hyperbole functions as a cue to the speaker's mocking, scornful, or contemptuous attitude. For example, in (14), the speaker exaggerates the extent of her excitement only to ridicule the expectation that the film would be exciting. Similarly, in (15), the speaker exaggerates the extent to which the chosen house might be thought to be an excellent spot for a romantic weekend, only to ridicule the expectation that it might be thought so.

What hyperbole does then is to exaggerate the claim literally expressed, making it less credible, so that it's unlikely to be taken at face value. By heightening its ridiculousness, it can thus function as a cue for the hearer to look for other interpretation than literal. This does not mean that the hearer has to infer the hyperbolic content by scaling down the literal claim to a weaker claim. If that were so, then the weaker claim would be a less suitable claim to be derided ironically. So, hyperbole is a cue rather than a full-blown content used as input for irony to build on.

Carston and Wearing make precisely this point when they say that the object of the ironical attitude is the proposition literally expressed:

> the thought that is metarepresented and dissociated from [...] is the literal proposition expressed rather than a representation containing an ad hoc concept recovered by pragmatic weakening of the encoded meaning [...] If it were first adjusted, then that clue to the intended ironic meaning would be lost and even if a dissociative attitude were recognised the proposition echoed would less obviously be a thought to be derided (2015: 88).

This is important because the ironic ridiculing attitude is expressed toward the literal claim, and not toward the claim resulting from a hyperbolic scaling down or scaling up. Indeed, as Carston and Wearing (2015: 84) note, when hyperbole is used ironically, it may be used to convey mockery toward the proposition literally expressed.

Imagine, for example, I utter (19) in response to you serving me a considerable portion of cake, after I've told you I'm on a slimming diet.

(19) This cake is tiny.

Clearly, it's not the case that the cake is small; after all it's a normal size portion. It's just bigger than I wanted. So, if there is a sense in which I'm exaggerating, it's not exaggerating how small it is, but rather how big it is. Thus, I'm not only hyperbolic, but also ironic because I say something I don't mean. What I mean instead is that you gave me a bigger piece of cake than I expected, thereby drawing attention to how much this fell short of my expectations.

Carston and Wearing are careful to note that if such cases are used to express any ridiculing or mockery, that is due to irony, and not to hyperbole. This is evidence for them that hyperbole is not in the business of expressing a characteristic tone of voice, like irony does. On the other hand, it has been suggested by Kreuz and Roberts (1995) that the ironic tone of voice may be confounded with the presence of hyperbole, contending that it may be the case that "the ironic tone of voice is nothing more than the use of exaggeration". I don't have the space to delve into this issue here, but clearly there are multiple uses of irony in the absence of hyperbolic exaggeration.[3] Notwithstanding, Kreuz and Roberts are right in pointing out that hyperbole has significant effects on the perception of irony, making it more manifest in some cases that the speaker has ironic intent. Carston and Wearing also note that "the excessiveness of the metarepresented propositional content plays a very helpful role in cueing the dissociative attitude of the speaker" (2015: 88).

So, if the attitude expressed in hyperbolic irony is the characteristic ironic mockery, what does hyperbole add to the mix? Here I want to draw attention to an interesting effect that arises out of mixing irony and hyperbole, which hasn't received much attention. This concerns the idea of *attitude transfer* from the perspective that the speaker pretends to be putting forward (call it *F*) towards the perspective which she presents as object of ridicule (call it *G*).[4] The suggestion is that by giving due weight to the role of pretence in understanding irony, we can see what role hyperbole plays in the mixing. Essentially, the hyperbole helps

---

3 In obviously ironic utterances – where the utterance clearly sits in contrast to the known facts – there is less need for such cues (such as sarcastic intonation), and skilled users of irony may minimise these extra linguistic cues in order to slow the listener's inference of the ironic implicature. This is a common strategy among British speakers who relish appearing sincere to a naive audience, relying on the hearer's perception of a clash with known facts. This is culturally regarded there as being funnier.

4 Thanks to John Barnden for encouraging me to explore this point.

boosting the pretence by making the pretend thought/perspective F that is put forward even more ridiculous than it would have otherwise been, had the speaker used a non-hyperbolic vehicle.

For example, imagine we've completed a long, arduous trail, climbing various hills through undergrowth. At the end you are totally distressed showing me all the nasty scratches you've got along the way. In response I say:

(20) My darling, soon you'll need a blood transfusion.

Here the target of ironic ridicule is the fact that the addressee's complaints could be found a justifiable source of lamentation. Thus, by way of exaggerating the pretence the speaker has more free room of manoeuvre to put the hearer in the mind of a related thought/perspective G, as long as the pretence can be taken to allude to or echo specific expectations related to the situation at hand.[5]

There is a further implication of exploiting hyperbole for ironic purposes. The mockery or ridiculing attitude one would have toward the kind of pretend thought/perspective (F) can be transferred towards the targeted thought/perspective (G), though it will be a less strong attitude toward G than toward F. Nevertheless, there is a correlation in the strength of the evaluation from F to G: the more ridiculous the pretence associated with the literal claim, the more heightened the ironic attitude expressed. Thus, for example in (19), were I to describe the cake as "minuscule", "microscopic", instead of "tiny" or "small", we might expect that I was able to express a greater sense of frustration or dissatisfaction with the waiter who ignored my request. In short, there is a certain correlation between the degree of ridiculousness of the claim put forward, and the intensity of the mocking attitude towards anyone who would entertain such a claim.

Wrapping up, we might ask the same question that we asked about hyperbolic metaphor. Here, it would be: what kind of compound, if any, do we have from mixing hyperbole and irony? The answer is that the mixing, again, doesn't yield a compound with a structure similar to that of ironic metaphor where metaphor and irony condition and constrain one another. Instead, the speaker is making primarily an ironic point, if only a bit more colourful and forceful due to hyperbolic tinges. The overall effect of using hyperbole is not to convey a weaker claim than literally stated, but to exploit the exaggeration for ironic purposes. This thus makes the ironic point more emphatic, and thereby eliciting a more heightened attitude or affect.

---

[5] See Currie (2006), Wilson (2006), Clark, H. H. and R. J. Gerrig. (1984), Kumon-Nakamura et al. (1995), Walton (1990, 2017), Popa-Wyatt (2014).

5 Conclusion

In this paper I looked at cases of hyperbole mixing with metaphor and irony, respectively. The starting point was whether we can think of such mixtures as a figurative compound along the lines familiar from ironic metaphor compounds. I've argued this a temptation we should resist. This is because when hyperbole mixes with either metaphor, or irony, the result is not a new encompassing compound where one figure builds on another. Instead, the figure that is primarily communicated is coloured with hyperbolic tinges. Hyperbolic metaphor is nothing more than a metaphor with a more emphatic point. Hyperbolic irony is nothing more than irony with a more emphatic point. So, what else does hyperbole bring to the mixing pot? I suggested we should think of hyperbole in hyperbolic figures as being an interpretive effect, modulating the characteristic effects of the figure it mixes with. This is why hyperbole is so versatile in mixing with all sorts of figures of speech.

References

Athanasiadou, Angeliki. 2017. Irony has a metonymic basis. In Angeliki Athanasiadou & Herbert L. Colston (eds.), *Irony in Language Use and Communication*, 201–215. Amsterdam & Philadelphia: John Benjamins.

Barker, J. Stephen. 2017. Figurative speech: pointing a poisoned arrow at the heart of semantics. *Philosophical Studies* 174 (1). 123–140.

Barker, J. Stephen & Mihaela Popa-Wyatt. 2015. Irony and the dogma of sense and force. *Analysis* 75. 9–16.

Barnden, John. (this volume). Uniting irony, hyperbole and metaphor in an affect-centred, pretence-based framework.

Bezuidenhout, Anne. 2001. Metaphor and What is Said: A Defense of a Direct Expression View of Metaphor, Midwest Studies in Philosophy 25. 156–186.

Bezuidenhout, Anne. 2015. The Implicit Dimension of Meaning: Ways of "Filling In" and "Filling Out" Content. *Erkenntnis* 80. 89–109.

Burgers, Christian, Elly. A. Konijn & Gerard. J. Steen. 2016. Figurative Framing: Shaping Public Discourse Through Metaphor, Hyperbole, and Irony. *Communication Theory* 26. 410–430.

Camp, Elisabeth. 2006. Contextualism, Metaphor, and What is Said. *Mind & Language* 21 (3). 280–309.

Camp, Elisabeth. 2012. Sarcasm, pretence, and the semantics-pragmatics distinction. *Noûs* 46. 587–634.

Carston, Robyn & Catherine Wearing. 2011. Metaphor, hyperbole and simile: A pragmatic approach. *Language and Cognition* 3 (2). 283–312.

Carston, Robyn & Catherine Wearing. 2015. Hyperbolic language and its relation to metaphor and irony. *Journal of Pragmatics* 79. 79–92.

Clark, H. Herbert & Richard J. Gerrig. 1984. On the pretense theory of irony. *Journal of Experimental Psychology: General* 113. 121–6.

Colston L. Herbert. 1997. I've Never Seen Anything Like It: Overstatement, Understatement, and Irony. *Metaphor and Symbol* 12. 43–58.

Colston, L. Herbert & Raymond W. Gibbs. 2002. Are irony and metaphor understood differently? *Metaphor and Symbol* 17. 57–80.

Colston, L. Herbert & Jennifer O'Brien. 2000. Contrast of kind versus contrast of magnitude: the pragmatic accomplishment of irony and hyperbole. *Discourse Processes* 30 (2). 179–199.

Colston, L. Herbert & Shauna B. Keller. 1998. You'll never believe this: irony and hyperbole in expressing surprise. *J Psycholinguistic Research* 27 (4). 499–513.

Currie, Gregory. 2006. Why irony is pretence. In S. Nichols (eds.) *The Architecture of the Imagination*, 111–133. Oxford University Press, Oxford.

Fogelin, J. Robert. 1988. *Figuratively Speaking*. New Haven and London: Yale University Press.

Gibbs, W. Raymond. 2000. Irony in Talk among Friends. *Metaphor and Symbol* 15 (1/2). 5–27.

Gibbs, W. Raymond & Herbert L. Colston. 2007. *Irony in Language and Thought*. Hillsdale NJ: Lawrence Erlbaum.

Grice, H. Paul. 1989. *Studies in the Way of Words*. Cambridge, Mass.: Harvard University Press.

Kreuz, J. Roger & Richard M. Roberts. 1995. Two cues for verbal irony: Hyperbole and the ironic tone of voice. *Metaphor and Symbolic Activity* 10. 21–31.

Kreuz, J. Roger, M A. Kassler & L Coppenrath. 1998. The use of exaggeration in discourse: Cognitive and social facets. In S. R. Fussell & R. J. Kreuz (eds.), *Social and Cognitive Approaches to Interpersonal Communication*, 91–111. Mahwah, NJ: Lawrence Erlbaum Associates.

Kumon-Nakamura, Saki, Glucksberg, Samuel. & Brown, Mary. 1995. How about another piece of pie? The Allusional Pretense Theory of Discourse Irony. *Journal of Experimental Psychology: General* 124 (1). 3–21.

McCarthy, Michael & Ronald Carter. 2004. There's millions of them: hyperbole in everyday conversation. *Journal of Pragmatics* 36. 149–184.

Norrick, Neil. R. 2004. Hyperbole, extreme case formulation. *Journal of Pragmatics*, 36 (9). 1727–1739.

Popa, Mihaela. 2009. Figuring the Code: Pragmatic Routes to Non-literal. University of Geneva.

Popa, M Mihaela. 2010a. Ironic metaphor interpretation. *Toronto Working Papers in Linguistics* 33. 1–17.

Popa, Mihaela. 2010b. Ironic metaphor: a case for Metaphor's Contribution to Truth-conditions. In E. Walaszewska, M Kisielewska-Krysiuk & A. Piskorska (eds.), *In the Mind and Across Minds: A Relevance-theoretic Perspective on Communication and Translation*, 224–245. Cambridge Scholars Publishing.

Popa-Wyatt, Mihaela. 2014. Pretence and echo: towards an integrated account of verbal irony. *International Review of Pragmatics* 6. 127–68.

Popa-Wyatt, Mihaela. 2017. Compound figures: priority and speech-act structure. *Philosophical Studies* 174 (1). 141–161.

Popa-Wyatt, Mihaela. (ms.) Compound Figures, Communicative Intentions and Communicative Channels.

Popa-Wyatt, Mihaela. (forth.) Mind the Gap: Expressing affect with hyperbole and hyperbolic figures. In Gargett A. & J Barnden (eds.), *Figurative Thought and Language*. Amsterdam & Philadelphia: John Benjamins.

Recanati, Francois. 2004. *Literal Meaning*. Cambridge, Cambridge University Press.

Rubio-Fernández, Paula, Catherine Wearing & Robyn Carston. 2015. Metaphor and Hyperbole: Testing the Continuity Hypothesis. *Metaphor and Symbol* 30 (1). 24–40.

Stern, Josef. 2000. *Metaphor in Context*. Cambridge, MA: MIT Press.

Walton, Kendall. 1990. *Mimesis as Make-Believe: on the Foundations of the Representational Arts*. Harvard University Press, Cambridge, MA.

Walton, Kendall. 2017. Meiosis, hyperbole, irony. *Philosophical Studies* 174 (1): 105–120.

Wilson, Deirdre. 2006. The pragmatics of verbal irony: echo or pretence? *Lingua* 116. 1722–1743.

Wilson, Deirdre. 2017. Irony, Hyperbole, Jokes and Banter. In: Blochowiak J., Grisot C., Durrleman S., Laenzlinger C. (eds) *Formal Models in the Study of Language*. Springer, Cham, 201–219.

Wilson, Deirdre & Dan Sperber. 1992. On Verbal Irony. *Lingua* 87. 53–76.

Wilson, Deirdre & Dan Sperber. 2002. Truthfulness and relevance. *Mind* 11 (443). 583–682.

Wilson, Deirdre & Dan Sperber. 2012. *Meaning and Relevance*. Cambridge University Press.

Graham Watling
Denying the salient contrast
Speaker's attitude in hyperbole

Abstract: This chapter highlights "that which a speaker is particularly concerned to deny" (as well as its denial) as preeminent in hyperbole. Often this denial is a forceful portrayal of a speaker's attitude toward what is being denied, resulting in a gap between what is said and what is meant. In examples involving *you always* and *you never*, speakers put their attitude on display by the rhetorical strategy they employ, and particularly by their choice of what they choose to deny and contrast. This offers a window on one way that exaggeration is employed in hyperbole, through what speakers choose to deny, and the attitude which informs that decision. Additional examples are looked at, with a focus on the strategies employed in production and comprehension in denying some salient feature of the conversational context. Emphasis is given to speaker's attitude in producing hyperbole.

Keywords: hyperbole, affect expression, attitude, conventionalized expressions, implicature, discourse, context, irony

1 The salient contrast

Hyperbole is a speaker's overstatement of the magnitude of something – a quality, quantity, or frequency. In (1) we see an example of the characteristic discrepancy between what the speaker has said and what is meant (example is borrowed from Carston and Wearing 2015).

(1) This piece of cake is *tiny*
    (uttered at the moment that a child realizes that his sister has been served a piece of cake which is bigger than his own)

Following Walton (2017),[1] we can characterize that which is said (its literal meaning) as the *explicit content* (or EC) of the utterance, distinguishable from its *assertive content*

---

[1] See Popa-Wyatt (forthcoming) for an alternative development of Walton's account.

Acknowledgements: Thanks to Mihaela Popa, John Barnden, Shir Givoni, and one anonymous referee.

(AC), or what the speaker "means to get across" (Walton). The assertive content is what is potentially understood by the hearer of a hyperbolic utterance – that is, the intended message of the speaker. A third component is necessitated, which helps to derive the assertive content – the SC, or *salient contrast*[2] (Walton). The SC is what the speaker "especially means to deny" (113). Through knowing what the speaker especially means to deny,[3] the assertive content (AC) of the utterance is arrived at. For the sake of clarifying things, we can spell out exactly what the speaker means to deny here – that the piece of cake is normal or adequate in size and, by extension, that the speaker is satisfied with it. That the cake might be adequately small is something that is not applicable, or simply not of interest, in the discourse context at hand in (1). It is non-salient (a non-salient contrast). Figure 1 lays all of this out.

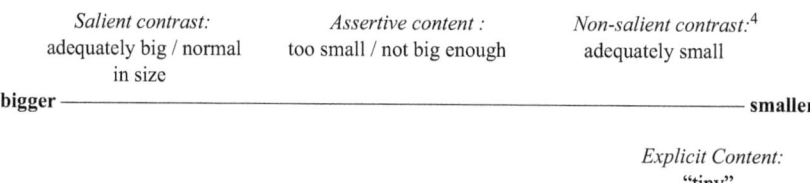

Figure 1: This piece of cake is tiny.

The speaker expresses an extreme position on this size scale (overstates how small the piece of cake is), and the hearer quickly takes an extra step to get to the message, moving down the scale to arrive at a modified point, what is most salient in the message (*not* SC), resulting in an understanding that the piece of cake is smaller than the speaker expected or wanted – i.e., "not big enough."[5]

---

2 Salient contrast (SC) should be understood as the thing being contrasted *against*. To place the SC as one point on a scale (as in the Walton model) defies the definition of contrast (between two things). A contrast occurs between two things. Walton's term will be stuck to for economy. It can be thought of as the salient contrast (to the explicit content), what the explicit content is contrasting *against*.
3 or *reject*. Both verbs are used interchangeably in this chapter – deny or reject the salient contrast.
4 A non-salient contrast is denoted in the analysis, following Walton. Indeed, this example could be re-examined and a discourse context could be imagined where the non-salient contrast (adequately small) could be contrasted against as the salient contrast, and made less exaggerative, somewhere to the right of "adequately small" on the scale. To paraphrase: "This cake is more than *adequately* small. It is downright tiny!"
5 Hyperbolic figures can portray a discrepancy between expectations or desires and reality (Carston & Wearing, 2015; Colston, 2015; Colston & Keller, 1998). In these cases, the expectations of the speaker are what is being contrasted against (the SC). However, it is not always the case that the SC is what is expected by the speaker. The EC of example (4) in this chapter, for instance, does not contrast with any expectations of the speaker.

This denial of the SC is the pivoting point upon which the core message of hyperbole is transmitted. How to deny the SC forcefully? By pushing to the contrary against it, by exaggerating. If the assertive content were to be stated literally, it could invite skepticism. "This cake is too small". By what objective standards? Who decided them? The term "too small" summons a certain set of criteria by which something can be measured objectively – simply, criteria as stipulated by the speaker or some other source, which will either obtain or not obtain. A hearer might doubt those criteria, but not the term itself.

On the other hand, the assessment of the piece of cake as tiny is an invitation to step into the shoes of the speaker as a subject, to see things as colored by the speaker's perspective. It is a more extreme assessment, and it is meant as an exaggeration (in the above example).[6] Exaggeration is a step into falsehood, into the imagined, into the mind of the speaker, into the imagination of making something what it is not. It is the strategy, the choice to use hyperbole, which portrays an attitude of the speaker, a choice to go further, a choice to see the piece of cake as something else. "Too small?" and then, going further, "Why, it's tiny!"[7]

2 Importance of the salient contrast in hyperbole

The denial of the SC is primary, but the way to deny and contrast it is through exaggeration. Exaggerations of quantity are sufficient at any obvious inflation of amount. Examples (2) and (3) are hyperboles that exaggerate quantities.

(2) I have told you a thousand times that . . . (Brdar-Szabó & Brdar 2010: 391)

(3) He missed the goal by at least 30 meters (Brdar-Szabó & Brdar 2010: 392)

The sort of quick and rough imprecision and approximation in number hyperboles is often present in hyperbolic formulations across the board. Such imprecision achieves a conservation of expenditure in production, and can result in greater communicative efficiency in comprehension, adequately exaggerating with some largely inflated number, enough to contrast against a more "normal" quantity in a clear and certain way, enough that the hearer looks to infer the salient contrast and, thereby, the assertive content.

---

6 *Tiny*, while exaggerative in the example, is not necessarily exaggerative.
7 If the speaker had said "positively miniscule" instead of tiny, the content of the AC would be similar. Both "tiny" and "positively miniscule" reject the same salient contrast, making for a similar and inexact AC. This will be returned to.

Once the salient contrast is rejected (through use of hyperbolic statement), it is up to the hearer to decide if an exaggeration of 100 meters rather than 30 meters is adding anything to the affective component. Similarly, in example (1) (the cake example), once the SC is forcefully denied in the hyperbolic expression, the hearer "gets the point". Would it enhance any affective component to say miniscule or microscopic? It is up for the hearer to decide. What is important, however, is that the SC is equally rejected whether the statement is tiny, microscopic, or miniscule.[8] Denial of the SC is one aspect of the hyperbolic expression, while the form of the expression itself is a separate factor. In an example such as (1), if the SC is already to include satisfaction (with cake size), the denial of that SC is dissatisfaction. Potential SC's in (3) are either "a normal amount to miss the goal by" or, in keeping with expectations and desires, perhaps the SC is "ball goes in the goal". Thereby, any distance that the goal is missed by is unsatisfactory. How "badly" somebody missed just adds to our dissatisfaction, and *how* badly is portrayed with distance from the goal in meters in some excessive (however, imprecise) amount.

For the purpose of this chapter, the idea of a salient contrast is useful in clarifying the nature of hyperbolic utterances and in analyzing them. While any assertion can be thought of as making a salient contrast[9] (also pointed out in Walton 2017), it is particularly useful in analyzing hyperbole. The analysis is made in two stages. First, the speaker chooses a salient contrast, what can be thought of as an input in the scalar models throughout this chapter. Second, the speaker pushes against it, exaggerating in the opposite direction.

3 Choosing a point on the scale to contrast against

Examples (1)–(3) deal with quantities on a scale. The salient contrast in (1)–(3) could be considered as some "normal" or expected amount from the point of view of the speaker – i.e., a normal or acceptable amount to miss the goal by (in [3]), or a normal or acceptable amount of times to tell somebody something (in [2]).

While Walton's (2017) salient contrast model deals strictly with examples of quantities being overstated, I will look additionally at examples of quality (and frequency). It does not make any significant change in the scalar model itself. As

---

8 This runs counter to the Correlation Principle as put forth by Peña and Ruiz de Mendoza (2017), and reflected in Popa-Wyatt (forthcoming), which suggests that greater intensification in a hyperbolic utterance corresponds with an intensification of the speaker's emotion.
9 Example: the salient contrast of "There was an earthquake in Los Angeles yesterday" is "There was not an earthquake in Los Angeles yesterday."

quantities can be assessed on a scale, so can qualities and frequencies.[10] The following example[11] is uttered by someone who is exaggerating a state (or quality) of feeling overwhelmed.

(4) I died. Right there. For real.
(referring to meeting someone greatly admired)

While size and quantity are clearly explicit in the explicit content of examples (1)–(3), the explicit content here only indirectly touches on overwhelmedness, stating the effect of being overwhelmed, with perhaps a twinge of metaphor. One logical consequence of someone or something (say, a machine) being overwhelmed is that it shuts down completely. Certainly, we cannot say for sure the extent to which this figure makes reference to something other than human. Maybe that is part of the usefulness of hyperbole in cases such as this – the open interpretation into its meaning or the salient contrast that is being denied, or that there could even be multiple possible salient contrasts, making for multiple possible ACs, all depending on exactly what is being measured on the scale.

An analysis of (4) provides one reason why hyperbole is necessary in our linguistic repertoire. The salient contrast in this particular example is what can be considered for the purpose of analysis the maximum possible literal expression of a quality (overwhelmedness). This is an SC that has nothing to do with a consideration by the speaker of what is normal, reasonable, expected, or acceptable. There is rather a will and a requirement by the speaker to go beyond literal norms in language, to deny any literal expression whatsoever of the sentiment of being overwhelmed. The representation of the AC in Figure 2 reflects this.

SC:	AC:	EC:
the maximum that can be conveyed literally—i.e., extremely overwhelmed	more than extremely overwhelmed*	"I died. Right there. For real."

less ———————————————————————————— more

Figure 2: I died right there for real.

The hyperbolic statement far exceeds any literally conveyable state of being extremely excited, overwhelmed, or just plain shocked. It highlights the quality

---
10 Frequencies can be considered to be quantities as well.
11 Example (4) was inspired by a series of similar examples in Popa-Wyatt.

by stretching it past the bounds of reason. While dying may have somewhat conventionalized associations (it scares me to death, for example), the speaker underlines that they actually died (for real) to pull it more to the extreme end of the scale, to deny the SC as forcefully as possible, seeming to say, whatever this SC is, any maximum reality-based amount of being overwhelmed, this (what the speaker means to convey) was more than that. It could similarly be imagined that a speaker could utter "I literally died," lest the reference to death be taken figuratively by the hearer, weakening the SC, thereby placing it somewhere more to the left on the scale, putting it into doubt.

In the forceful denial of the SC, what is left over is the AC, arrived at indirectly, more effectively than saying "not SC" in literal terms. The resulting AC here comes with a caveat: it should not be understood as an even stronger literal expression of what is communicated by the speaker. In the above figure, it is simply for the purpose of depicting a point on our scale, and it is useful in our analysis. What is the takeaway for the speaker? It is something other than that, much more than a paraphrase. It is what is left over in an unreal portrayal of a situation – something more abstract and subjective than the AC of "more than extremely overwhelmed". To revisit "too small" as an example, it could be said that there are some criteria (whatever they are) which could cause that distinction of smallness to obtain. In (4), there is not even a conjecturable set of criteria for overwhelmed that could be considered to be what the speaker means. To paraphrase the speaker, "I was so overwhelmed that I died." Death moves an extra step past overwhelmed, and this can be understood through a default interpretation of what overwhelmed means for humans in the aforementioned context.

The speaker pushes forcefully in the opposite direction on the scale, away from the salient contrast, as extremely as possible. What informs this decision is the attitude of the speaker toward the salient contrast – i.e., what the speaker seeks to deny. Was the speaker overwhelmed in example (4)? Well, no. The speaker was something more* than overwhelmed. The speaker's attitude also informs the creation and make-up of *what is contrasted against* (the SC). This will be addressed further in the following section.

4 What is contrasted against. The case of always and never

The preceding examples portray a gap firstly in the push of the explicit content away from the SC, resulting in an assertive content which is somewhere between the two. Saying (in the explicit content) more than what one means (the assertive content) is often taken to be a starting point in discussion of hyperbole. In the following analysis of examples (5) and (6), a short circuiting of this equation occurs. Or, rather, denying what is chosen as a salient contrast (*once*) necesitates a denial of *never* in the explicit content and, potentially, in the assertive content. That is to say, the exaggeration happens at the stage of choosing a salient contrast, in which that point on the scale (SC) reflects a state of affairs which has been made exaggerated by the speaker. Consider a couple discussing how they feel about different goings-on in the house.

(5) You *never* put the dishes away.

(6) You *always* leave the faucet on.

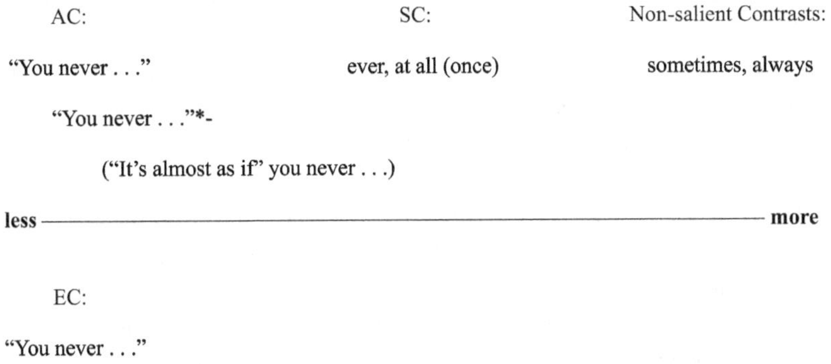

AC:	SC:	Non-salient Contrasts:
"You never . . ."	ever, at all (once)	sometimes, always
"You never . . ."*-		
("It's almost as if" you never . . .)		

less ———————————————————————————————— more

EC:

"You never . . ."

Figure 3: You never put the dishes away.

It is the attitude of the speaker which informs a rhetorical strategy in choosing the SC in the first place. One can imagine the speaker uttering (5) at the moment the dishes are found to not be put away. The attitude portrayed by the speaker is "If I can't count on you to do this just this once (even *once*), can I *ever* count on you?" The EC is the only available option in denying the SC. If one is rejecting "once" or "ever," the only utterance at one's disposal is "never".

A quick aside is warranted. In the following paragraphs, a potential AC of "never" (equal to the EC) is examined, but an allowance is made for a possible lesser, non-literal AC. An intended (or, by hearer's standards, potentially understood) *never**- with a subtraction sign – a lessened, or weakened, non-literal understanding of never – is included in Figure 3 for consideration as a possibility for the AC of the utterance.

According to Walton (2017: 115), "The contradictory of what is asserted often counts as the salient contrast". The assertion "you never put the dishes away" contradicts that the person being accused has "ever" or "even once" put the dishes away. Another way to showcase the attitude that brings the speaker to make this utterance is to paraphrase their hyperbole, following wording used by Walton (2017: 110).

(7) It is as though, almost as if, you never put the dishes away. You might as well never put the dishes away.

"You *might as well* (as far as I'm concerned) never ..." is similar to the "I can't count on you" attitude mentioned above, the attitude put forth by the speaker. In this example, it is not an easy path to know where the speaker stands and whether the speaker means what she says, while in example (4), it can be known, for example, that the speaker is not dead, precluding the possibility of taking the speaker at her word ("I died"). In example (5), it is harder to get a window on the speaker's beliefs.

There are two main points to be made here. A certain attitude of "You might as well never" or "Can I ever count on you?" 1.) is used in choosing the SC of "ever, at all (once)" as input of what is being denied (i.e, in intending to use hyperbole, a speaker, by design, chooses what is being contrasted against). Secondly, the explicit content "never" is the only way to deny this particular SC – to contradict *once* is to say "never," and one can go no further – there is nothing less frequent than *never*.

The hearer is free to understand what the speaker means to be something lesser than *you never* in its strictest sense. Its use is perhaps, even, somewhat conventionalized. This will be returned to in the next section. In spite of any of this, this figure itself, what it measures, is a frequency. Part of the work here, then, in arguing for an SC of "once, ever" should be to discount other greater frequencies on the scale as possible salient contrasts.

"Sometimes, always" is included as a non-salient contrast on the scale for our consideration. "Sometimes" as an SC could suit the utterance, if the speaker were choosing to acknowledge that as a possibility, or she knows that the hearer does put the dishes away sometimes but wishes to wrest that distinction away. Also, this suits our intuitions as a possibility. If someone tells us "you never do," we are likely to respond in a general way with "yes I do" (sometimes). Perhaps we even want to additionally argue that we always do, but that doesn't seem to be what our accuser had in mind when making the utterance. It suits our intuition that the hearer is working against what was *said* by the speaker (never), to try and re-frame things. The opposite of never is *once*, but the hearer wants to newly assert *sometimes*.

"Always" seems counterintuitive in any context as a consideration for this utterance's salient contrast, as this could imply those exceptions to the rule which would include "almost always" and "most of the time". If "always" were the salient contrast at hand to be considered, it would seem more intuitive that it would be chipped away at its edges by the speaker rather than reduced to an all-or-nothing "never".

Again, we have some indication that the utterance of (5) does occur in the context of the SC in Figure 3 simply by how the utterance is (often) understood. "Never" can be understood by the hearer in the strictest sense, to mean *not even once*, and the hearer would feel perfectly entitled to respond, "but you don't notice the instances where I *do* put the dishes away," to strike at the heart of the SC that the speaker is putting forth, to re-assert instanc*es*, plural, in an attempt to re-frame things away from *once*.

Is *never*, in its strictest sense, the intended message of the speaker? Is it the assertive content? To help answer this question, there is no middle ground betweeen zero and one. If the dishes are not put away once even, this necessitates its denial with never, and it just so happens that a middle ground (between once and never) cannot exist, making, at least, no possible number between zero and one available as the assertive content.[12] Does this indicate that the speaker means what she says? No. The salient contrast portrays a state of affairs that cannot possibly be meant because the speaker knows it is not true that the hearer has never put the dishes away. The speaker means what she says in the sense that the AC is the same as the EC,[13] but it is based on circumstances that the speaker knows are falsely portrayed, and it just turns out that the hardest way to push against this SC is the only way to push against it. The SC is once (1) and the EC moves as forcefully as possible away from it as it can with never (0). As it was the choice of SC to begin with that was disingenuous, it is an incidental downstream effect that the speaker does not mean what she says. This can also be instructive as to why, in expressions like these, never is often taken quite literally. Let us just assume for a moment that the hearer knows that the speaker is aware that it's a false portrayal. The hearer must look deeper to the speaker's intentions and their shared experience, and to the salient contrast being made to know that something doesn't add up. Then the hearer can decide whether the speaker means what she says.

Example (6) (depicted in Figure 4) goes in the other direction. "Could you ever turn of the faucet, just *once?* No, you always leave it on."

---

[12] Through what we have seen in past examples, however, we know that what is being talked about is not necessarily the only thing that is being communicated. Example (1) mentions cake size, but satisfaction with cake size is what is also communicated.
[13] If EC = AC, then the figure could be considered a literal statement, just one that is unrealistically strong. This will be returned to.

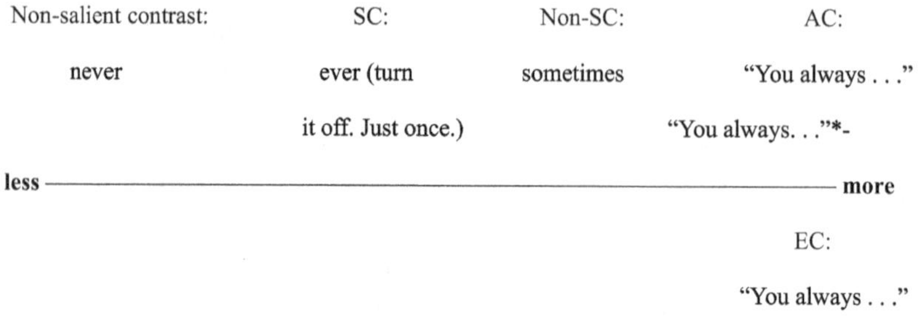

Non-salient contrast:	SC:	Non-SC:	AC:
never	ever (turn it off. Just once.)	sometimes	"You always . . ." "You always. . ."*-

less ── more

EC:

"You always . . ."

Figure 4: You always leave the faucet on.

Perhaps it is more natural to think of the speaker as asserting this for rhetorical purposes (while not actually believing that the accusee actually never turns off the faucet). This frames the situation under certain exaggerated premises, to portray an attitude of "I can't count on you," to portray the disappointment of the speaker.

Another way to look at this is that the speaker is invoking an imaginary scenario, providing a subjective perspective (perhaps a perspective where only the times that the faucet wasn't turned off are considered) and an invitation to step into her shoes. The exaggeration is in the perspective, leading to the choice of an exaggerated SC, and not in the explicit content. Hearers can choose to look past the imagined scenario to arrive at an AC of *sometimes*, or a looser use of *never*, but they certainly could not be faulted for taking the speaker at her word. "Never" is an attempt at amplifying the salience of the non-instances of dishes being put away while "always" attempts to amplify the salience of the positive occurrences of the faucet being left on.[14]

Peña and Ruiz de Mendoza (2017) apply a model for the construal and construction of hyperbole which is similar to past proposed models for metaphor in that it makes use of target and source domains. It can be instructive to think that this exact imagined scenario where the faucet actually is never turned off (source) is applied to a target (the situation that our interlocutors find themselves in at the time of the utterance). The imagined scenario, as well as the concomitant feelings of letdown on the part of the speaker and the portrayal of complete negligence on the part of the hearer, are conjured in the minds of the interlocutors and applied to the current situation.

---

14 (5) and (6) seem to take the attitude "as with this time, then with all times". It is the generalization of a binary distinction – the dishes are either put away or they are not, just as the faucet is off or on. Once is never when extrapolated and generalized. Example (6) employs a similar attitude of "as with this time, then with all times".

Like examples (1)–(4), the speaker is increasing a quantity along a scale, amplifying it, maximizing and exaggerating it to one extreme or another, but this time with an eye on a salient contrast that is imagined, to make a point, to portray an emotion, and to convey a feeling of disappointment. With example (1), the hearer knows that "tiny" is not really what the message is about, but rather the speaker's disappointment. In example (4), it is self- evident that the speaker didn't die. The hearer knows to make an adjustment based on what the explicit content is and that it should be discounted. In (5) and (6), the explicit content is not necessarily discountable. This leaves a door open to the speaker being taken at her word – it is pragmatically feasible that somebody never, ever puts the dishes away and, additionally, the content of what is said is bolstered by the contrast with *once*.

Hyperbole is commonly thought of as an exaggeration between what is said and what is meant. By that standard, if we propose the AC to be the same as the EC (never, always) in the preceding examples, they cease to be hyperbolic figures but, rather, unrealistically strong literal statements based on an exaggerated state of affairs. It is more useful, though, to expand our idea of what hyperbole is, to include the exaggeration that goes into constructing a statement and choosing a salient contrast, with a greater importance assigned to speaker attitude and perspective, as well as the speaker's intention to convey that attitude indirectly.

For the sake of argument, however, an alternative salient contrast that is similar to the one proposed for the cake example can be offered for (5) (and, as well, something similar for [6]) without greatly altering the attitude being conveyed. In the cake example it was a salient contrast that concerned the adequacy of the size of the cake. Here, we can also conjur the SC to be the speaker's judgement of adequate frequency for putting the dishes away – simply, often *enough*.[15] Figure 5 offers an alternative analysis of example (5).

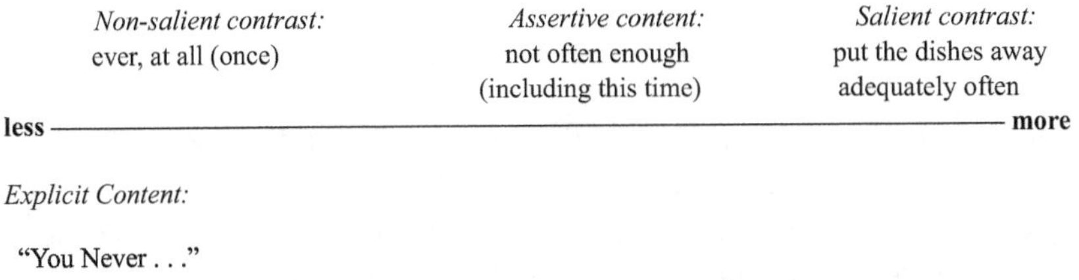

Non-salient contrast:	*Assertive content:*	*Salient contrast:*
ever, at all (once)	not often enough (including this time)	put the dishes away adequately often

less ——————————————————————————— **more**

Explicit Content:

"You Never . . ."

Figure 5: Alternative for you never put the dishes away.

---

15 A similar figure could be applied to the faucet example, with the salient contrast being turning off the faucet with adequate frequency.

Either this or the prior analysis/figure 3 for the same statement make for a similar attitude being portrayed.[16] What is intended (or understood) to be the attitude of the speaker might range from dissatisfaction, to disapproval, to disappointment. Whatever it is, it's not good, and it's not good enough. Attitudes themselves are completely scalar in either direction and somewhat vague – from very good (positive) to very bad (negative).

That is to speak of the attitude portrayed, or expressed. The content and what it implies differs, however, between the the two analyses/figures, with the SC of the former putting the hearer at a disadvantage because he or she can only strike at the validity of that particular SC – "ever, at all (once)". For the hearer to deny the statement would mean having done something only once, but the hearer knows that he has put the dishes away *more* than once. To protest is really only to say once instead of never, boxing the hearer in in their denial of the assertion. This is a very savvy strategy by the speaker to frame things this way. It is also an effective tool at the speaker's disposal to show how she feels. She wants for the hearer to take her seriously, for the hearer to understand her imagined situation, and also how disappointed she feels.

5 Conventionalized hyperbolic expression and speaker's attitude

While *never* and *always* are actual possibilities, the following examples express impossibilities in their explicit content, just as example (4) (*died*) does. The explicit content of (8) and (9) is readily discountable by a hearer due to its impossibility, necessitating an AC which is lesser because the EC is unattainable, or not pragmatically feasible.

(8) You're taking *forever* to finish this paper.

Certain hyperboles have implicatures that are iron-clad to their EC's. That is to say, *taking forever* is, in effect, just another way of saying "taking too long" across many contexts.[17] Less work is required by the hearer and, equally, less context sensitivity and less contextual clues go into their interpretation.

What can be said, however, is that they can work the same way as other hyperboles, contrasting quantity and frequency on a scale. It is more the case

---

[16] Again, there could even be multiple salient contrasts addressed in one same utterance.
[17] It is a *generalized* as opposed to conventionalized implicature.

that the implicatures themselves are doing the work in staking out the EC, AC, and SC. A possible implicate for *forever* might be "longer than normal" (in the view of the speaker). A perfect candidate for the SC in this case could be what is normal or expected as far as how long something *should* take in a given instance. Working backwards from the implicature of *forever* (taking too long), we can conjecture what is being contrasted (the salient contrast) – *not* taking too long or, again, taking a "normally" expected amount of time. All of this is to say that, we can conjecture the salient contrast here but, really, what is the point when this highly conventionalized expression – the utterance (the EC) – has the implicature of "taking too long" so closely associated with it? Figure 6 provides an analysis of figurative *forever*.

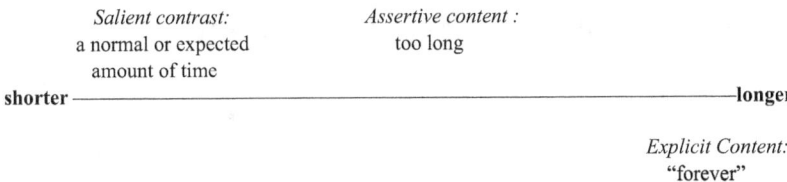

Figure 6: You're taking forever to finish this paper.

The speaker is portraying an attitude or perspective on how long it is taking somebody to do something – *too* long, in the speaker's opinion. There is no adjustment for the sake of trying to figure out what the speaker is getting at, as in (1) and (2). The attitude that goes along with it is part of the face value of the expression *forever* (*taking* forever). What is *forever* adding that its literal paraphrase, *too long*, cannot? *Too long*, like *too small* in the "tiny cake" example (1), begs the questions "By what objective standards?" Who decided those objective standards?[18] Forever takes the hearer directly to the speaker's subjective take on the situation, including the speaker's attitude, emotions, and perspective. The emotion portrayed comes from the intention of the speaker to use this particular phrase, *taking forever*, in certain contexts, a phrase that portrays a personal attitude more than *too long* does.

---

18 Cappelen and Lepore (2005: 21–22), in a useful discussion on comparative adjectives, discuss the reading of "That building is small". They state ". . . the building in question is not being said to be small for an object in general (whatever that may mean)" (21), implying again that the nature of such types of assessments as *small* is uncertain. Lasersohn (2005) argues that "truth values of sentences containing predicates of 'personal taste' such as fun or tasty must be relativized to individuals." Tiny, as compared to small, especially belongs in such a category, as well as other expressions covered in this paper, such as *so much* and *forever*.

(9) Sure, anytime.[19]
(Said in response to being thanked for help)

(9), as an utterance, takes having helped somebody once and reconfirms to the hearer a disposition to help again in the future. This once becomes *always* when generalized, and *once* is what is maximally contrasted against, to show that there is a disposition toward helpfulness in the future. It could be the case that, when "anytime" is said, the speaker actually does not have a favorable attitude toward what they have just done for the hearer, nor do they ever want to help the hearer again. The speaker is simply portraying exactly that – an attitude, as a nicety.

6 Intensification and affect in production and comprehension

Additionally, it must be noted that unclear concepts are going to be especially underspecified (inexactly) at a lexical level (Brdar-Szabó & Brdar 2010: 416). It was mentioned that example (4) ("I died") may be somewhat vague in what it is trying to express.[20] To take another example, someone might show their disdain for some occurrence by saying "it was the stupidest thing ever," painting the phenomenon as broadly and widely with *stupid* as possible, to intensify that characterization to its absolute maximum level. As unclear concepts are especially underspecified, language may seem inadequate when the moment comes to try to do justice to our strongest, most highly commited to emotions. How to *say* how we *feel*?

Intensification in language has real implications, something that can help to inform us of its place in hyperbole. (10) is an example where someone is talking about the amount of work to be done.

(10) I have *so much* work to do.

It is an intensified amount, but it asserts an intensified attitude toward a large amount of work. This includes the fact that there is a lot of work somewhere that, as of yet, is not done and needs doing. Stuff "to do," or remaining to be done,

---

[19] See Brdar-Szabó and Brdar (2010: 402) and Colston (2015: 54) for additional discussion of "anytime."
[20] Take, as an additional example, the underspecified expression *all over the place*, in the sense of "He threw up all over the place".

is negative (at a deficit), and it is not out of this realm until the work is done, to a point that we can "get ahead" (positive). The gap between things done so far and what is yet to be done helps to clarify the negative emotion, expressed as *so much* in the expression – an expression about a quantity of work that equally tells something about an attitude *toward* that work, readily picked up on by listeners.[21] Colston (2015: 75) states "Many kinds of figurative language have the pragmatic effect of both expressing a speaker's emotion and eliciting (the same or other) emotional states in hearers". As in metaphor (Zelinsky-Wibbelt 2010: 203), hyperbolic speakers "transform their internal representations into external behaviour," potentially showing or displaying their attitudinal or emotional state.

Such uptake of what the speaker is thinking occurs readily in conversations, to the extent that literal meaning of hyperbolic utterances goes unnoticed, as is accounted for in the follow up to the original hyperbolic utterance in (11).

(11) SPEAKER A: These are the shittiest . . . speakers on earth . . . besides the ones in the kitchen

SPEAKER B: And these are an improvement over my last ones. (paraphrased from Norrick, 2004, p. 1734, sourced from the SBCSAE)

Speaker B takes Speaker A's utterance of shittiest speakers on Earth as intended to indicate something about his beliefs about the speakers (they suck), replete with a subsequent contradiction (his last ones were shittier than the shittiest)[22] which is felicitous. As far as what has been understood by the utterance, there is no contradiction. The literal quality of the statement was not part of the interpretation, nor was it the intention of the speaker. Rather, the speaker was using hyperbole as a strategy for depicting his feelings about the speakers. This leads Gibbs (1994) to a reassessment of hearers' expectations, in light of Grice's (1975) quality maxim: that statements only need resemble the beliefs of the speaker, rather than match them perfectly (394). Attitudinal or emotional content can be roughly gauged as positive (good) or negative (bad) along some relative scale, not necessarily very exactly. This suits intuitions about how we talk – like, dislike, like a lot, really don't like, holding someone in high regard, holding someone in low regard. . .

---

21 *So much* is to "a lot" as *forever* is to "too long" as *tiny* is to "too small". The former of each pair indicates an affective component to a greater degree than the latter.

22 Which, incidentally, is another hyperbolic form in English: taking the superlative and relativizing it. Take, for example, worse than the worst, uglier than the ugliest, better than the best, etc.

7 Deriving the salient contrast

In example (12), the speaker, who has moments earlier checked into a temporary rental apartment, is talking to someone about an advertised guest room in the apartment. The speaker finds it to not be up to what she expected or might have wished for.

(12) Oh, actually it's just a tiny kid's bedroom with a bunch of toys in it.

She seems to imply "less than a guest room" in her assessment of the child's room. We can infer what criteria for a guest room she might be invoking by using her statement as an evaluation of what a guest room is not. It will be left to the reader to decide whether this example is hyperbole or not, whether *tiny* is, similar to *forever*, conventionalized hyperbole, and just how particular or fancy the speaker is being in what she considers a guest room. Through her utterance alone we will be able to construct the idea of a guest room that she is contrasting against.

Through her use of *just*, already, we can expect something that doesn't measure up. Being that it's for "kids," perhaps she had a room in mind that is more styled for adults, which includes a tidier presentation (something without a bunch of toys in it). By any other name, a guest room could be a "room for guests". The speaker's viewpoint puts some perspective on the thing in question, what a guest room should be in the speaker's opinion. The question under discussion is the guest room (idealized, or as expected), contrasted with the actuality of the situation as viewed by the speaker.

Example (13) as well as Figures 7 and 8 that follow, highlighting salient contrast in overstatement and understatement, are from Walton (2017: 114). The example is used by Walton to show how one same statement, depending on where the salient contrast lies, serves as understatement or overstatement, depending on what is of interest in the discourse context. In both cases, "a few dollars" is used to mean some moderate amount. The speaker necessarily dissociates from the "a few dollars" claim, making for an ironic statement.

(13) She was hospitalized for a month, and they had to spend a few dollars on medical expenses.

First, it helps to remember what a few dollars means in its most commonplace, literal sense. One goes to the store and spends a few dollars on some baseball cards and candy, around three dollars. Perhaps we can imagine a scenario for (13) in which the speaker's interlocutors are curious to know if any money was spent

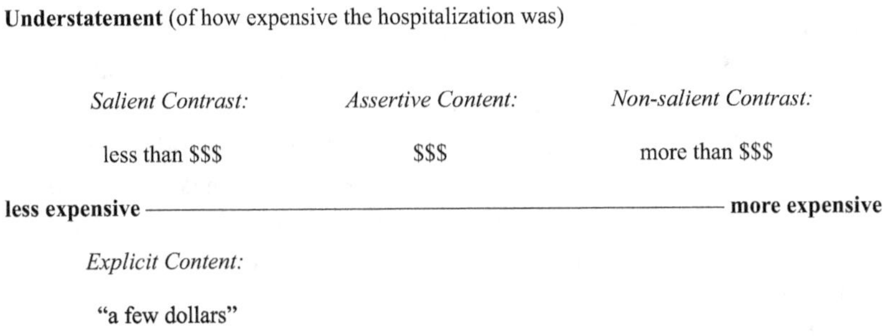

Understatement (of how expensive the hospitalization was)

Salient Contrast:	Assertive Content:	Non-salient Contrast:
less than $$$	$$$	more than $$$

less expensive ─────────────────────────────── more expensive

Explicit Content:

"a few dollars"

Figure 7: A few dollars on medical expenses understatement (from Walton 2017: 114)

at all. Was there much of a hospital stay? Perhaps they are hoping for the best case scenario (very little money spent, and the health issue was not very serious).

The speaker communicates that this was not the case. The "few" dollars that were spent stand in for a larger quantity, greater than the SC in the "conversational air" (Walton), and greater than (contrary to) the expression's literal meaning. According to Wilson (2006: 1724), ironical utterances intend to "draw attention to some discrepancy between a description of the world that the speaker is apparently putting forward and the way things actually are". The expression "a few dollars" puts forth a description of the world that is different from what is really there (a moderate amount). In an *echoic* account of irony, first proposed by Sperber & Wilson (1981),[23] speakers "tacitly dissociate [thems]elves from an attributed utterance or thought with a similar content" (Wilson 2006: 1722).

The thought or utterance with a similar content to the one expressed is anything to the effect of *that* the amount of money is only a few dollars. The utterance or thought is attributed to some conjectured other person, or to a group of people, or people in general, or even oneself at a different time, usually to "express a critical or mocking attitude to it" (Wilson 2006: 1724). However, Sperber and Wilson's echoic account does not preclude hopeful or wishful ironical echoes (1736). This is viable as a possible intention behind the speaker's utterance of (13) as understatement – a touch of irony as the speaker echoes not herself at a different time, but a self or anyone at all who sees the expenditures as only a few dollars, to echo a thought that the money is a less threatening and serious amount. What is the speaker's attitude to this echoed thought? It's not mockery, but approval or endorsement of it, to frame things in a more hopeful way, where the blow is lessened for the parties incurring the medical costs. Aside from endorsement, the statement is potentially humorous. Alternatively, the speaker could be mocking

---

[23] See also Sperber & Wilson (1986) and Wilson & Sperber (2012), among others.

the predicament of the people in question, saying "a few" dollars, but knowing that the medical expenses would hit the people in question hard enough – as if to mean, with a wink, "they're screwed". The speaker's dissociation from an echoed thought takes on its meaning only once the speaker's attitude *toward* that thought is made clear. A speaker has various means to help make this message clear. Wilson and Sperber (2012: 123) provide a list of examples of non-linguistic cues, all of which are suitable for this last example: "…an ironical tone of voice, a wry facial expression, a resigned shrug, a weary shake of the head."

"A few dollars" is readily applicable to any amount more than a few. Example (15) is a more outrightly ironic, clear example, as the distance between the understated amount and the actual amount spent is increased.

(14) Their Ferrari cost *a few dollars*

It's obvious what the speaker means because it's, well, a Ferrari. It's more understated, and more obviously ironic.

A purely hyperbolic utterance, on the other hand, is something that the speaker is particularly commited to – that is, a speaker stands squarely in their own shoes and it is clear that the attitude being expressed is of the speaker and the speaker is clearly "associated" with it. The nature of ironic statements and hyperbolic statements will be assessed further as part of the discussion of the overstatement reading of (13).

Overstatement (of how inexpensive the hospitalization was)

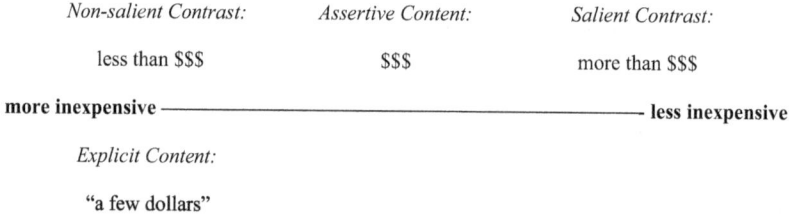

Figure 8: A few dollars on medical expenses overstatement (from Walton 2017: 114)

In the overstatement context analysis, *some* money was spent, and the point is not that it was a particularly small amount. There is not really a personal emotional reaction to something. There is no personal expectation toward the situation – things are being described just as they are, and it doesn't seem particularly typical of hyperbole. Try paraphrasing it as in the "never" example. It is as though, almost as if, they spent a few dollars(?). The explicit content is not highly exaggerative, nor highly contrastive as some of the previous examples, nor does it deny the salient contrast forcefully, in the sense of rejecting it. To speak metaphorically, the salient contrast is causing the explicit content to "drift" in its direction, pulled by the gravity of the SC in the discourse context, to arrive at the assertive content.[24] (Did they spend a lot of money? Yes, and then attenuating it….). It is a concession in the same direction as the SC. As in the case of the understatement, the explicit content expresses what it does only because it is denying the particular SC that is pertinent.

An imagined context provides the motivation for the utterance. We can think of the question under discussion being, perhaps, whether a huge amount of money was spent and the speaker doesn't deny that fact but rather concedes to it, to deny it only partially without fully endorsing it, thereby arriving at the affirmation that *some* money ($$$) was spent, without completely rejecting what is salient. It is rather splitting the difference between a few and a lot. The nature of the SC seems to play a part in this. A forceful denial is not what is called for in the mind of the speaker, but rather a biasing of it. It is hard to know what a forceful rejection of this SC would look like. Perhaps it could be example (15).

(15) Oh, they spent nothing

This is to downplay money's worth. This could be an ostentatious utterance made sincerely. Or, one could dissociate from the thought (or mentality), one which is attributed to an imagined person, perhaps of relative wealth, who dismisses a moderate sum ($$$) as a small sum (less than $$$). Or, alternatively, if it were a huge sum of money by any standard and the speaker echoed "nothing" or "close to nothing," it might indicate a snooty or snobbish attitude to a far-flung degree. In either possible context, the statement is ironic. It could be that the speaker is choosing to identify with that attitude for the moment – for the sake of humor or pretense (i.e, pretending to be fabulous) – or the speaker may have an intention to mock such a thought.

It is a good question, though, whether (15) uttered sincerely about a huge sum of money should be considered to be hyperbole proper. What is made pertinent by the statement in such a context seems to necessitate a newly revised SC, one that considers the potential effect that expenditures can have on people rather than how much money was actually spent – which, incidentally, was our imagined context in the understatement analysis for Figure 7. By saying "nothing," it

---

[24] This metaphor involving physical bodies in motion will be returned to.

negates any effect that such a large expenditure might have. If this is a hyperbolic statement, what would be the assertive content aside from the subtext gathered from (negation of) the implied SC? The nothing (zero dollars) seems here to be standing in for "no effect," both null quantities anological to each other. Perhaps (15) could alternatively be considered to be an (unironic) understatement again, due to the nature of the discourse context which seems to be brought about by the proposed SC. Or, perhaps, as an understatement, it is necessarily engaging in pretense and something very close to irony. This question will remain open. Such an utterance in such a context, while it does reject the SC in the way that we would like it to as hyperbole, seems to reframe the entire discourse context and our consideration of the entire figure.

To return to the more moderate overstatement depicted in the figure, it portrays a weakness in force by an *aim* toward a medium between the SC and EC through a tempered utterance which allows for the SC, unlike our prior examples which shoot for the moon in the opposite direction. Example (13) implies an openness to the SC with a modest biasing rather than an exaggeration against it, making it weakly hyperbolic in comparison. Contrary to all previous examples, it does not *forcefully reject* the SC.

Statements that are hyperbolic tend to push toward the extreme end of a hypothetical scale, usually when exceeding a point that is already toward one end of a scale. Hyperbole is potentiated when something that is already very big is made out to be even bigger, or something very small is made out to be tiny or nothing at all. Imagine a push to one end of the scale that is then further exceeded, perhaps in a portrayal of some exorbitant quantity of money. For example, "we were bleeding money out of our ears." Or, remember example (4). "I was so overwhelmed that". . . Well, how overwhelmed *were* you? Such examples are more emblematic of hyperbole.

As stated by Brdar-Szabó & Brdar (2010: 400), "...[p]robably one of the most prominent functions of hyperbole is intensification, i.e. to express the assertion that an entity possesses some property to a very high degree, that the circumstances and/or effects of an event are extreme, etc." While exaggeration can occur without limit toward the upper end of the scale, exaggeration ends at zero on the lower end. This does not inhibit hyperbole if and when the salient contrast is adequately contrasted within its bounds. As seen in the preceding examples, a meaningful denial hinges more on what the salient contrast is and a means of denying it sufficiently and with force. (16) is another example that shoots toward the lower end of the scale.

(16) He is so small that you can barely see him.
      (said in reference to a boy)

It is absurd because it lacks any poignance, and it lacks a context which provides a salient contrast to be pushed against. Perhaps the person is exceptionally small, but never this small. It's hyperbole in that it is exaggerating, sketching out a version of smallness that is quite extreme. It was questioned earlier whether miniscule or microscopic added anything as replacements to tiny in the tiny cake example. Is it just exaggerating for exaggeration's sake? It is hyperbole only to the extent that we can find something to contrast against. There is *some* contrast to be made, just from what we know about the size of humans, but more is needed.

There is a difference now if more context is provided. A teacher is counting students in a classroom and doesn't notice a particularly small student. There are practical implications that have to do with not being able to see someone in a crowded room. If a person is small, they might be hidden by a larger object. Or perhaps the teacher really means it in the sense of tiny objects that are so small that you can *barely* see them. The purpose of the statement is to exaggerate whether someone is even big enough to be countable (with countable being what is contrasted against). This example verges on hyperbole becoming a mixed figure with metaphor as it begins to necessitate the seeing of the child as something that he absolutely is not – something microscopic. Hyperbole achieves effectiveness through its discourse context and some salient contrast that it makes.

As in the above examples, the context gave us a reason *why* the utterance was made. The reason was to contrast something meaningfully, and its poignance came from establishing a salient contrast. This reason speaks to the motivations for why speakers use hyperbole and what compels them to make these utterances – *that* the cake is *too* small, *that* a speaker was *more than* extremely overwhelmed, to make these contrasts. In (16), a pertinent context and *why* a boy's unperceivability (at all) due to his size was worth mentioning.

For most of the examples shown here, even a default (without background information) reading of the utterance would indicate that the salient contrast lies in one direction or another on the relevant scale. In an example like "tiny cake," the shift of the salient contrast to some other end of the scale would completely change the nature of the utterance. As mentioned before, if it were indeed a salient *contrast* of "adequately small," *tiny* would say it's *more* than small enough. Or, if the cake simply met the distinction of "adequately small," the statement would become a confirmation. This piece of cake *is* (indeed) tiny (enough).

The value of the SC is its usefulness in analysis. Someone has said more than what they mean, but in regards to what point that is being rejected? This point is the point that is pushed against forcefully. To pick up again on the metaphor suggested in the overstatement analysis of (13), the salient contrast is the brick wall that the EC basketball is thrown at (with force), to bounce it back toward the EC. It starts the journey as the EC and, ounce bounced off the wall, it (the same ball) is the AC rocketing back toward where it started its journey (at EC). This is depicted in Figure 9.

(4) I died. Right there. For real.
    (Said about meeting someone greatly admired by the speaker)

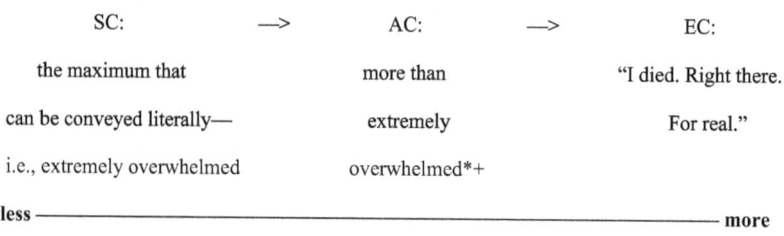

Figure 9: Return trip of the proverbial basketball

While the AC of example (13) drifted toward the SC, the AC in the rest of the examples is the basketball that has been thrown forcefully at the SC, bouncing back and continuing its trajectory in the direction of the EC. It is for this reason that a plus sign should be placed next to the paraphrasing of each AC, for it is propelled by the force of what is said (the EC is the basketball created, propelled by the intention of the speaker in the first place). The plus indicates where it is moving toward, which direction it looks toward in its meaning, pushing toward the meaning of the explicit content. The meaning of AC is more than its paraphrased meaning. The EC and the potential energy that is still unrealized in AC's trajectory toward its metaphorical destination sprinkles that extra plus on the assertive content, forever imbuing it with something that is not attainable through literal speech – i.e., everything implicated by the explicit content, limited only by the explicit content's irreality.

8 Concluding

Walton (2017), in offering the term salient contrast, applied it to quantitative examples. What has been offered in this current study is an application of the same idea of a contrastive point to hyperboles that deal with qualities and frequencies, in examples that are more emblematic of hyperbole. The cases of *never* and *always* showed that, in hyperbole, there is not only just a shift and adjustment on the scale between what is said and what is meant. Attitude and exaggeration are part of the input in hyperbole – an exaggeration of a state of affairs informs the input, specifically the choice for what is being contrasted against. In hyperbole there is no distinct isomorphic pairing of linguistic forms to hyperbolic meanings. Hyperbolic meanings are dependent on a salient contrast (and where it lies) as well as the nature of that contrast relative to a speaker's attitude and that speaker's subjective evaluation. It is informative to look at borderline examples. When is *tiny* hyperbolic? It is hyperbolic the more its use moves away from objective to subjective assessment. It is hyperbolic when used to describe something that is smaller than expected or wanted (thereby creating a salient contrast). In general, the production of hyperbole aims for the portrayal of some subjective attitude, while the comprehension of hyperbole is to pick up on that attitude.

References

Brdar-Szabó, Rita & Mario Brdar. 2010. "Mummy, I love you like a thousand ladybirds:" Reflections on the emergence of hyperbolic effects and the truth of hyperboles. In Armin Burkhardt & Brigitte Nerlich (eds.), *Tropical truth(s): The epistemology of metaphor and other tropes*, 383–427. Berlin & New York: De Gruyter.

Cappelen, Herman & Ernie Lepore. 2005. *A defense of semantic minimalism and speech act pluralism*. Malden: Blackwell.

Carston, Robyn & Cathering Wearing. 2015. Hyperbolic language and its relation to metaphor and irony. *Journal of Pragmatics* 79 (May). 79–92. http://doi.org/10.1016/j.pragma.2015.01.011 (accessed 6 May 2016).

Colston, Herbert L. 2015. *Using figurative language*. New York: Cambridge University Press.

Colston, Herbert L. & Shauna B. Keller. 1998. You'll never believe this: irony and hyperbole in expressing surprise. *Journal of Psycholinguistic Research* 27 (4). 499–512.

Gibbs, Raymond W., Jr. 1994. *The poetics of mind*. Cambridge: Cambridge University Press.

Grice, H. Paul. 1975. Logic and conversation. In Peter Cole & Jerry L. Morgan (eds.), *Syntax and semantics, vol. 3: Speech acts*, 41–58. New York: Academic Press.

Lasersohn, Peter. 2005. Context dependence, disagreement, and predicates of personal taste. *Linguistics and Philosophy* 28 (6), 643–686. http://doi.org/10.1007/s10988-005-0596-x

Norrick, Neal R. 2004. Hyperbole, extreme case formulation. *Journal of Pragmatics* 36 (9). 1727–1739. http://doi.org/10.1016/j.pragma.2004.06.006

Peña, María Sandra & Francisco J. Ruiz de Mendoza. 2017. Construing and constructing hyperbole. In Angeliki Athanasiadou (ed.), *Studies in figurative thought and language* [Human Cognitive Processing, 56], 42–73. Amsterdam & Philadelphia: John Benjamins.

Popa-Wyatt, Mihaela. (Forthcoming). Mind the Gap: Expressing affect with hyperbole and hyperbolic figures. In Andrew Gargett & John Barnden (eds.), *Figurative thought and language*. John Benjamins.

Sperber, Dan & Deirdre Wilson. 1981. Irony and the use-mention distinction. In Peter Cole (ed.), *Radical Pragmatics*, 295–318. New York: Academic Press.

Sperber, Dan & Deirdre Wilson. 1986. *Relevance: Communication and cognition*. Oxford: Basil Blackwell.

Walton, Ken. 2017. Meiosis, hyperbole, irony. *Philosophical Studies*. 174 (1). 105–120.

Wilson, Deirdre. 2006. The pragmatics of verbal irony: Echo or pretence? *Lingua* 116. 1722–1743.

Wilson, Deirdre & Dan Sperber. 2012. Explaining irony. *Meaning and relevance*. 123–145. Cambridge: Cambridge University Press.

Zelinsky-Wibbelt, Cornelia. 2010. Natural language processing: Minds, brains, and programmes. In Armin Burkhardt & Brigitte Nerlich (eds.), *Tropical Truth(s): The epistemology of metaphor and other tropes*, 177–212. Berlin & New York: De Gruyter.

Part II: **Diversity across languages**

Patrawat Samermit and Apinan Samermit
Thai irony as an indirect relational tool to save face in social interactions

Abstract: Irony in Thai has historically been examined as a form of sarcasm. This chapter extends the use of Thai irony to include hyperbole, jocularity, understatement, rhetorical questions, sarcasm as a way to negotiate social interactions. In particular, a corpus analysis of a popular Thai cooking show *Krua Khun Toy* found that irony in Thai can be used as a multifunctional relational tool that is humorous to help speakers save face for *both* themselves and their interlocutor. Thai irony is not necessarily about distancing oneself from an interlocutor, but rather maintaining social cohesion between the two through indirect speech. In this way, irony helps uphold Thai sociocultural values in interpersonal interactions, such as saving face and sharing empathy through humor, which are understood through specific embodied metaphors about the face, heart, and body. Finally, this chapter calls to light the importance of having a culturally-situated analysis of Thai figurative language to further examine the nuances of its functionality and use.

Keywords: Thai, verbal irony, sarcasm, social interactions, embodied metaphor, interpersonal dynamics, face saving, hyperbole, jocularity, rhetorical questions, heart, humor

1 Introduction

Imagine you are watching a Thai cooking talk show with four hosts and a guest chef from Bangkok. One of the hosts asks the chef, "Where is your restaurant located?" The chef takes two minutes to respond with an extremely long, detailed set of directions based on streets coming in from the north, south, east,

---

Acknowledgements: We'd like to thank Ray Gibbs and Nick Antrilli for their comments during the preparation of this manuscript and their undying support as we explored the relationship between our cultural identity, figurative language use, and how we use both in conjunction to walk through an ambiguous social world.

Patrawat Samermit, University of California, Santa Cruz, Department of Psychology
Apinan Samermit, University of Texas at Arlington, English Language Institute

https://doi.org/10.1515/9783110652246-007

and west parts of town. A co-host cuts off the chef and asks in a conversational tone, "Well, what if you're coming in from Rayong?", which is a city south of Bangkok. Non-Thai speakers might perceive this question to be literal where the co-host is trying to understand the location of the restaurant. However, when this interaction is stated in Thai, Thai speakers perceive it as a rhetorical question that sarcastically criticizes the chef's long-winded explanation through a joke. The irony in this statement is not only a linguistic or pragmatic device used conversationally, but a conceptual tool used to reinforce interpersonal dynamics (Gibbs & Samermit, 2017). In this case, it works to criticize the speaker in a way that helps him save face from embarrassment and openly accept criticism about his long-winded explanation. Immediately after the Rayong comment, this particular chef laughed along with the uproar of laughter from the crowd and co-hosts, marking his affiliation with them rather than embarrassment or scorn.

This use of ironic humor is one of many examples from a corpus we have collected and analyzed for instances of irony from *Krua Khun Toy*, a popular Thai cooking talk show. This research is in line with emerging literature on cross-linguistic studies of irony that seeks to identify different cultural markers and uses of irony (Escandell-Vidal & Leonetti, 2014; Leonetti & Escandell-Vidal, this volume; Okamoto, 2002; Yao, Song, & Singh, 2013) and assess their relationships with proposed mechanisms of irony (Colston, in press). This article adds to the literature by describing some culturally appropriate analyses on irony use in Thai. Much of the past literature on Thai irony has limited itself to examining sarcasm in Thai (Pengpanich, 1998; Jaroenkiatboworn, 2005), and is understudied beyond that. This exploratory analysis of irony in Thai extends its use to hyperbole, jocularity, understatement, rhetorical questions, and sarcasm as a way to negotiate social interactions.

This chapter demonstrates the use of irony in Thai to criticize others in an indirect, but positive way to maintain politeness and save face in social interactions. In this corpus, we have found that irony is used in Thai as a multifunctional relational tool that is often humorous to help participants in the conversations be indirectly polite (Srinarawat, 2005) and save face (Ukosakul, 2005) to maintain social cohesion, saving both the speaker's and listener's face. Directness, or stating explicitly what one believes, thinks, or acts, is considered to be inappropriate in many Thai social settings. Indirectness, or stating something explicitly that is different from the implied meaning, allows for the expression of one's stance without the risk of someone losing face. Indirectness includes irony and its family of forms, but may also include other forms of figurative language such as humor, metaphor, and metonymy, which are not analyzed in this chapter but invite further research.

2 Verbal irony mechanisms

One of the greatest difficulties in studying verbal irony is trying to define the term itself. There exists a basic, layperson understanding of irony as opposition, where one says the opposite of what one means. An example of this would be saying, "You're quite the early bird" to someone who has arrived very late to a meeting. A listener would understand that the comment is expressing the opposite sentiment to what is literally being expressed by picking up on things like intonation that express criticism or warning as a speech act (Haverkate, 1990). This common understanding of irony seems intuitive, but recent research calls into question the use of a specific tone of voice to mark verbal irony (Bryant, 2010; Bryant & Fox Tree, 2005) as it may not capture many aspects of ironic meaning (Gibbs, 1994), ironic action (Gibbs, 2007) or ironic thought (Gibbs & Samermit, 2017). For example, Kaufer (1981) questioned the opposition account of irony by indicating that non-declarative forms of irony, such as rhetorical questions, make it difficult to identify what the specific opposite belief is. A propositional understanding of irony may be too simplistic to account for the wide variety of ironic instances available in language.

Irony may extend beyond simple propositional equations in language to a more contextual, culturally sensitive, and embodied experience. In general conversation, people often use irony to convey attitudes and beliefs indirectly to be polite, humorous, to heighten or soften a harsh criticism, to show that one is in control of their emotions, and to avoid damaging social relationships (Colston, 1997; Dews, Kaplan, Winner, 1995).

Research on verbal irony, which is almost exclusively based on English, proposes different general mechanisms to achieve this indirect form of communication. For example, the Relevance-theoretic account of irony (Sperber & Wilson, 1995; Wilson & Sperber, 2012) proposes that a person explicitly echoes past and possible statements, beliefs, and social norms attributed to a group or individual. They propose that people use irony in this way to dissociate themselves from the opinion that is echoed, and to criticize it or its original speaker. Yus (2016) suggests that the identification of a speaker's intentional *affective attitude* (e.g., their feelings and emotions) provides a useful label to help explain a variety of non-propositional effects of an ironic utterance in the Relevance-theoretic account such as amusement, softened criticism, and praise. Additionally, the Pretense Theory states that an ironic speaker acts out someone else's actions and language so the listeners may identify the critiques the speaker has about the portrayed person's beliefs as well as the speaker's distance from the topic (Clark & Gerrig, 1984). Both of these theories extend the mechanism of irony beyond the confounds of pragmatic markers into the social realm, where beliefs, intentions, and attitudes are shared between the speaker and audience as a specific form of indirect critique and distancing.

Even so, ironic performances and language may not be consciously produced or even consciously registered as irony. Instead, the experience of irony may arise as emergent property from a broader, dynamic systems of interactions across our brains, bodies, and world (see Gibbs, 2012 for review), including our social one. Thus, irony may not be a simple linguistic or pragmatic device limited to conversations, but may be a conceptual tool used to explore interpersonal dynamics (Gibbs & Samermit, 2017) that are constrained and interpreted through contextualized, culturally-grounded interactions.

The experience of different emotions may be amplified by the use of irony. People feel more intensely criticized when receiving sarcastic criticism as compared to direct criticism (Toplak & Katz, 2000). The use of verbal aggression via sarcasm has been directly linked to the experience of anger and loss of self-esteem (Anastasia, Cohen, & Spatz, 1948). The use of jocularity, on the other hand, may leave an addressee feeling mirth and aid in the maintenance of a positive relationship with friends (Gibbs, 2000). Having a certain level of affiliation, such as with a group of friends at an informal dinner, may cause irony to elicit a more humorous experience and reaffirms the bond of social cohesion through shared play (Kotthoff, 2003).

The different social contexts in which irony is used may elicit different emotions, but it should be acknowledged that irony is not only about dissociating from one's emotions or other people. Rather, these various forms of irony can also be used as ways for speakers to relate with one another both verbally and emotionally, perhaps making irony an indirect relational tool in social interactions similar to humor.

2.1 Irony as a tool for interpersonal dynamics – an embodied view

It may be more accurate to consider irony an umbrella term covering a variety of figurative intentions where meaning is conveyed indirectly such as sarcasm (where speakers convey negative intent or criticism), jocularity (where speakers intend humor), rhetorical questions (where speakers literally ask a question that implies either a humorous or critical assertion), hyperbole (where speakers express nonliteral meaning by exaggerating the reality of the situation), and understatement (speakers state far less than is obviously the case; Gibbs, 2000). In English, these different forms of irony evoke different emotional responses: Sarcasm, rhetorical questions, and hyperbole cause people to feel more negatively, while understatement and satire evoke more neutral emotional reactions (Leggitt & Gibbs, 2000). Some forms of irony such as indirectness use the statement of positive words to diminish the sting of negative criticism compared to direct language (Dews & Winner, 1995; Dews, Kaplan, & Winner, 1995) while other forms, like sarcasm, are explicitly hostile with the purpose of mocking or attacking addressees (Toplak & Katz, 2000).

Verbal irony, much like humor, requires speakers to recognize others' implicit beliefs and attitudes through some form of communication. Both ironic and humorous language may be forms of encryption that require listeners to have a "key", or shared, specific implicit knowledge to recognize what is truly being implied by a speaker (Flamson & Barrett, 2008). This does not mean that all ironic acts are humorous, or that all humor is ironic, just that the two processes both require implicit knowledge to understand an exchange. To mark our possession of the "key", or shared access to underlying knowledge, beliefs, and attitudes, we laugh as a vocal signaling system to denote our social affiliation and in-group status (Flamson & Bryant, 2013), which can decrease tension while eliciting positive affect (Bacharowski, Smoski, & Owren, 2001).

The shared unlocking of an encrypted message, such as a sarcastic "Wow *that's* a look" can be used to soften the blow of harsh critiques by downplaying the seriousness of the message (Dews, Kaplan, & Winner, 1995), or enhance the amount of condemnation in a criticism (Colston, 1997) depending on what best reaffirms the social affiliation within that given context. Beyond this, the shared experience of humor that can arise from ironic statements can help us maintain relationships with people we understand to be "cognitively similar" to us in the hopes of continued cooperation, friendship, and collaboration (McElreath et al., 2003).

Through the sharing of implicit knowledge, both irony and humor can act as conceptual tools by which we negotiate interpersonal dynamics in understanding our metaphorical stance towards other people and their beliefs (Gibbs & Samermit, 2017; Samermit & Gibbs, 2016). Both experiences may both be motivated by the conceptual metaphor HUMOR/IRONY ARE A SPECIFIC BODILY DISTURBANCE or FORCE (Gibbs & Samermit, 2017) where we understand them through benign violations (think of tickling) on our bodies, which metonymically represent our sense of ego or selves. This is consistent with the benign violation theory of humor (McGraw & Warren, 2010; McGraw & Warner, 2014) that states we experience humor when three conditions are met: 1) something threatens our sense of what ought to be, 2) the threatening situation seems benign, and 3) a person maintains both interpretations at the same time. These threats may involve physical well-being, as with tickling, but extend to threats to one's psychological well-being, behaviors that break social norms, cultural norms, linguistic norms, norms of logic, and moral norms.

For example, in our corpus one of the hosts, Oh, makes a joke indicating that if someone wants dessert, they can steal pickled mangoes from the back of the guest chef's restaurant. Khun Toy, the main host, responds with โอ้โฮ กู กู ขโมยมาทำไม ตกนรกหมกไหม้ บ้า! (Transliterated: *oho khamoi maa tammai tok narok mok mai baa!*; Translated: [Whoa! Why would I steal it? You go to hell. Crazy!]) which at face value may seem like a literal chastisement. However, within the context of the interaction, the rhetorical question he responds with acts as a softer criticism, indicating that even thinking that of joking about stealing is not remotely okay. Additionally, the "go to hell" seems like a direct insult, but comes off a hyperbolic, sarcastic statement indicating that the thought of theft is one that is a massive violation, worthy of eternal damnation. Within this context, the use of sarcasm points to how the suggestion to steal breaks social norms, but is also recognized as being benign since it was only a suggestion, and not an act. This is emphasized by his final comment of "Crazy!", where *baa* has a specific connotation of acceptable absurdity. His use of this at the end of his utterance punctuates this cultural violation, but that it was benign because no one was hurt. This instance is responded to with laughter from all involved, including the guest chef whose restaurant would be the one hypothetically experiencing theft. This indicates that everyone understands the shared lesson of "theft is bad and if you do it, you are actually amoral and will go to hell."

Whether it is through a softened or heightened criticism of your friend, or the use of jocularity to evoke humor, irony can be used to communicate social intent and understanding that helps us negotiate ambiguous social relationships and social contracts. Irony's pragmatic, emotional, and social functions are often talked about as being performed mutually exclusively. However, recent studies have shown that the use of ironic sarcasm may simultaneously mute and enhance the negative comment, indicating that ironic language may need to be examined as serving multiple functions at once (Boylan & Katz, 2013). Additionally, it is important to acknowledge that the various theories and dimensions of irony discussed above were developed by analyzing acts of irony in English. If cognition and language are situated in our embodied and cultural context (Gibbs, 2006), then their functions must be examined cross-linguistically to identify similar underlying cognitive structures and mechanisms.

3 Thai social interactions and indirectness

The study of irony across languages requires an understanding of the cultural context in which it is being used. Most of the theories of ironic mechanisms, including those outlined above, have been defined within the context of the

English language. Colston (in press) suggests the need for more cross-linguistic documentation to identify the potential differences in function, as well as validation of theories of irony that have been proposed as universal. A few studies have recently identified specific cultural productions and functions of irony. For example, a fronting system used in Castilian Spanish has been identified that gives rise to a "verum focus" interpretation, or an emphasis that magnifies one meaning over another, that allows for a clearer ironic reading (Escandell-Vidal & Leonetti, 2014; Leonetti & Escandell-Vidal, this volume). Additionally, the use of politeness and honorifics in Japanese in different contexts, such as with positive and negative contents of the message or when addressing people with different power status, can cause a divergence in politeness levels that is read as ironic (Okamoto, 2002). Finally, Yao, Song, and Singh (2013) provide an examination of irony through the Chinese *bei* construction of passives, which acts as a pragmatic marker to help readers and listeners identify points of disapproval or critique. Our chapter hopes to add to this growing list of cross-cultural examinations of irony through an analysis of Thai irony within the context of Thai social interactions.

Thai studies of irony have not extended the argument beyond sarcasm (Jaroenkiatboworn, 2005; Pengpanich, 1998; Panpothong, 1996), and moreover they have not been integrated in to cognitive linguistic theories of irony. This view of irony as sarcasm may be due to the general difficulties in pinning down a definition for irony in English, making it difficult to translate the concept from English into Thai studies of pragmatics. Many existing studies address irony in a disembodied way that attempts to identify it through the use of language alone, decontextualizing its specific use within the Thai cultural context. We examine the cultural context of social interactions and communication within Thai culture in conjunction with general mechanisms proposed in English for a more contextualized view of Thai irony.

One of the core tenants of Thai social interactions revolves around the idea of saving face, or *raksa na,* where *"na"* means face but metonymically represents a sense of personhood (Sammakarn, 1975) or one's ego that must not at any cost be violated (Komin, 1990). This is related to the Chinese linguistic family tree from which Thai originates, where the face is metonymically and metaphorically understood as the "focus of interaction and relationships" and the "locus of dignity and prestige" (Yu, 2001). An analysis of Thai face idioms revealed that *na* describes four aspects of a person including one's personality, one's countenance or behavior, one's emotions, and the concept of honor (Ukosakul, 1999). The concept of face is not merely the loss of "public self-image that a person wants for himself" (Brown & Levinson, 1978: 61), but is more widely understood as a social component of self-identity that is understood as the acceptance of one's accomplishments and social position within society (Ukosakul, 2005). In this way, the conceptual metaphor of DIGNITY/PRESTIGE IS FACE that exists in Chinese (Yu, 2008) is also a prevalent conceptualization of self in Thai.

Thai identity is intrinsically tied to the perception of oneself not only as an individual, but as a member of society. It is important to protect our sense of honor, to provide others with a sense of honor, and avoid shameful behaviors that may cause another person to experience shame. A core component of Thai social interaction is to preserve your own face or, *raksa na eng*, while also helping others maintain face, *raksa nam cai kan* (Ukosakul, 2005). A person who acts in a way that is too confrontational or direct may cause someone to *sia na*, or lose face, causing the addressee to experience negative feelings such as public shame or anger (Ukosakul, 1999). Acting in a direct, confrontational way makes you someone that *mai hai na*, or does not provide face, while being the recipient of such actions can lead to a loss of face, *sia na*. A person can also *sia na* when they are disrespectful, behave dishonorably, or sometimes when they exhibit large emotions out of context in a way that affects others. Both of these – *mai hai na* and *sia na* – are undesirable states of self, and so Thai speakers often turn to different politeness strategies to help them save face. In communication, Thai speakers try to enact an attitude of respect towards others' egos and feelings and not impose on others (*krengcai*) with the use of communication to maintain harmonious relationships (Ukosakul, 2005; Komin, 1990).

To *raksa na* in Thai social interactions, Thai speakers will utilize many different politeness strategies that are performed as indirect communication, such as jokes and teasing, general avoidance of confrontation (Ukosakul, 2005), the interrogative form (e.g., the use of questions as indirect speech acts, and was not limited to rhetorical questions), and irony in the form of sarcasm (Srinarawat, 2005). At the most extreme end, when someone has a conflict with another person they may try to keep silent about a situation or *lop na*, or literally to "hide their face" and avoid the person (Ukosakul, 2005). On top of avoiding a person with which they have conflict, in actual interactions they may use other forms of indirect speech, such as vague, general terms (including hedging) when making a criticism or comment since a rejection of their ideas feels like a rejection of their ego (Komin, 1990).

In many cases, Thai speakers will use jokes and teasing to help lessen the possibility of interlocutors losing face in a situation where something critical or sensitive is being communicated. This use of humor as a form of indirect speech is particularly powerful since listeners regularly perceive the message as something that is not offensive, even when it is critical (Ukosakul, 1994). An analysis of spontaneous communication between Thai speakers completing a task together found that Thai speakers prefer to use intensifiers and spontaneous expressions to show involvement in the interaction (Aoki, 2010). The purpose of this type of communication was to create an amusing and fun atmosphere that plays in to the Thai value of *sanuk*, which is to experience a fun, enjoyable, or pleasant time with the purpose of strengthening relationships with each other. The use of humor, intensifiers, and self-disclosure create a light-hearted atmosphere where it is more difficult to *sia na*. By creating a *sanuk* atmosphere where people experience humor together, it becomes easier to identify others that share the "key" (Flamson & Barrett, 2008) to otherwise encrypted Thai social interactions: the need to save face (Ukosakul, 2005). In this way, Thai social relationships are characterized by a desire for affiliation and acceptance within an "affiliative society" (Wichiarajote, 1973), which can be maintained through various forms of indirect speech that are encrypted and decoded by those with like values.

Srinarawat (2005) showed that Thai participants preferred indirect speech to direct speech in situations that necessitated politeness. Srinarawat (2005) conducted a corpus analysis of contemporary Thai novels and found that the primary form of indirect speech was interrogative questions that functioned to criticize others (e.g., sarcasm), indicating that the use of indirect speech in Thai, such as humor and irony, are for the primary purpose of maintaining social relationships to *raksa na*. In this way, the imperative of Thai social interactions is to preserve the sanctity of one's body from violations for a sense of psychological well-being, which necessitates the use of irony and humor as a way to keep these violations benign (Samermit & Gibbs, 2016; Gibbs & Samermit, 2017).

4 Irony in Thai – moving beyond sarcasm

Previous analyses of irony in Thai have been limited to understanding it as just sarcasm produced through syntactic structures and Gricean maxims (Pengpanich, 1998; Srinarawat, 2005) and do not apply an analysis of cultural context, which can further elaborate on Thai irony's use and functions. Our analysis extends the understanding of irony in Thai to include other forms of irony such as sarcasm, jocularity, hyperbole, understatement, and rhetorical questions (Gibbs, 2000) and multifunctional combinations of them by analyzing ironic utterances within a culturally appropriate context: saving face in social interactions. Additionally, the use of humor in Thai irony may be another way to reduce tension (Bacharowski, Smoski, & Owren, 2001) and help save face by softening criticism (Ukosakul, 1994), which will be discussed in our analysis of the popular, unscripted cooking show, *Krua Khun Toy*, or Mr. Toy's Kitchen. Khun Toy and his three co-hosts (Oh, Nawat, and Ko) speak with a local guest chef about a special dish of theirs, watch a montage of the chef cooking it in their own restaurant, and then try it live in front of an audience. This show was chosen because of the unscripted nature of their interactions, where the co-hosts and chef talk naturally before and after watching the montage of the chef cooking.

To collect these instances of irony, two independent coders watched 20 episodes of *Krua Khun Toy*, and individually marked ironic utterances. The coders then validated each instance for irony (e.g., the expression of an opposite view from what is literally being said) across their results. The corpus only includes instances that both coders agreed upon as ironic. The corpus consists of 227 instances, averaging about 11 instances per episode, which were coded for sarcasm (where speakers convey negative intent or criticism), jocularity (where speakers intend humor), hyperbole (where speakers express nonliteral meaning by exaggerating the reality of the situation), understatement (where speakers state far less than is obviously the case), rhetorical questions (where speakers literally ask a question that implies either a humorous or critical assertion), and pretense (acting out someone else's actions or language or demonstrating pretend actions).

For one-third (35%) of these instances, there was more than one dimension of irony that co-occurred, making the raw count of ironic dimensions greater than the total instances of ironic utterances. For this reason, we report the coded dimensions of irony in percentages as is shown below. Of the 227 instances, jocularity was the most frequent second dimension, additionally making up 86% of the multifunctional instances of irony. We argue that irony in Thai, at least within our corpus, extends beyond the use of sarcasm, and is also used as jocularity, hyperbole, understatement, rhetorical questions, and pretense. The tone of voice for most of the ironic utterances was very straight forward and conversational, except for the presence slightly lengthened vowels in some instances of hyperbole and understatement. The use of sarcasm was not marked by any exaggerated prosody or enunciation. This speaks towards evidence that call into question the presence of a distinctive ironic tone of voice, which has been presumed to be a marker of irony (Bryant, 2010; Bryant & Fox Tree, 2005). However, we did not do any analyses of vocal patterns for the purpose of this paper and this remains a rich field for future research.

Table 1: The percentages of the different dimensions of irony that occurred within our corpus.

Irony Dimension	Jocularity	Sarcasm	Hyperbole	Rhetorical Question	Understatement	Pretense
Percentage of Instances	43%	23%	15%	11%	8%	1%

The use of various forms of indirect speech stems from the cultural desire to be polite and *raksa na*, or save one's own face and sense of honor, while also *raksa nam cai kan*, or helping others maintain their face as well. In our corpus, the speakers use mechanisms such as echoic mention, pretense, and sarcasm, but ultimately to create a sense of humor (jocularity) to help soften the blow of a critique. The purpose of irony in these interactions is to create an atmosphere of *sanuk*, or having a good time with each other to *raksa na*. Additionally, we present findings that a single instance of irony may have multiple functions, such as instances where speakers are expressing both rhetorical questions and sarcasm together. A culturally contextualized analysis indicates that the primary use of irony in Thai is to avoid confrontation to *raksa na* and produce jocularity.

4.1 A characteristically ironic Thai criticism

One example of a lightened criticism is when they are featuring a guest chef's special marinated pork, but a co-host, Ko, instead cooks the unmarinated meat that is on the table. Khun Toy, the main talk show host, is talking to the guest chef when he notices this and interrupts himself and Ko's actions as follows. The examples shown will be presented in Thai, Romanized Thai (italicized text), and the English translation (bracketed text) for each turn.

(1) Why??

    Khun Toy: เอ๊ะ คุณเอาหมูธรรมดากินทำไม นี่คุณเป็นอะไร
                     Eh! Khun aaw muu thammada kin thammai nii khun pen arai
                       [Hey! Why are you eating the unmarinated pork? What's going on with you?]

    Ko: อ้อ! เราขอโทษเอาหมูธรรมดาเก็บก่อนนะครับ
            oh! rau khothot aau muu thammada kep kon na krap
            [Oh! I am sorry, I am going to save the unmarinated pork first. (puts half cooked pork to the side)]

In this instance, Khun Toy uses a set of rhetorical questions to criticize Ko's haphazardly cooking of unmarinated meat. For example, *Khun aaw muu thammada kin thammai nii* can be translated as the present progressive tense: "Why are you eating the unmarinated pork?" However, it is actually understood as a question of future action, with a more accurate translation including dropped tense markers: *Khun [ja] aaw muu thammada [bpai] kin thammai nii*. The words *ja* and *bpai* mark the future progressive tense, but are regularly dropped in conversation. The colloquial translation of what is said comes out to "Why [are you going to] eat the unmarinated pork?" In this way, Khun Toy uses the imagined future action of eating as a way to criticize Ko's current actions of cooking the wrong piece of meat.

These questions are not literal as Khun Toy is not actually concerned with "why" or what's happening with Ko. The use of *thammai nii* as an interrogative marker makes the question rhetorical. *Thammai* translates into "why", but adding the *nii* exaggerates the question in a way that indicates that it was not sincere and the speaker does not desire a verbal answer. Khun Toy uses this syntactical form to hyperbolize the question and potentially mark it as an ironic utterance to listeners. His use of a hyperbolized rhetorical question enhances the negative comment to draw attention to Ko's mistake, making it more easily identifiable as sarcastic criticism. In this way, Khun Toy's criticism of Ko is softened through the use of a hyperbolized rhetorical question, which draws the focus to the action and not on Ko himself. The use of Thai syntax contributes to an ironic reading of these otherwise seemingly-literal sentences, similar to how different Spanish syntactic constructions may do the same (Escandell-Vidal & Leonetti, 2014; Leonetti & Escandell-Vidal, this volume).

The syntax of the second question indicates that this carelessness is not a personality trait of Ko's, but a current state of confusion that is happening *to* him. In this way, the multifunctional use of irony as both hyperbolized rhetorical question and sarcasm acts to draw attention to the mistake, but overall reduces the condemnation on Ko himself. In this way, the use of irony provided a potential action for the addressee to take to help him save face and remedy the mistake. This perspective of "you made a mistake, but it's not your fault necessarily" is picked up by Ko, who remedies his mistake immediately by removing the piece and making a joke that he is going to save this piece for later. Ko's picking up the humor and reciprocating it indicates that the ironic criticism is actually perceived as affiliative. This is one example of many in our corpus that demonstrates how the use of irony may be multifunctional, even within the context of criticism, to ultimately adhere to cultural values, such as saving face and creating an affiliative atmosphere.

4.2 Echoic mention and pretense in Thai irony

In our corpus we found that the use of echoic mention and pretense created an affiliative atmosphere through jocularity to help speakers save face, such as from experiencing emotional embarrassment or shame. The following transcript exemplifies the use of echoic mention and pretense to *raksa na* and create an affiliative atmosphere. In this episode, the guest chef presents her specialty dish, *magrood loy gao*, which is a Thai dessert made of brined kaffir lime piths (white part under the zest) in simple syrup (it's very good, please trust us). As the guest chef introduces the dish, one of the co-hosts, Ko, talks about how this dish makes him miss his father, since this was his favorite dish when Ko was a child. In the first few minutes of this episode, he cries as he describes a memory of his father giving him money to run down to the street and buy him a dish of it since his father recently passed away.

As Ko describes his memories of his father, Khun Toy hugs him and says, "It's okay, child, it's okay" before the following interaction. In this interaction, Khun Toy pulls away from the hug and looks up, pretending that he is searching the sky when he says the following:

(2) The Memory of Ko's Father

    Khun Toy: โก๊ะ ถ้าลูกมองไปสูงนิดเดียว เดี๋ยวจะเห็น...
                  Ko, thaa luuk moong pai suung nit diaw diaw ja hen-
                  [Ko, if you look up just a little bit, you will see-]

    Ko: -มะกรูด!!!
           -magrood!
           [-Kaffir lime!]

    Khun Toy: บ้า! คุณเห็นพ่อ
                  baa! khun hen pho!
                  [Crazy! You see your dad!]

The expression of extreme emotions in public spaces puts one at risk of *sia na*, or losing face (Ukosakul, 2005), by making others uncomfortable while revealing an intimate moment about oneself. As Ko is openly crying in front of a guest and audience, this situation is one of high risk of losing face. Khun Toy implicitly recognizes that this is a moment where he can help Ko *raksa na* by helping him temper his expression of sadness. Khun Toy engages in pretense here, taking on the language and body reminiscent of a mother speaking down to their young child to comfort him. He also engages in pretense by pretending to look up at the stars where he implies that Ko will see his father in heaven. The use of pretense here is not specifically to criticize Ko, as is proposed by Clark & Gerrig (1984), but to help relate to his emotionality and comfort him publicly. In this way, Khun Toy is trying to *raksa nam cai* Ko, and help him save face with an initially non-ironic moment of pretense.

Ko recognizes this interaction as one where Khun Toy is giving him an out for his emotionality and a chance to save face. His crying has created a sad atmosphere where he has potentially embarrassed himself, his co-hosts, the audience, and most importantly, their guest. He recalibrates the energy of the interaction by cutting off Khun Toy, who is trying to say his father is up above by stating that he would see kaffir limes above him. Ko is also engaging in the pretense as he looks up and points as well, and maintains the believable reality that above him would be kaffir limes on a kaffir lime tree. Ko uses the combination of pretense and jocularity to create a humorous response as everyone laughs. This use of irony helps him *raska na* for himself and for the audience. This use of jocularity – stating something opposite to what was believed to be above them (i.e., the deceased father in heaven) for humorous purposes – evokes a sense of *sanuk* (Aoki, 2010) that alleviates tension and reaffirms social cohesion by eliciting laughter (Bacharowski, Smoski, & Owren, 2001).

Khun Toy's response of *baa!*, which is used as a criticism, is sarcastic as on the surface it literally means "crazy". But semantically, the use of *baa* indicates an acceptance of the absurdity in this situation and indicates something along the lines of "Yes, that makes sense, but you're crazy for thinking it." Additionally, the use of this sarcastic utterance in this context is softened by the continuation of the pretense that Ko's father is up there, not just the kaffir lime, creating both an ironic and humorous understanding of the overall situation. In this way, the conjoined use of pretense, sarcasm, and jocularity helps 1) Ko *raksa na* in a moment where his emotionality would cause him to lose face, 2) use humor to reaffirm a sense of *sanuk* within the social interaction and maintain social cohesion and, 3) softly criticize Ko for taking advantage of the vulnerable situation.

This episode also has a good example of how echoic mention is used to simultaneously maintain an affiliative atmosphere, express criticism, and help Ko accept the said criticism while saving face. After they have eaten *magrood loy gao* at the end of the episode, Khun Toy talks about how this dish has been on Channel 3 before, and the last time it was, Ko also cried. As Khun Toy is talking, Ko leans onto the table and begins looking a bit sad again. Another co-host then initiates the following interaction:

(3) A callback to Ko's tears

  Nawat: ไม่เป็นไร คราวหน้าไม่ต้องร้องแล้ว เพราะว่าพอเห็นมะกรูดปั๊บ ให้มองขึ้นไปข้างบนแล้วเราจะเจอ...
     mai pen rai kraaw naa mai tong rong laew prawah pho hen magrood pap hai moong khuen pai khang bon laew rao ja jue...
     [Don't worry. Next time you won't cry because when you see kaffir lime, just look up and you will see...]

  Ko: มะกรูด
    magrood
    [Kaffir lime]

Khun Toy: ไม่ใช่ พ่ออยู่บนสวรรค์!
mai chai pho yuu bon sawan!
[No, No! (you will see) your dad in the heaven!]

Nawat begins with an almost exact echo of the interaction at the start of this episode. He again is engaging in pretense, where he is not only enacting a motherly figure, but also Khun Toy mere moments ago attempting to comfort Ko. The use of pretense here helps bring back the echo of an earlier moment for the purpose of partially criticizing Ko for taking advantage of Khun Toy's earlier sympathy, as well as to remind the audience of Ko's funny and irreverent reaction. Ko repeats the same line here (that he sees kaffir limes above and not his dad) as a way to maintain the pretense, acknowledge the criticism aimed at him, and bring back a sense of *sanuk*, which otherwise was at risk of being lost as he was on the verge of crying again. Here, Ko uses echoic mention by directly quoting himself to reduce tension. However, in the use of the exact same line, he is also acknowledging the criticism of himself before (*baa* – that he's acceptably absurd) is accurate by reenacting the inappropriate response and acting *baa* again. Khun Toy also engages in this pretense once again with another chastisement, reinforcing the social acceptance of Ko's absurd behavior. In this case, the echoic mention is an acceptance of criticism through jocularity, where the interaction reinstates a sense of *sanuk* and he continues to save face and maintain social cohesion.

4.3 Sarcasm

Previous papers on sarcasm in Thai look at it from a framework where the comments serve only to criticize others (Pengpanich, 1998; Panphotong, 1996). However, taking a step back to examine sarcasm from a more culturally situated approach, we found that sarcasm is indeed used to criticize others but in a fashion that softens the blow of the critique. This form of sarcasm clearly communicates the criticism, but in a way that helps the recipients of the critique *raksa na*.

In this example, the guest chef has prepared a special form of Thai barbecue called *moo kra ta*, where diners cook their own meat on a family-style Thai hotplate (a cross between Korean barbecue and Chinese hotpot – also delicious, trust us). The chef tediously marinated a special type of pork, which they watched and talked about in earlier parts of the episode, and it is now time to cook the meat atop the hotplate. Ko, Nawat, and Oh have all begun vigorously cooking and eating the meat, commenting on how good it is. Khun Toy continues to speak with the guest chef on the other side and talks back and forth with the co-hosts, but has not had the chance to try any meat. After a few minutes of this, Khun Toy transitions from complimenting the chef into the following:

(4) Khun Toy's Love

  Khun Toy: แล้วผมก็รักสามคนนี้มากๆ เพราะว่าผมก็พูดไปสิ
       ไม่ได้มีใครคิดจะปิ้งให้ผมสักชิ้นหนึ่งเลย
       lao phom ko rak saam khon nii maak maak prowaa phom ko phuut pai si mai dai mii krai kit ja ping hai phom sak chin neung leuy
       [And I love these three men very much because while I was talking, there was no one that thought of cooking a piece of meat for me!]

       ขอบใจที่ลืม ขอบใจมาก
       khop cai tii leum khop cai maak
       [Thank you for forgetting me. Thank you very much.]

  Oh: อ้าว ลืมลืมลืมลืม
       ao lum lum lum lum
       [Oh! We forgot! We forgot!]

  Nawat: (takes a piece of meat he's cooking for himself, dips it in sauce, gives it to Khun Toy)

Khun Toy uses sarcasm here in the form of positive, kind words stated in an incredibly sincere way, both in terms of his syntax, diction, and prosody, to criticize the others' inattention to his needs. This use of sarcasm is very similar to how it is used in English, where positive words are used for the purpose of criticizing another person (e.g., "You're a fine friend" when they have done something not very friendly). Within the context of the interaction, his profession of love for these three comes about unexpectedly. This expression of positive affiliation towards them paired with the comment that no one even thought of him allows for a softening of the criticism. By using a syntactic structure that prioritizes his love, Khun Toy is indicating that they are all generally honorable and lovable people – they simply were inconsiderate in this moment. Their inconsiderateness negatively affects him as he still has not eaten any meat, but this structure indicates that this is not a static characteristic of theirs – they are still lovable people. Additionally, he uses *khop cai*, which is used to express the sincerest form of thanks, as a way to ironically comment that he is the victim and is grateful to them for hurting him. Using the emphatic form may favor ironic interpretation, which has also been found in Spanish (Leonetti & Escandell-Vidal, this volume). In this moment, the ultrapolite form is used to both emphasize a sarcastic reading while pragmatically functioning as face giving. Sarcasm, in this way, is toned down by the politeness with which he is expressing his criticism to help them *raksa na*. His expression of love and the ultrapolite forms in which he speaks helps them continue to maintain their honor and save face.

The contrast between the politeness, love, and expressed criticism lead the audience, guest, and even the co-hosts to burst out laughing as Oh apologizes. The indirect ways in which Khun Toy criticizes the others evoke humor, though he is not necessarily using jocularity in this instance. This serves to help maintain social cohesion even though he has been forgotten by them. His comment shows that he has been violated by being forgotten, but his use of politeness strategies and indirect communication styles (choice of diction, syntax) indicate that at the same time, the violation is benign. In this way, Khun Toy is also indicating a moment where *he* was about to *sia na*, or be embarrassed or dishonored by being forgotten even though he is the host of the show. However, he also marks this violation as benign through his use of the ultrapolite *khop cai* and expression of love, emphasizing that long-term, there is affiliation and no bad blood. This creates a general sense of humor through which their social cohesion is maintained, and provides the others an opportunity to save face. They do so by indicating that it was not meant to be a personal slight ("I forgot, I forgot!") and remedying the error by feeding him meat. Sarcasm here is used in a way to indirectly criticize the others, but still help everyone in the interaction maintain their honor and save face.

4.4 Hyperbole

A previous analysis of spontaneous communication between Thai speakers shows they prefer to use intensifiers and spontaneous expressions to show involvement in the interaction (Aoki, 2010). In our corpus, we found that hyperbole is not only used to show involvement, but to implicitly communicate whether one has saved, lost, or gained face within the context of the social interaction. Hyperbole may not just be a figurative language device in Thai, but a means by which we can potentially give face, *hai na*, or tear at/break face, *chik na/hak na*, in a polite way. The use of hyperbole can also lead to the experience of humor as the exaggeration of reality may denote a benign violation (e.g., "that's not literally true, but it makes sense"), and lead to maintained social affiliation.

An example within our corpus of when someone uses hyperbole to *chik/hak na*, or tear away at/break face by tearing someone down a bit, is when a guest chef prepared *tum pa*, her specialized form of *som tum* (papaya salad) that is based on a notoriously spicy Isan (Northern Thai) dish called *gang pa*. As they are about to eat the dish, Khun Toy mentions that the producer, Aoi, for the show tried it before and leads into saying the following:

(5) Hot, Hot Hate

> Khun Toy: ผมเกลียดมากเลยนะครับ ไม่ชอบคุณอ้อยเลยนะครับ เพราะว่าเขาให้ใส่ลูกพริก 30 เม็ด ไปบอกว่าให้ใส่พริก 30 เม็ด แล้วก็กินกันซี๊ดกันทั้งสตูเลยครับ
> *phom kliat maak luey na khrap mai choop khun Aoi leay na khrap prowaa khao hai sai luuk prik saam sip met laew ko kin kan siid kan thang satu laey krap*
> [I hate [our producer, Aoi] very much. Do you know? I don't like Khun Aoi because she had the chef put 30 chili peppers [in this dish]. Everyone in the studio ate it and experienced how extremely spicy it was.]

In this instance, Khun Toy is purposefully being confrontational by way of using hyperbole. Within Thai social interactions, people often try to *lop na*, or hide their face, to avoid conflicts that they anticipate will arise (Ukosakul, 2005) or prefer the use of indirect speech when making criticisms to avoid a rejection of their ideas (Komin, 1990). However, Khun Toy is purposefully risking losing face by expressing a very strong negative emotion in public (Ukosakul, 1999), *kliat*, or hate. The structure of his emotional phrasing *phom kliat maak* (I hate her a lot) and *mai choop khun Aoi* (I do not like her) parallels the direct confrontation towards Khun Aoi and exaggerates the negative emotionality of it. The hyperbolization of his emotions towards her acts as a moment in which he may *chik na Khun Aoi*, or tear away at her face and make her lose status by being the recipient of such strong emotions.

However, the rest of his explanation helps Khun Aoi *raksa na* and save face because the reason he hates her is so trivial – she wanted the food to be spicy. The contrast between the exaggerated sense of emotions and the triviality of the amount of peppers is palpable to Thai speakers as listeners recognize that his hatred has no grounds. This contrast leads to us understanding that his hatred – an emotional violation – was truly benign, and we experience a wave of humor. This humor helps us (and probably Khun Aoi) identify that he's a bit upset, but that it ultimately was not that big of a deal. Khun Toy's use of hyperbole to inflate his hatred put him in a position to tear away at Khun Aoi's face and create a sense of social tension. However, his reason for why deflated that tension and allowed for humor to arise, helping Khun Aoi *raksa na*, relieve tension, and maintain a sense of social affiliation even though he did tear her down a bit.

Hyperbole can also be used in Thai to *hai na*, or give face by honoring another person. This function of hyperbole speaks towards the desire to maintain affiliation and acceptance within a predominantly "affiliative society" (Wichiarajote, 1973). The creation of this affiliative atmosphere may take form through the use of humor, or using different forms of irony such as hyperbole to emphasize another's greatness. In the following example, Khun Toy uses hyperbole to *hai na* to the guest chef. The guest chef is talking through his montage of how he cooks fried fish. Fried fish is a staple food in Thailand and is typically pretty easy. However, this chef's fish is widely regarded as being the most delicious. As they watch the montage, Khun Toy makes the following comments as the guest chef's cook prepares the fish:

(6) And wait – there's more!

    Khun Toy: ลูกยี่หร่า เอง แล้วยังมีอีกนะ เม็ดผักชี เรายังมีอีกนะ ใบกระวาน แล้วยังมีอีกครับ น้ำพริกปาปริกา แล้วตามด้วยออริกาโน่ แล้วตามด้วยน้ำผึ้งแท้
luuk yiiraa eng laew yang mii eiik na met phakchii laew yang mii eiik na baikrawaan laew yang mii eiik krap nam prik paprika laew taam duay oregano laew taam duay naam phueng thae
[Nutmeg, there's still more! Coriander Seed, there's still more! Basil leaves, there's still more! Paprika, followed by oregano! And then pure honey!]

In this instance, Khun Toy is literally expressing that there is yet more, and more, and more ingredients to add to this fried fish. He is only verbally noting that there are a bunch of ingredients in this fish, perhaps in a way that can be described as exasperated. But implicitly, he expresses a sense of being impressed by the level of difficulty and expertise it takes to prepare a dish of this kind, even though fried fish is normally pretty commonplace in Thailand. Khun Toy uses the repeated expression of the phrase *yang mii eiik*, or "there's still more!" to hyperbolize the number of steps necessary to cook this top-tier fish. The use of irony here does not *chik na*, which detracts from one's sense of self or honor, or even *raksa na*, which keeps one's sense of self or honor stable. Instead, the use of hyperbole specifically *hai na*, or gives face to the guest chef as Khun Toy denotes being impressed with the process it takes to create such a dish. His exaggeration here does not just maintain social affiliation but enhances it as the hyperbole functions as an implicit compliment.

Hyperbole within our corpus has been shown to help us change the status of our face or others' within social interactions, whether that is in the positive direction as we use it to *hai na*, or give face, or *hak na*, or break face.

4.5 Multifunctional irony in Thai

The final example exemplifies the way irony in Thai may be more complicated than having a single function per turn. The same turn can serve multiple ironic functions within a single interaction for the specific purpose of creating criticism and softening the blow at the same time to again, save face and *raksa na*. In this example, the guest chef had been living in America for 25 years prior to moving back to Thailand and opening her restaurant. During her introductions, one of the co-hosts asks her in Thai where she lived. She responds in perfect Thai that she had been living in Huntington Beach, California. Immediately upon her response is the following interaction:

(7) Thais and their Thai

> Nawat: โอ๊ย! พูดภาษาไทยได้นี่ครับ เดี๋ยวนี้เด็กไทยไปอยู่มาแค่เทอมเดียว ไอคิดว่า เออ..เออ..
> *Oh! Phuut phasa Thai dai nii krap dek thai pai yuu maa khae thuem diaw "ai kit wa Hmm... Hmm"*
> [Oh! You actually speak Thai. Nowadays, young Thai [students] go abroad for one semester and (Nawat pretends he can't speak Thai anymore) "I think... Hmm... Hmm (stuttering in English)"]

Nawat's initial shock at the guest chef's fluent Thai and first sentence comes off as sarcasm where he is indirectly criticizing her for the 25 years she has spent in America. It is an example of irony where the utterance does not indicate opposition, yet is ironic, which is in line with the proposals set forth by the Relevance Theoretic account of irony. His statement is literally neutral, but also asserts an implicit accusation of her former ex-patriotism from Thailand as he expected that she had completely forgotten the language. One feature that makes this statement particularly sarcastic is that he is marveling at her ability to speak Thai while *using* Thai for her to understand and interpret. Here, his sarcasm is not only directed towards her, but indirectly aimed towards other members of Thai society who have moved to America for a long time and have lost their language. The use of irony here is not only interpersonal commentary, but social as well.

However, the use of such a direct and potentially accusatory statement may put both him and the guest speaker at risk of losing face as Nawat was potentially too direct, and she was the object of the sentiment. Because of this, he follows up the sarcastic utterance with a rhetorical question about Thai students who go to America for a term (e.g., a semester or quarter) and lose their ability to speak Thai altogether. He engages in pretense as he acts out what one of these students might look like trying to speak Thai after being gone for 3–4 months, which is perceived as jocularity. The use of the rhetorical question is to pull the comment's directness away from the guest chef and towards criticizing the more generalized Thai society's students. The pretense then acts to humorously seal in this criticism on the subject of the students, specifically, and *not* on the guest chef. The immediacy of his transition into pretense creates a direct comparison between the pretend student who cannot speak Thai at all with the guest chef as a competent speaker of Thai who had just proven herself competent with the language. In this way, Nawat transitions the critique away from the guest chef onto the students through pretense and jocularity. His use of "You actually speak Thai" acts as a form of sarcasm at the same time that it is an understated compliment full of awe.

This use of multifunctional irony – a combination of pretense, rhetorical question, sarcasm, and jocularity in the same utterance, softens the effect of the criticizing comment by changing it into a compliment, and leaves them all laughing and feeling bonded over the fact that they all, in fact, can speak Thai better than the pretend students. His transition into a rhetorical question, pretense, and using the initial utterance as an understated compliment saves his face, *raksa na*, by softening a direct criticism, as well as gives face, *hai na*, to the guest chef by complimenting her Thai as better than Thai national students. This interaction is perceived overall to reinforce a sense of *sanuk* through how funny his immediate impression was, save his and the guest chef's face, and maintain social affiliation.

5 Discussion

Although the study of ironic mechanisms has largely stemmed from research on English, it is important to culturally situate the study of irony cross-linguistically. Doing so can help identify the universality of the different proposed mechanisms for irony while recognizing how irony functions differently within larger cultural contexts. Speaking or acting directly by stating one's explicit beliefs to another person can be considered inappropriate within most Thai social interactions, contrary to English interacts where directness is often valued. In Thai, indirect forms of speech allow for a politer way to convey one's stances to addressees (Srinarawat, 2005), and may include forms of figurative language such as irony, humor, metaphor, and metonymy. Within the context of saving face in Thai social interactions, it is possible that these forms of figurative language may be utilized when expressing highly emotional content so as to not be misunderstood as confrontational. As stated before, figurative language may rely on embodied simulation processes and be an effective way of communicating abstract concepts such as emotionality as our comprehension of metaphors (Gibbs, Lima, & Francozo, 2004; Gibbs, Gould, & Andric, 2006), fictive motion (Richardson & Matlock, 2007), humor (Samermit & Gibbs, 2016), and irony (Gibbs & Samermit, 2017; Colston, in press). This may allow us to understand figurative language as a culturally-situated framework by which we make meaning together, as in the expression of emotions (Kövecses, 2009).

The conceptual structure of humor and irony as benign bodily violations presents itself through systematic linguistic metaphors that map the relationship between our bodies and humor/irony as a FORCE that acts on them (Samermit & Gibbs, 2016; Gibbs & Samermit, 2017). Humor and irony evoke felt senses of bodily movement, similar to the experience of emotions (Kovesces, 2000) that act as an action tendency for us to move towards people we affiliate with and away from those we do not agree with (Samermit & Gibbs, 2016). The use of and experience of irony can be understood as a metaphorical force on our body that softens a violating blow on your psychological well-being or self-worth, making it more benign. The use of irony requires the recognition of shared implicit beliefs and attitudes, such as cultural values, and the communication of differing beliefs in a more benign way that results in some affective response. However, there have been few studies examining humor and irony in Thai, which invites further examination before concretely identifying the differences in their frequency of use and functions.

Previous studies have used television shows to glean estimates of the frequency and function of irony use (Dews, Winner, Nicolaides, & Hunt, 1995) and impoliteness (Culpeper, 2005) to help orient theories of irony in English. This corpus examined the use of irony in Thai on a cooking talk show to help explore different possible functions of irony in Thai. The examples provided here demonstrate how irony within a Thai context may revolve around the concept of saving face, or *raksa na*, within social interactions by making comments more indirect as a form of politeness. We also found that the use of irony in Thai is often to create a sense of jocularity or humor as a way to save face by reducing tension and maintaining social cohesion. While *Krua Khun Toy* was chosen for its unscripted interactions, the constraints of being TV hosts of a popular cooking show may have caused the speakers to use more figurative language like irony than occurs in spontaneous communication. Because of this, it is important for studies of Thai irony to extend beyond the realm of corpus analyses and to examine spontaneous communication across interlocutors, and we look forward to that novel body of research.

These findings on irony and face saving may be limited by the analysis of only the cooking talk show genre, which is meant to generally entertain and keep a positive attitude. Cooking talk shows as a genre, both in English and Thai, constrain its speakers to maintain a certain level of politeness and positivity. Severe face attacks are generally taboo as it would destroy the entertainment value and appeal of the talk show. However, cooking competition TV shows, like the American version of *Hell's Kitchen* (or most American versions of Gordon Ramsay's shows), raise their entertainment value by lowering the bar on politeness and increasing face attacks. Because of the politeness constraints on the cooking talk show genre, future research should compare the use of ironic forms across languages and TV genres (e.g., American English, British English, and Thai cooking talk shows and cooking competition shows, just as one example) to broaden an understanding of their functionality.

Thai irony within our corpus does not look exactly the same as irony has been proposed in English or in other papers examining Thai sarcasm, such as Pengpanich (1998). The experience of irony may act as a relational device that people use to relate to ambiguous situations as benign bodily violations in both English and Thai. Irony may be used more as a tool to identify some benign violation in the world, comment on it, and then emotionally detach from the oddity so as to not spend much more energy on it. In English, irony is often (but not always) emotionally unidirectional. It is a message that a speaker sends onto a listener to be affected by, however they may interpret it, and the speaker is allowed some sort of emotional detachment or dissociation from the topic at hand, as is indicated in the echoic mention and pretense theories (Wilson & Sperber, 2012; Yus, 2016; Clark & Gerrig, 1984). In English, the use of irony is sometimes about conveying the emotion or sentiment at hand onto a listener, without many broader implications or social impact for the speaker besides distancing themselves. The speaker may be put at risk of being seen as overly critical or sarcastic, but the use of irony does not put them at the same level of social risk as a Thai speaker would be in. Irony is a way for English speakers to engage with, brush off, and move on from some sort of benign violation that has just occurred.

However, irony in Thai feels like a more overt use of empathy and social cohesion through an indirect linguistic mechanism. Even though Thai speakers are using indirect speech, they are doing so to share *nam cai*, metaphorically water from the heart, by extending affiliation through what feels like a sincere expression of emotion through politeness strategies (e.g., not being too emotionally expressive, not being too direct). If the face in Thai represents the ego or self, then *cai*, or heart, metonymically stands in for our source of emotions and perhaps our cognition. This is similar to how the heart is used and understood in Chinese through the conceptual metaphor of THE HEART IS THE RULER OF THE BODY (Yu, 2008b), where it governs our affect, thoughts, and actions. Thai speakers avoid confronting people as much as possible because being direct is considered highly inappropriate in Thai culture, and a stain on the speaker. While it is also considered inappropriate at times in English-speaking cultures, directness is still accepted in private social interactions (e.g., a one-on-one conversation expressing how hurt/insulted one might be) and as a cultural value of individualism. However, in Thai culture, being direct in either private or public can cause a person to *sia na* and lose face. The speakers, themselves, are put at a higher risk of losing face than English speakers, even in the expression of their own emotions. Because of this, the use of irony can be considered emotionally bidirectional in Thai – the indirect message a speaker sends is not one they can dissociate from, even if they are putting it onto the listener. The way that indirect message is interpreted still as social implications for the speaker as well, and they cannot simply distance themselves from the topic at hand.

Thai people use irony because they have a sincere and implicit concern not only about themselves losing face, but about their interlocutor losing face as well. There is a social contract that stipulates a Thai speaker will help their interlocutor maintain face as much as their own and vice versa, *raksa nam cai kan*, which Ukosakul (2005) refers to as saving face. However, a more direct translation would be "taking care of the water of our hearts together", implying a greater shared social component to saving face than is originally translated. The *kan* is "together" – a key component in the use of Thai irony that is missing in English.

Because of this, when Thai speakers use sarcasm and other forms of irony, they are careful to *raksa na* and save face by avoiding using it as a direct confrontation to the listener as a way for them to take care of each other. Instead, they often use empathy and humor to soften the confrontation and to express that the speakers, too, were making themselves emotionally vulnerable in this expression. By expressing their emotions at all, the speaker puts themselves at risk of losing face, but they care enough about the other person to say something while making sure to *raksa na* to maintain social cohesion and uphold the social contract. Irony in Thai may be about shared emotional experience where both the speaker and the listener fully share in the mutual understanding (*kao cai kan* or metaphorically "entering our hearts") that it is in the interest of everyone to recognize this benign violation. However, should the irony go too far and be too direct or emotional, for example, then it is no longer in the interest of all the interlocutors involved and becomes a direct criticism, which is no longer interpreted as ironic. In a way, Thai irony relies heavily on a sense of vulnerability and empathy, which may not necessarily be the case in its use in English.

Finally, we must caveat our claims by acknowledging that the use of humor and irony in English can also serve multiple functions like Thai irony, where the ironic statement works bidirectionally to express solidarity between a speaker and listener. Leech (1983) proposed the *banter principle*, where a speaker may use sarcasm more as *banter* to show solidarity with a listener. Sarcasm or banter in this sense is when someone states something impolite or offensive, but at the same time is obviously untrue. This may help a listener save face by expressing solidarity, where the speaker shares that belief with them. Beyond banter, Dynel (2008) differentiates between *putdown humor*, which delineates an "us" versus "them" attitude through disparagement, and *teasing*, which may appear critical or harsh, but lacks true aggression. Teasing, in her view, also acts as a way to build cohesion between speakers through potentially humorous or sarcastic interactions. This view of sarcasm as banter and teasing moves beyond the view of irony that states it must involve an attitude of scorn or detachment (Wilson, 2017; Wilson & Sperber, 2012; Yus, 2016; Clark & Gerrig, 1984), and acts as a more analogous comparison to the multifunctional Thai use of irony. Indeed, Leech (2005) proposes that there may not be a true, categorical East-West divide in politeness overall, and that it may be more of a question of scale. Irony in English, like Thai, may already be multifunctional and used for social cohesion, and we invite further examination of these forms to identify functional overlaps with non-Western languages like Thai.

However, we hypothesize that if English and Thai speakers were asked to assess Thai ironic utterances, there may be some subtle differences in their interpretation. Specifically, Thai speakers will have the "key" to these ironic utterances by understanding that the irony is socially situated within a broader, social motivation of saving face. Specifically, if an English monolingual speaker and a Thai speaker is presented with a sarcastic exchange and asked, "Why did the speaker say that?", the Thai participant may recognize that the exchange has the underlying motivation to *raksa na*, where the speaker is trying to help the recipient save face. They may also perceive the message as bidirectional, where they can see that the speaker is putting themselves at social risk of being rude by making an ironic utterance. However, English speakers may interpret it as the speaker purposefully being critical or taking down the listener, with more of an emphasis on the social effect on the listener than speaker. We hypothesize they may not recognize any group-level social motivation to the statement, or any type of social risk to the speaker. Rather, the sarcastic utterance may be perceived as purely disparaging to the listener. Thai speakers may also perceive the sarcastic utterance to be funnier than English speakers, since they may recognize the use of irony as having that underlying social function of maintaining an air of *sanuk* or jocularity and jest for the sake of saving face. On the other hand, English speakers may perceive the same sarcastic utterances to be more critical. Finally, we hypothesize that there are some ironic statements that English speakers will recognize as literal while Thai speakers may recognize them as ironic.

Some of the instances presented here may not be interpreted as irony by non-Thai speakers who do not fully grasp the sociality present in our language. Some instances of opposition may be hard to identify or translate directly into English since many single words in Thai have behind them a multitude of social meaning. For example, the translation of both *baa* and *prasaat* is "crazy", but *baa* is perceived as a more socially acceptable absurdity/craziness while *prasaat* indicates someone seriously mentally ill and may be a threat. In a similar fashion, *chuy* directly translates into "incompetent" or "careless", but is packed with the social meaning of impeding others from their goals or embarrassing someone and causing them to lose face. Because of the nuances within the Thai language – from the choice of syntax, diction, and the metaphors used to talk about emotionality – it is imperative that Thai speakers be the ones to examine figurative language such as irony for ourselves. Much like other papers on cross-linguistic irony, it is our hope that this paper will be the first of many that uncovers the nuances of Thai irony and humor with culturally appropriate analyses and integration with theories from cognitive linguistics.

References

Anastasia, Anne, Cohen, Nadia, & Spatz, Dorothy. 1948. A study of fear and anger in college students through the controlled diary method. *Genetic Psychology*, 73, 243–249.

Aoki, Ataya. 2010. Rapport management in Thai and Japanese social talk during group discussions. *Pragmatics. Quarterly Publication of the International Pragmatics Association (IPrA)*, 20(3), 289–313.

Bachorowski, Jo-Anne, Smoski, Moria J., & Owren, Michael J. 2001. The acoustic features of laughter. *Journal of the Acoustical Society of America*, 110, 1581–1597.

Boylan, James, & Katz, Albert N. 2013. Ironic expression can simultaneously enhance and dilute perception of criticism. *Discourse Processes*, 50(3), 187–209.

Brown, Penelope, & Levinson, Stephen C. 1978. *Politeness: Some universals in language usage*. Cambridge, England: Cambridge University Press.

Bryant, Gregory A. 2010. Prosodic contrasts in ironic speech. *Discourse Processes*, 47, 545–566.

Bryant, Gregory A. & Fox Tree, Jean E. 2005. Is there an ironic tone of voice? *Language and Speech*, 48, 257–277.

Colston, Herbert L. 1997. Salting a wound or sugaring a pill: The pragmatic functions of ironic criticism. *Discourse Processes*, 23(1), 25–45.

Colston, Herbert L. in press. Irony as indirectness cross-linguistically: On the scope of generic mechanisms.

Clark, Herbert H. & Gerrig, Richard J. 1984. On the pretense theory of irony. *Journal of Experimental Psychology: General*, 113, 121–126.

Culpeper, Jonathan. 2005. Impoliteness and entertainment in the television quiz show: The Weakest Link. Journal of Politeness Research. *Language, Behaviour, Culture*, 1(1), 35–72.

Dews, Shelly, Kaplan, Joan, & Winner, Ellen. 1995. Why not say it directly? The social functions of irony. *Discourse Processes*, 19(3), 347–367.

Dews, Shelly, & Winner, Ellen. 1995. Muting the meaning: A social function of irony. *Metaphor and Symbolic Activity*, 10, 3–19.

Dews, Shelly, Winner, Ellen, Nicolaides, Natasha, & Hunt, Malia. 1995. Forms and functions of verbal irony found in children's and adults' television shows. American Psychological Association, New York.

Dynel, Marta. 2008. No aggression, only teasing: The pragmatics of teasing and banter. *Lodz papers in pragmatics*, 4(2), 241–261.

Escandell-Vidal, Victoria, & Leonetti, Manuel. 2014. Fronting and irony in Spanish. In Andreas Dufter & Álvaro Octavio de Toledo (Eds.). *Left sentence peripheries in Spanish: Diachronic, variationist and comparative perspectives* (pp. 309–342), Amsterdam: John Benjamins.

Flamson, Thomas J., & Barrett, H. Clark. 2008. The encryption theory of humor: A knowledge-based mechanism of honest signaling. *Journal of Evolutionary Psychology*, 6(4), 261–281.

Flamson, Thomas J., & Bryant, Gregory A. 2013. Signals of humor. *Developments in Linguistic Humour Theory*, 1, 49–74.

Gibbs, Raymond W. 1994. *The poetics of mind: Figurative thought, language, and understanding*. New York: Cambridge University Press.

Gibbs, Raymond W. 2000. Irony in talk among friends. *Metaphor and Symbol*, 15, 5–27.

Gibbs, Raymond W. 2006. Metaphor interpretation as embodied simulation. *Mind & Language*, 21(3), 434–458.

Gibbs, Raymond W. 2007. Why irony sometimes comes to mind: Paradoxical effects of thought suppression. *Pragmatics & Cognition*, 15, 229–251.

Gibbs, Raymond W. 2012. Are ironic acts deliberate? *Journal of Pragmatics*, 44(1), 104–115.

Gibbs, Raymond W., Gould, Jessica J., & Andric, Michael. 2006. Imagining metaphorical actions: Embodied simulations make the impossible plausible. *Imagination, Cognition and Personality*, 25(3), 221–238.

Gibbs, Raymond W., Lima, Paula Lenz Costa, & Francozo, Edson. 2004. Metaphor is grounded in embodied experience. *Journal of Pragmatics*, 36(7), 1189–1210.

Gibbs, Raymond W., & Samermit, Patrawat. 2017. How does irony arise in experience? In Angeliki Athanasiadou & Herbert L. Colston (Eds.), *Irony in language use and communication* (pp. 43–60). Amsterdam, The Netherlands: John Benjamins.

Haverkate, Henk. 1990. A speech act analysis of irony. *Journal of Pragmatics*, 14(1), 77–109.

Jaroenkiatboworn, Kanjana. 2005. *A Discourse Analyses of Joke in Thai*. Bangkok, Thailand: Chulalongkorn University doctoral dissertation.

Kaufer, David S. 1981. Understanding ironic communication. *Journal of Pragmatics*, 5, 495–510.

Komin, Suntaree. 1990. *Psychology of the Thai people: Values and Behavioral Patterns*. Bangkok: NIDA.

Kotthoff, Helga. 2003. Responding to irony in different contexts: On cognition in conversation. *Journal of Pragmatics*, 35(9), 1387–1411.

Kövecses, Zoltán. 2009. Metaphor, culture, and discourse: The pressure of coherence. In Jörg Zinken & Andreas Musolff (Eds.), *Metaphor in discourse* (pp. 11–24). Amsterdam, the Netherlands: John Benjamins.

Leech, Geoffrey N. 1983. *Principles of Pragmatics.* London: Longman.

Leech, Geoffrey N. 2005. Politeness: is there an East-West divide. *Journal of Foreign Languages*, 6(3), 1–30.

Leggitt, John S., & Gibbs, Raymond W. 2000. Emotional reactions to verbal irony. *Discourse Processes*, 29, 1–24.

McElreath, Richard, Boyd, Robert, & Richerson, Peter J. 2003. Shared norms and the evolution of ethnic markers. *Current Anthropology*, 44(1), 122–130.

McGraw, A. Peter, & Warren, Caleb. 2010. Benign violations make immoral behavior funny. *Psychological Science*, 21(8), 1141–1149.

McGraw, A. Peter, & Warner, Joel. 2014, *The humor code: A global search for what makes things funny.*, New York: Simon & Schuster.

Okamoto, Shinichiro. 2002. Politeness and the perception of irony: Honorifics in Japanese. *Metaphor and Symbol*, 17(2), 119–139.

Panpothong, Natthaporn. 1996. A pragmatic study of verbal irony in Thai. Honolulu, Hawaii: University of Hawaii at Manoa doctoral dissertation.

Pengpanich, Achara. 1998. A pragmatic look at sarcasm in Thai. In *Papers from the Fourth Annual Meeting of the Southeast Asian Linguistics Society,* (pp. 241–250).

Richardson, Daniel, & Matlock, Teenie. 2007. The integration of figurative language and static depictions: An eye-movement study of fictive motion. *Cognition,* 102, 129–138.

Samermit, Patrawat, & Gibbs, Raymond W. 2016. Humor, the body, and cognitive linguistics. *Cognitive Linguistic Studies*, 2, 32–49.

Sperber, Dan, & Wilson, Deirdre. 1995. *Relevance: Communication and Cognition (2nd edition).* Blackwell, Oxford.

Srinarawat, Deeyu. 2005. Indirectness as a politeness strategy of Thai speakers. In Robin Tolmach Lakoff & Sachiko Ide (Eds.), *Broadening the horizon of linguistic politeness* (pp. 175–193). Amsterdam, The Netherlands: John Benjamins.

Toplak, Maggie, & Katz, Albert N. 2000. On the uses of sarcastic irony. *Journal of Pragmatics*, 32, 1467–88.

Ukosakul, Chaiyun. 1994. A Study of the Patterns of Detachment in Interpersonal Relationships in a Local Thai Church. Deerfield, Illinois: Trinity International University (formerly TEDS) doctoral dissertation.

Ukosakul, Margaret. 1999. Conceptual Metaphors Motivating the Use of Thai 'Face'. Chiang Mai, Thailand: Payap University, master's dissertation.

Ukosakul, Margaret. 2005. The significance of 'face' and politeness in social interaction as revealed through Thai 'face' idioms. In Robin Tolmach Lakoff & Sachiko Ide (Eds.), *Broadening the horizon of linguistic politeness* (pp. 117–125). Amsterdam, The Netherlands: John Benjamins.

Wichiarajote, Weerayut. 1973. *The Theory of Affiliative Society.* Bangkok: College of Education, Prasanmitr.

Wilson, Deirdre. 2017. Irony, hyperbole, jokes and banter. In *Formal Models in the Study of Language* (pp. 201–219). Springer: Cham.

Wilson, Deirdre, & Sperber, Dan. 2012. Explaining irony. In Dirdre Wilson and Dan Sperber (Eds.) *Meaning and Relevance* (pp. 123–145). Cambridge University Press: Cambridge.

Yao, Jun, Song, Jie, & Singh, Michael. 2013. The ironical Chinese *bei*-construction and its accessibility to English speakers. *Journal of Pragmatics,* 55, 195–209.

Yu, Ning. 2001. What does our face mean to us? *Pragmatics and Cognition,* 9, 1–36.

Yu, Ning. 2008. Metaphor from body and culture. *The Cambridge handbook of metaphor and thought,* 247–261.

Yu, Ning. 2008b. The Chinese heart as the central faculty of cognition. *Culture, body, and language: Conceptualizations of internal body organs across cultures and languages,* 7, 131.

Yus, Francisco. 2016. Propositional attitude, affective attitude and irony comprehension. *Pragmatics & Cognition,* 23(1), 92–116.

Andreas Musolff and Sing Tsun Derek Wong

England is an appendix; Corrupt officials are like hairs on a nation's arm: Sarcasm, irony and self-irony in figurative political discourse

Abstract: In political discourse, metaphor production/use can serve to achieve irony and sarcasm, e.g. ridiculing (*Brexit: the kind of divorce that involves the police*), (apparent) self-effacement (*I am the toenail of the body politic*), or devastating critique (*the heart of Europe is rotten*). Can such sarcastic or ironical effects also be observed in responses to metaphor interpretation tasks? This paper looks at comprehension responses for the metaphor NATION-AS-BODY that include critical, ironical or sarcastic comments on the perceived 'health' or 'character traits' of the nation in question (e.g. *England is a body with feet designed for queuing; My nation have [sic] a mad mind*). We analyse such metaphor interpretations by speakers from English-L1 and Mandarin- or Cantonese-L1 backgrounds and highlight contrasting usage that calls for further investigation.

Keywords: Body politic, comprehension, discourse, irony, metaphor scenario, nation, person, sarcasm

1 Introduction

When asked to describe their nation in terms of a body,[1] some students in British university classes gave responses such as the following:

---

[1] The examples presented here are drawn from a corpus of questionnaire responses, which were collected 2011–2017 in three British universities (Aston University, Birmingham University, University of East Anglia). Special thanks go to the colleagues who helped to collect them: Jeannette Littlemore, Stefan Manz, Giulio Pagani, and Gabrina Pounds. The main task to be completed was to "apply the NATION-AS-BODY metaphor to [one's] home nation". In addition, social indicator information (first language, nationality, sex and age) was elicited which is largely omitted here (for details see Musolff 2016, 2017b).

Acknowledgements: Research for this paper has been supported by the Marie Curie Fellowship Programme of the European Union and the Senior Fellowship Programme of the Freiburg Institute for Advanced Studies (FRIAS). For helpful advice and suggestions on the draft we are grateful to the editors, Herbert L. Colston and Angeliki Athanasiadou.

Andreas Musolff, University of East Anglia
Sing Tsun Derek Wong, University of Oxford

https://doi.org/10.1515/9783110652246-008

(1) England is like an *appendix*, not very significant anymore but can still cause trouble and make you realise its there if it wants to.

(2) The *guts* of the country remain from when we had an empire.

(3) Don't talk about Oxford, *that is the fungal nail infection,* which we haven't got round to treating yet.[2]

This type of answer represents a minority; most of the responses follow the pattern of the following two examples:

(4) The *head of the body* represents the Queen of England, as she is in charge of the whole country and she is royalty. The features of the *head (eyes, nose, mouth and ears)* represent the different official people, such as politicians, the Prime Minister, the Government.

(5) Birmingham, right in the centre of the country, could be said to act as the *'heart', controlling the flow of the 'blood' through the main arteries,* including the M6 and M40 motorways [...].

Examples (4) and (5) compare Britain to a human body in subtly different ways: the former constructs the nation as an institutional/functional hierarchy starting from the 'top' political level, i.e. the Queen, as the *head* (which corresponds to the lexicalised metaphor of the *head of state*); the latter describes the nation as a "geobody" (Callahan 2009), i.e. it views the whole national territory as a human body and allocates landmarks to body parts that are associated analogically with socio-economic functions. These types of responses are generally descriptive and imply a neutral or positive evaluation of the "home nation"; occasionally, however, they can take on a humorous aspect as in the following example, which plays on national stereotypes about the British:

(6) The *heart* of Britain is essentially tea, with queues making up the *limbs*.

By contrast, the first three examples, though arguably also including humorous aspects, provide a distinctly negative evaluation, using as they do 'troublesome', 'lowly' and/or disgusting body parts and bodily conditions (*appendix,*

---

[2] These and further examples of questionnaire responses have been left in their original form, including spelling and grammatical mistakes; however, italics have been added to highlight words or passages that are analysed in detail.

guts, nail infection) to criticise a particular place in Britain or political/historical aspects of English nationality. Whilst the critical stance of these responses may be spelt out in explicit explanations such as (1), *"not very significant anymore but can still cause trouble"*, it has to be inferred from the choice of specific BODY source elements that imply a negative evaluation of the political target referent in question.

This inferential relation between BODY source reference and critical stance, which can turn the response into a more or less sarcastic utterance, as in (1) – (3), is the focus of our analysis. First, we will discuss how irony and sarcasm function in figurative political discourse in general and then go on to metaphor interpretation examples such as the above quoted ones from English-L1 students. Lastly we compare them with the responses by Chinese informants to the same task, which seem to show a different emphasis in the type of sarcastic metaphor use.

2 Political irony and sarcasm

Political discourse is replete with ironical and sarcastic utterances, e.g. as regards the 'front-stage' performances of political debate in parliamentary debates, election or referendum campaigns and interviews, but also in its many 'mediatized' incarnations of being reported and interpreted by journalists and other commentators, including internet users (Dedaić 2005; Gruber 2015; Ilie 2001, 2018: 318–319; Livnat & Hacohen 2013; Partington & Taylor 2018: 190–194; Sivenkova 2015). Like satire, irony and sarcasm often target a perceived discrepancy between a highly confident evaluative assertion and its contradiction by circumstances as they are known to the speakers and hearers (Abrams 1981: 167–170; Baym 2005: 263–270, Gray, Jones & Thompson 2009: 3–4; Zaltzman 2017). This 'contradictory' relationship inherent in irony and sarcasm is viewed in the relevance-theoretical account as "echoic" because the respective utterances implicitly refer to a contrasting proposition (Wilson 2006: 1722–1724); the competing *pretense*-theoretical account (Clark & Gerrig 1984; Currie 2006; Kumon-Nakamura, Glucksberg & Brown 1995), which bases itself on classic and neo-Gricean frameworks, holds that the ironical or sarcastic speaker *pretends* to speak as if he or she were another person who makes an utterance that contradicts common ground knowledge and exposes a failed expectation. Despite their differences, both accounts share the basic assumption that the speaker *implicitly dissociates* him- or herself from the content of a 'precedent utterance', whether echoed or pretended (Colston 2017: 30–36; Willison 2017: 65–77).

A prototypical example was supplied in December 2017 by an article in the left-leaning British newspaper, *The Guardian*, which commented on a defeat of the conservative-led government in a parliamentary vote on the United Kingdom's withdrawal ("Brexit") from the European Union (EU), which was inflicted by Conservative Members of Parliament (referred to as "Brexit rebels") who voted together with the opposition:

(7) Most of the Brexit rebels are lawyers. *Maybe experts are useful after all.* [...] Sovereignty is complicated [...]. It does nobody any favours to pretend the answers are easy. *Experts, it turns out, do understand a thing or two. And experts were among those who stepped up to a challenge last night to give parliament back some voice.* (Jolly 2017)

Read in isolation, the praise of the "experts" as being "useful after all" and "knowing a thing or two" about sovereignty may seem baffling because experts' competence (at least on issues that fall into their field of expertise) is normally not newsworthy or contentious. After all, why shouldn't Members of Parliament who are lawyers be trusted as "experts", i.e. as competent to decide complicated issues such as a country's sovereignty in relation to other nation states?

Example (7)'s seemingly pointless praise of experts only becomes "relevant" (Sperber & Wilson 1995) within the discourse-historical context of the British debate on "Brexit", as it has unfolded since 2015. In the run-up to the 2016 Brexit referendum, the conservative politician Michael Gove, leader of the "Vote Leave" campaign that advocated Britain's withdrawal from the EU, had famously dismissed "experts" in an interview on *Sky News*, as reported by another (conservative- and pro-Brexit-leaning) newspaper, *The Daily Telegraph*, at the time:

(8) The political editor of Sky News [= journalist Faisal Islam] began by challenging Mr Gove to name a single economic authority who backed Brexit. "I'm glad those organisations are not on my side!" retorted Mr Gove, with peculiar breeziness. *"I think people in this country have had enough of experts!"* he insisted, a minute later. (Deacon 2016).

Two paragraphs later, the *Telegraph* reporter highlighted a further dismissal of "experts" in the same *Sky News* interview when Gove was challenged to justify Vote Leave's claim that Britain sent "£350m a week" to the EU:

(9) *With extraordinary chutzpah*, Mr Gove said the figure was actually more than £350m. But the Treasury select committee and the UK Statistics Authority

have ruled it untrue, spluttered Mr Islam disbelievingly. Would he allow this figure to be checked out by independent auditors? No? Why not? *Ah, but Mr Islam, those people are mere experts.* (Deacon 2016).

The *Daily Telegraph* journalist seems to be at least partly fascinated by Gove's audacity to rubbish "expert" opinion, as his qualification of Gove's behaviour as an example of "extraordinary chutzpah" shows. Unlike Gove's statement cited in example (8), which dismisses experts in general, example (9) identifies the experts in question as the (usually highly regarded) official bodies of the "Treasury select committee" and "UK Statistics Authority" as well as "independent auditors". Still, in line with his general verdict, they are all disqualified by Gove as "mere experts" who do not match the competence of the "people in this country".

Gove's dismissal of the experts in the Sky News interview encountered massive criticism for being imprudent, offensive and populist.[3] The author of the 2017 *Guardian* article, from which example (7) was taken, could thus expect that her readers had retained an 'echo' of Gove's 2016 statement in their discourse-historical memory, which provided the platform for its ironical, implicitly dissociating metarepresentation (Wilson & Sperber 1992, 2012) even a year later. In order to understand the irony in (7) as cognitively and communicatively relevant, readers must notice that the statement in its literal version is redundant or pointless, and they must also be at least vaguely aware of the fact that a pro-Brexit politician in the past has questioned "expert" competence on Brexit-related issues. Only in this context can (7) be read as a case of irony, i.e. can it be viewed as "ironical" that Gove's 2016 criticism of experts was now, in 2017, being proven wrong.

For readers of (7) who might not be immediately aware of the implicature (that Gove's "expert"-bashing was wrong), the *Guardian* author helpfully spelled it out that the (legal) "experts" among the MPs had now 'done the right thing' (from her viewpoint), i.e. had defended parliament's sovereignty by voting against the government, precisely because of their legal knowledge or "expertise". The parenthetical clause, "it turns out", in the journalist's praise of the experts may even be viewed as crossing the borderline between irony and sarcasm, because it pretended, against her and the readers' shared knowledge, that the proposition "experts know a thing or two" might come as a surprise. She thus highlighted the contradiction between the preceding speaker's (Gove) position and the common-

---

[3] See e.g. Behr 2016; Henley 2016, *The Economist* 2016a, b; Wright 2016. For Gove's later attempt to relativise the impact, see D'Ancona 2017: 35–36.

place truism that experts "know a thing or two", so that Gove appeared as ridiculously incompetent and out of sync with common sense. This contrast arguably weakened the ironical implicitness and introduced instead an explicitly disdainful, i.e. sarcastic, face attack.

In the following, related example, such an *explicit* disdain of the current speaker, another *Guardian*-commentator, for the expert-bashers is even more obvious:

(10) The Outers had a success during the referendum in persuading many voters to ignore the "so-called" experts on the other side [...] You may recall that some of *those much-derided experts* did predict that Brexit would trigger a fall in the value of the pound [...] *Now some of the consequences of Brexit are beginning to knock on the door. The loudest knock – more of an almighty crash, actually – is the tumble in the value of the pound*. (Rawnsley 2016b)

Here, the journalist specifically reminded his readers ("Recall....") of the gist of the anti-expert warning of pro-Brexit politicians ("Outers") and explicitly contrasted it with what he saw as its factual disproval, i.e. the vindication of the experts' predictions. His stance towards the warning was as critical as his colleague's in (7), but instead of relying on an implicit ironical inference he foregrounded the discrepancy as being a demonstrable fact and thus, its conclusion as a certainty; hence, outright sarcastic.

The "expert" examples show that both irony and sarcasm in political discourse can be realised by a speaker/writer referring to a 'precedent utterance' that he or she assumes to be still alive in her audience's memory, so that mentioning it can be contrasted with a statement about a contrary state of affairs pertaining, which exposes its falsity and/or absurdity. The readers' assumed recognition of the precedent utterance and its contrast with the current state of affairs (as implicitly or explicitly evaluated by the writer) can increase writer-reader intimacy (Blakemore 1992: 170).

3 Ironical and sarcastic metaphor usage in politics

Echoic utterances can of course include figurative use of language as its 'precedent',[4] and examples of metaphor-irony combinations are easy to find in political discourse. The metaphor of Brexit as a divorce, for instance, has generated

---

[4] For discussions of the interplay of metaphor and irony (and hyperbole) see Barnden 2017; Burgers et al. 2016; Carston &Wearing 2015; Giora 2003: 69–102; Partington 2011: 1792–1793; Wilson 2006: 1735–1739.

many ironical and sarcastic evaluations of the UK-EU separation. Following the Brexit referendum, EU Commission President J.-C. Juncker was quoted with a warning that the UK-EU division would not be an "amicable divorce," to which he added, sarcastically pretending that someone could be nostalgic about the past relationship: "It was not exactly a tight love affair anyway" (Dathan 2016). Later, a German Member of the European Parliament, E. Brok, stated that "if you have a divorce you have to pay up on your obligations". Held to that standard, the UK government's reluctance to agree the "divorce bill" was in his view "like a husband running away from the family and their children." (Roberts, Syal & Boffey 2017). And when reviewing the progress of the first phase of negotiations later that year, a *Guardian* columnist judged that the divorce could "transition to a lengthy period of driving round to [the] ex's house at night, sitting in the car outside with a bottle of vodka, and texting a cocktail of pure venom and pleas to get back together, until the police are called" (Hyde 2017).

In these cases, the metaphorical depiction of the UK ending its EU membership in terms of the ending of a marriage is used as a platform to pour scorn at the UK government's EU-political performance. The underlying metaphor POLITICAL SEPARATION-AS-DIVORCE itself carries no specific evaluative bias but its conceptual enrichment into a stance-taking and even minimally narrative "scenario" (Musolff 2006, 2017a) provides a conceptual focus that can be exploited for irony and sarcasm.[5]

A further EU-related metaphor scenario that underwent similar sarcastic denunciation was the slogan, *Britain at the heart of Europe,* initially launched by in 1991 by the then Prime Minister, John Major, as an optimistic promise of a 'healthy' British policy engagement with the EU (Musolff 2017a: 131). Through repeated disqualification of that *heart* (= political centre of the European Union) as being *diseased, close to a coronary, hollow, dead, dying, rotten,* Major's HEALTHY HEART scenario was turned into that of a desperate MEDICAL CONDITION (see examples 11, 12). In addition, by recontextualising this scenario with negatively-valued BODY-related concepts, Eurosceptic politicians and media aimed at exposing Major and other proponents of the optimistic version as either naïve or duplicitous (example 13).

(11) [...] if Mr Major wanted to be at the heart of Europe, it was, presumably, *as a blood clot.* (Marshall 1994).

---

[5] The general DIVORCE metaphor, with various scenarios (BAD/NEUTRAL/AMICABLE DIVORCE), belongs in a tradition of figurative conceptualisations of international relations as LOVE-MARRIAGE-SEPARATION narratives, which in some cases have been turned into soap opera-like sagas (see e.g. Đurović & Silaški 2018, Musolff 2001; Politics@Surrey 2017).

(12) After a long period of cautious equivocation, the prime minister [= Tony Blair] had [...] "shifted up a gear" in his ambition to lodge Britain at its rightful place in the heart of Europe. And then, abruptly, *the heart of Europe got sick*. (*The Economist* 1999)

(13) Tony Blair says he wants Britain to be at the heart of Europe. Well it looks this morning *as if Europe is showing us its backside*. (*The Sun* 2001).

In less sarcastic, i.e. more ironical uses of the *heart of Europe* metaphor the discrepancy between the current and precedent utterances was left implicit, which presupposed the readers' willingness to join the writer in the dissociation from the echoed utterance. One example for such ironical usage was the fictitious answer by the then incumbent Prime Minister, David Cameron, in a spoof-conversation with Commission President Juncker, which was supposedly 'reported' in the *Financial Times* in 2014:

(14) Juncker: So just to clarify. Aside from not joining the euro, you want to limit the free movement of people, cut the power of the European Court and the European Parliament [...] This is quite a list of demands, David. What do we get in return?
Cameron: *A Britain at the heart of Europe,* of course. (Shrimsley 2014)

Here, Cameron is (mock-)quoted as employing the *heart of Europe*-slogan to justify Britain's opt-outs from key EU-policy initiatives. The fictitiousness of this spoof-dialogue adds an extra layer of meta-irony (Musolff 2017a: 130–132, 137), but this rests on the basic effect of contrasting the echoed positive-sounding slogan with the negative state of affairs. The readers of (14) are invited/expected to infer from Juncker's summary that Britain's engagement with European Union policy amounts to nothing much, which is of course incompatible with Cameron's claim.

A relatively rare case in political discourse is *self-irony*. Its rarity may be explained with the respective speaker's communicative risk of being 'too successful' in terms of own face-loss. This risk may, however, be a ploy to use a 'fishing for compliments' tactic. For instance, at a time when he was starting his political career (which would take him to the office of Prime Minister in 2019) the Conservative politician Boris Johnson put himself down in a classic metaphorical understatement as,

(15) "a mere toenail in the body politic" (*The Independent on Sunday*, 20/11/2005)

Johnson 're-issued' the *toenail*-metaphor in 2009 in an interview on BBC, in which he linked the by now rather facetious self-deprecation (given that by now he was

Mayor of London and already part of the Conservative Party elite) to his inability to prevent the then still incumbent Labour government from passing EU-friendly legislation:

(16)   "as a mere Mayor of London, *as a mere toenail in the body politic*, it may be difficult to have a referendum" (BBC, *Newsnight*, 05/10/2009).

By casting himself as being at the 'lowest' rank of the *body politic* hierarchy, Johnson derided his own stance/status as part of the political system. However, even in 2005 Johnson was known to be highly ambitious and by 2009 he had already advanced in his career. His self-derogation could therefore be understood as insincere and even weakly implicating strengthened self-endorsement, i.e. the conclusion that he was much more important than *a toenail in the body politic*. We will take up this aspect of self-irony again later when considering cases of (collective) Self-effacement concerning speakers' identification with their nation.

4 Irony and sarcasm in metaphor interpretation

Returning to the examples from the NATION-AS-BODY questionnaire, this section focuses on the question of how they combine metaphor with irony or sarcasm. In examples (1)-(3) we had detected sarcasm, due to the explicitly derogatory depiction of the target as a *fungal nail infection,* an *appendix,* or *guts.* However, in comparison with the journalistic texts reviewed in the previous section, the communicative motivation of the questionnaire answers is different. They are not parts of texts produced to comment on political topics but responses to the task of interpreting the NATION-AS-BODY metaphor, i.e. they are examples of how the informants *understood* and *reapplied* the metaphor. The survey has yielded so far 1212 completed questionnaires,[6] which revealed five main types of conceptualisations, with four of them focusing on the BODY source concept, i.e. NATION AS A HIERARCHICAL FUNCTIONAL WHOLE, AS GEOBODY, AS PART OF LARGER BODY and AS PART OF THE SPEAKER'S BODY, and a fifth variant that focused on NATION AS PERSON- conceptualisations.[7]

---

[6] With the generous help of colleagues, the survey was administered in three British universities (see above) and in Higher Education institutions of 20 more countries. The respondents were undergraduate and postgraduate students of language- and communication-related subjects.

[7] The last group of interpretations, which make up 20% on average across the national samples, were not prompted by the task question, which only asked for BODY-focused answers (see

Let's go back to the initial examples, which are repeated here for convenience (to avoid confusion, their original numbering is retained here; afterwards the continuous numbering of examples will be resumed):

(1) England is like an *appendix*, not very significant anymore but can still cause trouble and make you realise its there if it wants to.

(2) The *guts of the country* remain from when we had an empire.

(3) Don't talk about Oxford, that is the *fungal nail infection*, which we haven't got round to treating yet.

In (1) – (3), the source concepts of the mappings, i.e. APPENDIX, GUTS and NAIL INFECTION do not belong to what might be called the 'canonical', highly valued parts of the human body[8]; furthermore, they are elaborated in such a way as to highlight their problematic status (e.g. *causing trouble, reminiscent of the (lost) Empire, needing treatment*). They are thus clearly critical of their target referents and in this respect they resemble irony; however, there is hardly any implicitness in their dissociation. Hence, it seems more plausible to treat them as sarcastic, i.e. similar to the denunciations of *the heart of Europe* by Eurosceptics mentioned earlier.

However, even this comparison may be questioned, as there is no indication in (1) – (3) of a precedent utterance that is echoed or pretended. *Prima facie*, they would then be neither ironical nor sarcastic. Against this doubt, it can be argued that whilst there is no explicitly attributed, preceding public or mental representation that they contrast with, there is the 'canonical' *body politic* hierarchy (from top/*head* down to bottom/*toe*), which serves as the presupposed scenario that lets readers infer that ascribing APPENDIX-, GUTS- and NAIL INFECTION-status to a part of the nation implies a negative evaluation and an emotional/ attitudinal dissociation by the speaker, just as in the cases of TOENAIL-, BLOOD CLOT- or DYING HEART-ascriptions (see above). The 'precedent' for the dissociating inference is then not an utterance or thought (whether real, imagined or pretended) but the metaphor scenario of the NATION AS A (HIERARCHICALLY ORDERED) BODY itself.

In this context it is revealing that across all 'national' samples, such critical, dissociating uses of the BODY-or PERSON-metaphor for one's own nation are clearly

---

above). This finding underlines the close relationship between the NATION-AS-BODY and NATION-AS-PERSON metaphors.

[8] For the Western tradition of canonical body hierarchy, going back to Hippocrates, Aristotle and Galen, see Jouanna 2012: 325–327, Schiefsky 2007: 379–382.

a minority. The English L1-sample (n=134)[9] includes a sizeable sub-sample with almost 50% of answers containing criticism)' the overall much larger Chinese sample (n=344) includes a much smaller sub-section of critical answers (4.1% of questionnaires). There may be various reasons for these results (sample size, influence of social context and schooling), but it seems reasonable to assume that allocating a positive BODY-image/status to one's own "imagined nation" (Anderson 2006) and its prominent parts is the default scenario in the use of *body politic* metaphors. In line with this assumption, we have found that the questionnaire corpus is dominated by positively slanted depictions of the nation's *well-functioning head/ brain, healthy heart, powerful arms* etc. By comparison, the negative, possibly sarcastic examples such as (1)-(3) stand out as exceptional. In the following subsections we give exemplary overviews of English L1-and Chinese responses from the NATION-AS-BODY survey, whose *potential* ironical/sarcastic status will be discussed in the concluding section (for a list of scenarios and sub-concepts included in critical ironical answers from both samples see the appendix at the end of this chapter).

4.1 English-L1 examples

The main targets of sarcastic BODY-focused conceptualisations in the English-L1 sample are places, regions, and social groups of the respondents' home nation (Britain, USA, New Zealand), which are ridiculed as representing lowly, disgusting or diseased parts or organs of the national body:

(17) The *backside* of England is Hull.

(18) The politicians are the *tongue* [of England], *sometimes talking rubbish.*

(19) Florida is the *wrinkles & parting lines* [of America].

(20) The *head* [of New Zealand] is the white guys in charge. They also double as the *asshole*.

The 'part-vs.-whole' conceptualisation also works the other way round: the whole nation is viewed as an organ or part of a larger body, usually without specification

---

[9] Special thanks for the collegial help in collecting the US and New Zealand data are due to Professors Theresa Catalano (University of Nebraska-Lincoln), Ning Yu (Pennsylvania State University) and Takashi Shogimen (University of Otago).

of that body, but focusing on a stereotypical negative feature e.g. *uselessness*, as in example (1), or *disappearance, pain*:

(21) England used to be *like hair in that it grew as it colonized and was all cut off during its decolonization*.

(22) America = *Lower back. You really need it and it is a very key part. It also gives a lot of people pain.*

On the other hand, the whole nation can be explicitly portrayed as one body that appears deficient in terms of the *state of health* and needs *medical* attention:

(23) The *heart of Britain is sick*, and Scotland looks at England as if England were a *transplant it wants to reject*. Britain as a nation is *not long for this world*.

(24) [America] *is fat*. [...] It's [sic] fat is a combination of *future pregnancy, a bloaded past and an uncontrollable metabolism*. It's [sic] *brain* is *bipolar and completely disjointed in the middle*.

(25) New Zealand needs a *liver transplant*.

Among PERSON-conceptualisations of the nation, we also find potentially sarcastic cases. They all seem to focus on *male* nation-*persons*, if we include the *Frankenstein* example in (27), which is based on a confusion between the protagonist of M. Shelley's novel, i.e. "Dr. Frankenstein", and his creation, the "monster"):

(26) England is an *old man continuously talking* about the Commonwealth that has grown up and no longer belongs to it.

(27) [...] *like Frankenstein*, [America has] *an abnormal brain* commanding the body, which is causing our country to act and react with more negativity and distastefulness in ways contrary to the moral norm.

(28) New Zealand is like a *little brother chasing* after the nations of the world and *clamouring for attention*.

Characterising one's own nation as a *grumpy old man, Frankenstein('s monster)* or *attention-seeking little brother* is both dissociative and explicit, i.e. closer to sarcastic denigration than to ironical relativization. We will consider the pragmatic status of these examples further after comparing them with those of the Chinese cohort.

4.2 Mandarin- and cantonese-L1 examples

As in the English-L1 sample, many critical *body*-based conceptualisations in the Chinese sample[10] concentrate on allocations of places or political institutions in the home nation to body features or conditions that can be viewed as being either superfluous or detrimental to the nation's *appearance* or *health*. *Hair*, as a not existentially necessary body feature can be found in the Chinese sample as well as in the English-L1 sample (see example 21) but with a stronger focus on its reappearance after falling out, which can be viewed both positively and negatively:

(29) Taiwan – *hair* – *we can live without hair. [But] to have hair is a more beautiful fashion.*

(30) The head of the government: *hair (if one goes down, always some other one will grow up).*

(31) Corrupt officials are like *hairs [sic] on a nation's arm being shaved off but later appearing to your eyes again.*

More drastically, 'problematic' places are identified as a *disease* or as *body parts* or *organs that can get injured* and *hurt*:

(32) Taiwan: potential *disease, maybe one time/finally we have to fight against it.*

(33) Tai Wan is the *elbow, it can hit others and get harm easily.*

(34) Tibet: *stomach (sometimes you feel uncomfortable).*

Deficiencies of China as a whole are pointed out in terms of *illnesses* or its enormous size viewed as a sign of obesity:

(35) My nation like a *blind*. It *can't see* the desire of the citizens.

---

[10] In the social indicator information, most respondents from both mainland China and Hong Kong entered "Chinese" as their L1; only a few informants specified "Mandarin" or "Cantonese". As systemic linguistic differences between Mandarin and Cantonese were not an important parameter of our investigation, this vagueness has no bearing on the results. Nevertheless, we must take into account that nearly 10% of the overall Chinese sample were produced by students in or from Hong Kong, where the political culture is different from that of the People's Republic of China.

(36) My nation like a *deaf*. It doesn't listen to the citizens.

(37) Our nation is like a *heavy giant,* he [...] has some *illness due to obesity.*

On the other hand, a depiction of China as part of a larger body occurs only once – and only by way of a comparison with a cancerous growth:

(38) [China] is not welcomed by lots of nations [,] like a *tumour inside human body.*

The remainder of dissociating Chinese uses are *person*-focused conceptualisations, e.g.:

(39) My nation *have* [sic] *a mad mind.* It supress [sic] the citizens when it wants.

(40) My home nation is an *arrogant bitch. She always bitching about others but never herself.*

Whilst the identifications of not 'fully integrated' as problematic body parts or organs (examples 29, 32–34) only occur in the samples from mainland students, the criticisms of China as a whole and in particular the personalised conceptualisations (examples 35–36, 38–40) come form the Hong Kong sub-sample. For both these trends, the respective socio-political contexts (i.e. official integration ideology in the "People's Republic of China" on the one hand, pro-independence movements in the administratively separate city of Hong Kong) seem to be plausible motivating factors. In either case, the Chinese responses differ from the English L1-sample by being more specifically political.

5 Discussion

The questionnaire responses presented above as examples (1) – (3) and (17) – (40) invite critical, dissociating evaluations of the respective political target referents. Such criticism is of course not ironical or sarcastic *per se*; it would require a 'precedent' utterance or thought that is incongruous with the context of its 'current' echo to identify it as such, as in the examples from political comments that we discussed earlier (7–16). Nevertheless, the "figurative framing" (Burgers et al. 2016) supplied by the NATION AS BODY metaphor and its scenarios seems to us to provide a ground for arguing that the critical evaluation examples can be considered to be at least *possible* candidates for sarcastic interpretations. Viewed in this perspective, the questionnaire task provides the 'preceding utterance', to which the informants' utterances respond. As argued above, the task may be considered as suggesting a positive answer, given that the target referent is always the informant's *home nation*. The fact that the overwhelming majority of responses (respectively, 51% and 95.9% in the two cohorts reviewed here) is descriptively neutral or proudly patriotic seems to bear out this assumption. Responses that articulate a critical stance towards one's own nation's deficient *appearance, status in body-hierarchy, state of health* or *personal character* may be seen as expressing projected self-criticism, insofar as the authors depict their collective national identity as *diseased, unseemly, dysfunctional* or, in the personalisation cases, *psychologically and morally deficient*.

Unlike the cases of apparently personal self-effacing metaphor use, which we considered in examples (15) – (16), such collective self-effacement is not aiming at a 'fishing for compliments' effect, as its contradiction would not enhance the respective speaker's own face. The NATION AS BODY and NATION AS PERSON scenarios framed in the questionnaire task presuppose a default positive condition (NATION AS HEALTHY BODY or NATION AS GOOD/ COMPETENT PERSON), which serves as a counter-foil against which the responses highlight the perceived shortcomings of the nation or its specific parts. This highlighting effect rules out any implicitness or irony; instead, it sarcastically exposes the discrepancy between the default positive precedent and the current deprecation of the target referent as a *disease, an injured organ, a perishable piece of hair, a Frankenstein monster* or an *immoral* or *psychologically unstable person*.

Regarding differences between the two cohorts of respondents, the contrast in overall percentages (49% and 4.1%) indicates a far greater reluctance on the part of the Chinese informants to engage in critical and sarcastic metaphor use than the English L1-cohort.[11] This finding is reinforced by the observation that low-status/taboo concepts (*asshole, appendix, guts, Frankenstein*-likeness) are avoided by Chinese respondents altogether; even when critical of their nation or parts of it, they prefer inoffensive and utility- and/or competence-focused source concepts (e.g. *hair, elbow, child*-status).[12] This makes an intriguing contrast to the relatively high degree of politicisation in the target-references (unruly provinces, corrupt officials) in the same cohort. The motivation for these results is not yet

---

[11] Figures for individual sub-concepts (see appendix) are too low to derive reliable conclusions.
[12] Another factor to be taken into account is the relative greater size of the female majority (62%) in the Chinese cohort than that in the English-L1 cohort (58%). In the latter, it is mainly male respondents who assign taboo-body parts as analogies.

clear and makes further comparative interdisciplinary research necessary, e.g. interviews with informants and experimental elicitation.

In this chapter, we have studied the interplay of irony, sarcasm and metaphor in political discourse. We established that, just like other public or mental representations, metaphor scenarios can serve as conceptual 'precedents' for achieving pragmatic effects of irony and sarcasm in utterances which allude to them through 'echoic mention' or 'pretense' and express a dissociative attitude and semantic contradiction. This dissociation aspect concerns the argumentative-evaluative bias or slant of the precedent metaphor scenario (e.g. in the assumption 'that the heart of Europe is healthy', which is denounced as being untrue, unrealistic, ridiculous etc.). Depending on the degree of explicitness of the alleged contrast between echoed/pretended scenario and the context of the current utterance, the latter is closer to either end of the irony-sarcasm continuum: if the contrast is assumed to be fully obvious to speakers and hearers (e.g. in British Eurosceptic circles, 'that the EU is dead'), denunciations of the assumed scenario (HEALTHY HEART) tend to be maximally explicit and thus more sarcastic dismissals than ironical criticisms. Conversely, the less obvious and more ambiguous the alleged contradiction is, the more implicit and ironical the dissociative bias of utterance is, as we observed in examples (7) and (14).

We also discussed examples from a questionnaire task eliciting responses for describing the informants' respective "home nation" as a body, as part of a larger questionnaire corpus (Musolff 2016, 2017b), with particular attention to comparing answers from the English-L1 and Chinese cohorts. In both samples, a minority of responses qualified as *potential* cases of sarcasm, due to their dissociating-critical bias. However, for these responses to count as sarcastic, the required relationship to the conceptual 'precedent' rests on their interpretation as implying an echo of the questionnaire task that is biased in favour of positive NATION-AS-BODY/PERSON scenarios. The critical conceptualisation of one's own nation (or parts of it) as a *disgusting or deficient body part*, as an *illness* or as a *bad character-trait* can then be viewed as fulfilling the 'contradiction condition' of sarcasm. In socio-pragmatic terms, it involves a self-effacement in terms of the collective national self and thus runs counter the mainstream tradition of uses of the NATION-AS-BODY/PERSON metaphor as an expression of national pride (Anderson 2006; Auestad 2014; Musolff 2010). If corroborated by further findings, the analysis of sarcastic responses to nation conceptualisation may contribute to building a theory of figurative collective (self-)irony.

References

Abrams, M. H. 1981. *A Glossary of Literary Terms*. New York: Holt, Rinehart and Winston.

Anderson, Benedict. 2006. *Imagined Communities. Reflections on the Origin and Spread of Nationalism*. London: Verso.

Auestad, Lene (ed.). 2014. *Nationalism and the Body Politic: Psychoanalysis and the Rise of Ethnocentrism and Xenophobia*. London: Karnac Books.

Baym, Geoffrey. 2005. The Daily Show: Discursive Integration and the Reinvention of Political Journalism. *Political Communication* 22. 259–276.

Blakemore, Diane. 1992. *Understanding Utterances. An introduction to Pragmatics*. Oxford: Blackwell.

Burgers, Christian, Elly A. Konijn & Gerard J. Steen. 2016. Figurative Framing: Shaping public discourse through metaphor, hyperbole and irony. *Communication Theory*. 26. 410–430.

Callahan, William A. 2009. The cartography of national humiliation and the emergence of China's geobody. *Public Culture* 21(1). 141–173.

Carston, Robyn & Catherine Wearing. 2015. Hyperbolic language and its relation to metaphor and irony. *Journal of Pragmatics* 79. 79–92.

Clark, Herbert & Richard R. Gerrig. 1984. On the pretense theory of irony. *Journal of Experimental Psychology: General* 113. 121–126.

Colston, Herbert L. 2017. Irony performance and perception. In Angeliki Athanasiadou & Herbert L. Colston (eds.), *Irony in Language Use and Communication*, 19–41. Amsterdam: John Benjamins.

Currie, Gregory. 2006. Why irony is pretence. In Shaun Nichols (ed.), *The Architecture of the Imagination*, 111–133. Oxford: Oxford University Press.

D'Ancona, Matthew. 2017. Post Truth: *The New War on Truth and How to Fight back*. London: Ebury Publishing.

Dedaić, Mirjana N. 2005. Ironic denial: *tobože* in Croatian political discourse. *Journal of Pragmatics* 37(5). 667–683.

Đurović, Tatjana & Nadežda Silaški. 2018. The end of a long and fraught marriage: Metaphorical images structuring the Brexit discourse. *Metaphor and the Social World*, 8(1). 25–39.

Giora, Rachel. 2003. *On our Mind. Salience, Context and Figurative Language*. Oxford: Oxford University Press.

Gray, Jonathan, Jeffrey P. Jones & Ethan Thompson. 2009. The State of Satire and the Satire of State. In Jonathan Gray, Jeffrey P. Jones & Ethan Thompson (eds.). *Satire TV: Politics and Comedy in the Post-Network Era*, 3–36. New York: New York University Press.

Gruber, Helmut. 2015. Policy-oriented argumentation or ironic evaluation: A study of verbal quoting and positioning in Austrian politicians' parliamentary debate contributions. *Discourse Studies* 17(6). 682–702.

Ilie, Cornelia. 2001. Unparliamentary language: Insults as cognitive forms of confrontation. In: René Dirven, Roslyn Frank & Cornelia Ilie (eds.), *Language and Ideology II: Descriptive cvognitiev approaches*, 235–263. Amsterdam: John Benjamins.žž

Ilie, Cornelia. 2018. Parliamentary debates. In: Ruth Wodak & Bernhard Forchtner (eds.), *The Routledge Handbook of Language and Politics*, 309–325. London: Routledge.

Jouanna, Jacques 2012. *Greek Medicine from Hippocrates to Galen. Selected Papers*. Transl. Neil Allies, Ed. Philip van der Eijk. Leiden: Brill.

Kumon-Nakamura, Sachi, Sam Glucksberg & Mary Brown. 1995. How about another piece of pie: The allusional pretense theory of discourse irony. *Journal of Experimental Psychology: General* 124, 3–21.

Livnat, Zohar & Gonen Dori-Hacohen. 2013. The effect of irony in radio talk-back programmes in Israel. In: Anita Fetzer (ed.), *The Pragmatics of Political Discourse: Explorations across cultures*, 193–218. Amsterdam: John Benjamins.

Musolff, Andreas. 2001. Cross-language metaphors: *parents* and *children*, *love*, *marriage* and *divorce* in the *European family*. In Janet Cotterill & Anne Ife (eds.), *Language across Boundaries*, 119–134. London: Continuum.

Musolff, Andreas. 2006. Metaphor Scenarios in Public Discourse. *Metaphor and Symbol* 21(1). 23–38.

Musolff, Andreas. 2010. *Metaphor, Nation and the Holocaust. The Concept of the Body Politic.* London/New York: Routledge.

Musolff, Andreas. 2016. Cross-Cultural Variation in Deliberate Metaphor Interpretation. *Metaphor and the Social World* 6(2). 205–224.

Musolff, Andreas. 2017a. Irony and sarcasm in follow-ups of metaphorical slogans. In Angeliki Athanasiadou & Herbert L. Colston (Eds.), *Irony in Language Use and Communication*, 127–142. Amsterdam: John Benjamins.

Musolff, Andreas. 2017b. Metaphor and Cultural Cognition. In: Farzad Sharifian (ed.), *Advances in Cultural Linguistics,* 325–344. New York: Springer.

Partington, Alan. 2011. Phrasal irony: its form, function and exploitation. *Journal of Pragmatics* 43(6). 1786–1800.

Partington, Alan & Charlotte Taylor. 2018. *The Language of Persuasion in Politics. An Introduction*. London: Routledge.

Patterson, Annabel M. 1991. *Fables of Power: Aesopian Writing and Political History*. Durham, NC: Duke University Press.

Peltonen, Markku. 2009. Political rhetoric and citizenship in *Coriolanus*. In David Armitage, Conal Condren and Andrew Fitzmaurice (eds.), *Shakespeare and Early Modern Political Thought*, 234–252. Cambridge: Cambridge University Press.

Politics @ Surrey. 2017. *Three Unhelpful Metaphors For Understanding Brexit.* https://blogs.surrey.ac.uk/politics/2017/04/28/three-unhelpful-metaphors-for-understanding-brexit/ (accessed 20/12/2017).

Schiefsky, Mark J. 2007. Galen's teleology and functional explanation. *Oxford Studies in Ancient Philosophy* 33. 369–400.

Shakespeare, William. 1976. *Coriolanus*. Ed. P. Brockbank. London: Methuen & Co.

Sivenkova, Maria. 2015. Metacommunicative follow-ups in British, German and Russian political webchats. In Elda Weizman & Anita Fetzer (eds.), *Follow-ups in Political Discourse*, 109–135. Amsterdam: John Benjamins.

Sperber, Dan & Deirdre Wilson. 1995. *Relevance. Communication and Cognition*. Oxford: Blackwell.

Willison, Robert. 2017. In defense of an ecumenical approach to irony. In Angeliki Athanasiadou and Herbert L. Colston (eds.), *Irony in Language Use and Communication,* 61–83. Amsterdam: John Benjamins.

Wilson, Deirdre. 2006. The pragmatics of verbal irony: echo or pretence? *Lingua* 116. 1722–1743.

Wilson, Deirdre & Dan Sperber. 1992. On verbal irony. *Lingua* 87. 53–76.

Wilson, Deirdre & Dan Sperber. 2012. Explaining irony. In Deirdre Wilson & Dan Sperber, *Meaning and Relevance*, 123–145. Cambridge: Cambridge University Press.

Political press text examples

Behr, Rafael. 2016. Brexit earthquake has happened, and the rubble will take years to clear. *The Guardian*, 24 June 2016.
Dathan, Matt. 2016. Brexit will not be 'an amicable divorce' – it wasn't exactly a tight love affair anyway:' EU leaders tell Britain to 'urgently' trigger formal process to leave Brussels (after a VERY continental breakfast) *Daily Mail*, 25 June 2016.
Deacon, Michael. 2016. 'It's Project Lies!' Michael Gove takes on the audience – and the experts. *The Daily Telegraph*, 03 June 2016.
Henley, Jon. 2016. Why Vote Leave's £350m weekly EU cost claim is wrong. *The Guardian*, 10 June 2016.
Hyde, Marina 2017. Coming next, a Brexit divorce: the kind that involves the police. *The Guardian*, 08 December 2017.
Jolly, S. 2017. Most of the Brexit rebels are lawyers. Maybe experts are useful after all. *The Guardian*, 14 December 2017.
Marshall, Andrew. 1994. Mixed metaphors spell out post-Maastricht doubts. *The Independent*, 11 September 1994.
Moore, Suzanne. 2014. Nigel Farage: a pustule of resentment on the body politic. *The Guardian*, 23 April 2014.
Rawnsley, Andrew. 2016a. Brexit: a journey into the unknown for a country never before so divided. *The Observer*, 26 June 2016.
Rawnsley, Andrew. 2016b. Welcome to Poundland, where life is bliss if you're a foreign buyer. *The Observer*, 16 October 2016.
Rawnsley, Andrew. 2017. The more they say they are all happy the more sceptical you should be. *The Observer*, 10 December 2017.
Roberts, Dan, Rajeef Syal & Daniel Boffey. 2017. May dismisses reports of frosty dinner with EU chief as 'Brussels gossip'. *The Guardian*, 10 May 2017.
Shrimsley, Robert. 2014. David Cameron opts out to keep Britain at heart of Europe. *Financial Times*, 30 October 2014.
The Economist. 1999. Moses Blair and his promised Euroland. *The Economist*, 18 March 1999.
The Economist. 2016a. Divided we fall. [Leader]. *The Economist*, 10 June 2016.
The Economist. 2016b. A tragic split. [Leader]. *The Economist*, 25 June 2016.
The Sun. 2001. When is the refugee camp in Calais to be shut? *The Sun*, 03 September 2001.
Wright, Ben. 2016. There's a sinister strain of anti-intellectualism to Gove's dismissal of 'experts'. *The Daily Telegraph*, 21 June 2016.
Zaltzman, Andy. 2017. 'Satire has had a busy year': how to laugh at the year that was. *The Guardian*, 29 September 2017.

Appendix

	English L1	Mandarin or Cantonese L1
BODY PARTS/ORGANS		
ANUS/ASSHOLE/BACKSIDE	3	
APPENDIX (IRRELEVANT)	3	
ARMPIT (GROSS)	1	
BACK (ACHING)	1	
BELLY BUTTON (LESS IMPORTANT)	1	
BRAIN (INDECISIVE, BIPOLAR, DISAGREEMENT, ABNORMAL)	4	1
ELBOW (CAN HURT)		1
FEET (LOW STATUS, DESIGNED FOR QUEUING)	2	
FRECKLES	1	
GUTS (= REST OF EMPIRE; LOW STATUS)	1	
HAIR	3 (MESSY, ALL FELL OFF, HIGH BUT NO POWER)	3 (NOT ESSENTIAL FOR SURVIVAL)
JOINTS, KNEES (PAINFUL, ON ITS KNEES)	2	1
LUNG (OF SMOKER)		1
LOWER BACK (PAIN)	1	
NAKED (WITHOUT EMPIRE)	1	
SCARS	1	
SMALL	3	
STOMACH (CAN BE UNCOMFORTABLE)		1
TOE (LOW STATUS)	1	
WRINKLES	1	
YOGA (IN NEED OF)	1	
ILLNESS/INFIRMITY		
BLIND/SHORT-SIGHTED		2
CANCER/TUMOUR	1	1
DEAF		2
NAIL INFECTION	1	
OBESITY/GLUTTONY	1	2
OLD AGE	4	

	English L1	Mandarin or Cantonese L1
SICK/PATIENT/WEAK/AILMENTS/POISONED/ ATROPHYING/ NEEDING (LIVER) TRANSPLANT	7	5
PERSON		
CHANGEABLE/MULTIPLE PERSONALITIES		2
CHILD	1	3
FEMALE		1
FRANKENSTEIN	2	
MALE	3	4
PESSIMIST	1	
POOR/GREEDY		2
MOUTHY, LIKES GOOD COMPLAINT. TALKING RUBBISH	4	1
POLITE ARROGANCE	1	
TEA DRINKER	2	
WET IN TERMS OF AUTHORITY	1	
SUM	60	33

Victoria Escandell-Vidal and Manuel Leonetti
Grammatical emphasis and irony in Spanish

1 Introduction

It is widely assumed in the literature that irony is a pragmatic phenomenon: in other words, irony is not encoded, but inferred (Searle 1979; Grice 1975; Clark and Gerrig 1984; Gibbs 1994). The trigger for the ironic interpretation is the obvious 'incongruence' between the assumption expressed by the utterance and the actual state-of-affairs (Colston 2000). This contrast suggests that the speaker cannot be seriously committed to entertaining the thought expressed. In the framework of Relevance Theory (Sperber and Wilson 1986/1995 and subsequent work), irony is further analysed as simultaneously "echoing a thought attributed to an individual, a group or to people in general, and expressing a mocking, sceptical or critical attitude to this thought" (Sperber and Wilson 1986/1995:125). Thus, when a speaker utters *What a lovely day!* on a stormy morning, she provides information about the content of an attributed thought with the intention of showing her own dissociative attitude towards that thought (Sperber and Wilson 1981; Wilson and Sperber 1992, 2012; Curcó 2000; Wilson 2006; Yus 2009; Rosales Sequeiros 2011).

In all these approaches, recognising that the speaker is being ironic crucially depends on contextual cues. It has been noted in the literature, however, that certain factors can favour, or make more accessible, ironic interpretations, such as prosody and changes in the fundamental frequency (Gibbs 2000; Bryant and Fox Tree 2002, 2005; Attardo et al. 2003; Bryant 2010, 2011; Padilla García 2012) and gestural cues (Gibbs 2000; Bryant 2011; Attardo et al. 2003, 2011; Gonzalez-Fuentes et al. 2015).

For Spanish, Escandell-Vidal and Leonetti (2014) have argued that some sentences can easily elicit an ironic interpretation based on their syntactic form even in the absence of a (previous) context. This is the case of constructions involving non-focal, or '*verum* focus'-inducing fronting (hereinafter, VFF) (see Leonetti and Escandell-Vidal 2009; Escandell-Vidal and Leonetti 2009, 2014), like those in (1), and verb-subject-object word order (Leonetti 2014), like those in (2).

(1) a. *¡Contenta me tienes!*
      Happy   me.OBJ have.PRS.2SG
      'You've sure made me happy!'

Victoria Escandell-Vidal, Departamento de Lingüística General, Estudios Árabes, Hebreos, Vascos y de Asia Oriental, UCM
Manuel Leonetti, Departamento de Lengua Española y Teoría de la Literatura, UCM

https://doi.org/10.1515/9783110652246-009

b. *¡A buenas horas llegas!*
   At good hours arrive.PRS.2SG
   'It's a fine time for you to arrive!'

(2) *¡Estoy yo para canciones!*
    Be.PRS.1SG I for songs
    'I'm in a fine mood for songs!'

The fact that these sentences can receive an ironic interpretation even without a context (see Giora et al., this volume for a related proposal) seems to suggest that irony is encoded in these cases, thus providing a counterargument to the initial assumption that irony is not encoded, but rather inferred. However, as argued in Escandell-Vidal and Leonetti (2014), these constructions encode not irony, but rather different degrees of emphasis. When emphasis is expressed by grammatical means, as in sentences like (1)–(2), it can favour ironic interpretations by making it easier to imagine, or accommodate, a state-of-affairs not congruent with the proposition expressed. In this sense, like prosodic and gestural cues, grammatical emphasis merely plays a facilitating role in irony without encoding it in any direct way.[1,2]

2 Hypotheses

Elaborating on these ideas and assumptions, in this paper we seek to test if there is any significant correlation between different means of expressing intensification and grammatical emphasis, on the one hand, and the saliency of ironic interpretations, on the other.

---

[1] The investigation presented in this paper forms part of the research project "The Semantics-Pragmatics Interface and the Resolution of Interpretive Mismatches" (SPIRIM), funded by the Spanish Ministerio de Economía y Competitividad (FFI2015-63497-P). A previous, shorter version was presented at the *6th International Conference on Intercultural Pragmatics and Communication* (University of Malta, La Valletta, May 2014) and published in Spanish as Escandell-Vidal and Leonetti, (2015). We are grateful to the editors of this special issue for their kind invitation to participate, and also to the two reviewers for their careful and insightful comments on a previous version.

[2] The problem we face with irony in Spanish is the same one that Michaelis and Feng (2015) face in their analysis of the syntax of sarcasm in English (specifically, the analysis of so-called *split interrogatives*: like "What is this, Spain?"). However, our approach is different: while they assume that the expression of a sarcastic judgement is an encoded function of English split interrogatives, we maintain that irony is not conventionally associated with the constructions we analyse – except when they become formulas.

Our main hypothesis is that ironic interpretations are favoured by the accumulation of grammatical resources that encode intensification and emphasis (such as exclamative intonation, exclamative syntax, polarity focus structures, marked word order and certain lexical choices). This predicts a scalar result: the more the grammatical resources used for intensification in a sentence, the higher the bias of its interpretation towards an ironic reading without a context. Thus, intensification and emphasis do not encode irony, though their concentration in a sentence facilitates it.

We assume that there is a difference between intensification and emphasis. Intensification is the use of grammatical means to express a high degree of some property, as in *wh*-exclamatives. Emphasis, in turn, is reactive intensification, in other words, intensification used to reject or cancel an assumption, as in the *Verum*-focus cases illustrated below. Sentences involving emphasis expressed by grammatical means need to activate and make salient the assumption they are meant to reject: they act as presuppositions triggers, and therefore they need first to activate the corresponding contrary proposition in order to reject it. This is what favours irony without the need to rely on contextual data. Sentences involving intensification, in contrast, will not trigger such a strong effect because they do not carry any presupposition that can make particularly salient any other proposition.

This general hypothesis can then be broken down into four predictions:
1. Declarative sentences will be preferentially interpreted in their literal meaning.
2. Declarative sentences with exclamation marks – i.e., exclamative intonation – will be preferentially interpreted as literal, though there will be an incipient tendency to make their interpretation more dependent on the context.
3. Exclamative sentences (i.e., sentences with exclamative syntax, marked either by *wh*-fronting or predicate fronting with right-dislocation of the subject) will show a stronger tendency to mark their interpretation as context-dependent, with an incipient tendency to receive ironic readings.
4. Sentences with grammatical marking for emphasis (*VerumFocus*-inducing fronting, marked word order, use of <*ir* + *a* + infinitive> periphrasis) will receive the highest scores for ironic interpretations.

The overall prediction is, therefore, that sentences containing more grammatical features for emphasis (emphatic syntax, marked word order) will be interpreted more straightforwardly as ironic compared to neutral sentences and sentences with intensification. To test these predictions, we carried out an informal survey to determine what kind of sentences are more likely to receive ironic readings in the absence of any contextual or prosodic cue.

3 The survey

3.1 Design

A total of twenty sentences in Spanish were presented in the questionnaire. On the basis of their grammatical properties, they can be grouped into five different categories:

- Declarative sentences with evaluation expressed by lexical means and with no grammatical intensifiers, exemplified in (3).

(3) a. *La película fue muy aburrida.*
   The film be.PST.3SG very boring
   'The film was very boring.'

   b. *Armó un buen lío.*
   Raise.PST.3SG a good mess
   'S/He kicked up a fuss.'

- Declarative sentences with exclamation marks, with or without lexical evaluation, exemplified in (4).

(4) a. *¡Hoy hace un día espléndido!*
   Today make.PRS.3SG a day splendid
   'It's a lovely day!'

   b. *¡A las ocho llegaremos!*
   At the eight arrive.FUT.1PL
   'We'll arrive at eight!'

- Exclamative sentences with *wh*-fronting, as in (5), or an inverted order, either by right-dislocation of the subject, as in (6a), or by subject inversion in the VSX pattern, as in (6b).

(5) a. *¡Qué bonito!*
   What beautiful
   'How lovely!'

   b. *¡Cuánto tiempo sin verte!*
   How much time without see.INF.you.OBJ
   'I haven't seen you in such a long time!'

(6) a. *¡Sensacional, esta película!*
    Great, this film
    'What a great film!'

  b. *¡Tienes tú mucha prisa por terminar!*
    Have.PRS.2SG you much hurry for finish.INF
    'You're in a big hurry to finish!'

– Sentences with VFF (XVS word order), exemplified in (7).

(7) a. *Algo sabrá...*
    Something know.FUT.3SG
    'S/he must know something.'

  b. *¡Mucho interés tienes tú en la conferencia!*
    Much interest have.PRS.2SG you in the conference
    'You're sure interested in the conference'

  c. *¡Menudo coche se ha comprado!*
    Small car REF have.PRS.3SG bought
    'That's some car he's bought!'

  d. *¡Para fiestas estoy yo!*
    For parties be.PRS.1SG I
    'I'm in a fine mood for parties!'

  e. *¡Bastante trabajo tengo ya!*
    Enough work have.PRS.1SG already
    'As if I didn't have enough work already!'

  f. *¡Buena impresión debimos producir!*
    Good impression must.PST.1PL cause
    'A fine impression we must have made!'

  g. *¡A buenas horas llegas!*
    At good hours arrive.PRS.2SG
    'Fine time for you to arrive!'

  h. *¡Muy enterado te veo!*
    Very informed you.OBJ see.PRS.1SG
    'You sure know a lot about it!'

  i. *¡Eso mismo le dije!*
    That same s/he.OBJ tell.PST.1SG
    'That's exactly what I told him/her!'

– Sentences with VFF (XVS word order) or with VSX order, plus the verbal periphrasis <*ir a* + infinitive> (roughly equivalent to '*be going to* + infinitive'), exemplified in (8).

(8) a. ¡A   ti   te   voy   a   dejar yo el   coche!
       To   you.OBL you.OBJ   go.PRS.1SG   to   lend   I   the   car
       'Yeah, right, I'm going to lend you my car!'

   b. ¡Te   va   a   esperar Eva   hasta las ocho!
      You.OBJ   go.PRS.3SG   to   wait   Eva   until the eight
      'Yeah, sure Eva's going to wait for you until eight!'

   c. De   poco   te   va   a   servir   quejarte...
      of   little you.OBL   go.PRS.3SG   to serve   complain
      'Little good it'll do you to complain.'

Before we move on to a description of the remaining features of our survey, some observations about the list of grammatical patterns in (3)–(8) are in order. Aside from the examples in (3), which are simple declarative sentences, all these constructions can be qualified as exclamative constructions (Michaelis 2001, Bosque 2017, Villalba 2017): this explains most of their common properties and gives some internal coherence to the list. That said, they show clear differences. In (4) we find cases of so-called *declarative exclamatives*, that is, intonational-only exclamative sentences; in (5) the central, prototypical pattern of *wh*-exclamatives is represented – although the examples contain just *wh*-phrasal exclamatives, instead of full sentential structures; (6a) exemplifies *binomial exclamatives*, predicative verbless clauses with the predicate in initial position and the subject typically right-dislocated (Bosque 2017:32–34, Villalba 2017:611); (6b) is a case of exclamative sentence with VSX order, an option that has received little attention in the literature on Spanish, but which is close to other cases of verb-subject inversion in exclamatives (Michaelis 2001:1048); the examples in (7) represent another productive schema for verb-subject inversion, here triggered by fronting of a constituent, and XVS order as a result – labelled *focal*[3] and *polarity* exclamatives in Bosque (2017:25–28), and *rhetorical exclamatives* in Andueza (2011);

---

[3] The term *focal* is due to the (controversial) assumption that the fronting operation in (7) should be analysed as focus movement of a phrase to a left peripheral position. In Leonetti and Escandell-Vidal (2009) and Escandell-Vidal and Leonetti (2014) we argued that this kind of fronting cannot be analysed as a case of focus fronting, since the fronted phrase is not interpreted as a focus. The same holds for so-called *emphatic polarity exclamatives* obtained from the fronting of *bien* 'well' (Bosque 2017:27–28).

and finally, (8) shows the combination of VSX and XVS patterns with a futurate periphrasis. This series of grammatical options clearly suggests a strong link between the expression of irony and the syntax of exclamatives. How all these ingredients interact in the interpretive process will be the topic of the discussion in Section 5.

3.2 Participants

One hundred and forty-seven native speakers of Spanish volunteered to participate in the experiment. They were mostly students of the degree in Spanish Language and Literature at the UNED (an on-line national university covering the whole of Spain and abroad), though we allowed them to pass the questionnaire on to friends and relatives to obtain a more representative sample in terms of age and educational level. Ninety-five participants (65%) were women. As for age range, 77 of our informants (52%) were between 30 and 45 years old; 53 (36%) were between 46 and 60; and ten (7%) were between 18 and 30. The sample covered all regions of Spain, the largest groups coming from Madrid (38 participants, 26%), Andalusia (33 participants, 23%), Castilla-León (16 participants, 11%) and Castilla-La Mancha (13 participants, 9%). Other regions provided between one and six participants. This distribution is of interest because it means that more than 70% of the participants were from monolingual Spanish-speaking areas. All the participants but one had at least a secondary education.

3.3 Procedure

Participants were sent a hyperlink to access the survey. They were informed that completing the survey entailed their prior consent and that no personal data would be collected. They were first sent to a training page where the experiment was explained. They were told that this was a survey on irony and were given some examples of sentences in context to illustrate what we meant by irony and how the interpretation of an utterance can vary from its literal, "face-value" meaning to the ironic, antiphrastic[4] meaning, depending on the context. Participants were

---

4 In this survey we limited the interpretations offered to antiphrastic interpretations. We did this for two main reasons: first, antiphrastic interpretations are the prototypical instances of irony; and second, they are the interpretations that an untrained participant will recognize most easily. However, we are not claiming that antiphrasis is the only way in which ironic interpretations are obtained and that irony is always achieved by uttering a sentence with a content that the speaker

then told that in the experiment they would read isolated sentences with different structures. For each sentence, they had to choose an interpretation using a 5-point annotated Likert scale, where five possibilities were offered, from the literal reading to the ironic, antiphrastic one (*Never ironic, Seldom ironic, It depends on the context, Often ironic, Always ironic*), plus an *Other* option to mark other possible interpretations not captured by the scale. The two extreme interpretations were specified by means of an explicit statement to make the intended interpretation completely clear. The centremost option on the scale indicated the neutral point, where the ironic value of the utterance would be entirely context-dependent. The participants were instructed to make their choice as quickly as possible so that their response would reflect their instinctive, unpremeditated intuitions. The presentation of the examples was randomized to avoid any training effect. Therefore, the order in which the examples are discussed below does not reflect the order in which they were presented to the test subjects.

4 Results and discussion

4.1 Hypothesis #1: Declarative sentences will be preferentially interpreted in their literal meaning

In the results of our survey, the two neutral, unbiased declarative sentences (see (3) above) obtained the highest scores for the literal, non-ironic interpretation. As shown in figures 1 and 2 below, 106 informants (72%) preferred the literal interpretation over the ironic one in the case of *La película fue muy aburrida*, and 107 (73%) favoured a literal reading in the case of *Armó un buen lío*. The strength of this result is confirmed by the fact that 19 informants (13%) chose 'Seldom ironic' as their preferred option in the former instance and 16 (11%) of them did so in the latter, so altogether non-ironic interpretations scored 85% and 84%, respectively. In both cases, the option 'It depends on the context' obtained a similar percentage (13% and 11%, respectively), which, according to the standard view of irony as a contextual phenomenon, should be the default choice. The fact that few informants interpreted these sentences as ironic shows a strong preference for literal interpretations.

---

does not endorse. Returning to our initial example, a speaker is ironic when she says *I love calm and sunny days!* in the middle of a terrible storm. This shows that what counts is the mismatch between the content of the utterance and the actual state-of-affairs that triggers the ironic interpretation, regardless of the fact that the speaker does indeed love calm and sunny days.

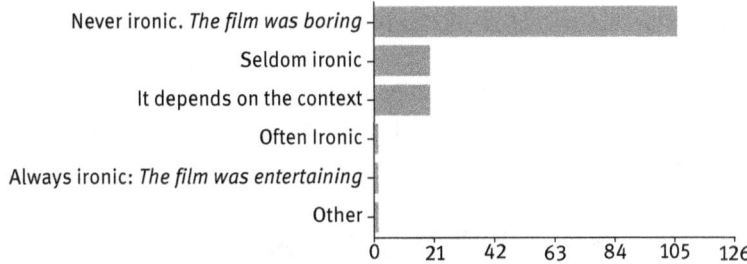

Figure 1: *La película fue muy aburrida* ('The film was very boring').

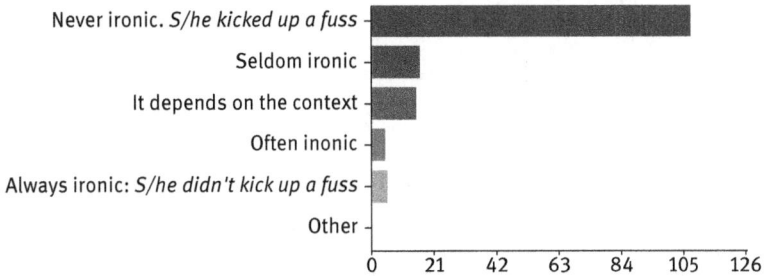

Figure 2: *Armó un buen lío* ('S/he kicked up a fuss.').

The two sentences contain a judgemental evaluation expressed by lexical means, but this fact has not helped to bias the interpretation towards the pole of irony. This seems to provide a first piece of support for our initial hypothesis that only when intensification is expressed by grammatical means can it be strong enough to favour an ironic reading.

4.2 Hypothesis #2: Declarative sentences with exclamation marks will be preferentially interpreted as literal, though there will be an incipient tendency to make their interpretation more dependent on the context

The data show that the answers obtained for declarative sentences with exclamation marks (see ex. (4)) are consistent with our predictions. For the sentence *¡Hoy hace un día espléndido!* (see Fig. 3 below), 60 informants (41%) chose the literal interpretation, but 31 informants (21%) left some room for an ironic interpretation, and a significant number of informants (45 cases; 31%) marked the option that the interpretation would depend on the context.

A similar distribution was obtained for the sentence *¡A las ocho llegaremos!* (see Fig. 4), where 74 informants (50%) preferred the literal interpretation, 17 (12%) chose 'Seldom ironic' and 42 (29%) favoured 'It depends on the context'. In both cases, though the interpretation still falls on the side of literal readings, there is more diversity in the answers.

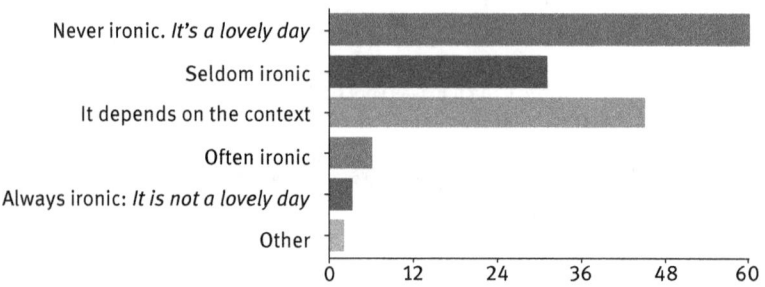

Figure 3: *¡Hace un día espléndido!* ('It's a lovely day!').

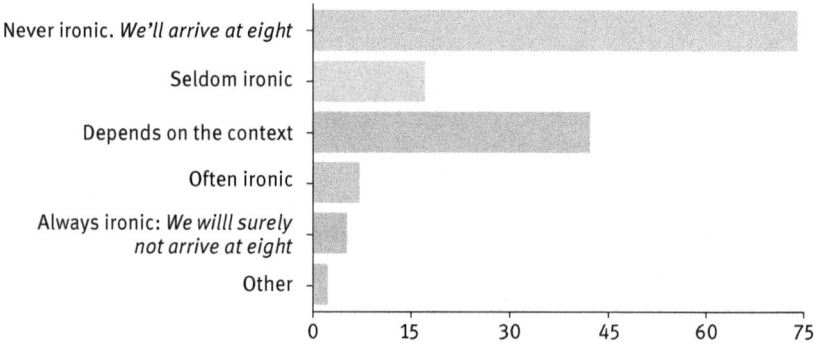

Figure 4: *¡A las ocho llegaremos!* ('We'll arrive at eight!').

4.3 Hypothesis #3: Exclamative sentences will show a stronger tendency to mark their interpretation as context-dependent, with an incipient tendency to yield ironic readings

Exclamative sentences combine prosodic marking (cued textually by exclamation marks) with specific forms of syntactic marking (either by *wh*-fronting or marked word order). Our prediction is that syntactic marking will begin to shift the informants' preferences towards the pole of irony. The data obtained seem to support this prediction.

Sentences with *wh*-fronting (see ex. (5)) obtained a neutral interpretation, where it is the context that provides the relevant data to decide whether the interpretation can be ironic or not. In the case of *¡Qué bonito!* (Fig. 5), 95 informants (65%) chose the neutral option, where the interpretation is entirely dependent on the context. The remaining responses were distributed evenly between the literal interpretation (11%) and the ironic interpretation (8%), with a balanced result for the other intermediate options (4% and 11%, respectively). The results for this example, then, are closer to a normal Gaussian distribution.

In the case of *¡Cuánto tiempo sin verte!* (Fig. 6), the neutral option was again preferred by a majority (71 informants; 48%), though the remaining responses are closer to the pole of literal interpretations (24% and 17%), to the detriment of ironic readings (3% and 1%). In any event, it is worth noting that no other structure shows such a marked preference for neutrality as syntactic exclamatives with *wh*-fronting.

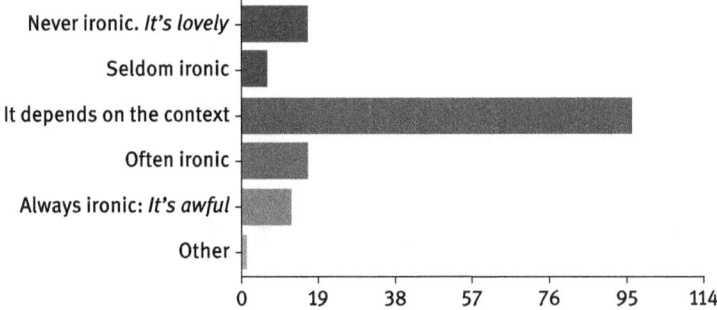

Figure 5: *¡Qué bonito!* ('How lovely!').

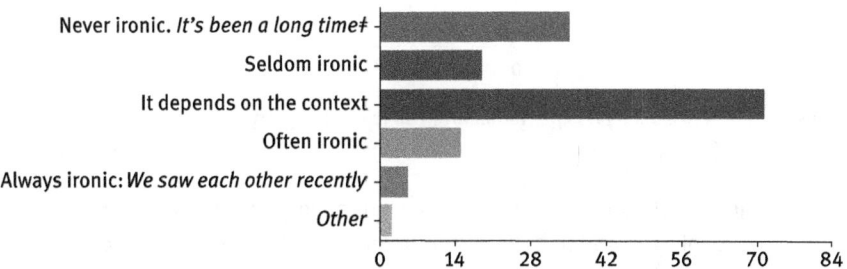

Figure 6: *¡Cuánto tiempo sin verte!* ('I haven't seen you in such a long time!').

A similar picture is obtained for exclamatives with right-dislocation of the subject and verb-initial orders (see ex. (6)). In *¡Sensacional, esta película!* (Fig. 7) the literal interpretation still predominates (70 cases; 48%), but the percentages favouring neutral interpretations are higher in comparison with declaratives with 24 informants selecting 'Seldom ironic' (16%) while 43 prefer the context-dependent option (29%).

The preference for neutral and ironic interpretations is clearer in ¡Tienes tú mucha prisa por terminar! (Fig. 8), an exclamative with VSO word order (see (6b) above). In fact, the preferred option here is the ironic reading, with 39 cases (27%), followed by the neutral, context-dependent option, with 35 cases (24%) and the 'Often ironic' option (31 cases, 21%). In the aggregate, the bias towards ironic interpretations represents 48% of the answers, twice the score of the set of answers favouring a literal interpretation (25%).

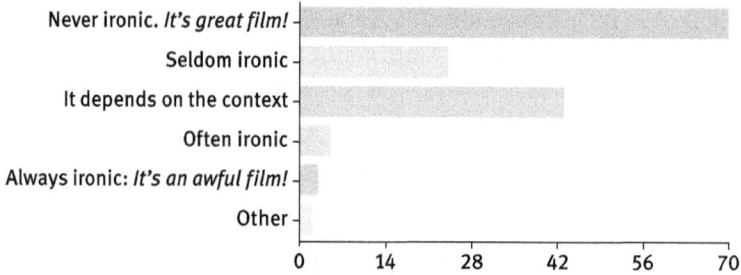

Figure 7: ¡Sensacional, esta película! ('What a great film!').

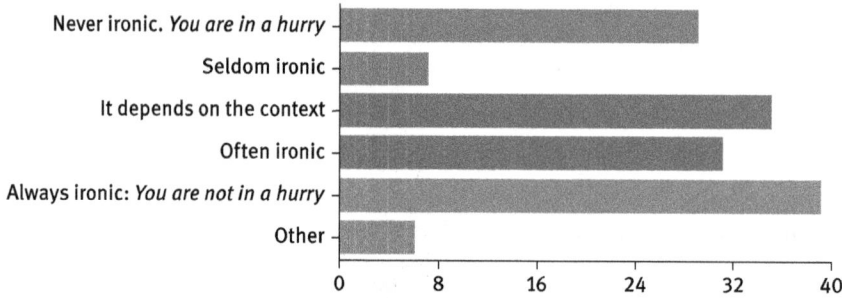

Figure 8: ¡Tienes tú mucha prisa por terminar! ('You're in a big hurry to finish!').

The divergent evaluations of these two exclamative patterns by our informants calls for an explanation. We believe that at least three factors may be conspiring to make the ironic interpretation more salient in the case of ¡Tienes tú mucha prisa por terminar!. The first factor concerns the kind of "mocking, sceptical or critical attitude" that the speaker is able to communicate by means of irony: in ¡Sensacional, esta película! the dissociative attitude does not necessarily target the hearer, whereas in ¡Tienes tú mucha prisa por terminar! the hearer is clearly the target, which makes the ironic reading particularly salient and easy to grasp. The second factor is the presence of two different interpretations that can be seen as ironical in *¡Tienes tú mucha prisa por terminar!* – the same situation that we also perceive in example (7b) (see 4.4 below): one is the basic antiphrastic reading, equivalent to 'You don't seem to be in a hurry to finish' and implying a critical remark like *Come on, hurry up!*; the other is not antiphrastic, and consists in asserting that the hearer really is in a hurry and, at the same time, suggesting that it is because of some hidden reason which is not the one that we might in principle expect, thus communicating a dissociative attitude on the part of the speaker (but not the same attitude as in the antiphrastic reading). The availability of two varieties of ironic interpretation in *¡Tienes tú mucha prisa por terminar!* clearly favours the bias toward irony in the informants' intuitions. Finally, a third relevant factor is the syntax of the two examples. While the grammatical pattern of *¡Sensacional, esta película!* can only be accompanied by an exclamative intonational contour, which suggests that it is intrinsically exclamative, the VSX pattern of *¡Tienes tú mucha prisa por terminar!* is potentially acceptable as an ironic comment and indeed might well be interpreted as such even in the absence of exclamative intonation. This means that VSX, despite not being intrinsically exclamative, is particularly appropriate for the expression of irony (see Escandell-Vidal and Leonetti 2014: §5; Escandell-Vidal and Leonetti 2019), as shown by the bias observed in our results.

A striking feature of the syntax of (6b) is the presence of the subject pronoun *tú*. As Spanish is a null subject language, it could perfectly well be omitted (*Tienes mucha prisa por terminar*), but then the salience of the ironic reading is considerably weakened (note that when the subject is null the sentence no longer exhibits VSX order). Though it is not easy to come up with a principle that would justify the insertion of an overt subject pronoun here, we believe that the motivation lies in the need to make the VSX pattern "visible", with all the interpretive consequences this entails. The main effect is to force an all-focus reading of the sentence (Leonetti 2014). The question is why, and to what extent, this should favour irony. We will deal with this issue again in section 4.4. At this point, there is at least one conclusion that we can safely draw: the link between syntactic structure and ironic interpretation must be seen as a multifactorial issue.

4.4 Hypothesis #4: Sentences with grammatical marking for emphasis will receive the highest scores for ironic interpretations

The examples used to test this prediction fall into two main categories, being either sentences with '*verum* focus'-inducing fronting VFF (XVS order; see ex. (7)) or sentences that combine XVS or VSX with the <*ir* + *a* + infinitive> periphrasis (see ex. (8)).

4.4.1 Sentences with XVS order

The sentences with XVS seem to show a mixed behaviour. A significant subgroup (*Algo sabrá...*, *¡Bastante trabajo tengo ya!* and *¡Eso mismo le dije!*; ex. (7a–c)) shows a bias towards literal interpretations very similar to that of declaratives with exclamation marks (see 4.2). A second, equally significant subgroup (*¡Mucho interés tienes tú en la conferencia!*, *¡Menudo coche se ha comprado!*, *¡Para fiestas estoy yo!*, *¡Buena impresión debimos producir!*, *¡A buenas horas llegas!*, and *¡Muy enterado te veo!*; ex (7d–h)) shows a strong preference for ironic readings.

The sentence *Algo sabrá...* (Fig. 9) is interpreted literally a majority of the time (61 cases, 41%), followed by context-dependent readings (40 cases, 27%), while ironic readings represent a total of only 30 cases (20%). The bias in favour of literal interpretations is more marked for *¡Bastante trabajo tengo ya!*, with a distribution very similar to that of declaratives (Fig. 10), where 98 informants (67%) chose the literal interpretation, whereas the remaining options receive relatively meagre percentages, all between 5% and 10%.

Finally, the sentence *¡Eso mismo le dije!* (Fig. 11) stands in an intermediate position, with 91 informants (55%) selecting the literal reading, and the ironic interpretations representing a residual 6% only.

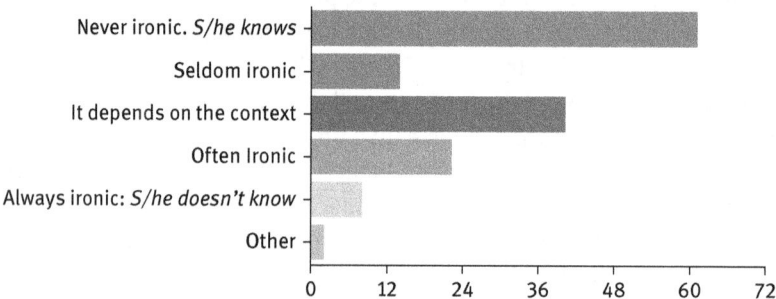

Figure 9: *Algo sabrá...* ('S/he must know something').

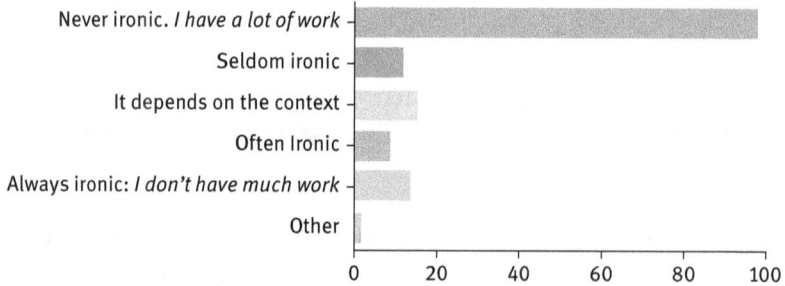

Figure 10: *¡Bastante trabajo tengo ya!* ('As if I didn't have enough work already!').

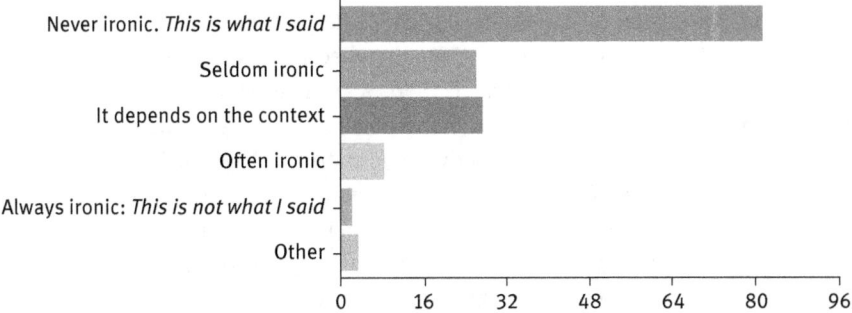

Figure 11: ¡Eso mismo le dije ('That's exactly what I told him/her!').

The second subgroup in the XVS category, by contrast, shows a very significant bias towards ironic interpretations, as if it were the mirror image of the first group. For the sentence ¡Mucho interés tienes tú en la conferencia! (Fig. 12), if we add the 58 cases (39%) of 'Always ironic' to the 51 cases (35%) of 'Often ironic', we get an aggregate score of 109 cases (74%) of ironic interpretations. Only 24 informants (16%) chose the context-dependent option, and the literal interpretations show only residual figures. Among the reasons why informants preferred ironic interpretations, we should mention that the sentence can have two different readings, both of which can be perceived as "ironic", similarly to what we saw with (6b). On the one hand, the sentence can be used to ironically express the notion that the addressee has no interest at all in the conference – in other words, the antiphrastic interpretation, and on the other, it can be also used to convey the idea that the addressee has little interest in the content of the conference, though possibly a great interest in other secondary aspects, such as who is going to attend the conference. In either interpretation, there is a clash between the encoded content and the actual state-of-affairs, together with a dissociative attitude on the part of the speaker, so both interpretations count as ironic.

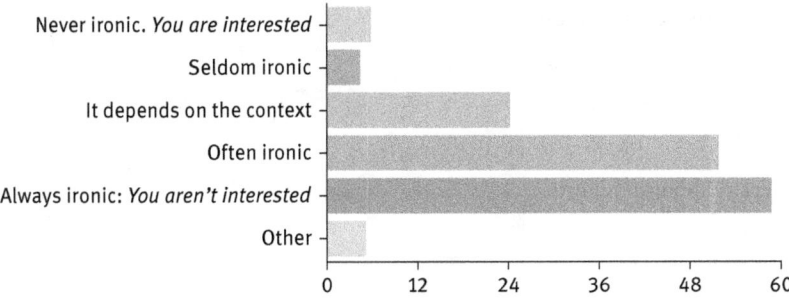

Figure 12: ¡Mucho interés tienes tú en la conferencia! ('You sure are interested in the conference!').

The interpretation of the sentence *¡Para fiestas estoy yo!* (Fig. 13) was almost unanimously ironic: 114 informants (78%) labelled it 'Always ironic' and another 18 (12%) judged it 'Often ironic', which yields a grand total of 90%, the remaining options eliciting insignificant scores. The pattern of answers shows a very consistent, shared intuition across a large body of informants. The reason is, we think, that the predicate *estar para fiestas* is actually a 'negative polarity item' which requires a negation. *No estar para fiestas* is an idiom, so an ironic interpretation simply adds the missing negation. Therefore, the grammatical properties of the sentence trigger a negative interpretation, in much the same way as do other negative polarity items in rhetorical interrogatives, such as when *Did you ever lift a finger for him?* is interpreted as 'You never lifted a finger for him' (see Bosque 1980: 106–108 for the link between irony and negative polarity items). As a result, irony is not encoded directly here but rather favoured by the grammatical properties of the sentence.

In *¡Menudo coche se ha comprado!* (Fig. 14), the preferred option is the 'Always ironic' interpretation (53 cases; 36%), followed by the neutral option (46 cases, 31%). If we add the score for 'Often ironic' (17 cases, 12%), the preference for the

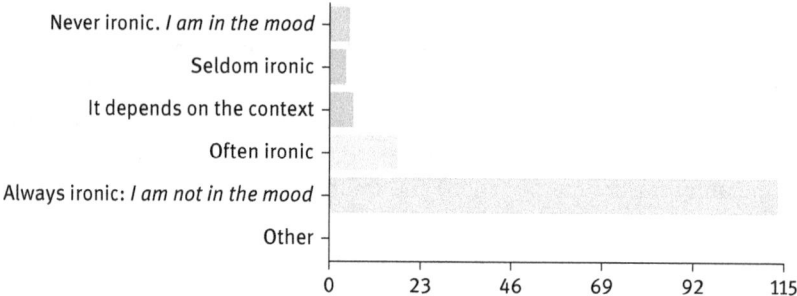

Figure 13: *¡Para fiestas estoy yo!* ('I'm in a fine mood for parties!').

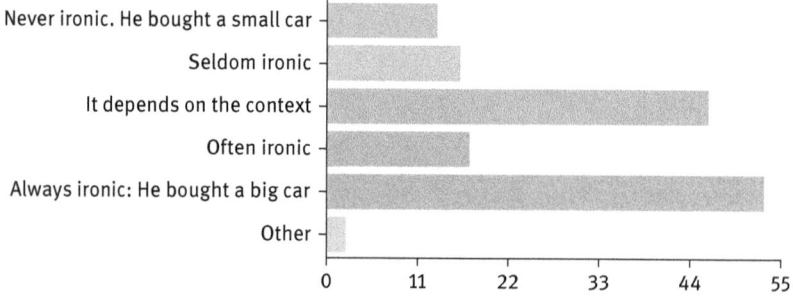

Figure 14: *¡Menudo coche se ha comprado!* ('That's some car he has bought!').

ironic readings rises to 48%. In this case, the fact that 20% of the informants selected the literal interpretation is totally unexpected, given that what *menudo coche* implies is that the car is very big, or very expensive, or very flashy, and not that it is small or insignificant, as the literal meaning of the adjective *menudo* encodes. What we have here is probably a case of reanalysis of the meaning of *menudo*. When this adjective occurs before the noun – a marked word order in Spanish – it works as a sort of idiomatic intensifier. This has led the informants to assume that the literal meaning of *menudo* is 'big', not 'small', which can explain the diversity of judgements obtained.

The interpretation of *¡Buena impresión debimos producir!* (Fig. 15) shows a strong bias in favour of ironic readings (a total of 68%: 67 responses for 'Always ironic', 46%, and 35 for 'Often ironic', 24%). These results contrast with those elicited by a closely related sentence, *¡A buenas horas llegas!*, with similar syntax and lexical choice, but here the bias towards the ironic interpretation is stronger. In fact, this is the sentence that produced the greatest consensus (Fig. 16), with 121 informants (82%) choosing 'Always ironic' and another 15 (10%) choosing 'Often ironic', to yield a total of 92%. In fact, this sentence has become an idiom with an antiphrastic interpretation, which surely biased the results for this question.

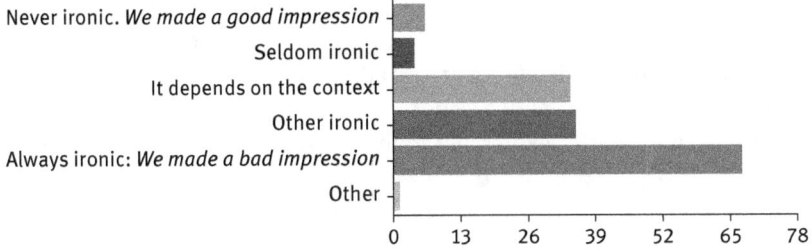

Figure 15: *¡Buena impresión debimos producir!* ('A fine impression we must have made!').

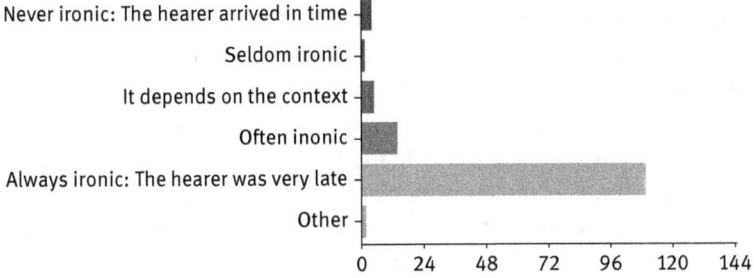

Figure 16: *¡A buenas horas llegas!* (Fine time for you to arrive!).

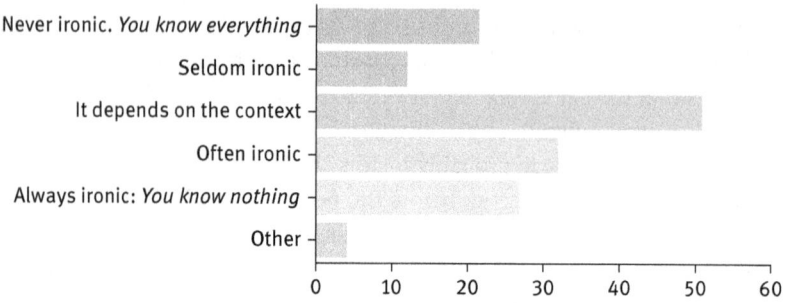

Figure 17: ¡Muy enterado te veo! ('You sure know a lot about it!').

Finally, ¡Muy enterado te veo! (Fig. 17) shows a similar distribution, with a less marked bias towards ironic interpretations, and a strong preference for the context-dependent option.

To sum up, within the class of sentences with XVS word order there are two distinct groups: one where the preference falls on the side of literal interpretations, and one favouring ironic interpretations. The difference can be explained, we think, by a number of factors. First, irony is never encoded in any of the examples under consideration. At most, syntax can favour certain readings to various degrees, but a certain amount of choice is always available to the speaker. Furthermore, the bias towards ironic interpretations increases when other resources are added, such as the fronting of evaluative adjectives or, as we will see later, the use of the <ir + a + infinitive> periphrastic structure. On the other hand, not all the contents are equally apt for expressing ironic remarks. For instance, the future and indefinite in *Algo sabrá…* and the weak quantifier in *¡Bastante trabajo tengo ya!* are not good candidates for argumentative inversion, particularly because they do not favour the expression of a dissociative attitude. This shows again that irony is not encoded. It can be favoured by some syntactic structures, but lexical choices and world knowledge also play a very significant role in the interpretation.

A reviewer raises a very interesting question related to our perspective: what proportion of a construction's interpretations need to be ironic before we can say that it 'encodes' irony, rather than just being a trigger for an ironic interpretation? In this paper we have taken a strong monosemous approach, trying to avoid the multiplication of meanings in the grammatical system and therefore leaving identification of the intended interpretation to the utterance's interaction with its context. Thus, in the cases we have examined here it is the context that makes it possible to determine whether the interpretation is ironic or not. Of course, the more frequent an interpretation, the higher the likelihood that it will become grammaticalized. This is probably the case with *menudo* ('small, minute'), which in the expression '*Menudo* + [noun]!' automatically elicits an ironic interpretation – an interpretation that has almost completely replaced the original meaning in Spanish speakers' consciousness.

4.4.2 XVS with <*ir* + *a* + infinitive> periphrasis

Our last group of examples of sentences with XVS order is that in which this grammatical resource is combined with the <*ir* + *a* + infinitive> periphrasis. This construction places focus on the initial phase of an event, triggering the inference that, once initiated, the event will necessarily and inevitably occur. This component of epistemic necessity is what underlies the speaker's strong commitment, which makes any incongruence more salient (see Escandell-Vidal and Leonetti 2014).

Informants showed a strong preference for literal readings for the sentence *De poco te va a servir quejarte...* (103 answers, 70%, for 'Never ironic' and 20 more, 14%, for 'Seldom ironic', making a grand total of 84%) (Fig. 18). These results seem to contradict our initial predictions. There are various possible reasons for this behaviour, however. On the one hand, the utterance was presented to informants as text followed by ellipsis points, a graphic representation which does not favour emphatic readings, and on the other, as in other examples considered above like *Algo sabrá...* and *Bastante trabajo tengo ya*, the occurrence of a weak quantifier does not facilitate strong emphatic interpretations either. It is worth noting that if we had presented the example with an intensifier like *mucho* 'much', as in *De mucho te servirá quejarte* (lit. 'You will gain a lot from complaining'), the interpretation would have been clearly biased towards the irony pole. Again, syntactic form plays a major role, but it can be overridden by the effects of lexical choices.

The sentence *¡A ti te voy a dejar yo el coche!* (Fig. 19) received a very high number of answers for the ironic readings (91%, of which 112 answers, 76%, for 'Always ironic', and 22 answers, 15%, for 'Often ironic'). Crucially, none of the informants chose the literal interpretation and only one of them marked 'Seldom ironic'.

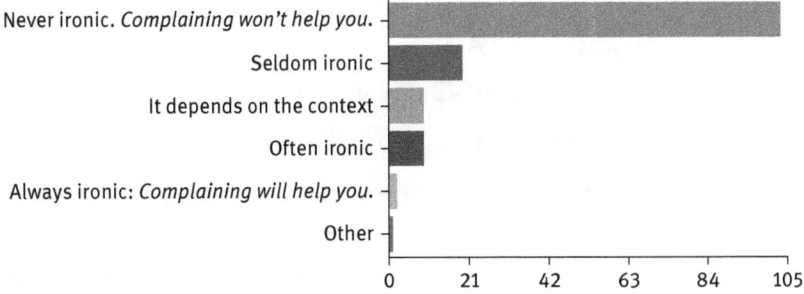

Figure 18: *¡De poco te va a servir quejarte!* ('Little good it'll do you to complain!').

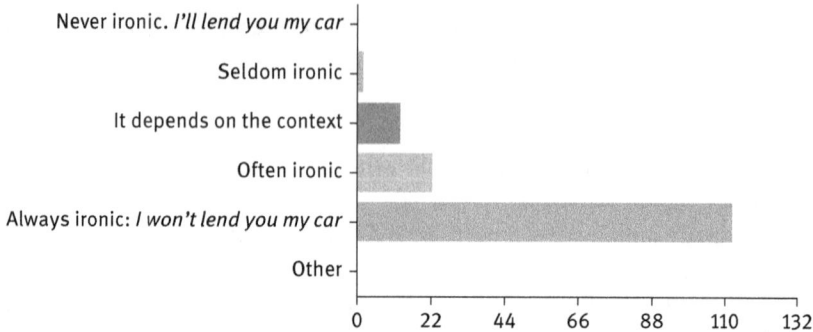

Figure 19: *¡A ti te voy a dejar yo el coche!* ('Yeah, right, I'm going to lend you my car!').

The results for *¡A ti te voy a dejar el coche!* (Fig. 19), with fronting and a radical preference for ironic interpretation, contrast with the scores obtained for the sentence *¡Te va a esperar Eva hasta las ocho!* (Fig. 20), with VSX order but without fronting (the initial clitic is irrelevant here). In this case ironic interpretations still predominate (74 cases, 50%, for 'Always ironic', and 26 cases, 18%, for 'Often ironic'), literal readings attracting only 9% of responses), but the utterance leaves considerable room for ambiguity – in fact, an exclamative but non-ironic reading is perfectly acceptable. The differences between these two sentences may seem unexpected, since the <*ir* + *a* + infinitive> periphrasis is present in both of them. However, there is a syntactic factor that can explain the differences in scores. In the first sentence VFF combines with an additional mark for emphasis, namely, the doubling of the fronted second person pronoun, which occurs twice, once in its full strong form, introduced by the preposition *a* (*a ti*) and then again in its clitic, weak form (*te*). By contrast, in the second sentence there is VSX order, but we have neither fronting nor clitic doubling. Thus, apparently, the sentence with more marks for emphasis receives higher ratings as ironic. This highlights the importance of '*verum*

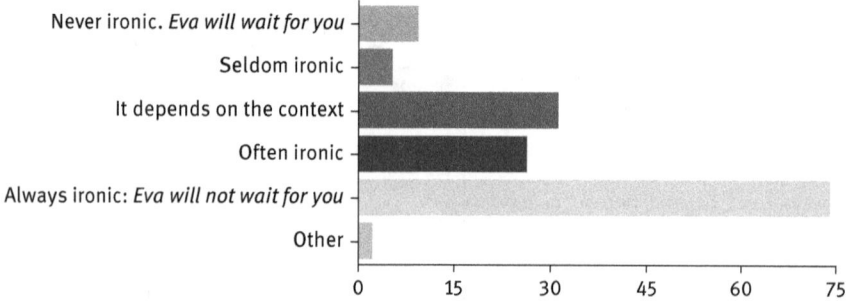

Figure 20: *¡Te va a esperar Eva hasta las ocho!* ('Yeah, sure Eva's going to wait for you until eight!').

focus'-inducing fronting as a possible trigger for ironic readings, and at the same time raises the question as to why clitic doubling should be relevant.

We cannot offer a fully articulated answer here, but we would like to note certain facts that may help to justify bringing clitic doubling into the overall discussion. Clitic doubling is grammatical – actually, obligatory – in all varieties of Spanish with strong pronouns as objects, but resorting to the bare clitic pronoun, without doubling, is always an available option. If the object is in focus, doubling is required, since the clitic alone is unable to express focal information. This is not the case with *¡A ti te voy a dejar el coche!*, but in this example doubling is needed to allow fronting (cf. **A ti voy a dejar el coche*). The crucial data come from contexts where doubling is not licensed by focus structure and has no apparent motivation. For instance, in *¡Te va a esperar Eva...!* doubling of the direct object is optional (*¡Te va a esperar a ti Eva...!*): it is of interest to observe that with doubling the bias towards ironic interpretations is reinforced. Doubling has essentially the same effect that the presence of a strong subject pronoun in postverbal position may have (in competition with the null option), as already mentioned with respect to (6b). The minimal pairs in (9) and (10) illustrate this point (both include the futurate periphrasis).

(9) a. Si   sigues   así,   vas   a   llegar   muy   lejos.
       If   go-on.PRS.2SG   So,   go.PRS.2SG   to   arrive   very   far

    b. Si   sigues   así,   vas   tú   a   llegar   muy   lejos.
       If   go-on.PRS.2SG   so,   go.PRS.2SG   you   to   arrive   very   far
       'If you go on like this, you are going to get very far.'

(10) a. Vete   a   decirle   que   lo   haga.
        Go.REF.IMP.2SG   to   tell.him   that   it.OBJ   do.PRS.SUBJ.3SG

     b. Vete   tú   a   decirle   que   lo   haga.
        Go.REF.IMP.2SG   you   to   tell.him   that   it.OBJ   do.PRS.SUBJ.3SG
        'Go tell him to do it!'

In (9) and (10) the two options – null subject/overt subject – are compared: in both cases the version with an overt pronoun is almost obligatorily interpreted ironically (with readings equivalent to 'If you go on like this, you are not going very far', for (9), and 'Don't dare to tell him to do it!', for (10)), whereas its counterpart can receive a literal interpretation as well. The key factor is the insertion of a strong pronoun in a context where a simple clitic or a null subject could have been used. Since strong pronouns are traditionally associated with emphasis in grammatical descriptions of null subject languages, it is not surprising that their presence counts as a marker of emphasis, possibly through contrast and the evocation of contextual alternatives. In our examples, the effect is strengthened by the fact that we have second person pronouns: this surely favours the expression of a critical attitude towards the hearer. The common feature for strong pronouns in all cases we observed is that they are interpreted neither as topics nor as narrow foci. The role of pronouns in the relative saliency of ironic interpretations deserves a detailed study that we cannot carry out here, but hopefully these brief notes can shed some light on certain aspects of the results in our survey.

5 The grammatical ingredients of emphasis

The hypothesis that irony is favoured by the grammatical expression of intensification and emphasis is confirmed by the results of our survey. Emphasis plays the role of making the incongruence between utterance and context more easily noticeable. As noted above, all emphatic constructions in the survey belong to the typology of exclamative sentences or are closely related to them. At this point, it is worth discussing in more detail the connections among all the constructions involved.

Exclamatives can be defined as grammatical structures which convey an emotional attitude on the part of the speaker towards a certain state of affairs, this attitude usually reflecting surprise with respect to a situation that is judged to be non-canonical or unexpected. Exclamatives express propositions which the speaker assumes to be true.

A facet of the grammar of exclamatives that is seldom discussed is their informational articulation (see § 4.3). In *wh*-exclamatives (like (4)), focus falls on the degree value of some gradable predicate (for instance, in *How tall she is!*, on the degree variable in a proposition like 'She is tall at degree d'), and the rest of the propositional content is a single, unarticulated informational chunk, which represents the background. We would like to stress that the remaining exclamative schemas we reviewed share this property of lacking informational articulation (topic comment, focus/background).

Binomial exclamatives (like (6a), *¡Sensacional, esta película!*) at first sight contradict this generalization, since they contain a clear partition: the subject is right-dislocated. However, we believe that the true exclamative –despite the presence of exclamation marks in writing – is actually only the predicative constituent in initial position; the subject is right-dislocated merely to comply with the condition related to informational structure, as a means of obtaining a single informational chunk that presents an unexpected state of affairs, once the topical subject has been "expelled" from the core predication. If these observations are well founded, binomial exclamatives no longer serve as a counterexample anymore for the condition regarding information structure.

As for exclamatives built on marked orders (XVS, VSX; see §4.4), the generalization holds, since both patterns give rise to informational chunks without internal articulation, as shown in Leonetti and Escandell (2009) for XVS and in Leonetti (2014) for VSX in Spanish. In the first case, overt constituents in the sentence form a single informational region that acts as the background with respect to narrow focus on the sentence polarity; focus on polarity is a way of emphasizing the truth of a contextually known proposition, and explains why the construction is perceived as emphatic (note the parallel with the basic properties of exclamatives mentioned above).

In the second case (VSX), there is no aboutness topic – though there could be an initial 'stage topic' – and the sentence is assigned an all-focus, thetic interpretation. Thus, the two orders are interpreted differently, but both give rise to the absence of internal informational divisions. It is interesting to recall that even in unmarked SVO sentences coupled with exclamative intonation (for instance, *Eleanor has bought a new bike!*), the expression of surprise and unexpectedness of new information correlates with an all-focus, thetic reading, in other words, with the absence of informational partitions.

The common feature in all these constructions is informational packaging: the propositional content forms a single informational unit, because focus is limited either to a degree value (*wh*-exclamatives) or to the polarity (VFF), or because focus extends to the whole predication (binomial exclamatives, VSX). Emphasis is rooted in the interpretation of focus. It may derive (a) from focus on a degree that is beyond the speaker's expectations; (b) from focus on the polarity and the consequent strong assertion of the propositional content; (c) from focus on the whole clause, which is presented as new information (this implies that the speaker is unaware of such information and gives rise to the expression of surprise and unexpectedness). The set of constructions under discussion includes thetic sentences, mirative expressions and exclamatives: this confirms that they are closely related constructions, as argued in García Macías (2016) on the basis of cross-linguistic data. Then, it should not be particularly shocking that they are all appropriate linguistic tools for the expression of irony.

6 Conclusions

With this survey we have attempted to gather some preliminary data to understand why some sentences seem to receive an ironic reading even out of context.

Our claim is not that irony is encoded, but rather that there are certain grammatical resources that can facilitate ironic interpretations. We have explored the correlation between ironic readings and grammatical resources for intensification and emphasis. Our data show that the more emphatic a sentence, the greater the likelihood that it can receive an ironic interpretation. This interpretive bias can be explained along the lines of Sperber and Wilson's approach to irony. In their view, irony consists of echoing a thought and communicating an attitude of distance towards it (typically, because that thought does not actually correspond to the state-of-affairs it intends to represent). When the content of an utterance is clearly incongruent with the actual state-of-affairs, the stronger the emphasis, the more noticeable the incongruence. Put in other words, intensification and emphasis can contribute to making the incongruence more salient.

References

Andueza, Patricia. 2011. *Rhetorical Exclamatives in Spanish*. Columbus: The Ohio State University dissertation.

Attardo, Salvatore, Jodi Eisterhold, Jennifer Hay & Isabella Poggi. 2003. Multimodal markers of irony and sarcasm. *Humor* 16 (2). 243–260.

Attardo, Salvatore, Manuela Maria Wagner & Eduardo Urios-Aparisi. 2011. Prosody and humor. In Salvatore Attardo, Manuela Maria Wagner & Eduardo Urios-Aparisi (eds.), *Prosody and Humor*, 189–201. Amsterdam: John Benjamins.

Bosque, Ignacio. 1980. *Sobre la negación*. Madrid: Cátedra.

Bosque, Ignacio. 2017. Spanish exclamatives in perspective. In Ignacio Bosque (ed.), *Advances in the Analysis of Spanish Exclamatives*, 1–52. Columbus: The Ohio State University Press.

Bryant, Gregory A. 2010. Prosodic contrasts in ironic speech. *Discourse Processes* 47 (7). 545–566.

Bryant, Gregory A. 2011. Verbal irony in the wild. *Pragmatics & Cognition* 19 (2). 291–309.

Bryant, Gregory A. & Jean E. Fox-Tree. 2002. Recognizing verbal irony in spontaneous speech. *Metaphor and Symbol* 17 (2). 99–117.

Bryant, Gregory A. and Jean E. Fox-Tree. 2005. Is there an ironic tone of voice?. *Language and Speech* 48. 257–277.

Castroviejo Miró, Elena (2008). Deconstructing exclamations. *Catalan Journal of Linguistics* 7. 41–90.

Clark, Herbert H. & Richard J. Gerrig. 1984. On the pretense theory of irony. *Journal of Experimental Psychology*: General 113 (1). 121–126.

Colston, Herbert. 2000. On necessary conditions for verbal irony comprehension. *Pragmatics and Cognition* 8 (2). 277–324.

Curcó, Carmen. 2000. Irony: negation, echo and metarepresentation. *Lingua* 110. 257–280.

Escandell-Vidal, Victoria & Manuel Leonetti. 2009. La expresión del *Verum Focus* en español. *Español Actual* 92. 11–46.

Escandell-Vidal, Victoria & Manuel Leonetti. 2014. Fronting and irony in Spanish. In Andreas Dufter & Álvaro Octavio de Toledo (eds.), *Left Sentence Peripheries in Spanish: Diachronic, Variationist and Typological Perspectives*, 309–342. Amsterdam: John Benjamins.

Escandell-Vidal, Victoria & Manuel Leonetti. 2015. Factores sintácticos en el reconocimiento de la ironía en español. Un estudio empírico. In *Studium Grammaticae. Homenaje al profesor José A. Martínez*, 269–284. Oviedo: Universidad de Oviedo.
Escandell-Vidal, Victoria & Manuel Leonetti. 2019. Futuro y miratividad. Anatomía de una relación. *Estudios lingüísticos en homenaje a Emilio Ridruejo*, vol. I, 385–402. Valencia: Publicacions de la Universitat de València.
García Macías, José Hugo. 2016. *From the Unexpected to the Unbelievable: Thetics, Miratives and Exclamatives in Conceptual Space*. Albuquerque: The University of New Mexico dissertation.
Gibbs, Raymond. 2000. Irony in talk among friends. *Metaphor and Symbolic Activity* 15. 5–27.
González-Fuentes, Santiago, Victoria Escandell-Vidal & Pilar Prieto. 2015. Gestural codas pave the way to the understanding of verbal irony. *Journal of Pragmatics* 90. 26–47.
Grice, Herbert Paul. 1975. Logic and conversation. In Peter Cole & Jerry L. Morgan (eds.), *Syntax and Semantics, vol. III. Speech Acts*, 41–58. New York: Academic Press.
Leonetti, Manuel. 2014. Spanish VSX. In Karen Lahousse & Stefania Marzo (eds.), *Romance Languages and Linguistic Theory 2012*, 37–64. Amsterdam: John Benjamins.
Leonetti, Manuel & Victoria Escandell-Vidal. 2009. Fronting and Verum Focus in Spanish. In Anderas Dufter & Daniel Jacob (eds.), *Focus and Background in Romance Languages*, 155–204. Amsterdam: John Benjamins.
Michaelis, Laura. 2001. Exclamative constructions. In Martin Haspelmath, Ekkehard König, Wulf Österreicher & Wolfgang Raible (eds.), *Language Universals and Language Typology. An International Handbook,* 1038–1050. Berlin: De Gruyter.
Michaelis, Laura & Hanbing Feng. 2015. What is this, sarcastic syntax?. *Constructions and Frames* 7 (2). 148–180.
Padilla-García, Xosé. 2012. ¿Existen rasgos prosódicos objetivos en los enunciados irónicos?. *Oralia* 14. 203–224.
Rosales-Sequeiros, Xosé. 2011. Irony, relevance and pragmatic interpretation in Spanish. *Language Sciences* 33. 369–385.
Searle, John. 1979. *Expression and Meaning: Studies in the Theory of Speech Acts*. Cambridge: Cambridge University Press.
Sperber, Dan & Deirdre Wilson. 1981. Irony and the use-mention distinction. In Peter Cole (ed.), *Radical Pragmatics,* 295–318. New York: Academic Press.
Sperber, Dan & Deirdre Wilson. 1986/1995. *Relevance: Communication and Cognition*. Blackwell: Oxford.
Villalba, Xavier. 2017. Exclamatives, imperatives, optatives. In Andreas Dufter & Elisabeth Stark (eds.), *Manual of Romance Morphosyntax and Syntax*, 603–646. Berlin: De Gruyter.
Wilson, Deirdre. 2006. The pragmatics of verbal irony: echo or pretence?. *Lingua* 116. 1722–1743.
Wilson, Deirdre & Dan Sperber. 1992. On verbal irony. *Lingua* 87. 53–76.
Wilson, Deirdre & Dan Sperber 2012. Explaining irony. In Deirdre Wilson & Dan Sperber, *Meaning and Relevance*, 123–145. Cambridge: Cambridge University Press.
Yus, Francisco. 2009. Saturación contextual en la comprensión de la ironía. In Leonor Ruiz Gurillo & Xosé A. Padilla García (eds.), *Dime cómo ironizas y te diré quién eres*, 309–331. Bern: Peter Lang.

Part III: **Diversity across media**

Herbert L. Colston
Eye-rolling, irony and embodiment

Abstract: Eye-rolling is a wide-spread human nonverbal behavior associated with a number of attitudinal positions and corresponding language forms. People commonly roll their eyes, along with a host of related behaviors, for instance, as stand-alone disapproval and other meaningful displays. Eye-rolling is also a frequent accompaniment of verbal irony and other figurative, indirect and direct forms of language also associated with disapproval or other relevant attitudes concerning referent topics. To-date, though, relatively little research has investigated this prevalent human communicative behavior other than some documentations of its common practitioners and discourse residences, including as a form of social aggression and as a complex response by women (demonstrating "contempt") to sexist humor (Goodwin & Alim, 2010; LaFrance & Woodzicka, 1998; Underwood, 2004). The following chapter accordingly offers a brief overview of some observed parameters of eye-rolling and related behaviors, as well as several potential accounts to explain their usage for disapproval and related displays and as complements of verbal irony. Different ways to frame explorations into eye-rolling as communicative behavior are also provided. An empirical test of one of the proposed accounts, under one of the considered evaluative frameworks is then presented to demonstrate one means of addressing eye-rolling as a complex embodied human communicative behavior. Questions and issues that future research into eye-rolling and ally behaviors are likely to face are then considered.

Keywords: eye-rolling, verbal irony, disapproval displays, embodiment, nonverbal behavior, co-speech gesture, gesture

In a widely viewed international news story from summer 2017, German Chancellor Angela Merkel was recorded on camera at the G20 economic summit in

---

Acknowledgements: Portions of this work were presented at the 2017 International Cognitive Linguistics Conference in Tartu, Estonia (Colston, 2017, July), and as part of an address at the Alberta Conference on Linguistics in Edmonton, Canada (Colston, 2017, November).
   The author would like to thank Caelaan Marrville for assistance with the experimental portion of the work.
   This research was partially supported by the Office of the Vice President, Research (VPR) at the University of Alberta, and the Social Sciences Research Council (SSHRC) of Canada.
   The author declares no conflicts of interest with respect to authorship or publication of this work.
   Please address any correspondence concerning this research to: colston@ualberta.ca

---

Herbert L. Colston, University of Alberta

https://doi.org/10.1515/9783110652246-010

Hamburg, Germany, rolling her eyes in apparent response to a presumed patronizing conversional turn by Russian President Vladimir Putin. As reported in the New York Magazine at the time, ("Angela Merkel Rolling Her Eyes at Putin Is the Perfect GIF You Didn't Know You Needed", Kircher, 2017):

> Attention, please: Eye-rolling 101 is officially in session. Your teacher today is none other than German Chancellor Angela Merkel, who appears to have the ocular move down pat. Chancellor Merkel demonstrated her skills today while speaking with Russian President Vladimir Putin during the G20 summit in Hamburg. It's unclear exactly what the two world leaders were discussing, which means we can't know for certain what Merkel meant by her eye-roll. Perhaps she'd had enough of whatever Putin was yapping about and sent her eyes skyward in hopes of shutting him up ('Okay, Angela: So a priest, a rabbi, and a duck walk into a bar …'). Or, maybe, it was an emphatic agreement with something the Russian had just said ('The coffee at this shindig is terrible this year!'). Either way, take notes on her form – the brow raise, the chin lift, the slight gulp at the end – and study up. If you're going to roll your eyes, this is the way to do it.

Although the content of Putin's comment which supposedly elicited this communicative act by Chancellor Merkel is not widely known, and as suggested by the New York Magazine piece the gesture could mean a variety of things, it appears to nonetheless have involved, according to many commentators, some form of dismissal by Putin of a preceding contribution by Merkel. Putin begins his turn with a curt head shake, as if he was saying Merkel was incorrect about something in her immediately preceding contribution. He then follows this gesture by talking at Merkel but without looking at her at which point she performs the eye-roll gesture. Many commentators thus took this turn by Putin to be an instance of "mansplaining", or a condescending and superior patriarchal attitude occasionally adopted by men, and sometimes women, demonstrating their assumption of superior expertise about some content relative to their female (usually) conversational partner(s). On this view, Merkel was accordingly expressing her disapproval of this behavior on Putin's part, through her poignant earnest eye-roll gesture.

Or, consider another possibility of an eye-roll gesture used with irony. Imagine a speaker using an eye-roll gesture not as a stand-alone disapproval display, but rather as a cue accompanying a sarcastic comment such as, "How typical of my sister, always arriving on time", when the sister is actually arriving late for some engagement, as per her usual behavior.

Although some limited work has investigated eye-rolls of this nature, almost none of it comes from a cognitive linguistic or psycholinguistic perspective – looking into potential underpinnings of this particular gesture, why it bears the suite of meanings it often does, how it interacts with speech, how it is understood, acquired, etc. Previous work has documented instead how eye-rolls are often used for social aggressive purposes, often by girls, women, and disrespectfully treated groups of people – the latter as a complex response to demeaning humor (Goodwin & Alim, 2010; LaFrance & Woodzicka, 1998; Underwood, 2004). This published work has come from Linguistic Anthropology, Feminist Studies and related disciplines seeking to document complex communicative and expressive behaviors cohering with particularized experiences in the groups addressed.

But given recent calls for greater incorporation of nonverbal communicative behaviors in our attempted understandings of linguistic production, comprehension and usage processes in Cognitive Linguistics and Psycholinguistics (Kelly, 2001; Stec, 2012), it behooves researchers from these backgrounds to pay greater heed to eye-rolls and related behaviors in our attempts to understand meaningful linguistic communion. Accordingly, the following chapter will offer first some potential parameters of observed eye-rolls as a communicative behavior, including related behaviors used for similar purposes. This will serve the initial need to establish a sense of the domain of eye-rolls and related behaviours within human discourse. This treatment will be accompanied by a brief analysis of how people label eye-roll recordings on a website devoted to posting catagorizeable GIFS, including snippets of recorded eye-rolls and related behaviours with the labeling hashtag; "eyeroll".

Some potential accounts of eye-roll production and comprehension, some adapted from existing accounts of verbal irony with others stemming from accounts of embodied meaning more broadly construed, are then offered. A brief empirical evaluation of one of these accounts is also provided. This evaluation demonstrates one view that eye-rolls might be considered a deeply embodied, multiply-determined experiential, and expressive communicative system, which serves both as a marker of irony but also as a stand-alone disapproval display. Detachment and optimality are discussed as key underpinnings of this account.

Finally, some potential research questions and concomitant ramifications for methodologies and scopes of theorizing are offered to catalyze future work on eye-rolling. It is hoped that this initial look at some lay categorizations of eye-rolls, the discussion of potential theoretical underpinnings as well as consideration of questions for research going forward will lay a foundation for more specific empirical, experimental and observational work on this interesting expressive and communicative phenomenon.

1 Eye-rolling parameters

An interesting initiation into the range of eye-rolls and related behaviors is possible by searching internet websites with the search term, "eye-roll" and then simply observing the content posted. Of course such collections will contain a wide variety of authentic, staged, acted, canned, animated, exaggerated, minimalist and many other types of eye-rolling and related behavior. But such an initial nonscientific perusal can nonetheless provide at least a sense of the range of complex and interrelated behaviors people display involving subtle to not-so-subtle expressions involving their eyes. These behaviors will range from full-blown rolling of eyes with gaze directions traversing the complete arc from initial extreme lateral gaze to one side, moving through looking upward to ending with gaze directed to the opposite side of the onset direction, to much more subtle hazing of visual focus, eye-widening, eyelid-fluttering, slight gaze aversions, eye-crossings, complex mixtures of the above and many other similar behaviors.

One can readily see from such content that eye-rolling can be used as a stand-alone disapproval display or as an accompaniment to speech. Eye-rolls are also often used as co-speech gestures with verbal irony and other related language. Eye-rolls can also be used as initial displays in conversational interactions or as free or back-channel responses. They are also often carefully positioned amid other discourse content to enable subtle timing manipulations, in part to leverage pragmatic effects (Colston, 2015) but also to cleft discourse participants into those witnessing the display versus those left out of the expressed message. Eye-rolls are also often conducted with lengthy durations (e.g., several seconds), with subtle sequences of intermixed other expressive behaviors to create an elaborate mini-performance of great nuance and complexity.

Many other forms of nonverbal behavior are also incorporated with eye-rolls and similar eye gestures. Among these are other facial expressions and emotional displays. A variety of head and body movements are used along with eye-gestures. As mentioned earlier, speech is also a frequent accompaniment of all these behaviors but so are other varieties of vocalizations. Other hand and body gestures including stance and spacing expressions are also used with eye-rolling.

In short, eye-rolling in situ as well as in performed and acted situations is incredibly complex and involves a huge suite of related nonverbal activity. Isolating eye-rolling as a unit of analysis might thus be a bit of an artificial endeavor. But it remains useful to at least consider possible meaningful underpinnings of eye-rolling along with similar behaviors, as many of them might share embodied sources. This could explain both why people produce them but also why they're useful for comprehension by observers. Indeed, these production and comprehension motivations might stem from similar underpinnings in that eye-rolls could arise from deeply embodied experiences of speakers/performers in situations motivating eye-rolling, including the experience of irony. But the leaking out, as it were, of these embodied experiences in speakers/performers also might serve to enhance the uptake of the expressed states of the speakers by hearers (viewers), such that eye-rolls serve comprehension success as well.

Given this potential mutual function of expressive catharsis and comprehension enhancement, it might be useful to look briefly at how people label publicly posted recordings of eye-rolls, including authentic and other performances as contained on websites as previously mentioned, to get a sense of what people think eye-rolls are doing. Accordingly, the following brief analysis of eye-roll GIFS posted on the website, "tenor.com" – a widely-used video website devoted to posting GIFS that allow posters to provide labels for their shared recordings.

2 How people label eye-rolls

The website tenor.com (https://tenor.com/search/eyeroll-gifs) enables people to post short videos in GIF format and to include labels of the GIFS in the form of hashtags. A search of the hashtags on this site using the term "eyeroll" was conducted on July 6, 2017. The total number of returned hits was not available, but an estimation based on the length of the available scroll of included files on the computer screen suggested an enormous number, likely at the very least in the thousands. It is also unknown how the returned files were sorted by the website software (e.g., based on date of posting, randomized, etc.). Accordingly, the GIFS were simply viewed sequentially starting with the first one displayed. Recordings which did not appear to contain instances of genuine eye-rolls or very similar gestures were omitted. But of the remaining recordings, the first one hundred unique hashtags were captured to provide a snapshot of people's conceptualizations of eye-rolls. The full results of this observation are reported in Table 1. Among the post hoc rough categories created here for the hashtags were the following, with selected verbatim exemplars provided (note lack of mutual exclusivity):

Negativity:	"awful", "lame", "stupid", "dislike"
Unexpectedness:	"confused", "why", "what the hell"
Emotion:	"irritated", "angry", "embarrassed"
Irony:	"hilarious", "okay fine", "it's starting to annoy me"
Parallel Behaviors:	"deep breath", "eye palm", "face palm", "groan"
Unimportance:	"bored", "don't care", "unimpressed"
Denial/Refusal:	"nope", "can't", "let's not"
Rhetorical Questions:	"are you kidding", "really", "seriously"
Miscellaneous/Interesting:	"fuck my life", "shit I put up with", "migraine", "bruh"[1]

---

[1] "Bruh", according the online "Urban Dictionary", is an abbreviation for "brother", which itself could be an abbreviated form of the common American English exclamation or exasperation expression, "Oh, brother".

Table 1: Verbatim First 100 Unique Hashtag Labels of "Eyeroll" GIFS Posted on Tenor.com, July 6, 2017.

Angry	Get out	Puhlease
Annoyed	God	Really
Are you kidding	Groan	Rude
Argh	Gross	Sad
As if	Halt	Sassy
Attitude	Hate	Seriously
Awful	Hate-you	Shake my head
Blech	Head banging	Shrug
Boo hoo	Headache	Sick
Bored	Hilarious	Side eye
Bruh	I don't know	Sigh
Bullshit	Irritated	Skeptical
Bummer	Starting to annoy Jesus	So done
Can't	Lame	So what
Come on	Leaving	Stressed
Confused	Let's not	Stupid
Cry me a river	Mad	Suspicious
Deep breath	Meh	Shit I put up with
Depressed	Migraine	Twitch
Dislike	Moan	Ugh
Dismissed	Naw	Unamused
Don't care	No	Unbothered
Done	Nope	Unhappy
Duh	Not	Unimpressed
Ehh	Not into it	Upset
Embarrassed	Oh brother	Wait
Enough	Oh no	What
Exasperated	Oh please	What the hell
Eyepalm	Okay fine	Whatever
Facepalm	OMG	Who cares
Frustrated	Over it	Why
Fuck my life	Patience	WTF
Get it together	Pissed	You idiot

It thus appears, based on this informal perusal of people's posted labels for publicly shared eye-roll recordings, that eye-rolls serve as generic disapproval displays, for contextualized events which might be unexpected by participants or witnesses, which might conjure negative emotions, which fail to impress the performer of the eye-roll or an observer (i.e., the poster of the recording), which may be difficult to assimilate into belief systems, and that generate varieties of figurative and related language which also serve similar expressive goals. Among the latter are verbal irony, ironical rhetorical questions and other clever forms of language play (e.g., profanity, slang) or relevant parallel expressive behaviors or verbalizations (e.g., "groan").

3 Possible accounts of eye-rolls

Given the invocation of verbal irony and related forms of figurative language in the presence of eye-rolls, along with resemblances in their functionality, one might begin a discussion of possible accounts of eye-rolls – their meaning motivations, their potential embodied nature, etc. – by extending accounts of verbal irony to address eye-rolls. Still other accounts might arise from other sources such as viewing eye-rolls as an epiphenomenon of something else (e.g., mere disapproval) or considering eye-rolls as a form of deep-seated embodied expression. We'll begin though with the relatively simple explanation that eye-rolls are nothing special in their own right, but instead just serve as acquired markers or cues for ironic intent.

3.1 Eye-rolling as a cue for expressed irony

Akin to discussions about tones of voice and other markers, claimed by some studies (disputed by others) to serve as cues to verbal ironic intent (Neshkovska, 2015; Bryant & Fox Tree, 2005; Rockwell, 2000; Attardo, Eisterhold, Hay & Poggi, 2003; Kreuz & Roberts, 1995), eye-rolling has also been claimed on occasion to serve as a mere cue for irony. Whether eye-rolling has concomitant, coincidental or epiphenomenal other underpinnings aside for the moment, some scholars have viewed eye-rolling as simply a useful cue to hearers of speakers' ironic intent in using verbal irony. It could be, for instance, that eye-rolling serves as an indicator of a speaker's figurative intent, perhaps by distinguishing a speaker's figurative utterance performance from more earnest non-figurative behavior (i.e., the interlocutors maintaining eye contact with serious facial expression conducted on the part of the speaker). Of course eye-rolling would have to be viewed as an optional clue by this account since it doesn't always accompany expressed irony.

Or, eye-rolling could be a disapproval cue, for whatever underlying reasons, such that its coupling with ironic commentary helps hearers glean speakers' intended meaning to express disapproval, despite the typically positive semantic meaning of the surface forms of sarcastic utterances. On this view the eye-roll and its indication of disapproval are specifically coupled with verbal irony to aid the comprehension of the ironic commentary, also ultimately as an expression of disapproval.

Another possibility is that eye-rolling isn't used as a cue for irony per se, but rather both eye-rolling and ironic language stem from a core source process, such that the eye-rolling can *end up* as a cue, but only due to happenstance – because it is a common correlate of irony, not as an indicator cum indicator of ironic intent itself. This view can align with more embodied approaches discussed below. But in a simple form, one needn't invoke the embodied underpinning for this account to work. Verbal irony and eye-rolling could just both be means of expressing disapproval such that they appear together in people's expressions of negativity.

Implicit in this consideration of eye-rolling as a marker or cue for irony, either directly or coincidentally, is a discussion about whether eye-rolling is an acquired behavior or not. Although little research speaks to the prevalence of eye-rolling as a universal or broadly dispersed human expressive behavior, it seems likely that some degree of variability in its usage exists across human cultures. It is of course difficult to ascertain if this variability, assuming of course it exists with validity, is due to mere cultural variability in acquisition (i.e., some cultures have and therefore likely perpetuate eye-rolling, where other cultures likely discourage it), or whether eye-rolling is a relatively universal and embodied/emergent display of disapproval but is just influenced by norms of expressivity (i.e., it might be considered extremely rude to use eye-rolling as an expression of disapproval in some cultures despite its possible embodied nature, where in other cultures its usage is licensed or even encouraged). Resolution of this issue awaits future research. For the present we'll simply consider ways in which it seems plausible that eye-rolling is embodied. For the moment, though, we'll continue first with extensions of accounts of verbal irony for the explanation of eye-rolling.

3.2 Eye-rolling as pretense

One very influential account of verbal irony involves the idea that speakers of irony are actually acting out how a hypothetical or mimicked other person might express themselves in some situation. This portrayal is made to be transparent by the performers however, to enable their genuine attitude – typically oppositional to the one being portrayed, to remain apparent. So, on this view an ironic speaker is simply pretending, but making their pretense obvious (Clark & Gerrig, 1984).

Eye-rolling on this view could therefore just be part of the performer's depiction of the character being portrayed. Consider that, in typical cases of verbal irony, the actor portrays a person who might actually and perhaps bafflingly appreciate the currently ongoing set of contextual events, despite those events frequently being negative, undesirable, unpreferred or simply unexpected (e.g., extremely lengthy lines are encountered at a security check-point in an airport). The actor might then portray their character as happy about this outcome or as oblivious to reality ("Oh look, how wonderful, there's a line!", or, "Oh look, there's hardly anyone in line!!").

This belittling portrayal serves several functions; to distinguish the portrayed character's attitude from the speaker/actor's, to mock or make fun of the portrayed character and/or their attitude, all to serve the ultimate function of pointing out the situation at hand is undesirable, is not what should have occurred, and that anyone appreciating the actual situation is worthy of distain (Colston, 2015). It could thus be that the eye-rolling behavior serves this belittling function – to make the portrayed character appear unable to maintain physical control of themselves, as in being unable to control their predominant sensory system, vision, espoused in their noticeably ungainly gaze control, or perhaps through the character's weakness – eyes rolling back indicative of someone about to lose hold on consciousness.

Of course it remains possible that a mixture of these marking, epiphenomenal or irony-extended accounts underlie eye-roll behavior, along with more embodied accounts to be discussed next. And indeed the mixture of accounts itself could vary according to the individualized characteristics of given instances of irony taking place in realistic contexts. Future research should also bear on these possibilities. But for now please consider accounts that place eye-rolling much more deeply in other grounded perceptual, cognitive, social and linguistic functional processes, as an expressive system deeply embodied in core psychological and physiological systems.

3.3 Eye-rolling as embodied

On this view, eye-rolling is meaningful in and of itself because it reflects a complex range and interaction of deeply embodied processes which constitute people's experience and conception of irony, concomitant in unexpected, undesirable situations, including the frequent partner experience of disapproval. Five different permutations of this view will be presented. They'll be discussed for the sake of clarity as if separable accounts in themselves, but no strict claims are intended as to their independence. The five views are in order, **Detachment** (*gaze aversion*), **Appeal** (*metaphorical directions*), **Physical Experiences** (*fatigue, impact*), **Lack of Control** (*gaze anomalousness*) and **Embodied Irony** (*body/eyes dichotomy*). Two important cross-characteristics of these views will also be discussed, **Experience Yoked with Demonstrativeness** and **Optimality**.

3.3.1 Detachment

The **Detachment** account argues that speaker/actors leverage off our dominant sensory system, vision, and our normally displayed patterns of interest and awareness with respect to vision, in order to express disapproval. As a species of primate, we are most dependent upon vision to gain information about, and to function within our worlds. Accordingly, all else held equal, we tend to look at things of interest to us, and not look at things we find less interesting. A similar pattern holds for things we find *desirable* and *undesirable*, things we *like* and *dislike*, etc. Where we tend to look is thus a straightforward indicator of our attitudes about or opinions toward things in our environment. Most simply put, we tend to look at what we like and look away from what we dislike. We can thus use this pattern to powerfully communicate to other people when we dislike or disapprove of something. We can make a poignant display of not only not looking at something, but more forcefully, taking an active role in deliberately looking away from that something. It is as if we are indicating to other people, "Look at me looking away from this", when we perform an eye-roll – using gaze detachment as an active indicator of our experienced disapproval.

One could then ask the reasonable questions as to why eye-rolling often takes the form of looking upward, and why it often involves motion? If active displayed and performed gaze aversion is the core process underlying eye-rolling as an indicator of the performer's disapproval, then why wouldn't we just avert gaze in any direction? Why do we tend toward upward gazing, and often with motion? The answer might simply involve minimizing ambiguity in gaze aversions. Looking upward may be the least ambiguous indicator of overt gaze aversion because gaze aversions in other directions could be confused with other things. The motion could perform a similar function – for gaze to not alight on any one point could diminish the possibility of misinterpreting the gaze to be directed *at* something else in the environment. Some of these hypotheses, admittedly speculative at this point, were actually put to an initial empirical test in the experiment reported below, and it turns out they may have some validity. For now, though, let's continue with the other possible embodied explanations for eye-rolls as disapproval displays and accompaniments of verbal irony.

3.3.2 Appeal

Another version of an embodied explanation of eye-rolling, the **Appeal** account, invokes a suite of conceptual metaphors involving directions. A number of very general conceptual metaphors linking the directions *up* and *down* with varying social status, authority, knowledge, wisdom, expertise and related target domains have been claimed by scholars working in the conceptual metaphor framework (Lakoff & Johnson, 1980). We often seem to conceptualize expertise, powerful status, knowledge-holding, correctness, properness, wisdom, etc. with *up*, and the oppositional dimensions of these constructs with *down*. So we say things like, "look up to some people", "look down upon some people", "take the high road", "take the low road", "high brow", "low brow", "I have this from the highest authority", "that is a low-down thing to say", "she's the top woman in her field", "he is low on the totem pole", "he works in the highest levels of government", "she's just an underling", "she's at the top of her game", "this University is going downhill", etc.

Accordingly, when we encounter situations not to our liking one could argue that our looking upward amounts to a gestural appeal to a "higher", more knowledgeable, all-knowing, etc., authority of some sort, or at least a demonstration of one's feeling the need to make such an appeal. This appeal could involve perhaps seeking commiseration on our plight from an all-knowing entity, a deity perhaps, or just a hypothetical knowledgeable person with an understanding of the situation and its having gone awry somehow. Or the appeal could involve desiring an intervention of some sort, again from an authority of some type, who comes bearing sage corrective advice to alleviate the situation. Or it could involve a plea for rescue from the situation in some manner. The point is that the speaker/actor of the eye-roll makes manifest the idea that they don't like being in the undesireable situation they've found themselves in through looking or perhaps even physically reaching, in a directions metaphorically related to different domains from which assistance might be obtained, generally up.

3.3.3 Physical Experience

The third permutation of an embodied underpinning of eye-rolling could involve demonstrations of, or indeed actual experiences of, how a person might physiologically or even **Physically Experience** being in undesirable situations. Negative, undesirable, unwanted, etc., experiences pose a physical and emotional strain on us. We must exert energy to react to and cope with these negative situations which we may not have to exert in comparable desirable situations.[2] This stress can produce fatigue, which has highly visible effects on a human body.

---

[2] Both strongly negative and strongly positive situations can be stressful for people, but negative situations in comparison to neutral, non-remarkable expected situations (i.e., things turning out as expected with no surprises) might be relatively more burdensome.

Fatigue can cause people to droop their heads forward, to have their limbs go limp, to have their mouths hang open. Indeed, such physical reactions are commonly seen when facing unwanted situations, as are eye-rolls. Fatigue can also manifest itself, though, by causing our heads to hang, and our eyes to roll, *backwards*. This physical reaction bears great similarity to eye-rolling, which might be a generified portrayal of this manifestation of physical fatigue.

Negative situations are also commonly conceptualized metaphorically as our being impacted by some form of physical object or force. This is shown in common linguistic constructions such as, "I was hit with a lawsuit", "We got slammed during the lunch rush", "The bad news hit her really hard", etc. Eye-rolling might also bear physical characteristics to our being impacted from the front by some object or force. Such an impact might throw our heads backward, causing our gaze to be cast upward. Eye-rolling could thus also be a demonstration, perhaps with enhancement via eye movement, of how our bodies would react to being impacted by some oncoming force – metaphorically standing in for the negative situation which descends upon us. One other twist on this physical experience approach could be an indication that the impact on us or fatigue produced within us is so strong as to nearly render us unconscious – eye rolls can also resemble a person's physical response to being on the cusp of passing out.

Also, particular emotional experiences might also be associated with gaze directionality. When people are saddened, perhaps related to the fatigue response, they will often hang their head or direct their gaze downward. Such gestures could also be somewhat related to the appeal mechanism in that when people feel disappointed, dejected, saddened, they may identify with weak social status, or with more generic negativity associated metaphorically with the direction down (i.e., as in feeling "low", "down", or having "sinking" feelings, etc.).

3.3.4 Lack of control

The fourth manifestation of embodiment underlying eye-rolling was mentioned previously in the eye-roll-as-pretense discussion. In that section eye-rolling was considered a means of acting out a character who had **No Control** over their vision (i.e. gaze direction). This was done as part of the belittling portrayal of a person actually liking or misunderstanding the negative situation at hand. Under a more embodied account of eye-rolling, though, a speaker/actor of an eye/roll could be demonstrating *their own* physical reaction, related to fatigue and/or being impacted by some force, to experiencing a negative situation. The person may not feel they have control over the negative events impacting them, otherwise the person might have prevented those events from happening. So this demonstration of a lack of control is not portraying another person's reaction but rather is showing the speaker/actors own response to the negative events and then experienced lack of control over matters.

3.3.5 Embodied irony

Finally, an eye-roll gesture could espouse a degree of **Irony** itself in that it could demonstrate a dichotomous relationship existing between our bodies and our vision. Under normal circumstances, our bodies and our vision behave in alignment. What our bodies are oriented toward (i.e., directions in which we are moving, objects to which we are reaching, things for which we are seeking, etc.) coheres with what our vision is attending to (i.e., looking where we are going, looking at what we're reaching for, using our vision to search our environment, etc.). Eye-rolling could be an active demonstration of a cleft in this normal relationship where we show our vision going off in a direction contrary to where our bodies are located or oriented. We are here, present in the current situation (usually a negative, undesireable one), but we show our vision as being somewhere else. This is similar to the gaze aversion process discussed previously, but the current account focuses more on the dichotomy being displayed (i.e. we are present [bodily] but also absent [visually], at the same time), rather than just our deliberately looking away from something.[3]

3.3.6 Demonstrativeness and Optimality

Underlying all of these embodied possibilities are two common themes or characteristics. One involves the degree of **Demontrativeness** on the speaker/performer's part. In each of the accounts, even if a speaker/performer is genuinely and actively experiencing a physical reaction to the negative situation, as in the case of fatigue, they are still actively making that experience visible to interlocutors, at least to a degree. It is as if they wish to demonstrate to interlocutors that they are having that experience. Or if they're not fully having the experience (i.e., not genuinely looking up to appeal to a higher authority) they are *invoking* that experience to make it visible to their interlocutors (i.e., *this is what it looks like for a person to appeal to a higher authority*).

---

[3] This could be related to the contradictions involved in verbal irony, espoused in various accounts (e.g., contrast [Colston, 2000], negation [Giora, Livnat, Fein, Barnea, Zeiman & Berger, 2013], pretense [Clark & Gerrig, 1984], among others [See Colston & Gibbs, 2007, for a review]).

The second theme involves **Optimality**. People might avert their gaze from something for a wide variety of reasons. People might also look up, as if appealing to a higher authority, but they might also look up merely to contemplate something. Perhaps to eliminate visual distractions for a moment to concentrate on their thoughts. People might also experience fatigue or impact also because they are reacting to the *complexity* of something rather than to its negativity. If someone is asked a complex, deep-reaching question, for instance, they might have a visible fatigue reaction just because they divert energy and resources to contemplating the question. Or they might have a visible impact reaction out of recognition of the quality of the question, perhaps as just a raw reaction or also partly to express acknowledgment to their questioner of their respect for the quality of the question. Such a diversion of resources could also manifest as a visible appearance of lessoned control over peripheral processes (like gaze direction).

So, people seeking, unconsciously or with more deliberateness, to convey the more embodied mechanisms discussed earlier as their motivations for eye-rolling (e.g., detachment, appeal, physical reactions to negative situations, etc.) would need to optimize their performances within the given context to disambiguate their expressions from some of the alternative possibilities discussed immediately above. So a degree of optimality is warranted on the speaker/performer's part to make as clear as possible what it is they wish to express.

3.3.7 Eye-rolling: Grappling with motivational complexity

Given the preceding brief discussion of optimality as an underlying theme of the different embodied and other motivational accounts discussed, plus the wide variety and similarity of some of those accounts themselves, a brief consideration of the complexity entailed in explaining eye-rolling is warranted. Parsimony, as a value in science, encourages us to look for the perfect crossroads between maximizing explanatory power while minimizing explanatory complexity. In the current situation, parsimony would likely direct us to thus single out one or a few of the explanations reviewed above, which best achieve this sweet spot.

But given the complexity and nuance of peoples' expressions in complex often undesirable situations, such a parsimony-driven approach may not be most useful. In situations such as those producing eye-rolling behavior, people are faced with a complex suite of often contradictory emotions, feelings, social norms, varieties of behavioral expectations and other factors influencing how they express themselves. On one hand, people are displeased at the negative situations and accordingly feel frustration, anger, etc. People also might feel compelled to express these feelings. But social norms may also inhibit or even fully squelch expression of some of these experiences. People's reactions to negative situations may also produce different reactions directed at different targets (e.g., anger at one interlocutor who partially caused the negative situation yet commiseration and comradery with other interlocutors who are sharing in the collective misery). People might also feel conflicts between wanting to purely express their feelings versus wishing to demonstrate an unrattled mastery over the situation and perhaps behave in such a way as to maximize successful resolution of the situation. In short, people face a gauntlet of potentially conflicting pragmatic effects they might experience and might wish to produce in other people, for which figurative language, especially verbal irony, is uniquely suited to address and accomplish (Colston, 2015). Eye-rolling and related nonverbal behaviors, with all their potentially nuanced similar yet separable embodied underpinnings might also provide the complexity to address this complex of pragmatic effects.

So it might behoove our attempts at understanding eye-rolling to lessen our usual value of parsimony and embrace the complexity of potentially underlying motivators of eye-rolling. Acknowledging how speakers/performers might cobble together different embodied and other motivators of eye-rolling for use in differing situations might service our understanding of the phenomenon. Speakers/performers might for instance customize their eye-rolling, verbal irony crafting and other expressive performance factors for different contexts, pulling from the full grab-bag of motivators in this process.

Indeed, a number of other forms of multiply-determined or multiply-produced human activities can serve as broad metaphors for eye-rolling and verbal irony expressivity. Democracy, as a decision-making system cobbles together input from a wide diversity of differing perspectives. But the majority-rule component nonetheless allows for a definitive choice to be made while allowing other perhaps dissenting voices to have felt included in the process.[4] Large collective music ensembles like orchestras or choirs also cobble together widely diverse sound productions from different musical instruments or human voices. But with careful design, these collectives can produce beautifully artistic nuanced and layered music that achieves some of the highest levels of human artistic expression – although greatly differing, the collective sounds align to produce incredibly powerful expressions. Finally, continuing with the musical metaphor, even very complex harmonies can be achieved when individual contributing voices misalign in interesting ways – even conflicting misalignments in collective endeavours can produce meaningful broad outcomes.

---

4 Assuming of course that democratic systems are designed and conducted to be inclusive, fair, transparent and trustworthy, which in practice often isn't the case.

So, although the experimental demonstration to be discussed next begins an empirical exploration of eye-rolling by carving out just one or two of the embodied processes discussed above for evaluation, it should be stressed that the true complexity of actual eye-rolling and verbal irony usage in genuine human contexts may far exceed this demonstration. As researchers conduct further evaluations of eye-rolling underpinnings, this underlying complexity is best kept vividly in mind.

3.4 Eye-rolling: A brief empirical study

As discussed above, one embodied account of eye-rolling puts major emphasis on the use of demonstrative gaze aversion as the mechanism for expressing disapproval. A brief discussion was also held earlier concerning alternative reasons for gaze aversion, which a speaker/performer of eye-rolling would likely wish to optimally nullify in order to disambiguate the meaning of her expression – perhaps to solidify the desired conveyance of disapproval. These alternatives will be revisited here in discussion of an empirical study to evaluate this potential embodied underpinning of eye-rolling' disapproval expression.

People avert their gaze from target things in their visual environment for a variety of reasons. A person might discover an object of new interest in their environment (e.g., a particular title on a bookshelf catches their eye). People might be distracted while conversing (e.g., one interlocutor in a conversation might be distracted momentarily by some activity taking place near the conversational locale). People also look away as mentioned earlier to contemplate something, perhaps simply to reduce visual distractions but also possibly as an indicator of that contemplation itself taking place (i.e., *Look at how I'm thinking about what you said*). A speaker/performer may also avert their gaze as a means of drawing an interlocutor's attention toward something, as a means of referring (i.e., *See the clean kitchen over there that I just slaved in for an hour*). People also look away because they're searching their environment for something (i.e., *Where did I put my phone?*). And of course, people may look away to avoid seeing something they dislike, either as pure avoidance or as a more meta-intended indication of avoidance in looking at something (i.e., *look at me looking away from this*).

So, if a speaker/performer wishes to express the latter of these gaze-aversion motivations, perhaps to express stand-alone disapproval or to accompany an utterance of verbal irony or other form of expressed disapproval, they'll need to somehow maximize the potential for the disapproval display interpretation over the other possibilities.⁵ One way of doing this might be revealed by considering the common *directions* of gaze aversion in all the motivations just discussed.

Although we live in complex three dimensional environments with objects and material all around us, it nonetheless seems reasonable to say more of those surrounding things lie in directions horizontal to our current location or below us, relative to being above us. In a gravity environment most things will be held to the ground, as will our own bodies. As such there is probably more stuff around and beneath us than there is above us, all else held reasonably equal. So, if a person finds a new interest in their environment, is distracted by something, is referring to an object or is searching their environment for something – *it seems likely that they will avert their gaze in a horizontal or downward direction, rather than upward*. Only the contemplation and avoidance/disapproval motivations seem to break with this rule, which might not be an accident. It could be that gaze averted upward is more likely to be interpreted as indicative of disapproval (or contemplation), rather than one of the other possibilities since those other options are likely to involve horizontal or downward directed gaze aversion. It is also possible that the strong linkage between downwardness and negativity metaphorically could also lend strength to downward gaze aversions as means of expressing disapproval.

To test these possibilities, the following experiment put people in situations where they would see faces averting their gaze in different directions. The faces were presented to the experimental participants as people being seen while they were overhearing, and then reacting to, short broadcast news items. The participants were then asked to rate, using a rating scale, the degree of approval or disapproval the observed people were experiencing toward the stories, based on the reactions observable in the people's faces.

3.4.1 Experiment

The experiment presented 24 undergraduates with 48 appropriately counterbalanced, randomly sorted, short news items, each depicting some news relevant to living in a university city in western Canada. One third of the items were negative in content, another third were neutral, the remaining third were positive. Each item was shown with a face doing a gaze aversion in one of eight directions. The participants were told they were seeing images of people overhearing news items and reacting to them. The participants were then asked to rate the degree of approval or disapproval being shown by the overhearers.

---

5 Assuming of course the person wishes to avoid ambiguity in their display, which may not be the case.

3.4.2 Methods

3.4.2.1 Participants

Twenty four undergraduate students from a western Canadian university participated as part of a course requirement. Participant gender was not specifically recorded but approximately three fifths of the subject pool used for the study are typically female. All participants reported being native English speakers.

3.4.2.2 Materials

Forty-eight stories, written by the experimenters depicted news items described as being overheard by the participant, as if on an internet video a person near the participant is playing aloud. (e.g., "Doctors are predicting a shortage of flu vaccine for the coming winter", "Skiing conditions in Banff are forecast to be average this winter", "Students committing to using all e-texts in their classes at the University can get free textbooks for one year"). In one third of the stories, the polarity of the news was designed to be moderately negative (e.g., the flu shortage story). In another third the news was neutral (the skiing conditions story), and the remaining third were designed to be positive (e.g., the free textbook story). Example stories are shown in Table 2.

Table 2: Example News Stories used in the Experiment.

Negative
Extremely cold temperatures are predicted for the upcoming winter.
All university students will have to pay for internet access starting next year.
Fast food chains in the area are goint to close at 9:00 p.m. to cut late night eating.
The price of gasoline in the province will go up 25% in the next two years.

Neutral
Envelopes are going on sale at Target next week.
Construction projects at the university are proceeding on schedule.
New waste cans are being installed in downtown train stations.
Electricity rates are expected to stay the same going into next year.

Positive
Local bars are giving students $2.00 drinks throughout exams.
Canadian residents with student loan debt can now qualify for free books.
Studies show that sleeping late can lead to higher levels of productivity and intelligence.
There is a new flavor of Kraft Dinner made of 80% super foods.

The stories were paired with cartoon faces shown with gaze aversion taking place in one of eight directions, described for convenience here using compass directions with upward being "North": N, NE, E, SE, S, SW, W, NW. Example faces are shown in the Appendix. Stereotypical gender of the faces was balanced across male and female. A variety of moderately varying appearances in terms of hair style skin tone and other facial and head features were used.

Eight different sets of the lists of stories were prepared such that the story-polarity/gaze-aversion-direction pairings were counterbalanced across the sets. For instance, in set one, the flu shortage story would be paired with a face looking N. In set two that story would be paired with a face looking NE, etc. An equal number of participants viewed each set resulting of counterbalancing of the variables across the study.

Participants used a seven point rating scale to record each of their responses. The scale was depicted approximately as shown here (note smaller numbers indicate greater disapproval – participants did not see numbers with the rating scales):

Greatly   Greatly
Disapprove   Approve
|------------|------------|------------|------------|------------|------------|------------|

coded as   *coded as*

1   7

3.4.2.3 Design & procedure

The design was a simple two-variable within-participants manipulation, with type of story (negative, neutral and positive) and gaze aversion direction (N, NE, E, SE, S, SW, W, NW) as the independent variables. Rated level of expressed approval/disapproval of the overhearers was the dependent variable.

Participants were met in the lab facility in a non-descript quiet lab room equipped with computer stations. Either undergraduate or graduate student research assistants explained the task, read aloud the instructions for the task, and answered any questions by the participants. The task was presented and data collected on lab computers. Participants first worked with five practice stories, not included in subsequent analyses, to familiarize themselves with the task. Participation then completed the task individually. Participants were debriefed and released upon completing the task.

3.4.3 Results and discussion

Since gaze aversion direction was the only variable of interest, planned comparisons on all the pairs of different gaze directions were conducted. Comparisons of the story polarity levels were also conducted but only for service as a manipulation check.

To summarize briefly, the experiment revealed a clear pattern in that gaze aversions directed upward expressed the greatest amount of disapproval (expressed about overheard news stories).[6] Gaze aversions directed downward revealed the next greatest level of disapproval, and lateral gaze aversions (directed leftward or rightward) displayed the least amount of disapproval. Aversions of gaze directed toward the corners (upward left, upward right, downward left and downward right) fell generally in the middle – between upward and downward aversions in terms of the level of disapproval indicated, but as with upward and downward directions, showing more disapproval than lateral aversions. Mean disapproval ratings by gaze aversion direction are reported in Table 3.

Table 3: Mean Disapproval Ratings by Gaze Aversion Direction.

Gaze Aversion Direction:	N		S		W		E
Mean Rating:	3.38	<	3.87	<	4.30	=	4.53
Gaze Aversion Direction:	NW		NE		SW		SE
Mean Rating:	3.33	=	3.61	=	3.40	=	3.48

NOTES: 1. Smaller Numbers Correspond to More Disapproval.
    2. Significant Differences indicated by < or >.
    3. Significatn Differences based on omnibus one-way ANOVA, followed by pairwise T-tests, all using $p < .05$.

The levels of disapproval for the story types were consistent with the polarity of the stories – serving as a nice manipulation check. Ratings on the negative stories showed more disapproval than both the neutral and positive stories, which did not differ from one another.

The results thus confirm the predictions for upward gaze aversions to be most disapproving since most of the embodied mechanisms (e.g., gaze aversion, appeal, etc.) involve an association of maximal expressed disapproval with upward gaze aversions. Since fewer of the embodied mechanisms stack on the downward gaze aversion direction as a means of expressing disapproval, that

---

[6] All claims of differences reached statistical significance (Omnibus ANOVAs, followed by pairwise T-tests, all at $p < .05$).

direction produced the second highest level of disapproval. Since the corner-directed aversions have components of upwardness and downwardness, it makes sense too that they fall closer to the pure upward and downward produced levels of disapproval, with aversions directed laterally expressing the least amount of disapproval since none of the embodied mechanisms really speak to gaze aversions taking place laterally.

This study attempted to isolate one small factor people use in eye-rolling, gaze aversions directed in different directions. The study was able to confirm what many of the embodied mechanisms predict – upward gaze aversions will express the most disapproval, followed by downward directed ones. Gaze aversions in lateral directions would be the weakest disapproval displays since they could occur for a wider variety of reasons other than avoidance/disapproval relative to upward and downward aversions.

Other studies adopting similar techniques on other presumably embodied eye-rolling processes should also be undertaken (e.g., motion, directionality, subtle approximations of eye-rolling, etc., plus many other peripheral characteristics [e.g., duration, couplings with other nonverbal components, etc.]). But such somewhat artificial experimental tasks need to be accompanied by many other types of methodologies (e.g., more indirect experimental measures [eye-tracking], observational, corpus-based, methodologies, etc.). I've also often advocated blending these types of methodologies for particular advantages. For instance, authentic examples of genuine eye-rolls and similar behaviors captured in observational or elicitation studies could be used as materials for experimental studies. Such blends produce unavoidable compromises in that for example some concerns in experimental design will have to be tolerated to gain the authenticity of the genuine recorded materials. But so long as other more pure experimental and other techniques are all coalescing on reliable results, such shortcomings can be worth tolerating.

Another approach would be to adopt sophisticated multivariate statistical and modeling techniques to assess causal and other underlying mechanisms in authentically captured eye-rolling and related behavior. Indeed, given the immense level of complexity in eye-rolling and related behaviors themselves, along with linguistic complements and background context characteristics, this approach might be an important way to tackle the nuance in eye-rolling as a versatile expressive behavior.

3.5 Eye-rolling: Issues for future research

The current study evaluated one of the potential embodied underpinnings of how eye-rolling functions. This mechanism also speaks a little as to why eye-rolling might often accompany verbal irony. Gaze aversions can serve as indicators of disapproval based on the principle that people tend to look toward things they like and away from things they dislike. Gaze aversions directed upward also tend to express a greater degree of disapproval relative to gaze aversions aimed in other directions. Upward aversions were argued to produce this disapproval maximization because other gaze aversion directions could be confusable with other motivators besides disapproval expression for averting gaze. So upward isn't special in any particular respect according to the gaze aversion explanation. Upward is just least ambiguous in indicating one is averting their gaze just to look away rather than for some other less disapproving reason. Upward gaze aversions are thus most able to express disapproval. This is why they can readily accompany verbal irony commentary which also often involves disapproval expression – eye-rolling bolsters the intention of using verbal irony, to express disapproval.

Of course future work could also address the other embodied potential underpinnings of eye-rolling. For instance, upward gaze aversion might be special after all in that the upward direction is metaphorically associated with authority, wisdom, etc., as the appeal mechanism claims. So should evidence be found to support the appeal mechanism then the above account of the gaze aversion functionality would require revision. Indeed, many of the embodied mechanisms could also be playing a role as well, so future studies should attempt to tackle multiple of these mechanisms at the same time. Such investigations could look at each of the other potential embodied underpinnings and how all these mechanisms might interact with one another.

But a number of other broader questions might also be posed of eye-rolling, irony and embodiment. Is eye-rolling different when used for stand-alone disapproval displays versus when coupled with ironic expression? Does eye-rolling carry a more diluted disapproval effect when accompanied by verbal irony, for instance, due to its more complex roll of disambiguating the irony along with being a disapproval display. Or does the disapproval of the ironic commentary itself carry some of the weight of the overall disapproval expression such that the eye-rolling contributes less of an expression of disapproval? One could also investigate what factors affect the prevalence of eye-rolling? It has been speculated here that eye-rolling would vary in its prevalence across cultures, regions, languages, etc. So determining mediators of this variability would be interesting. Still other questions could be asked about the other effects of eye-rolling, including pragmatic effects and others. What does eye-rolling do to addressees, other comprehenders and speakers themselves, perhaps dependently on some of the performance variables afforded by eye-rolling? Looking into the explanatory power of the pretense and other irony accounts for the usage and effects of eye-rolling is another direction future research could take. In short, there is no lack of interesting directions to explore eye-rolling as an expressive behavior, on its own and when coupled with verbal irony and other commentary.

3.6 Conclusion

This chapter has made the claim that eye-rolling is a deeply embodied, multi-determined experiential, expressive and communicative system, which may operate alone or may be accompanied with verbal irony and other kinds of language. The paper also provided limited evidence to support claims of detachment (via gaze aversions) and optimality (optimizing disapproval over other possible interpretations of gaze aversion) as components of interpreting eye-rolling. These claims will of course have to be reconsidered as more research is undertaken on eye-rolling and other possible underpinnings, embodied ones as well as others, of its ability to express disapproval and nuanced collections of other meanings.

References

Clark, Herbert H., & Richare J. Gerrig. 1984. On the pretense theory of irony. *Journal of Experimental Psychology: General 113(1)*. 121–126.

Colston, Herbert L. 2000. Contrast of kind versus contrast of magnitude: The pragmatic accomplishments of irony and hyperbole. *Discourse Processes 30(2)*. 179–199.

Colston, Herbert L. 2015. *Using figurative language*. Cambridge, UK: Cambridge University Press.

Colston, Herbert. L. 2017. *On the complexities of embodied irony: Considerations of eye-rolling and other multi-modal evidence*. Paper presented at the 14th International Cognitive Linguistics Conference, Tartu, Estonia, July.

Colston, Herbert. L. 2017. *On the complexities of verbal irony production: Eye-rolling and other multi-modal accompaniments*. Paper presented at the Alberta Conference on Linguistics, University of Alberta, Edmonton, Canada, October.

Gibbs, Raymond. W., & Herbert L. Colston. (eds.). 2007. *Irony in language and thought: A cognitive science reader*. Mahway, N.J.: Lawrence Erlbaum.

Giora, Rachel, Elad Livnat, Ofer Fein, Anat Barnea, Rakefet Zeiman, & Iddo Berger. 2013. Negation generates nonliteral interpretations by default. *Metaphor and Symbol 28 (2)*. 89–115.

Goodwin, Marjorie. H., & H. Samy Alim. 2010. "Whatever (neck roll, eye roll, teeth suck)": The situated coproduction of social categories and identitites through stancetaking and transmodal stylization. *Journal of Linguistic Anthropology 20(1)*. 179–194.

Kelly, Spencer D. 2001. Broadening the units of analysis in communication: Speech and nonverbal behaviours in pragmatic comprehension. *Journal of Child Language 28(2)*. 325–349.

Kircher, Madison M. 2017. Angela Merkel rolling her eyes at Putin is the perfect GIF you didn't know you needed. *New York Magazine*. July 7.

LaFrance, Marianne., & Julie A. Woodzicka. 1998. No laughing matter: Women's verbal and nonverbal reactions to sexist humor. In J. K. Swim & C. Stangor (eds.), *Prejudice: The target's perspective*, 61–80. San Diego, CA, US: Academic Press.

Stec, Kashmiri. 2012. Meaningful shifts: A review of viewpoint markers in co-speech gesture and sign language. *Gesture 12(3)*. 327–360.

Underwood, Marion. K. 2004. Glares of contempt, eye rolls of disgust and turning away to exclude: Non-verbal forms of social aggression among girls. *Feminism & Psychology 14(3)*. 371–375.

Appendix

Example Faces Used in the Experiment

Vera Tobin
Experimental investigations of irony as a viewpoint phenomenon

Abstract: If the experience of irony involves a special kind of perspective taking, as theorized in the viewpoint theory of irony (Tobin & Israel, 2012; Tobin, 2016), are people more inclined to interpret a statement as sarcastic when it appears with a congruent viewpoint arrangement? This study investigated the question with evaluative statements of the genre investigated in Riloff et al. 2013, paired with images of scenes in which people are and are not looking at other people as they speak. As predicted, participants were significantly more likely to interpret an utterance as sarcastic when it was shown with a scene of multiple embodied viewpoints. This effect was stronger in scenes showing two interlocutors (speaker and hearer) than it was in scenes showing speaker, hearer, and a third (bystander) figure. These data support the theory that irony is meaningfully a figure of viewpoint.

Keywords: viewpoint, perspective-taking, mental spaces, situational irony, dramatic irony, "view of a viewpoint", zoom-out configurations, bystanders, evaluative statements, Amazon Mechanical Turk, sentiment analysis, intersubjectivity

1 Introduction

Research on irony in linguistics and cognitive science has focused almost exclusively on verbal irony. The term "irony" in its full diversity, however, can refer to phenomena including cosmic irony, dramatic irony, and ironic modes of appreciation, with many others between. These sorts of irony are, indeed, so various that many researchers argue that they should not be considered together as a natural class (see, e.g. Wilson 2006). The viewpoint theory of irony (Tobin and Israel 2012; Tobin 2016) holds that these diverse phenomena do have shared cognitive underpinnings: when people construe a situation, a remark, or an attitude as ironic, they are taking a particular complex "view of a viewpoint" that that unites the many kinds of irony.

Acknowledgements: Many thanks to Max Zimon and Aaron Weinberg for their assistance collecting data and preparing materials for display online, and to Hannah Kent for assistance with gathering visual reference materials for stimuli.

Vera Tobin, Department of Cognitive Science, Case Western Reserve University

https://doi.org/10.1515/9783110652246-011

Meanwhile, many accounts of irony, from the classical descriptions in Cicero and Quintilian (Butler 1921) to Attardo (2000) and Lear (2011) have suggested that its major defining feature is a special kind of incongruity, especially involving opposites. A situation is ironic, it seems, if what is expected is the opposite of what occurs, especially if an action brings about what it was intended to prevent, or prevents what it was intended to bring about. An utterance is ironic if the speaker's true feelings are in some way the opposite of what she seems to be saying. People reliably deem sentences sarcastic, for example, when they take them to be ascribing a positive sentiment to a negative situation (Riloff, Qadir, Surve, De Silva, Gilbert, and Huang 2013).

This study investigated whether people would be more likely to interpret sentences as involving this kind of relevant incongruity if the theorized "view of a viewpoint" was made more accessible through visual priming. As Sweetser (2012: 13) observes, "there is no more powerful icon for... viewpoint than an actual body with an actual inherent viewpoint." If the experience of irony involves a special kind of perspective taking, people should be more likely to take an evaluative statement as sarcastic when they are primed with that viewpoint arrangement, and less likely when they are primed with a different one or none at all.

To test this hypothesis, we solicited judgments of sarcasm vs. sincerity for evaluative statements of the genre investigated in Riloff et al. 2013, paired with images of scenes in which people are and are not looking at other people as they speak. As expected, participants were indeed significantly more likely to interpret an utterance as sarcastic when it was paired with scenes presenting multiple embodied viewpoints. However, this effect was stronger in scenes showing only two interlocutors (speaker and hearer) than it was in scenes showing speaker, hearer, and a third (bystander) figure.

2 The viewpoint theory of irony

The viewpoint theory of irony offers a complement to prevailing theories of irony in cognitive psychology and linguistics as, for example, a form of echoic mention (Sperber and Wilson 1981 1998) or pretense (Clark and Gerrig 1984). Unlike these accounts, the viewpoint theory does not treat irony primarily as a particular kind of operation on a proposition or a particular kind of speaker behavior. Instead it defines irony in terms of a special kind of stance on the part of an *interpreter*, one that may obtain for either a speaker or a hearer (or for a bystander, for that matter; see also Gibbs 1996 on "irony as a mode of thought").

In other words, "ironic utterances, like ironic situations, are distinguished by the sort of interpretive process they evoke" (Tobin and Israel 2012: 31). One advantage of this approach is that it provides a way to capture commonalities across verbal, situational, and dramatic ironies. It also situates irony in a theoretical framework, Mental Spaces Theory (Fauconnier 1985 1997), which also handles a wide array of non-ironic linguistic phenomena, such as presupposition (Fauconnier 1997), conditional constructions (Dancygier and Sweetser 2005), verb tense and aspect (Cutrer 1994), negation (Dancygier 2012), and polarity (Israel 2011).

In the viewpoint account, acts of ironic understanding in general, including verbal, dramatic, and situational ironies, all involve a distinctive way of accessing a proposition or scene. Attention "zooms out" from some focused content to a higher viewpoint from which the original viewpoint is reassessed. A meaning is accessed from one vantage (the ironized viewpoint) and then, simultaneously or soon after, re-accessed from a higher vantage (the ironic view). This relation is described in terms of layered mental spaces (Fauconnier 1985 1997).

For instance, Figure 1 illustrates two parallel zoom-out scenarios, one for a classic situational irony and one for a classic verbal irony. Diagram 1a depicts the circumstance in which dying of thirst while surrounded by (salt) water is understood as an ironic fate, as in Coleridge's "water, water every where, nor any drop to drink". Diagram 1b depicts a canonical example of sarcasm, in which a displeased party remarks "Beautiful weather!" as a derisive comment on a sudden downpour.

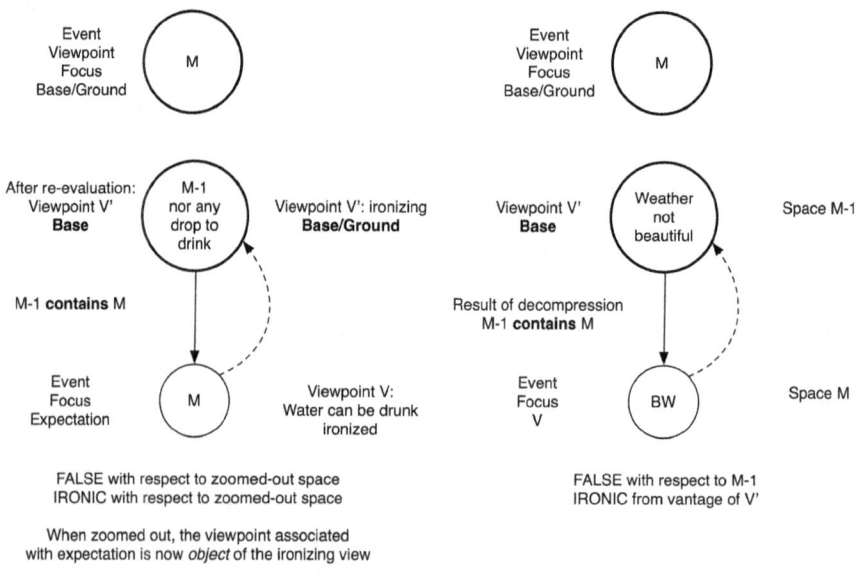

Figure 1: Water and weather.

In both cases, the irony involves a mental space configuration where that which is manifest – the outcome of events or the ostensible point of the speech act – is positioned as notably incongruous with the circumstances of its own production. To achieve ironic understanding, an ironist must construct at least two mental spaces. One is a putative Base space (in Figure 1, marked as "M") that contains both the to-be-ironized proposition and a Viewpoint (V) associated with it: a normative expectation about thirst and water, for instance, or a positive sentiment toward the current wet weather. The other is a space (M-1) that serves as a higher ground from which space M and its associated viewpoint can be considered – at a distance.

According to the viewpoint theory, taking an ironic view of events or of an utterance always depends on this kind of complex viewing arrangement. This is the case whether the ironist taking this view-of-a-view is the thirsty sailor noting the ironies in his own misfortune, the Ancient Mariner reporting on it, Coleridge inventing it, or a reader contemplating it; and whether she is the speaker, hearer, or overhearer of a sarcastic remark about the rainfall. In all cases, irony is a matter of construal, and arises from the flow of attention from one space to a higher-level Viewpoint space from which the focused event or utterance and its associated viewpoint are viewed from afar.

The effect is to present the ironized content from two vantages at once: the ironic (V') and the ironized (V). If a sailor in the Ancient Mariner's crew can appreciate the irony of his situation, he is, in that moment, taking a sort of outside view of his circumstance. If a person contemplating the rain that has disrupted her picnic plans can partake in a sarcastic comment about it, she too is stepping outside the simplest or most immediate perspective on events, at least for the duration of the sarcasm.

Thus, ironic understanding depends on construing a statement, situation, or sentiment as subject to multiple disjunct views.[1] This account is appealing in that it captures an element of ironic experience that many commentators have invoked to describe what makes irony more than mere opposition. This quality is what Wayne Booth (1974: 36) has called irony's "movement" to a "wiser, wittier" vantage, the sense that it involves "a leap or climb to a higher level." Similarly, John Haiman (1998: 80) observes that sarcasm and its relations crucially "allow one to express the difference between a behaving and a scrutinizing self," while Michaelis and Feng (2015: 149) note that what distinguishes the sarcastic func-

---

[1] Dramatic ironies also depend on making us acutely aware of the availability of and difference between (at least) two incompatible views on a single situation: by generating and highlighting a salient gap between character and audience understanding. See Tobin (2016) for more discussion of dramatic irony in this framework.

tions of English Split Interrogative constructions from their sincere counterparts is that they express "a dissociative *Doppelurteil*, or double judgment."

The question arises: does this kind of conceptually divided or doubled perspective correspond in any way to physical viewpoint? If so, will seeing physical viewing arrangements that correspond to particular conceptual viewpoint arrangements make those conceptual arrangements more accessible? Might images of people looking at other people affect participants' judgments of whether a given utterance is sarcastic or sincere?

3 Constructions of sarcasm and sincerity

Both the viewpoint theory of irony and the volume in which this chapter appears have a strong interest in exploring the diversity of irony's forms and functions. However, a controlled exploration of the above question requires a substantially constrained focus on a small subset of potential ironies.

Sarcasm and other forms of verbal irony are famously dependent on context (Wallace, Kertz, and Charniak 2014; Bamman and Smith 2015), and even constructions that are conventionally ironic in sentiment can themselves be used meta-ironically (Haiman 1998). That said, there are expressions that do seem to evoke an ironic interpretation as their primary meaning, even in the absence of paralinguistic cues or other contextual support. Some are stock phrases that supply what Michaelis and Feng (2015: 148) nicely call "preassembled wit," such as *Yeah, right* or *Good luck with that*. These phrases can, indeed, travel so far down the path of conventionalization that the strictly literal sense may not be available at all, or only with substantial extra work. For instance, Horn (2001) discusses the example of *fat chance*, which is, as far as I know, essentially never used to suggest that the relevant likelihood is in fact large. Haiman (1998: 57), for his part, claims that "the closest approach to a pure syntacticization of the [nonexistent] sarcastive [mood] is the word order exemplified in" expressions such as *A fine romance this is! A fine friend you turned out to be!* and *Some party this is!*

Rachel Giora and colleagues have also done important work demonstrating that certain constructions, particularly negative constructions modifying positive concepts at the high end of a scale, generate ironic interpretations by default. They have shown that most people prefer a sarcastic interpretation of statements such as *He's not the smartest* or *Thoroughness is not her greatest strength* when no additional context is supplied (Giora, Fein, Metuki, and Stern 2010; Giora, Livnat, Fein, Barnea, Zeiman, and Berger 2013; Giora, Drucker, Fein, and Mendelson 2015). Furthermore, these same expressions are processed more quickly and readily when they are presented in a sarcasm-supporting context than when they are presented in a context that supports a literal/sincere interpretation (Giora et al. 2010, 2013, 2015).

In the present study we wanted to avoid constructions that were strongly associated with sarcasm by default in this way. Additionally, to allow for ambiguity between sarcastic and sincere interpretations of the target sentences, we needed to avoid sentences with internal incongruities, as these tend to invite sarcastic interpretations (Giora 2016; Partington 2011), and to withhold any specific contextual information about the speaker's intentions, affective stance, or other relevant details that could either invite or inhibit an ironic interpretation. However, it was also important to choose expressions that were readily amenable to ironic interpretation. In the absence of any evaluative content, it can be difficult (though certainly not impossible, given sufficient context) to construct an interpretation of an utterance as sarcastic.

To strike this balance, we can turn to one very frequently described genre of sarcastic remark. These begin with *I love* or another expression of strong affection (*I adore...*; *I'm loving...*; *I really enjoy...*) and go on to pick out some situation or state towards which the speaker wishes to direct some sarcastic ridicule. This is the sort of not-too-subtle sarcasm found in examples from Twitter (Riloff et al. 2013) such as *I love waiting forever for the doctor* and *Oh how I love being ignored*.

When a speaker's ostensible affections are, as in these examples, directed at a situation stereotypically or locally marked as negative or undesirable – feeling sick, perhaps, or *this stupid exam* – the odds are strong that something sarcastic is afoot. And indeed this combination is a common template for everyday sarcastic remarks. This is how the algorithm presented in Riloff et al. (2013) is able to learn to recognize "negative situation phrases" by looking at n-grams following the word *love* in a large set of tweets previously marked as sarcastic. But sarcasm can also arise in these contexts even when the relevant situation is expressed in neutral or positive terms.

Many of the expressions in the González-Ibánez, Muresan, and Wacholder (2011) sarcasm corpus (generated by using the Twitter API to collect tweets including the hashtags #sarcasm or #sarcastic), for example, follow this pattern. Here are a few they cite as illustrative (p. 592):

(1) I can't express how much I love shopping on black Friday.
(2) @UserName that's what I love about Miami. Attention to detail in preserving historic landmarks of the past.
(3) @UserName im just loving the positive vibes out of that!

Note that in examples (2) and (3), the sarcast piles on ostensible markers of positive feeling well past the initial *love*. Understanding these remarks as sarcastic requires unpacking not only the initial declaration of love but also the alleged "positive vibes" mentioned by speaker 3 and speaker 2's suggestion that Miami displays attention to detail in preserving historic landmarks (instead, we may safely imagine that the occasion for this remark was a failure to do exactly that). But it is equally possible to structure sarcastic remarks that drop the pretense of positivity partway through, as seen in the examples from Riloff et al. and in the constructed variations (4) and (5) below:

(4) That's what I love about Miami. A complete lack of attention to detail in preserving historic landmarks of the past.
(5) @UserName im just loving the negative vibes out of that!

Meanwhile, Raymond Gibbs and colleagues have pointed out that the *I love* template may often be used sarcastically in yet another way: "Speakers may also mean what they literally say but still intend their utterances to be understood as irony, as when a mother says to her teenage son *I love children who keep their rooms clean* just as she has discovered that her son, once again, failed to clean his room" (Gibbs and O'Brien 1991: 525) or when a frustrated motorist observes sardonically *I love people who signal* after another driver pulls into her lane without signaling (Gibbs 1986: 4).

All of these variations mean that by deploying such constructions with semantically light and/or neutral complements, we can avoid explicit or conventional internal incongruities while also leaving open the ready possibility of sarcastic interpretation.

4 Study: Scenes and judgments

In this study, participants were shown line drawings of one or more people conversing, paired with short captions, and were asked how likely they thought it was that the speaker of the caption sentence was being sarcastic. All participants were native speakers of English, and all were paid for participating.

4.1 Participants

Two hundred and seventy participants (117 female; 152 male) were recruited via Amazon Mechanical Turk online. Subjects were screened by questionnaire, Amazon's localization and user qualification tools, and our records of Worker ID numbers to restrict participation to workers inside the United States, and to exclude participants under the age of 18, those who were not native speakers of English, and those who had participated in previous studies with our lab.

In Mechanical Turk, participants ("workers" in Amazon's terminology) browse a list of tasks available to them, and of the compensation they can receive for completing them, posted by "requesters." By default, these tasks ("HITs") are sorted by how recently they have been posted, and they remain open until the specified number of workers have completed the task or the requester closes the HIT. Studies of Mechanical Turk as a participant pool and as a recruitment tool suggest that both the timing and duration of HIT postings affect the quality and diversity of responses. The demographics and experience level of participants vary depending on whether an experiment is conducted at night or by day, and whether it is conducted on a weekday or a weekend (Arechar, Kraft-Todd, and Rand 2017). Participation rates are sensitive to recency (Chilton, Horton, Miller, and Azenkot 2010) – that is, potential participants respond in much greater numbers to recently posted tasks – and while participants working in Mechanical Turk have been found to be more attentive to instructions overall than college students who participate in psychology studies in person (Hauser and Schwarz 2016), Mechanical Turk participants who respond early in data collection tend to be even more attentive than their counterparts who respond later in the same posting period (Paolacci and Chandler 2014). For these reasons, participants for this study were recruited through several smaller batch postings distributed across different times of the day and week, rather than in a single large group.

4.2 Materials and procedure

The sentences used in this study were drawn from a set of 260 sentences originally developed for a study (Tobin and Zimon in prep) investigating the influence of "constructions of intersubjectivity" (Verhagen 2005) on judgments of irony. Following Riloff et al. (2013), all of these sentences are variations on the form *I love* + neutral complement or *I hate* + neutral complement. Nine hundred and seventy five native speakers of English evaluated sentences of these types with no additional modifiers (e.g. "I like that guy") as well as sentences with modifiers from four categories: intensifiers (e.g. "really"), evaluative adverbs (e.g. "unfortunately"), modal adverbs (e.g. "certainly"), and discourse particles (e.g. "well"), on a 9-point scale from "definitely sarcastic" to "definitely sincere." Sentences were presented in isolation, with no accompanying image or other contextual cues. In order to prevent judgment fatigue, each participant was given a randomly ordered selection of eight sentences from the larger set, yielding 30 judgments per sentence.

The present study looked at sentences that had received neutral ratings from those 975 participants, with mean ratings near 5 and a balanced distribution of judgments. From the set of sentences that met these criteria, we chose six that were balanced between *I love* and *I hate* and which represented a range of different complements and modifiers across the set. These are presented in Table 1.

Table 1: Target sentences, their mean ratings (1="definitely sincere"; 9="definitely sarcastic"), and standard deviations from the norming study (Tobin and Zimon in prep).

Sentence	Mean	SD
I sure do love that guy.	4.87	2.47
No, I love my job.	5.13	2.77
Yes, I hate seeing people.	4.74	2.57
Obviously, I hate the idea.	4.90	2.69
Really, I love to hear that.	5.00	2.75
I definitely hate doing nothing.	5.54	2.50

The images paired with these sentences were also drawn from a larger pool, again selecting for neutrality, in this case based on ratings by three student research assistants. Only scenes that all three assistants rated independently as "neutral" on rankings of positive/neutral/negative mood were selected for the study. Individual figures were assembled into six different scenes with one-, two- and three-person variations. See Figure 2 for the full set of scenes in their three-person variations, and Figure 3 for an example of the three variations of one of these scenes.

Figure 2: All six possible scenes, each displayed in its three-person variation.

Figure 3: One-, two-, and three-person variations for one of the six scenes.

Following instructions and a warm-up task, each participant answered the question "Do you think this person's statement is more likely to be sarcastic or sincere?" for six image-sentence pairs, as shown in Figure 4.

We created eighteen different stimulus sets for this stage of the study. Each set included all six of the sentences in Table 1, paired with different cross-sections of the scene image set. Participants in each group saw one image from each of

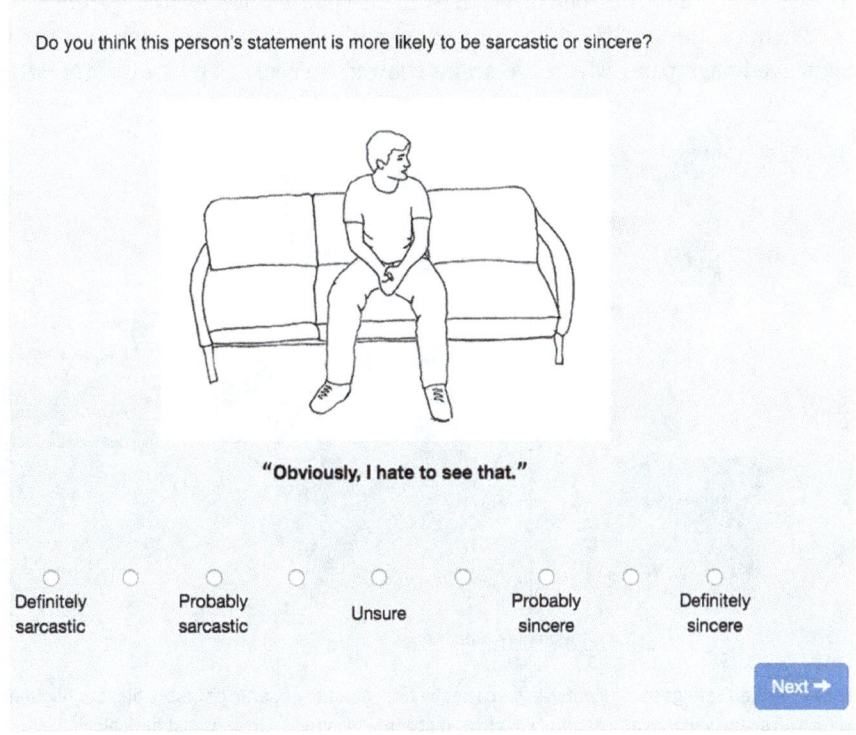

Figure 4: Screenshot of stimulus and query, as presented to participants via Mechanical Turk.

the six different scenes: two in the speaker-alone configuration, two in the speaker-hearer configuration, and two in the speaker-hearer-overhearer configuration, counterbalanced in pairings across sets. This allowed us to collect fifteen ratings apiece for each possible sentence/image pairing, while ensuring that every participant saw a balanced set of stimuli, with no repeated elements.

4.3 Results

As expected, participants rated utterances as significantly more likely to be sarcastic when they were paired with images of scenes showing multiple viewpointed figures than when they were paired with scenes featuring a speaker alone. Participants consistently judged utterances least likely to be sarcastic when they were paired with speaker-alone images across the set as a whole. Interestingly, however, the effect did not vary monotonically with the number of people visible in the scene. Sentence-image pairs with two people were the most "sarcastic," followed by pairs with three, followed by pairs with one. The overall rating spread for one-, two-, and three-person scene/sentence pairings is shown in Figure 5.

Each of these differences proved significant in paired sample t-tests. Sentence-image pairs where the scene showed a speaker and hearer ($M=5.91$)

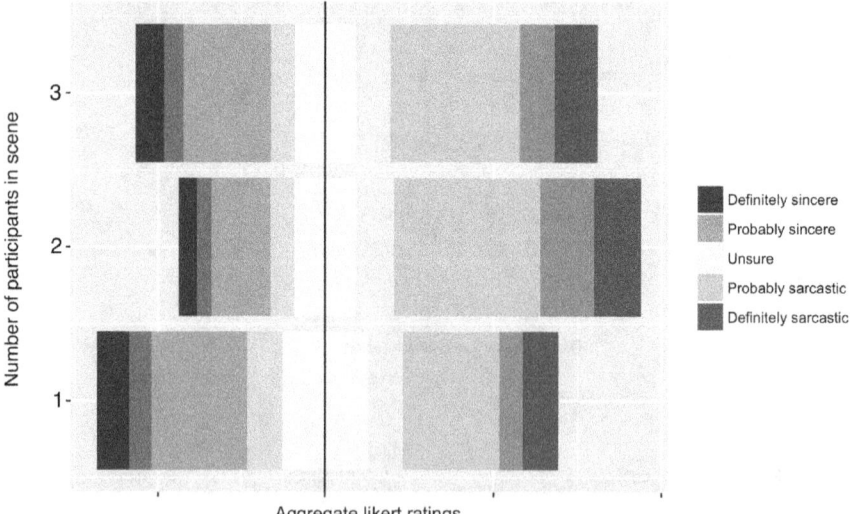

Figure 5: Likert ratings for sincerity vs. sarcasm, by total number of participants visible, aggregated across all scene variants and sentences, aligned at zero ("unsure"). The leftmost dark block corresponds to ratings of "definitely sincere" while the rightmost, darkest block corresponds to ratings of "definitely sarcastic." Width of each block corresponds to the number of ratings received.

yielded significantly higher sarcasm ratings than those showing a speaker alone (M=5.03); $t(1097)$= 6.599, p < .001. Sentence-image pairs where three people were visible (M=5.42) also yielded significantly higher sarcasm ratings than the speaker-alone pairings; $t(1097)$= 2.813, p < .001. However, sarcasm ratings for two-person scene pairings were also significantly higher than the ratings for their three-person counterparts; $t(1097)$= 3.63, p < .005.

The same general trend, in which speakers alone seemed most likely to be sincere, while the two-person version of scenes typically had the strongest pro-sarcasm effect, holds within cross-sections of image-sentence pairs: across variations for all six sentences (Figure 6), and also across sentences for all six scenes (Figure 7).

Across the board, then, judgments of sarcasm were, as hypothesized, sensitive to the number of embodied viewpoints visible in a scene. However, the observed effect is not simply a case of more viewpoints yielding more irony. Something more specific is going on.

In the viewpoint theory of irony, the classic zoom-out configuration of what we might call basic ironies rests not on a general proliferation of viewpoints, but on a single "step back" to a view of the ironized viewpoint. Because irony is both slippery and productive, it is certainly possible to construct ironies in which

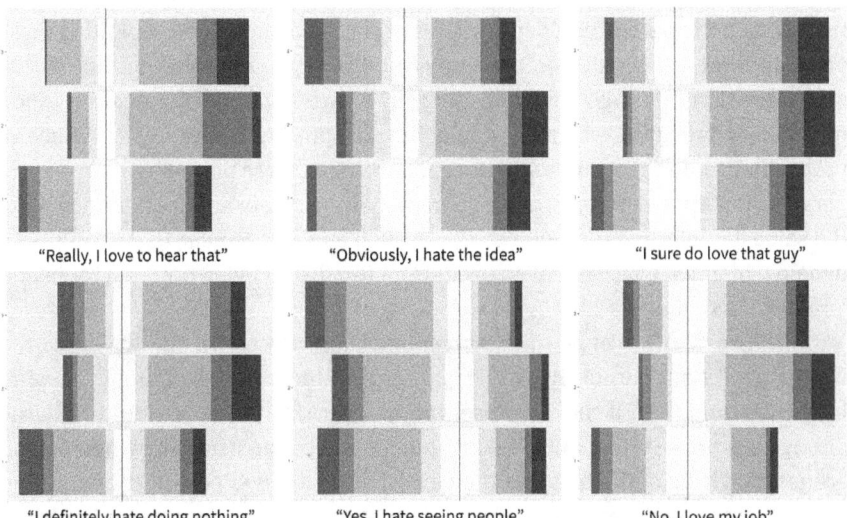

Figure 6: Likert ratings for sincerity vs. sarcasm by number of participants visible, aggregated across all scene variants, for each sentence in the set. Again, a Likert spread weighted toward the right corresponds to more sarcastic ratings for the sentence in question. One-person scene variations are at the bottom of each set; three-person variations at the top.

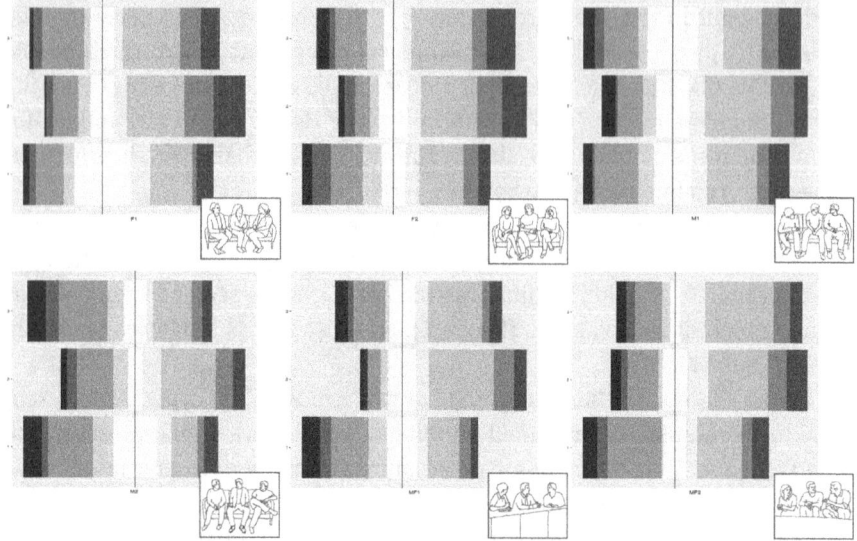

Figure 7: Likert ratings by number of participants visible, aggregated across sentences, for each of the six possible scene variants.

viewpoints proliferate, sometimes in ambiguous or destabilizing ways. Literary, theatrical, and pop-cultural deployments of irony are famous for exploiting these possibilities (e.g. Booth 1974; Brooks 1948, 1951); so too are various kinds of rhetorical evasion that take advantage of irony's capacity for piling distance upon distance or providing plausible deniability for putting dangerous or offensive propositions into a discourse without committing to those propositions *in propria persona*. But appreciating a canonical verbal, dramatic, or situational irony, as in the sarcastic interpretation of a sentence such as *I love to hear that*, involves "a dynamic blended construal of an event from *two* distinct viewpoints" (Tobin and Israel 2012: 31, italics added).

The two-figure scenes thus correspond most closely to the hypothesized interpretive stance underlying the particular kinds of verbal irony on offer in this stimulus set. It makes sense, then, that these prompts would have the strongest positive effect on speakers' judgments of sarcasm. The three-person scenes, by virtue of the fact that they incorporate the two-person configuration within their larger scene, do make the two-part viewpoint configuration available in a way that the one-person scenes do not. This fact is reflected in their significantly higher sarcasm ratings. However, for these (potential) verbal ironies, the presence of a third figure serves to militate or dilute this effect, rather than reinforcing it.

5 Discussion

This study asked whether visible, physical viewing arrangements corresponding to the viewpoint theory's hypothesized conceptual viewpoint arrangements would make those conceptual arrangements more accessible. The answer, at least provisionally, is yes. These findings provide preliminary but encouraging empirical support both for the longstanding intuition that irony depends on or invokes some kind of doubled, divided, distancing viewing arrangement of an ironized perspective, and for the specific depiction of that arrangement put forward in the viewpoint theory's Mental Spaces account.

That said, it is important to note that while these results are compatible with the viewpoint theory, other qualities of irony may also partly or wholly explain the pattern of judgments we see here. In particular, the natural discourse ecology of verbal irony is both interactive and private, suggesting an interactive but constrained conversational scene. The canonical situation of verbal irony is one in which the ironist performs a special kind of affective evaluation for a special kind of audience. There is, or can be, an element of complicity in irony. This is the quality that Wayne Booth (1974: 304) says "creates a sense of collusion" between speaker and hearer, or author and reader, "against those who do not get [the] point." If irony is fundamentally a sort of afffective conspiracy, it makes sense that the presence of some interlocutor or interlocutors more readily triggers an ironic interpretation than a solo scene, in which no co-conspirator is present. Meanwhile, the private nature of irony could explain why the presence of more interlocutors dilutes the effect or makes the ironic interpretation less obvious.

This last point is an especially interesting one to take up in more detail. Under the current study design, one might justifiably argue that Booth's collusion-exclusion model of irony predicts that the speaker-hearer-overhearer scenarios would most fully capture the canonical ironic scene. Booth argues that irony is "always [...] a device for excluding as well as for including" and indeed that the included parties "cannot but derive at least part of their pleasure from a sense that others are excluded" (p. 304). But this strong view of irony as necessarily and always predicated on exclusion may not be correct. The current state of research suggests that verbal ironies are often deployed in circumstances where speakers not only expect their ironic intentions to be broadly obvious, but also fail to think of them as involving any ambiguity at all (as in the case of "preassembled wit," as discussed above, or see, e.g. Epley and Kruger 2005; Giora et al. 2010).

If, however, scenes of complicity and exclusion do generally evoke ironic interpretations, and this association partly or wholly drives the findings in this study, we might expect the presence of a third party, especially one in a position outside the speaker-hearer interaction, to make the ironic interpretation most obvious of all. It did not. It is still worth investigating, however, whether we would find different patterns of judgments for scenes in which the speaker is facing away from the bystander as they are in the present study, versus scenes in which two or more interlocutors are positioned as multiple hearers facing the speaker. Specifically, we would at least expect the dilution effect to be stronger (that is, for the difference between judgments for two-person and three-person scenes to be greater) in the multiple-hearer condition. To investigate this question more closely, a follow-up study can look at scenes which differ categorically in this way.

An additional important question not answered by the present study design is the influence of facial expression in the depicted interlocutors. Although all of the scenes were rated as neutral/ambiguous by our raters in the absence of the stimulus sentences, people can be very sensitive to small differences in facial expression, especially in circumstances where (unlike the situation that obtained for the original raters) they are hunting for clues to use in making sense of ambiguous social situations. For this reason, follow-up studies can explore more stylized representations of multiple viewpoints. This approach will also have the advantage of allowing us to tease apart the effect of simply presenting multiple representations of viewing from the effect of presenting a potentially more or less conspiratorial conversational scene.

Finally, as shown in Figure 7, each of the stimulus sentences did interact with the number of scene participants in the reported 2 > 3 > 1 pattern. But the stimulus sentences, matched though they were for the distribution of sarcasm/sincerity judgments they received in the absence of any accompanying image, differ from one another in terms of the grounding viewpoint situations they themselves evoke. The anaphora of "I love to hear that," for example, readily suggests a previous utterance by an interlocutor (where "that" refers to "what you just said") while "I love my job" does not. We would expect the former sentence to make the viewpoint of the (an) other participant more salient than the latter. According to our working hypothesis, this fact should itself make an ironic interpretation more available. And indeed, in each of the stimulus sentences, there is some word or phrase (an evaluative adverb, a discourse marker, or an intensifier) that makes the dialogic, intersubjective scene more salient than it might otherwise be. This moderate evocation of intersubjectivity is, we think, responsible for the distribution of ratings these particular sentences received in the prior study. Preliminary analysis (Tobin and Zimon in prep) suggests that loading up multiple such elements in a single sentence does increase the probability of an ironic interpretation. What is not yet clear is how these different constructions of intersubjectivity interact differently, or similarly, with representations of multiple viewpoints in a visible scene. The number of judgments collected in the present study is not sufficient to draw meaningful conclusions about this interaction. In general, a larger and more diverse data set, amenable to more sophisticated multifactor analysis, will help to shed more light on all of these questions. More work is needed.

Is there anything else we can do with these results? Irony has received increasing attention in recent decades as a technical problem for natural language processing, especially in computational approaches to sentiment analysis (e.g. Littman and Mey 1991; Utsumi 1996; Tepperman, Traum, and Narayanan 2006). That work is driven largely by practical, rather than, or in addition to, theoretical concerns. The basic objective is to distinguish sarcastic from literal uses of language partly as a goal in its own right, but especially because of the threat that irony poses to the accurate diagnosis of attitudes and opinions from natural language data. Without tools for detecting sarcasm, these systems can be badly misled by, for example, circumstances in which "words [...]. have a strong polarity but are used sarcastically, which means that the opposite polarity was intended" (Riloff et al. 2013: 1).

As Wallace et al. (2014: 512) note in their aptly titled paper "Humans require context to infer ironic intent (so computers probably do, too)," there are limits to what can be done to close this gap using systems that look only at features within a target utterance, because "the exact same sentence can be both intended ironically and unironically, depending on the context (including the speaker and the topic at hand). Only obvious verbal ironies will be recognizable from intrinsic features alone." And indeed, just as humans are better at diagnosing ironic intentions in rich contexts where they have access to not only background information about the speaker and ongoing topics of conversation, but also rich paralinguistic cues, linguists have found that prosodic and other non-lexical elements of the discourse stream can be among the most reliable predictors of verbal irony. These elements of interest include things such as the speaker's intonation, gestures and facial expression (see, e.g., Colston, this volume), and both speaker's and hearer's laughter during and after a target remark (Bryant 2010; Eisterhold, Attardo, and Boxer 2006).

The results of this study suggest that the presence and arrangement of other people in a discourse setting are also valuable places to look for features that are predictive of sarcasm, rather than focusing solely on features of an utterance. Sarcastic interpretations are more accessible in circumstances in which multiple viewpoints – especially two viewpoints – are made visually accessible as part of the mise-en-scene, or where the view-of-a-viewpoint arrangement is otherwise already salient at the time the target content is presented.

It may seem on first consideration that while these variables may influence third-party judgments of ambiguous utterances, they are not necessarily very useful as a diagnosis of the correct interpretation of a speaker's sentiments. After all, isn't the number of people visible in a conversational scene essentially a matter of happenstance, independent of the intentions and circumstances driving speaker attitudes and intentions in that scene? People can be sarcastic by themselves, to an audience of one or many, in the presence of overhearers or not. I would argue, however, that the presence and arrangement of discourse participants may, at least in certain settings, capture important information about a range of contextual factors that may also predict something about speaker intentions. In addition to the follow-up studies discussed above, I present two avenues for future research to investigate these implications.

First, in many circumstances where we have access to large quantities of multimodal data of language in use – that is, the kind of video data that lends itself readily to computational approaches to sentiment analysis – that material is the product of choices and behaviors not only on the part of the speakers whose utterances are on display, but also on the part of camera operators, producers, directors, editors, and others. These choices about, for example, what to include in the video frame, camera angle and distance, the arrangement and position of performers on screen, and juxtapositions of shots across cuts, are not arbitrary. They reflect the judgments of humans, who are themselves pursuing discourse goals through those choices. These aspects of a scene will surely never be dispositive predictors of irony by themselves, but is plausible that, in constructing these scenes, production teams may systematically (if not necessarily consciously) opt to frame shots in ways that encourage audiences to interpret remarks ironically when that interpretation is desired.

Second, it is possible that speakers' confidence in the transparency of their own sarcastic intentions may reflect some implicit awareness of their interlocutors' sensitivity to visible viewpoint arrangements in taking remarks to be sarcastic or sincere. It is important to note that people are famously quite bad at estimating how easy it is to detect their communication intentions in general, and sarcastic intentions in particular (Epley and Kruger 2005; Keysar 1994; Kruger, Epley, Parker, and Ng 2005). Nonetheless, their efforts at disambiguation may turn out to vary in ways that are sensitive to these factors, even if the product still overestimates communicative transparency.

In conclusion, these data support the theory that irony is, in a real sense, a figure of viewpoint. Ironic interpretations were more readily accessible when anchored in, or primed by, congruent embodied viewpoint arrangements in a relevant, visible scene. Now that this basic relationship has been established, more research about the details and parameters of this effect are warranted. In addition to the avenues of investigation described above, we can empirically test other viewpoint variations, to help us understand how drawing attention to speaker viewpoint can under different circumstances enhance the impression of either sarcasm or sincerity. For instance, direct eye contact, which can make visible viewpoint more prominent in any scene, has elsewhere been associated with impressions of both sincerity and manipulativeness (Weir and Wrightsman 1990). Examining these factors can also help shed light on how various kinds of conceptual "distance" – ironic or otherwise – are grounded in embodied experience of interpersonal scenes.

References

Arechar, Antonio A., Gordon T. Kraft-Todd, & David G. Rand. 2017, Turking overtime: how participant characteristics and behavior vary over time and day on Amazon Mechanical Turk. *Journal of the Economic Science Association* 3 (1), 1–11.
Attardo, Salvatore. 2000, Irony as relevant inappropriateness. *Journal of Pragmatics* 32 (6), 793–826.
Bamman, David & Noah A. Smith. 2015. Contextualized Sarcasm Detection on Twitter. ICWSM, 574–77.
Booth, Wayne C. 1974. *A rhetoric of irony*. Chicago: University of Chicago Press.
Brooks, Cleanth. 1948. Irony and "ironic" poetry. *The English Journal* 37 (2), 57–63.
Brooks, Cleanth. 1951. Irony as a principle of structure. *Literary Opinion in America* 2, 729–41.
Bryant, Gregory A. 2010. Prosodic contrasts in ironic speech, *Discourse Processes*, 47 (7), 545–66.
Butler, Harold E. 1921. *The Institutio Oratoria of Quintilian, Vol. 3*. London: William Heinemann Ltd.
Chilton, Lydia B., John J. Horton, Robert C. Miller & Shiri Azenkot. 2010. Task search in a human computation market, *Proceedings of the ACM IGKDD Workshop on Human Computation*, 1–9.
Clark, Herbert H. & Richard J. Gerrig. 1984. On the pretense theory of irony, *Journal of Experimental Psychology: General*, 113 (1), 121–126.
Colston, Herbert L. (this volume). Eye-rolling, irony and embodiment.
Cutrer, L. M. 1994. *Time and tense in narrative and in everyday language*. San Diego: University of California dissertation.
Dancygier, Barbara & Eve Sweetser. 2005. *Mental spaces in grammar: conditional constructions*. New York: Cambridge University Press.
Dancygier, Barbara. 2012. Negation, stance verbs, and intersubjectivity. In Dancygier, Barbara & Eve Sweetser (eds.), *Viewpoint in language: A multimodal perspective*, 69–96. Cambridge: Cambridge University Press.
Eisterhold, Jodi, Salvatore Attardo & Diana Boxer. 2006. Reactions to irony in discourse: Evidence for the least disruption principle. *Journal of Pragmatics*, 38 (8), 1239–1256.
Epley, Nicholas & Justin Kruger. 2005. When what you type isn't what they read: The perseverance of stereotypes and expectancies over e-mail, *Journal of Experimental Social Psychology*, 41 (4), 414–422.

Fauconnier, Gilles. 1985. *Mental spaces: Aspects of meaning construction in natural language.* New York: Cambridge University Press.
Fauconnier, Gilles. 1997. *Mappings in thought and language.* Cambridge: Cambridge University Press.
Gibbs, Raymond W. 1986. On the psycholinguistics of sarcasm. *Journal of Experimental Psychology: General* 115 (1), 3–15.
Gibbs, Raymond W. & Jennifer O'Brien. 1991. Psychological aspects of irony understanding. *Journal of Pragmatics* 16 (6), 523–30.
Giora, Rachel, Ofer Fein, Nili Metuki, & Pnina Stern. 2010. Negation as a metaphor-inducing operator. In Horn, Laurence R. (ed.), *The expression of negation,* 225–56. Berlin: Mouton de Gruyter.
Giora, Rachel, Elad Livnat, Ofer Fein, Anat Barnea, Rakefet Zeiman, & Iddo Berger. 2013. Negation generates nonliteral interpretations by default, *Metaphor and Symbol* 28 (2), 89–115.
Giora, Rachel, Ari Drucker, Ofer Fein, & Itamar Mendelson. 2015. Default sarcastic interpretations: On the priority of nonsalient interpretations. *Discourse Processes* 52 (3), 173–200.
Giora, Rachel. 2016. When negatives are easier to understand than affirmatives: The case of negative sarcasm. In Larrivée, Pierre & Chungmin Lee (eds.), *Negation and polarity: Experimental perspectives,* 127–43. Cham: Springer Switzerland.
González-Ibánez, Roberto, Smaranda Muresan, & Nina Wacholder. 2011. Identifying sarcasm in Twitter: a closer look. *Proceedings of the 49th Annual Meeting of the Association for Computational Linguistics: Human Language Technologies: Short Papers Volume 2,* 581–86.
Haiman, John. 1998. *Talk is cheap: Sarcasm, alienation, and the evolution of language,* Oxford & New York: Oxford University Press.
Hauser, David J. & Norbert Schwarz. 2016. Attentive Turkers: MTurk participants perform better on online attention checks than do subject pool participants. *Behavior Research Methods,* 48 (1) 400–407.
Horn, Laurence R. 2001. Flaubert triggers, squatitive negation and other quirks of grammar. In Hoeksema, Jack, Hotze Rullmann, Víctor Sánchez-Valencia & Ton van der Wouden (eds.), *Perspectives on negation and polarity items,* 173–200. Amsterdam: John Benjamins.
Israel, Michael. 2011. *The grammar of polarity: Pragmatics, sensitivity, and the logic of scales.* Cambridge, UK: Cambridge University Press.
Keysar, Boaz. 1994. The illusory transparency of intention: linguistic perspective taking in text.. *Cognitive Psychology,* 26 (2), 165–208.
Kruger, Justin, Nicholas Epley, Jason Parker & Zhi-Wen Ng. 2005. Egocentrism over e-mail: can we communicate as well as we think? *Journal of Personal Social Psychology* 89 (6), 925–36.
Lear, Jonathan. 2011. *A Case for Irony.* Cambridge: Harvard University Press.
Michaelis, Laura A. & Hanbing Feng. 2015. What is this, sarcastic syntax? *Constructions and Frames* 7 (2), 148–80.
Paolacci, Gabriele & Jesse Chandler. 2014. Inside the Turk: Understanding Mechanical Turk as a participant pool. *Current Directions in Psychological Science* 23 (3), 184–88.
Partington, Alan. 2011. Phrasal irony: Its form, function and exploitation. *Journal of Pragmatics* 43 (6), 1786–800.
Riloff, Ellen, Ashequl Qadir, Prafulla Surve, Lalindra De Silva, Nathan Gilbert & Ruihong Huang. 2013. Sarcasm as Contrast between a Positive Sentiment and Negative Situation.

Proceedings of the 2013 Conference on Empirical Methods in Natural Language Processing, 704–714.

Sperber, Dan & Deirdre Wilson. 1981. Irony and the use-mention distinction. *Radical Pragmatics* 49, 295–318.

Sperber, Dan & Deirdre Wilson. 1998. Irony and relevance: A reply to Seto, Hamamoto and Yamanashi. In Carston, Robyn & Seiji Uchida (eds.), *Relevance theory: Applications and implications*, 239–255. Amsterdam: John Benjamins.

Sweetser, Eve. 2012. Introduction: Viewpoint & perspective in language and gesture, from the ground up. In Dancygier, Barbara & Eve Sweetser (eds.), *Viewpoint in language: A multimodal perspective*, 1–24. Cambridge: Cambridge University Press.

Tepperman, Joseph, David Traum & Shrikanth Narayanan. 2006. 'Yeah Right': Sarcasm Recognition for Spoken Dialogue Systems. *Ninth International Conference on Spoken Language Processing*.

Tobin, Vera & Michael Israel. 2012. Irony as a viewpoint phenomenon. On Dancygier, Barbara & Eve Sweetser (eds.), *Viewpoint in language: A multimodal perspective*, 25–46. Cambridge: Cambridge University Press.

Tobin, Vera & Max Zimon. In prep. Irony and markers of intersubjectivity.

Tobin, Vera. 2016. Performance, irony, and viewpoint in language. In Cook, Amy & Rhonda Blair (eds.), *Theatre, performance, and cognition: Languages, bodies, and ecologies*, 54–67. London & New York: Bloomsbury Methuen.

Verhagen, Arie. 2005. *Constructions of intersubjectvity: Discourse, syntax, and cognition.* Oxford: Oxford University Press.

Wallace, Byron C., Laura Kertz & Eugene Charniak. 2014. Humans require context to infer ironic intent (so computers probably do, too). *Proceedings of the 52nd Annual Meeting of the Association for Computational Linguistics (Volume 2: Short Papers)*, 512–516.

Weir, Julie A. & Lawrence S Wrightsman. 1990. The determinants of mock jurors verdicts in a rape case. *Journal of Applied Social Psychology* 20 (11), 901–19.

Wilson, Deirdre. 2006. The pragmatics of verbal irony: Echo or pretence? *Lingua* 116 (10), 1722–43.

Sabina Tabacaru
Faces of sarcasm
Exploring raised eyebrows with sarcasm in French political debates

Abstract: This paper explores the use of facial expressions in sarcasm, following new paths in Cognitive Linguistics and humor research related to multimodality (Tabacaru and Lemmens 2014; Tabacaru 2019). The aim is to emphasize the speakers' intentions of letting their hearers know of their humorous/sarcastic intent. We focus on the pragmatic use of facial expressions, particularly raised eyebrows, one that highlights their use in the switch of frames (Coulson 2005) in figurative language, which would make it possible for hearers to understand that the speaker is being critical of their interlocutor. We align with a layered mental space configuration (Clark 1996; Fauconnier 1984) as discussed by Brône (2008), which allows speakers to build new sarcastic meanings on the common ground that is already shared intersubjectively among discourse participants.

Keywords: facial expressions; sarcasm, layers, gestural triggers, humor

1 Introduction

The topic of humor, and specifically that of irony and sarcasm, has recently received more attention in the field of Cognitive Linguistics. Particularly, the development of multimodality has shown how humor exploits creativity for new meanings to emerge in interaction (Brône & Feyaerts 2003; Kotthoff 2006; Priego-Valverde 2009; Colston 2017; for sarcasm specifically, see Tabacaru and Lemmens 2014 and Tabacaru 2019). Feyaerts and Oben (2014) focus on the importance of meaning coordination among interlocutors. Speakers create their utterances for an addressee who is also part of the same common ground and the same social context (see Kristiansen and Dirven 2008). For example, for speakers "[w]hat is necessary is to coordi-

---

Acknowledgments: I would like to thank Amina Maghraoui for her assistance with the annotation process. I am grateful to Herbert Colston, Vera Tobin, and Hannah Leykum for their comments on previous versions of this article, as well as an anonymous reviewer for their comments and suggestions.

Sabina Tabacaru, Université Paris 8, TransCrit (EA1569)

https://doi.org/10.1515/9783110652246-012

nate predictions, to read the same message in the common situation, to identify the one course of action that their expectations of each other can converge on. They must 'mutually recognize' some unique signal that coordinates their expectations of each other" (Schelling 1960, as quoted in Klein and Orsborn 2009: 181).

On the topic of sarcasm, this idea centers the discussion on how speakers manage to get their (humorous/sarcastic) meanings across and make their hearers understand their utterances. This is an issue that has long been debated in linguistics (cf. Grice 1975) and multimodality should therefore not be overlooked when discussing sarcasm in interaction.[1] According to Gallagher & Hutto (2008: 20) "[...] in situations of social interactions, we have a direct perceptual understanding of another person's intentions because their intentions are explicitly expressed in their embodied actions and expressive behaviors. This understanding does not require us to postulate or infer a belief or a desire hidden away in the other person's mind." This can be done by focusing the attention on multimodality and how speakers constantly express their intentions through a set of tools they have at their disposal: not only words but also gesture, tone of voice, gaze, body position, etc.

In this article, we aim to show how facial expressions (particularly eyebrow movement) play a central role in getting these sarcastic utterances across and alerting the viewers of their intentions. We consider that all types of multimodal elements contribute to meaning construction in interaction, such as mentioned before. Following research on eyebrow movement previously done on sarcasm in English (Tabacaru and Lemmens 2014), our aim here is to see if these gestural triggers are also used with other types of data and other languages.

We align with a view on sarcasm that centers on its critical aspect, thus targeting someone/something in particular (a person, group of people, institution, etc.; for more on sarcasm, see Tabacaru 2018).

In the following, we briefly present the theories that have been used to analyze sarcastic turns in Cognitive Linguistics and then discuss recent studies on multimodality in humor, followed by examples taken from French political debates.

2 Irony and sarcasm in Cognitive Linguistics

Sarcasm has frequently been compared to irony (either as a mechanism of it or at the same level with it; see Gibbs 2000 or Feyaerts 2013). Since Grice (1975), several theories have been used to understand and tackle irony and sarcasm in all their

---

[1] Norris (2004: 1) notes, for instance, that "all interactions are multimodal."

complexity. Traditionally, in pragmatics, irony has been seen as figurative language that means the opposite of what is thought/intended by the speaker (Grice 1975; Coulson 2005). The question whether irony and sarcasm represent the same thing or not (see also Attardo 2000) is not the aim of this paper. A discussion in a recent article (Tabacaru 2018) explains the difference between the two, which are still presented as part of the same category. Generally, the two are closely connected, but "the main distinction between irony and sarcasm is that the latter implies the existence of some kind of target towards which criticism is addressed" (Tabacaru 2018: 190).

Within the field of Cognitive Linguistics, various perspectives can be used to account for these categories, theories such as the space structuring model (Coulson 2000, 2015) or the Salience Principle (Giora 1997, 2003) highlighting the idea of frame-shifting and prototypicality (see Brône 2017 for a summary of these theories). For instance, Coulson's (2000) space structuring model revolves around conceptual blending, allowing representations and possibilities between the real and the pretended world in sarcastic turns.

Brône (2008, 2010) discusses a model that combines Clark's (1996) layering model and Fauconnier's (1984, 1994; Fauconnier and Turner 1998) mental spaces theory. Clark's layering model has been used to discuss different linguistic phenomena, humor included (see Brône 2008, 2010, who discusses the case of hyper-understanding). Humor would involve a contrast between two meanings (see also Koestler 1964 and the idea of bisociation), so, a contrast between two layers of meaning. According to Fauconnier (1997: 11), mental spaces "are partial structures that proliferate when we think and talk, allowing a fine-grained partitioning of our discourse and knowledge structures." These structures consist of elements organized in cognitive models and frames. As such, a linguistic form has different possible readings depending on the context in which it occurs. Fauconnier further notes (2004: 662) that:

> [m]ental spaces proliferate in the unfolding of discourse, map onto each other in intricate ways, and provide abstract mental structure for shifting anchoring, viewpoint, and focus, allowing us to direct our attention at any time onto very partial and simple structures while maintaining an elaborate web of connections in working memory and in long-term memory.

The account of humor proposed by Brône (2008) in relation to hyper-understanding can be seen in Figure 1 below. The pretense space is built on the discourse base space; the latter constituting the common ground on which speakers operate:

This account can easily apply to sarcasm as this mechanism implies a switch between two interpretations. Take for instance the following example, located in Spain in the mid-thirties, and discussed in Veale, Feyaerts, and Brône (2006):

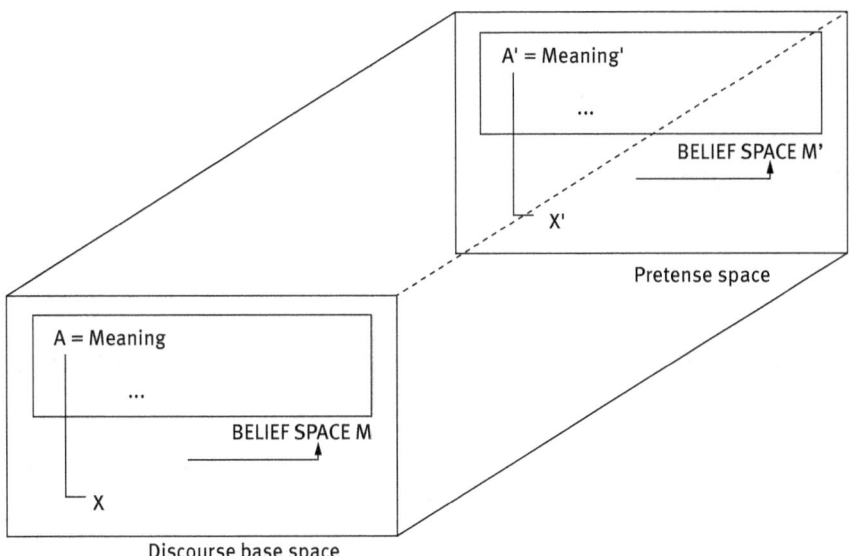

Figure 1: Layered mental space configuration for the base space and the pretense space according to Brône (2008).

(1) Opposition M.P. (referring to the Prime Minister) (S): But what can we expect, after all, of a man who wears silk underpants?
Prime Minister (H): Oh, I would never have thought the Right Honorable's wife could be so indiscreet!

In this case, humor relies on the different meanings added to the context by the different speakers. For S, the *silk underpants* represent a reference to homosexuality and mentioning them gives access to the social stereotypes around it; H rather gives to this comment the meaning of cuckolding. H "turns the tables" using common knowledge that underwear is not publicly visible. The second meaning is thus added as a pretense, non-serious space, built on the first interpretation intended by S. Common knowledge thus gives access to the different frames (the association to homosexuality by the use of *silk underpants* and the fact that underwear is visible in intimate contexts, as intended by H).

Following the pattern presented above, sarcasm will be created in discourse as a second discourse space built from common ground. Following previous studies (Colston 1997; Lee and Katz 1998; Mesing, Williams, and Blasko 2012; Averbeck 2013; Hanks 2013, among others), and as stated above, sarcasm implies the existence of a target (a person, a group of people, an institution, etc.), whether present or absent, towards which the speaker addresses some criticism (see Tabacaru 2018).

The question thus raised in recent years deals with knowing when speakers are being sarcastic. As highlighted by certain researchers (Rockwell 2000, see also below or Clark and Gerrig 1984), there can be a tone of voice used to mark sarcasm/irony in interaction. On top of that, gestural markers can be used for the same purpose: to emphasize the parts of speech that are to be interpreted as sarcastic. In the following, we present the idea of gestural triggers as markers in sarcastic interactions.

3 Markers of humor: The case of gestural triggers

Yus (2003: 1299) points out that there are clues in the context "that indicate that what is being said or about to be said, should not be taken seriously." On a similar note, Fauconnier (1997: 125) remarks that "[e]rrors, jokes, literary effects, and atypical expressions use the same cognitive operations as everyday language, but in ways that actually **highlight** them and can make them more **salient**" (emphasis added).

This hypothesis has been tested in different studies and from different perspectives. Rockwell (2000), for instance, considers that gestures and/or specific intonation are often used by speakers to emphasize parts of their speech. She carried out experiments revealing that speakers are able to recognize a sarcastic tone, showing that "sarcasm appears to exhibit a clear pattern of vocal cues" (2000:493). Rockwell (2001) and Attardo *et al.* (2013) link certain facial expressions, such as eye rolling and rapid blinking, to the use of sarcasm. Thus, speakers inform the hearer(s) that the meaning is sarcastic/ironic (see also Colston [this volume] on the role these expressions have in discourse). Attardo (2003) also notes that laughter may play the role of a marker of humorous intentions.

Burgers and van Mulken (2017: 390) present an overview of humor markers that include linguistic markers such as metaphor, hyperbole, change of register, etc., paralinguistic markers such as prosody and tone of voice (see Attardo *et al.* 2003) and visual markers that include facial expressions, kinesic, and pictorial elements. It seems then than speakers would make their intentions known to the hearer(s), especially in interaction.

Studies in psychology have debated over the meaning of facial expressions, specifically of eyebrow movement, associated to emotions such as surprise, rage, fear, sadness, etc. Both Darwin (1872/1998) and Ekman gathered data from speakers in different countries, comparing the results regarding these expressions. Ekman discussed the similarity between facial expressions and emotions across cultures and the fact that people are able to correctly recognize these (see for instance Ekman and Oster 1979; Darwin and Ekman 1998). Moreover, Ekman describes eyebrow movements in terms of *underliners* (1979: 184) that provide emphasis in a certain context. Similar to vocal cues, these eyebrow movements indicate that a word is important (Krahmer and Swerts, 2007; Birdwhitstell (1970) also notes their accentuation role). Similarly, Bouvet (1996) notes the role of raised eyebrows in sign language as markers of a certain segment in the sentence on which the whole interpretation depends. For Weast (2008), raised eyebrows mark the distinction between statements and questions in American Sign Language despite the speakers' emotional state.

These facial expressions have been linked to humor (Rockwell 2001), more recently with sarcasm or hyper-understanding (Tabacaru and Lemmens 2014; Tabacaru 2019). Occurring frequently with this type of data, they play the role of "gestural triggers", i.e., indicators of a space-shift, from the serious to the non-serious discourse space: "*gestural trigger* refers to the gesture that guides the hearer to interpret the utterance as humorous and contributes to meaning construction (i.e. how the hearer interprets the message)" (Tabacaru and Lemmens 2014: 20). The authors conclude on the semantic-pragmatic nature of these gestural triggers, the former focusing on the expressions of human emotions while the latter represents an underliner in speech (similar to vocal cues, as mentioned earlier). In the case of humor, these facial expressions underline the important parts of a speaker's utterance, the ones carrying the switch from the discourse base space to the pretense space.

Therefore, given the role eyebrow movement seems to play not only in human emotions but also and particularly in interactions, we investigate their occurrence in French, with a focus on television debates. Tabacaru and Lemmens (2014) and Tabacaru (2019) apply this research to staged interactions, which, similar to the case of Rockwell (2000) are played out by actors who exaggerate the reactions in order to make their emotions/intentions known to an audience that is watching. A different set of data (therefore, more spontaneous interactions) would make it possible to see if these eyebrow movements are also used and if their role in sarcasm is central to the message as a whole.

4 Data and methodology

We investigate the use of *gestural triggers* in a different set of data in order to show how speakers use these cues to make their sarcastic intent known to the hearers/audience. The speakers will use facial expressions on core parts of their message in order to show they are being sarcastic towards their interlocutor. A previous study carried out on a large number of examples from two American-television series (*House M.D.* and *The Big Bang Theory*) found that facial expressions were frequently used as a marker in order to switch from the serious to non-serious discourse (Tabacaru and Lemmens 2014; Tabacaru 2019). Given these were scripted exchanges in drama (*House M.D.*) and situation comedy (*The Big Bang Theory*), actors are expected to use markers to make their intentions known to an audience (see Rockwell 2000 for similar results for prosody). In the world of theater (see Lapaire 2015; Lapaire and Duval 2017), actors are expected to "perform" their actions and emotions, thus making their intentions known to the audience/public. It can thus be assumed that in scripted exchanges, actors are expected to highlight their reactions and discourse. This was similar to Rockwell's (2000) findings regarding sarcastic tone of voice, since she used actors who were able to emphasize the tone for the public to recognize.

We chose to focus our attention on uses of facial expressions in another language than English (see Tabacaru 2019 for an analysis of English interactions), gathering data from the 2017 French presidential elections, which would also represent more spontaneous uses of sarcasm and facial expressions. Although the candidates are well prepared for political debates (knowing their adversaries' campaigns and knowing how to persuade and talk about their own political approaches and opinions), the previous scandals surrounding the 2017 French elections made the debate the perfect environment for them to use sarcasm, targeting the others' programs or position in recent events. Some of these scandals included Fillon's misuse of public funds by creating fake jobs in France as well as accusations against Le Pen for creating fake jobs at the European Parliament. Moreover, the recent raise of populism in Europe made the candidates either align with the views (Brexit, for example) or completely oppose these positions, which meant that they are likely to disagree and be overtly critical of the others.

The examples presented below are translated from French and given in original version in the footnotes because of the frequent references to the original version. They come from *Le Grand Débat*,[2] the political debate prior to the presidential elections in France in 2017 which presents all eleven candidates for the first round.[3] The debate lasted 3h50m and was broadcast live on television in April 2017. The media estimated the total viewers to more than 6 million people[4] and was widely discussed on social media given recent events involving the candidates (mainly the fake jobs offenses mentioned earlier, which will be discussed in

---

2 Le Grand Débat (© BFMTV and CNEWS).
3 The official list can be found here: http://candidat-2017.fr/candidats.php
4 According to ozap.com (http://www.ozap.com/actu/audiences-le-debat-a-11-reunit-6-3-millions-de-telespectateurs-sur-bfmtv-et-cnews/523434).

some of the examples below). This debate was not intended as humorous, so the candidates and/or journalists do not intend to amuse the public. When the audience starts laughing and because of the number of candidates and the time allocated to each of them, the journalists request them to stop laughing. This means that common ground could not be enriched freely for sarcastic turns, which happened nonetheless. The debate highly amused viewers who took to social media to discuss lines and reactions from the candidates. Because of the non-humorous nature of the debate (as opposed to a stand-up comedy show, for instance, or a show that is aimed to amuse the public), two researchers watched the debate independently, which was then annotated in terms of the humorous/sarcastic exchanges and facial expressions. Given the previous study related above, the focus was on raised eyebrows, although other gestures, which play a central role for the message, will be mentioned in the examples below.

5 Raised eyebrows and sarcasm

The following examples present sarcasm used with raised eyebrows. These raised eyebrows will be explained in terms of the role they play for the hearers to understand the sarcastic meaning intended by the speaker. Context is given for each example in order to explain the way speakers aim at targeting their opponents.

For example, below, Marine Le Pen targets François Fillon bringing up the Institut Montaigne, a think tank based in Paris, closely related to Fillon through its ex-president[5] who is said to have inspired Fillon's presidential program. Le Pen raises her eyebrows when being sarcastic and also shrugs when uttering *I suppose*. The raised eyebrows appear in bold and can be seen in Figure 2 below:

Institut Mon[taigne]   *[I su]ppose*

Figure 2: Raised eyebrows in example (2).

---

5 An article in French discussing this can be found here: https://blogs.mediapart.fr/danyves/blog/060317/que-ce-soit-fillon-ou-macron-l-institut-montaigne-et-axa-sortent-vainqueurs-et-le-ci

(2) Le Pen: So, Mr Fillon said earlier,
he presented totally unbelievable (*lit. delirious*) numbers
which must come again from the **Institut Mon**taigne, I suppose.[6]

Note also the use of the epistemic *must* and the adjective *unbelievable*, referring to the numbers Fillon presented prior to Le Pen's intervention. This is preceded by her frowning (see video stills above) which would underline the idea of difficulty in believing something.[7] Le Pen implies here that the numbers are not real, invented maybe by Institut Montaigne in order to help Fillon's campaign. The French adjective *délirants* implies the idea of being crazy, delirious even in order to believe in such numbers/results. She raises her eyebrows when uttering *Institut Mon[taigne]* which highlights the role she gives to the Institute in the existence of these numbers. Given the common ground and the knowledge surrounding the Institut Montaigne (i.e., having helped Fillon's campaign), mentioning its name confirms she is being sarcastic and that she doubts the numbers given are real. Le Pen also says *again*, highlighting the unlikelihood of these numbers being real, given the assumption that the same Institute is helping Fillon with his campaign. The fact that she shrugs while uttering *I suppose* (not shown in the videos stills above) could imply the idea that she does not know this for sure, but she assumes that to be the case since the numbers cannot be real.

Her raised eyebrows mark the core part of her sarcasm since she attacks at the same time the Institut Montaigne and Fillon, not only the latter and the numbers he presented. Mentioning the source of the numbers (although not mentioned by Fillon himself during the debate) and raising her eyebrows would switch the discourse to the non-serious space, further suggesting that everything coming from Institut Montaigne cannot be believed/real. This should be obvious for anyone knowing of the past experiences with Institut Montaigne or following the news.

In the example below, Poutou (who is a worker at the Ford company) is directly targeting the Front National (most commonly known by the acronym FN), Le Pen's political party, regarding an episode just prior to the elections when her party was accused of fake jobs offenses as well (similar to the scandal surrounding Fillon's campaign). When the police wanted to question the members, they mentioned they have political immunity and refused to discuss the issue with the police. The raised eyebrows are shown in bold and in Figure 3 below:

---

[6] Original version: « Alors, Monsieur Fillon a dit tout à l'heure, a donné des chiffres complètement délirants, qui doivent venir encore de l'Institut Montaigne, je suppose. »

[7] In interaction, frowning is said to show hostility or withdrawing approval (for example, Kraut and Johnston 1979 or Arndt and Janney 1987).

Workers' immunity

we go

Figure 3: Raised eyebrows in example (3).

(3) Poutou: And **the worst** is that
on top of that,
FN,[8] who claim to be **against** the system,
don't even bother,
they protect themselves thanks to the laws crated by the system
thanks to parliamentary **immunity**
so they refuse to go to the **police** when summoned,
so, laid back
so **all this** shows
Le Pen: So, you agree with the police on this one?
Poutou: this shows
Yeah, when we are summoned by the police, you see, we don't
have **workers' immunity**
Sorry, we go[9]

---

[8] Front National, Le Pen's party.
[9] Original version : **Poutou** : Et le pire c'est qu'en plus, Le FN, qui se dit anti-système, ne s'emmerde pas du tout, se protège grâce aux lois du système, grâce à l'immunité parlementaire, et donc nous refuse d'aller aux convocations policières, donc pénard, donc tout ça, ça illustre... **Le Pen** : Sur ce coup-là vous êtes pour la police ? **Poutou** : ça illustre... ouais, quand nous on est convoqués par la police, nous, vous voyez, on n'a pas d'immunité ouvrière, désolé, on y va...

Several elements are uttered while the speaker raises his eyebrows: *the worst, against, immunity, police, all this* in the first part of his reply to the journalist and the elements *workers' immunity* and *sorry, we go* in his reply to Le Pen. The first part of Poutou's speech already builds on sarcasm, since he highlights these elements to target FN and Le Pen through the distinction between what they say (being against the system) and what they do (refusing to answer questions because the system protects them). When Le Pen intervenes to ask if he agrees with the police, he further emphasizes his sarcastic tone by comparing her situation (and her party's) to his own: there is no such thing as *workers' immunity*, they have to obey the rules like everyone else. He raises his eyebrows when uttering *workers' immunity* and *sorry, we go*, elements which build the sarcastic space already built on the common ground he just explained in the first part of his reply. In French, the word *ouvrière* (*workers'*) is built as an adjective to compare with *parlementaire* (parliamentary) in order to mark the distinction between the two situations. He also uses the present tense without any modal (such as 'must' or 'have to'), presenting this scenario as a fact rather than a hypothesis. Compare the video stills in Figure 3 showing him with a neutral face in the first and last frame and raising his eyebrows during his reply directed to Le Pen in the second and third video stills.

Other sarcastic utterances also come from Poutou, on the topic of salaries among politicians and corruption at these levels (since it happened so often prior to the 2017 campaign). These utterances represent reactions to the question asked by the journalist. Similar to above, raised eyebrows are marked in bold. When uttering *as much* (Fr. *moins*) he also tilts his head:

(4) Poutou: We think that we should limit the salaries of politicians
maximum the average salary of an employee
We have to stop the possibility of holding multiple offices
Journalist: And that will make them less corrupt?
If we reduce their salaries?
Poutou: for starters... **they won't chase after the position so much**
For a start we think
Eh it won't pay as much
And the other thing that could be advantageous is
That maybe they want to raise more easily the minimum wage and salaries
Because that **will affect them directly**[10]

---

10 Original version : **Poutou** : Nous on pense qu'il faut limiter le salaire des politiciens, maximum le salaire moyen d'un salarié, il faut arrêter le cumul des mandats... **Journaliste** : Et ça les

The first part of his speech is uttered as an answer to the issues of high salaries among politicians and is meant as a stand for his political views. When the journalist asks him if this is a solution for the corruption problem among politicians, his answer is uttered with raised eyebrows, marking the sarcastic targeting of the situation nowadays. The video stills are shown in Figure 4 below:

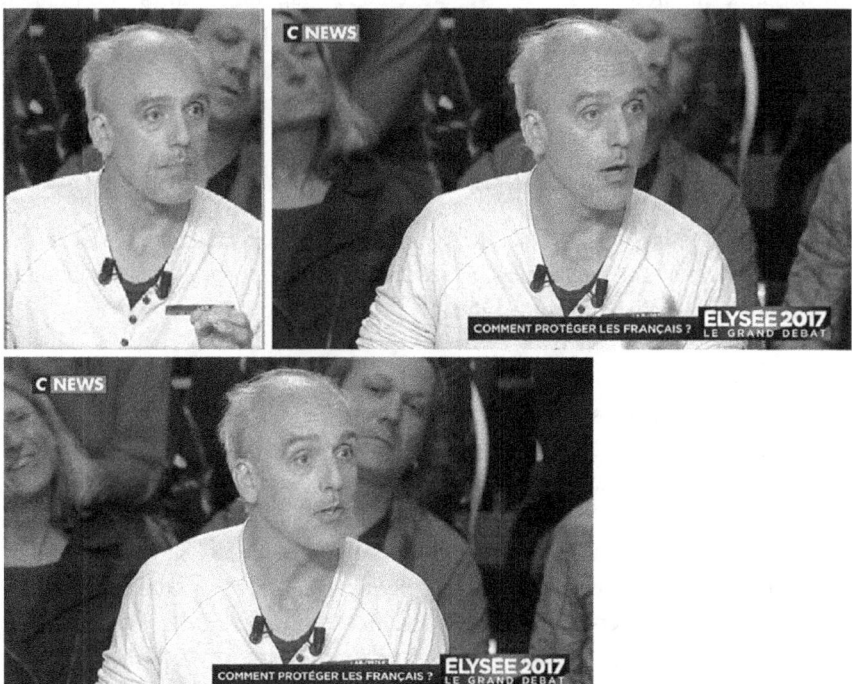

Figure 4: Raised eyebrows for example (4)

The two points raised by his answer are uttered with raised eyebrows (continuously raised, as can be seen from the camera filming – but the camera also switches focus and films the other participants during his reply) and can be perceived as sarcastic/humorous (the public laughs after his intervention, see also third image where the woman in the back is seen laughing). The target of

---

rendra moins corrompus, de baisser leurs salaires ? **Poutou** : Ben, au moins ils courront moins après le poste, déjà, on pense, hein, ça sera moins payé...et l'autre truc qui euuuh l'autre truc qui peut être avantageux c'est qu'ils ont peut-être envie d'augmenter plus facilement le SMIC et les salaires puisqu'ils sont directement concernés.

his sarcasm are all the politicians who try to make the most money out of the position, taking advantage of multiple offices and thus multiple salaries and forgetting what the average person makes since they are not affected by such issues. Building on common ground (what everyone knows and all the scandals surrounding the 2017 French elections), he shifts to the sarcastic space where these solutions would solve the problems related to corruption. The raised eyebrows mark the pretense space here, since he is imagining what would happen if politicians earned the same as any person and it is specifically the two points that are highlighted with use of raised eyebrows (politicians doing everything in their power to get one or several positions and politicians wanting to raise the minimum wage since that would affect them directly). He uses for both points the future tense and not the conditional to further emphasize his being sarcastic about the state of affairs.

Another example is (5) below, where Macron sarcastically answers the comment made by the journalist (the raised eyebrows appear in bold), whom he thinks is being sarcastic towards him:

(5) Journalist: What do you reproach to the elected representatives, you who have never been elected yourself?
    Macron: **Indeed,** I aspire to be elected, that did not get past you.
    It's the...the **reason why I am here tonight**.[11]

In this exchange, Macron answers to what he interprets to be a sarcastic question from the journalist, given his age and experience compared to the other candidates. Although he keeps a straight face when uttering *that did not get past you*, he raises his eyebrows when uttering *indeed* and *reason why I am here tonight*, accompanying his speech with hand gestures. The raised eyebrows are shown in the video stills in Figure 5 below.

The word *indeed* is uttered with his brows raised and, although he keeps a straight face and lowered his eyes when uttering *that did not get past you*, he further raises his eyebrows when continuing his sarcastic answer (*reason why I'm here tonight*). It might be argued that Macron did not want to further highlight he was being sarcastic since the verb échapper (*to get past you*) is obviously intended to answer the journalist for what he takes as sarcasm. He further explains the reason he is at a *great debate*, i.e., in order to get elected, which he had never

---

[11] **Journalist**: Qu'est-ce que vous reprochez aux élus, vous qui ne l'avez jamais été ? **Macron** : En effet, j'aspire à le devenir, ça ne vous a pas échappé. C'est le...la raison de ma présence ce soir.

Past you   *the reason*

Figure 5: Raised eyebrows in example (5).

been before, and this is also uttered with raised eyebrows to further emphasize the evidence of his presence there.

This is similar to what happens earlier in the debate when the same journalist makes a comment on the way he sees Europe (i.e., European Union). Macron raises his eyebrows to show that he does not agree with the use of the term *naïve* to qualify his perspective on the EU:

(6) Journalist: Emmanuel Macron, you, your Europe, is very very open, very generous, wouldn't it be a little naïve?
    Macron: **I thank** (nods, tilts head) **you** for this characteri**zation** (*lit. qualifying term*).[12]

His answer also contains a head nod with the head titled to his left. If a nod denotes agreement (Lee and Marsella 2010), it can be argued here that Macron is being sarcastic since he will not agree with the way the journalist is describing his view of the EU (note the use of *very very* in the journalist's question). In the most traditional sense of the concept of sarcasm, his nod here would be the opposite of what he means. The raised eyebrows happen at the beginning of his reply on the subject *Je* and direct object *vous* in French (*I thank you* here in the text), to show that he understood the journalist's criticism. The raised eyebrows are also used at the end of the French adjective *qualificatif*, which could be interpreted as "Thank you for the compliment". His eyebrow movement is shown in Figure 6 below:

---

12 Journalist : Emmanuel Macron, vous, votre Europe, est très très ouverte, très généreuse, est-ce qu'elle n'est pas un peu naïve ? **Macron** : Je vous remercie de cet..quali.. ce qualificatif.

I [thank] you   [characteri]zation

Figure 6: Raised eyebrows in example (6).

In this example, when he first raises his eyebrows (*I thank you*), it could also be a sign of surprise (Ekman 1979) since he perceives the criticism addressed by the journalist to his politics; this could indeed have surprised him on the spot. But the word *qualificatif* followed by the brow movement cannot be a sign of surprise anymore; rather, a sarcastic way of responding to criticism while not showing anger. It is a more polite way to rephrase her criticism under the term *qualificatif* instead of pointing it out as a criticism. The eyebrows would then emphasize the term in this exchange.

Another example is given below; here, one of the candidates turns the tables on what was intended as a criticism towards the whole group of elected representatives. Lassalle answers the journalist's question by shifting the attention from the intended target back to her. Both speakers use sarcasm in their speech, therefore the raised eyebrows are marked in bold for both of them:

(7) Journalist: [...] you, who defend the municipalities
                        You say it's the most important step
                        It's the alpha and the omega of the rebuilding of French **moral improvement and so**ciety
                        There are also **corrupt** elected representatives
     Lassalle: But, listen, there's **everything everywhere**, madam
                        Maybe there are **even** [corrupt] **journalists**
                        You never know[13]

---

13 Journalist : [...] vous, qui défendez les communes, vous dites c'est l'échelon le plus important, c'est l'alpha et l'oméga de la reconstruction de la moralisation et la société françaises, y a aussi des élus locaux corrompus... **Lassalle** : Mais, écoutez, y a de tout partout, Madame. Peut-être qu'y en a même chez les journalistes, on sait jamais.

Sarcasm here is possible by repeating the same structure in French [*il*] *y a* (*there is*) that the journalist introduced in her already sarcastic summary of Lassalle's policies: *y a aussi des élus locaux corrompus* (*there are also corrupt local representatives*). By repeating the structure and inserting *en* (*there is of*), Lassalle does not need to repeat the word *corruption* but just to shift the focus on journalists instead of elected representatives that were the target of the journalist's sarcasm. We focus here on both speakers' raised eyebrows, shown in Figure 7 below.

Moral improvement   *corrupt*

Everything   *journalists*

Figure 7: Raised eyebrows in example (7).

As shown below, both of them use raised eyebrows in their discourse which highlight parts of their sarcastic message. The journalist shows criticism towards Lassalle's idea that municipalities are the most important element for rebuilding French society on a moral level. She then points out that corruption also exists among these local elected representatives, which would mean that this political level is not as moral as Lassalle would want people to think.

Especially, the words *moral improvement* (*moralisation*) and *corrupt* (*corrompus*) are uttered with raised eyebrows by the journalist and they represent the core parts of the sarcastic message in this case, since she wants to highlight that there is corruption in these 'lower' layers as well. She also mentions that these layers are, according to Lassalle, *the alpha and the omega* of French improvement, which is an exaggeration of Lassalle's words, also intended as sarcastic.

In his answer, Lassalle first replies with *there is everything everywhere* (*de tout partout*) meaning that you will get all sorts of elements in every layer of any field, not just in politics. He then adds maybe *even journalists*, shifting the focus from the politicians (his domain) to journalists (her domain). Both these elements (*everything everywhere*) and (*even journalists*) are uttered with raised eyebrows (there is also a head tilt and a hand gesture when saying *everything*), emphasizing this shift of attention from one domain to another. This is also built on the common ground already presented by the journalist since she introduces his political perspectives, even if only to mock them.

6 Discussion: Sarcastic intentions marked by speakers' facial expressions

The examples presented here show that speakers signal/underline their sarcastic intentions to hearers. Gesture and facial expressions go *hand in hand* with their sarcastic meaning, emphasizing the intentions of the speakers to make their message understood by the hearers.

Raised eyebrows specifically have been connected to showing surprise (Ekman 1979, Wilkinson and Kitzinger 2006) or used in interrogatives (in Sign Language; see Zeshan 2004). Interestingly, regarding sign languages, raised eyebrows seem to be used also in conditional constructions (Pfau and Quer 2010).

In studies on humor and sarcasm, raised eyebrows have been linked to the core message, central to the shift between frames, layers, and interpretations. The speakers mark their shift to the pretense space with eyebrow movement, making in this way their intentions known to the hearers. In previous studies, however, this concerned staged interactions, whereas the examples presented here come from more spontaneous uses of sarcasm. Even if the candidates know some of the topics that will be discussed, they constantly answer each other and interact to what is previously said by their opponents. This highlights the use of these raised eyebrows in interaction, as a way of responding to or creating sarcasm. In examples (5), (6), and (7), raised eyebrows are used to respond to the sarcasm that was already present in their interlocutor's utterances and also turn the tables on the interlocutor (such as (7) above where Lassalle focuses on corrupt journalists instead of corrupt elected representatives). In examples (5) and (6), raised eyebrows are used to sarcastically acquiesce and respond to sarcastic remarks (such as *the reason why I'm here tonight* in (5) and *I thank you for this characterization* in (6)). In examples (2) and (3), raised eyebrows mark hints to elements that create the pretense space: *Institut Montaigne* in (2) and *workers' immunity* in (3). In example (4), they mark the whole scenario that takes place after Poutou's program would be implemented, making politicians' salaries as low as everyone else's.

In all these cases, they play a central role for understanding the intention of the speaker since they are meant to underline these salient elements in order for the shift of frames to take place for the audience. All the sarcastic implications are then 'triggered' with the use of facial expressions, not only through use of verbal components. Even though these represent some examples of uses of sarcasm in a particular setting, they show the role these expressions have especially since they are used at particular times by the speakers. The setting in the above examples is complex since it involves different journalists, politicians, and an audience (sitting behind the candidates) with cameras filming from different angles. This might have an impact on the use of these expressions as well (showing the intentions to an audience at home/in the studio or to the person involved in the exchange, whether it is a journalist or an opponent).

7 Conclusion

In this article, we explored facial expressions in sarcasm and how speakers make their intentions known to the audience/hearers. By exploring raised eyebrows specifically, we showed how they play a role in understanding the sarcastic turns since they mark important parts of the speakers' utterances that hold the sarcastic implications. We thus mainly focused on the pragmatic side of such *gestural triggers* (Tabacaru and Lemmens 2014) that would underline the sarcastic parts of the message, although earlier studies (such as Ekman 1979, among others) focused on their semantic role (as expressions of human emotions). Even though some of these examples can still fit the 'surprise' effect of facial expressions, the examples presented here mainly show them as triggering the pretense space from the part of the speaker with the use of sarcasm. As gestural triggers, facial expressions are used to mark the link between literal and figurative language, 'real' and pretense worlds. They make the link allowing hearers to switch to another frame, understanding, in the case of sarcasm, the criticism addressed by a speaker to an interlocutor.

However, a number of elements were involved in an approach such as this one and it is important to note the drawbacks that such a technique implies. Mainly, one has to consider the way such debates are filmed. Given there were several candidates with different political views and this was broadcast live, the camera does not always immediately react to the speaker (as sometimes the candidates react to something that is said by the opponent). This means that the facial expressions are difficult to explore if the camera does not zoom in on the speaker or does not film the speaker at all. Other times, the camera focuses on the person that is the target of the speaker's sarcasm, thus limiting the audience's view on the latter's facial expressions. Another case involves filming several faces from afar, thus limiting the noticeability of a facial expression. It is also noteworthy that some speakers either wear glasses or have a fringe that covers the forehead; in these situations, it is very difficult to discern if raised eyebrows are being used (especially when the camera films them from the side or from a distance). Finally, we followed here previous studies that dealt with facial expressions and sarcasm (Tabacaru & Lemmens 2014) and we focused on raised eyebrows specifically by taking into consideration the results of such studies. Other elements should not be overlooked when interpreting humorous/sarcastic corpora. When interacting, speakers do not only use one expression/gesture, but several (gaze, posture, manual gestures, even tone of voice, etc.) whose role should be explored in future studies to show they are used in this type of interactions. For example, Le Pen's shrug in example (3) adds to the meaning of *I suppose*, used here for sarcastic purposes. The head nods and tilts, gazes and other non-verbal elements in these exchanges also play a role in the way meaning is constructed and understood.

To sum up, we investigated here when and how speakers make their sarcastic intentions known through certain facial expressions. This may very well be a *grand débat* on its own, one that still needs (more spontaneous) data and exchanges across genres (political debates, stand-up comedy, movies, etc.) languages, and cultures. But, going back to even Gricean linguistics, speakers clearly cooperate and intersubjectively share a common ground. Understanding sarcasm means understanding all the complex ways in which people share that common ground.

References

Arndt, Horst & Richard W. Janney. 1987. *Intergrammar. Studies in anthropological linguistics*. Berlin: Walter de Gruyter.
Attardo, Salvatore. 2000. Irony as relevant inappropriateness. *Journal of Pragmatics* 32. 793–826.
Attardo, Salvatore. 2003. Introduction: The pragmatics of humor. *Journal of Pragmatics* 35(9). 1287–1294.
Attardo, Salvatore, Lucy Pickering, Fofo Lomotey & Shigehito Menjo. 2013. Multimodality in conversational humor. *Review of Cognitive Linguistics* 11(2). 402–416.
Birdwhistell, Ray. 1970. *Kinesics and context: Essays on Body Motion Communication*. University of Pennsylvania Press.

Brône, Geert. 2008. Hyper and misunderstanding in interactional humor. *Journal of Pragmatics* 40. 2027–2061.

Brône, Geert. 2017. Cognitive linguistics and humor research. In Salvatore Attardo (Ed.), *The Routledge handbook of language and humor*. 250–266. NY and London: Routledge.

Brône, Geert & Kurt Feyaerts. 2003. The cognitive linguistics of incongruity resolution: Marked reference-point structures in humor. University of Leuven, *Department of Linguistics preprint* no. 205.

Burgers, Christian F. & van Mulken, Margot J. P. (2017). Humor markers. In Salvatore Attardo (Ed.), *The Routledge handbook of language and humor*. 385–399. New York: Routledge.

Colston, Herbert. 1997. Salting a wound or sugaring a pill: The pragmatic functions of ironic criticism. *Discourse Processes* 23. 23–45.

Colston, Herbert. 2017. On the complexities of embodied irony: Considerations of eye-rolling and other multi-modal evidence. Paper presented at the *International Cognitive Linguistics Conference* (ICLC14), University of Tartu, 10–14 July 2017.

Colston, Herbert L. (this volume). Eye-rolling, irony and embodiment.

Clark, Herbert H. 1996. *Using language*. Cambridge: Cambridge University Press.

Clark, Herbert H. & Richard J. Gerrig. 1984. On the pretense theory of irony. *Journal of Experimental Psychology* 113. 121–126.

Coulson, Seana. 2005. Sarcasm and the space structuring model. In Seana Coulson & Barbara Lewandowska-Tomasczyk (Eds.), *The literal and the nonliteral in language and thought*. 129–144. Berlin: Lang.

Darwin, Charles. 1872. *The Expression of the Emotion in Man and Animals*. London: John Murray.

Darwin, Charles & Paul Ekman. 1998. *The Expression of the emotion in man and animal*, 3rd edition. New York: Oxford University Press.

Ekman, Paul. 1979. About brows – emotional and conversational signals. In Mario von Cranach, Klaus Foppa, Wolf Lepenies & Detlev Ploog (Eds.), *Human Ethology*. 169–248. Cambridge: Cambridge University Press.

Ekman, Paul, and Oster, H. 1979. Facial expressions of emotion. *Annual Review of Psychology* 30. 527–554.

Fägersten, Kristy Beers. 2016. *Watching TV with a Linguist*. NY: Syracuse University Press.

Fauconnier, Gilles. 1984. *Espaces Mentaux*. Paris: Les éditions de minuit.

Fauconnier, Gilles. 1994. *Mental spaces: Aspects of meaning construction in natural language*. Cambridge: Cambridge University Press.

Fauconnier, Gilles. 1997. *Mappings in thought and language*. Cambridge: Cambridge University Press.

Fauconnier, Gilles. 2004. Pragmatics and cognitive linguistics. In Laurence R. Horn & Gregory L. Ward (Eds.), *The Handbook of Pragmatics*. 657–674. Oxford: Blackwell Publishing.

Fauconnier, Gilles & Mark Turner. 1998. Conceptual integration networks. *Cognitive Science* 22 (2). 133–187.

Feyaerts, Kurt. 2013. Tackling the complexity of spontaneous humorous interaction. An integrated classroom-modeled corpus approach. In Leonor Ruiz-Gurillo & Maria Belén Alvarado Ortega (eds), *Irony and humor*. 243–268. Amsterdam & Philadelphia: John Benjamins Publishing.

Feyaerts, Kurt & Bert Oben. 2014. Tracing down schadenfreude in spontaneous interaction. Evidence from corpus linguistics. In Wilco Van Dijk & Jaap W. Ouwerkerk (Eds.),

'Schadenfreude': Understanding pleasure at the misfortune of others. 275–291. Cambridge University Press.

Gallagher, Shaun & Daniel D Hutto. 2008. Understanding others through primary interaction and narrative practice. In Jordan Zlatev, Timothy P. Racine, Chris Sinha & Esa Itkonen (Eds.), *The shared mind. Perspectives on intersubjectivity*. 17–38. Amsterdam/Philadelphia: John Benjamins.

Gibbs, Raymond W. 2000. Irony in talk among friends. *Metaphor and Symbol* 15 (1–2). 5–27.

Grice, Paul. 1975. Logic and conversation. In Peter Cole & Jerry L. Morgan (Ed.), *Syntax and semantics*, Vol. 3, Speech Acts. New York: Academic Press.

Hanks, Patrick. 2013. Creatively exploiting linguistic norms. In Tony Veale, Kurt Feyaerts, & Charles Forceville (Eds), *Creativity and the Agile Mind. A multidisciplinary study of a multifaceted phenomenon*. 119–138. Berlin: Walter de Gruyter.

Klein, Daniel B. & Aaron Orsborn. 2009. Concatenate coordination and mutual coordination. *Journal of Economic Behavior and Organization* 72. 176–187.

Kotthoff, Helga. 2006. Pragmatics of performance and the analysis of conversational humor. *Humor: The International Journal of Humor Research* 19(3). 271–304.

Krahmer, Emiel & Marc Swerts. 2007. The effects of visual beats on prosodic prominence: Acoustic analyses, auditory perception and visual perception. *Journal of Memory and Language* 57(3). 396–414.

Kraut, Robert E. & Robert E Johnston. 1979. Social and emotional messages of smiling; An ethological approach. *Journal of Personality and Social Psychology* 37(9). 1539–1553.

Kristiansen, Gitte & René Dirven. 2008. *Cognitive sociolinguistics: Language variation, cultural models, social systems*. Berlin: Walter de Gruyter.

Lapaire, Jean-Rémi. 2015. Living speech – or the bodily life of language. SKASE Journal of Theoretical Linguistics 12 (3). 528–541.

Lapaire Jean-Rémi & Hélène Duval. 2017. To the Lighthouse (1927): a choreographic re-elaboration. *Miranda* 15 (online).

Lee, Christopher J. & Albert N Katz. 1998. The differential role of ridicule in sarcasm and irony. *Metaphor and Symbol* 13(1). 1–15.

Lee, Jina & Stacy C Marsella. 2010. Predicting speaker head nods and the effects of affective information. *IEEE Transactions on Multimedia* 12(6). 552–562.

Mesing, Joslyn, Danielle Williams & Dawn Blasko. 2012. Sarcasm in relationships: hurtful or humorous? *International Journal of Psychology* 47. 724–724.

Norris, Sigrid. 2004. *Analyzing multimodal interaction: A methodological framework*. New York: Routledge.

Pfau, Roland & Quer Josep. 2010. Nonmanuals: their grammatical and prosodic roles. In Diane Brentari (Ed.), *Sign language*. 381–402. Cambridge: Cambridge University Press.

Priego-Valverde, Béatrice. 2009. Failed humor in conversation. In Neal R. Norrick & Delia Chiaro (Eds.), *Humor in interaction*. 166–183. Amsterdam/Philadelphia: John Benjamins Publishing Company.

Rockwell, Patricia. 2000. Lower, slower, louder: vocal cues to sarcasm. *Journal of Psycholinguistic Research* 29(5). 483–495.

Rockwell, Patricia. 2001. Facial expressions and sarcasm. *Perceptual and Motor Skills* 93, 47–50.

Schelling, Thomas C. 1960. *The Strategy of Conflict*. Cambridge: Harvard University Press.

Tabacaru, Sabina. 2018. When language bites: A corpus-based taxonomy of sarcastic utterances in American television series. *Pragmatics & Cognition* 24(2).186–211.
Tabacaru, Sabina. 2019. *A Multimodal Study of Sarcasm in Interactional Humor*. Vol. 40 of *Applications of Cognitive Linguistics*. Berlin: De Gruyter Mouton.
Tabacaru, Sabina & Maarten Lemmens. 2014. Raised eyebrows as gestural triggers in humor: The case of sarcasm and hyper-understanding. *European Journal of Humor Research* 2(2). 18–31.
Veale, Tony, Kurt Feyaerts & Geert Brône. 2006. The cognitive mechanisms of adversarial humor. *Humor: International Journal of Humor Research* 19(3). 305–338.
Weast, Traci Patricia. 2008. Questions in American Sign Language: A quantitative analysis of raised and lowered eyebrows. Doctoral dissertation.
Wilkinson, Sue & Celia Kitzinger. 2006. Surprise as an interactional achievement: reaction tokens in conversation. *Social Psychology Quarterly* 69 (2). 150–182.
Yus, Francisco. 2003. Humor and the search for relevance. *Journal of Pragmatics* 35. 1295–1331.
Zeshan, Ulrike. 2004. Interrogative constructions in signed languages: cross-linguistic perspectives. Language 80. 7–39.

Hannah Leykum
A pilot study on the diversity in irony production and irony perception

Abstract: Speakers differ in the way and extent to which they highlight irony acoustically and / or visually. Some speakers express irony quite subtly, others make use of specific irony markers. Moreover, the extent to which irony is marked differs depending on the utterances, situations, and common grounds between speaker and listener. In addition, listeners differ in their ability to detect irony.

Keywords: Irony production, irony perception, cochlear implant, acoustic analysis, Standard Austrian German

In the present pilot study, audio and video recordings of one speaker producing 33 short utterances once in an ironic manner and once in a literal manner are analysed. Moreover, a perception experiment is conducted to investigate the irony recognition of six normal-hearing and two cochlear-implant listeners. The acoustic and visual characteristics of the recordings combined with the recognition rate and response times of the two groups of listeners and with ratings of the items obtained from an online questionnaire help to understand the complex processes involved in verbal irony production and perception.

The analyses revealed that ironic utterances of the speaker mainly differed from literal realisations of the utterances in mean fundamental frequency (F0), duration and intensity of the utterances, and the minimum and maximum value of F0 within each utterance. Concerning the facial expression during the utterances, the analyses revealed less smiles and more movement of the eyebrows during ironic utterances. In most cases, several characteristics were used jointly to mark the irony. All normal-hearing listeners and one of the cochlear-implant listeners correctly recognised the ironically and literally intended utterances with a detection rate of above 80 %. Regression analyses revealed that the listeners most likely used word duration, word intensity, mean F0, SD of F0, and HNR cues for their judgements of acoustically presented stimuli. The occurrence of smiles, frown and eyebrow raising were used to classify the utterances when only the video was presented.

Hannah Leykum, Acoustics Research Institute, Austrian Academy of Sciences, Vienna, Austria

https://doi.org/10.1515/9783110652246-013

1 Introduction

Verbal irony has important communicative and social functions by either bonding or distancing speakers and listeners (Gibbs and Colston 2002). According to Grice (1989), irony is a conversational implicature by which the speaker violates the maxim of quality: "Do not say what you believe to be false" (p. 27). In irony, the speaker's statement conveys the opposite meaning of what is said. Although Grice's definition has been a matter of debate, it is agreed that in verbal irony, some inconsistency between the literal expression and the conveyed meaning is to be observed. Cutler (1974) describes irony as "saying what you mean without meaning what you say".

Several forms of irony are distinguished in theoretical treatises; Gibbs (2000), e.g., describes five types: jocularity, sarcasm, hyperbole, rhetorical questions, and understatements. Dews and Winner (1999: 1580) base their classification on the communicative functions of irony and differentiate between "ironic criticism" and "ironic praise", the latter being less commonly used. In ironic criticism, a positive expression conveys a negative meaning, whereas in ironic praise, a negative expression is meant to convey a positive meaning. Anolli, Ciceri, and Infantino (2002) refer to these two types of irony as "blame by praise" and "praise by blame". Although verbal irony, especially ironic criticism, entails the risk of possible negative effects on social relationships, i.e., introducing distance between speaker and listener, most researchers agree that the use of verbal irony implies a muting or minimising function of the negative meaning expressed by the speaker (Dews, Kaplan, and Winner 1995; Pexman and Olineck 2002) or even a face-saving function (Jorgensen 1996). In the evaluation of verbal irony, a gradual aspect is introduced by Colston (2002), who showed that the degree of perceived negativity of a situation is biased by prior negative or positive comments on a specific scenario. This prior information leads to either assimilation or contrast effects, which influence the degree of the perceived negativity of the situation, i.e., the degree of condemnation of the speaker. To summarise, speakers with normal hearing make extensive use of various, often subtle forms of verbal irony to convey their opinions on persons or situations. In order to take an active part in daily social life, it is important to be able to understand ironic messages.

Whether and how ironic expressions are realised or not depends on the relationship between speaker and listener(s). Both for production and understanding of verbal irony, shared common grounds, attitudes and experiences form a prerequisite (Averbeck and Hample 2008).

Verbal irony is prominent in interpersonal communication. It occupies approximately 8% of the interaction among friends (in a study on Californian students (Gibbs 2000)) and occurs frequently in popular television shows (e.g. investigated for North American TV shows (Dews and Winner 1999)), in political television debates (e.g. in France: Tabacaru (this volume); or in Finland: Nuolijärvi and Tiittula (2011)), and in social media (e.g. Khokhlova, Patti, and Rosso 2016).

In order to avoid misunderstandings, especially when an unambiguous context is missing, most speakers underline ironic utterances by using paraverbal cues (e.g. slower speaking rate, lower fundamental frequency (F0)). Normal-hearing listeners use these cues to recognise irony. Especially, F0 and intensity values help listeners to distinguish between ironic and literal utterances (Schmiedel 2017). However, when the auditory input is reduced, the ability to detect irony might be reduced. This is the case for listeners with cochlear implants (CIs), widely used auditory prostheses that restore auditory perception in the deaf or severely hard-of-hearing. Due to technical limitations, cochlear-implant listeners have great difficulties in F0 perception (Carlyon and Deeks 2015). Therefore, the use of F0 information for the detection of irony is probably impaired, raising the question whether cochlear-implant listeners are nevertheless able to detect irony in short context-free utterances.

The aim of the study is two-fold: On the one hand, the acoustic cues present in verbal irony of one speaker of Standard Austrian German will be analysed. On the other hand, the perception of irony by normal-hearing and cochlear-implant listeners will be investigated. Since irony is often additionally conveyed by characteristic facial expressions (see e.g. Attardo et al. 2003) and since cochlear-implant listeners show audio-visual synergy effects (e.g., Winn et al. 2013; Alghamdi et al. 2015), video recordings are included to analyse their influence on the irony perception of both hearing groups.

1.1 Irony processing

Some theories assume a two-stage processing of verbal irony (e.g. Grice 1989; Dews and Winner 1999; Schwoebel et al. 2000; Giora 2002): The first step involves a literal processing of the meaning. The literal interpretation is then rejected on pragmatic grounds and the expression is subsequently reinterpreted. On the other hand, Gibbs (1994, 2002) assumes that verbal irony is accessed directly (Direct Access Model). He assumes that no additional cognitive processes are necessary in order to understand irony. Yet, it has to be considered that context plays a decisive role in the comprehension of irony, thus diminishing the role of language processing. However, a recent study (Deliens et al. 2018) revealed that the costlier processing of contextual cues is stopped as soon as non-contextual cues (visual and paraverbal) allow an ironic or literal interpretation of an utterance, even though the non-contextual cues lead to less accurate decisions (Deliens et al. 2018).

1.2 Irony production

In a study of Hancock (2004) 76.4 % of ironic utterances were marked with explicit cues in face-to-face communication between strangers. These cues were either verbal (e.g. use of amplifiers), paraverbal (prosody) or non-verbal (laughter, facial expression, gestures). In the present study only paraverbal (acoustic cues) and nonverbal (facial expression) cues of irony are investigated.

1.3 Acoustic cues

Verbal irony is highly context-dependent, because generally, a literal interpretation of ironic utterances is also possible. In addition, speakers and listeners must share a common ground; If shared expectations, attitudes, or experiences are missing, ironic expressions are usually avoided (Kreuz and Caucci 2009). Irony cues can be verbal, nonverbal, or paraverbal. If both verbal and nonverbal cues are missing in interaction (e.g., ambiguous utterances on the telephone), listeners have to rely on paraverbal cues in order to understand irony. The risk of misunderstanding of ironic expressions is reduced by applying disambiguating (e.g. paraverbal) cues. Overall fundamental frequency (F0), F0-contour, intensity, and duration are generally the most prominent paraverbal cues to indicate verbal irony. Acoustic analyses performed on German utterances of sarcasm/ironic criticism showed a lower average F0, smaller F0 variation, and longer segment durations in verbal irony (Schmiedel 2017; Nauke and Braun 2011; Scharrer and Christmann 2011). Scharrer and Christmann (2011) also found hyperarticulation of vowels. In addition, Schmiedel (2017) revealed a lower intensity and a higher Harmonics-to-Noise Ratio (HNR) for sarcastic utterances. Concerning voice quality, Niebuhr (2014) found a more variable, mainly breathier or tenser, voice quality for sarcastic utterances.

The use of specific F0-contours to indicate verbal irony appears to be language specific. Scharrer and Christmann (2011) found no signalling function of F0-contours in German, whereas in English (Cheang and Pell 2008; Chen and Boves 2018) or in French (Laval and Bert-Erboul 2005), F0-contours are used for expressing verbal irony. Equally, it seems to be language dependent whether the mean F0 is higher or lower in ironic utterances compared to literal utterances.

In Cantonese (Cheang and Pell 2009), in French (Laval and Bert-Erboul 2005; Lœvenbruck et al. 2013), and in Italian (Anolli, Ciceri, and Infantino 2000), the mean F0 was found to be higher in ironic utterances. Whereas in English (Rockwell 2000; Cheang and Pell 2009) and in German (Schmiedel 2017; Scharrer and Christmann 2011), the mean F0 is lower in ironic utterances.

1.4 Visual cues

In face-to-face communication visual cues (e.g. lip reading) are used to enhance speech perception, even by persons with normal hearing. The information of both modalities is combined to enable best possible speech understanding (Rosenblum 2008). Not only the lip shapes, but also the overall facial expression provides information which is used for speech understanding. This is especially important when listeners are confronted with irony. Irony is usually not only marked acoustically, but in addition a specific facial expression (= nonverbal cues) frequently emphasises the ironic intention of the speaker (Attardo et al. 2003; González-Fuente, Escandell-Vidal, and Prieto 2015; Rockwell 2001; Williams, Burns, and Harmon 2009). Irony is visually marked either by a "blank face" (Attardo et al. 2003), or by a combination of gaze deviation, mouth stretching and head tilt during or just after the utterance (González-Fuente, Escandell-Vidal, and Prieto 2015), or by a larger movement in the mouth region (Rockwell 2001). Caucci and Kreuz (2012) found significantly more slow nods, looks to the conversation partner, smiles, lip tightening and laughing in sarcastic utterances compared to literal utterances. The use of eyebrow raising (Tabacaru, this volume) and eye-rolling (Colston, this volume) in irony marking is under investigation in other chapters of this volume.

1.5 Irony perception

1.5.1 Irony perception by normal-hearing listeners

In total, the recognition rate of irony in auditory presented context-free stimuli is remarkably high. Ironic criticism is correctly identified by the listeners with a rate of approximately 70 % (Schmiedel (2017): 72.5 %; Nauke and Braun (2011): 80.5 %; Lœvenbruck et al. (2013): 79 %; Bryant and Fox Tree (2002): 67 %).

Regarding the perception of context-free ironic utterances, Schmiedel (2017) showed that normal-hearing listeners mainly rely on fundamental frequency and intensity values to distinguish ironic utterances from literal utterances. With synthetically manipulated stimuli, it was shown that for irony recognition in French the manipulation of duration, intonation and pitch range resulted in high recognition rates. The manipulation of only duration or only intonation resulted also in an enhance recognition rate compared to non-manipulated or only pitch-manipulated stimuli (González-Fuente, Prieto, and Noveck 2016). Equally, Bryant and Fox Tree (2002) showed the importance of acoustic information for the recognition of verbal irony. Voyer and Techentin (2010) revealed that listeners perceive subjective auditory differences between ironic, neutral and sincere utterances which they use for the recognition of irony. Especially, a perceived lower pitch and slower tempo are cues for ironic utterances.

In addition to the acoustic parameters, quite some studies show the importance of nonverbal cues in the recognition of irony (e.g., Rockwell 2001; Attardo et al. 2003). Normal-hearing listeners identify verbal irony significantly better when provided with visual cues (especially cues produced directly after the utterance) than without visual information (González-Fuente, Escandell-Vidal, and Prieto 2015).

1.5.2 Irony perception by cochlear-implant listeners

It is well known that cochlear-implant listeners have great difficulty in pitch perception (see e.g., Carlyon and Deeks 2015; Moore and Carlyon 2005; Gfeller et al. 2007), thus they have largely reduced access to F0 cues which are pivotal for several tasks like e.g. auditory irony perception. On the other hand, cochlear-implant listener have, despite their largely reduced dynamic range, reasonable intensity resolution (e.g., Kreft, Donaldson, and Nelson 2004; Loizou et al. 2000) which may allow them to use energy level cues for irony perception. In addition, cochlear-implant listeners show good temporal resolution (e.g., Zeng et al. 2008) which likely provides them access to duration cues for detecting irony.

Listeners with cochlear implants are able to recognise emotions above chance level, but less accurate compared to normal-hearing listeners (e.g., Ambert-Dahan 2014; Chatterjee et al. 2015; Luo, Fu, and Galvin 2007). Due to the similarities in the acoustic characteristics of emotional speech and the acoustic cues used to emphasis verbal irony (see e.g. Braun and Heilmann (2012) and Schmiedel (2017)), it is likely that cochlear-implant listeners are able to perform above chance level in auditory irony detection tasks.

Concerning the use of visual cues, it has been shown that in general speech understanding, cochlear-implant listeners show audio-visual synergy effects, resulting in large benefits from the combined presentation of auditory and visual information (e.g., Winn et al. 2013; Alghamdi et al. 2015).

2 Experiment 1: Bias of the utterances

2.1 Methods

In order to check several (literal positive) utterances for a bias towards the manner in which the items are used predominantly in everyday communication, an online questionnaire was conducted with SoSci Survey (Leiner 2014). A set of 40 short utterances of up to two words was chosen for the questionnaire (see Table 1).

Table 1: Utterances.

Ausgezeichnet! 'excellent'	*Cool!* 'cool'	*Danke!* 'thanks'	*Danke schön!* 'thank you'	*Ganz toll!* 'great'	*Gemütlich!* 'comfortable'
Genial! 'genius'	*Gerne!* 'with pleasure'	*Glückwunsch!* 'congratulations'	*Großartig!* 'magnificent'	*Fabelhaft!* 'marvellous'	*Fantastisch!* 'fantastic'
Herrlich! ≈ 'lovely'	*Interessant!* 'interesting'	*Ja fein!* ≈ 'great'	*Ja, gerne!* 'with pleasure'	*Köstlich!* 'delicious'	*Na klar!* 'of course'
Na schön! 'well'	*Na toll!* 'great'	*Perfekt* 'perfect'	*Prima!* 'fine'	*Riecht gut!* 'smells good'	*Sauber!* 'neat'
Schmeckt gut! 'tastes good'	*Sehr gut!* 'very good'	*Sehr nett!* 'very nice'	*Sehr schnell* 'very fast'	*Sehr schön!* 'very beautiful'	*Sehr toll!* 'very good'
So früh? 'so early?'	*Spannend!* 'exciting'	*Spitze!* 'great'	*Super!* 'super'	*Unglaublich!* 'incredible'	*Wahnsinn!* ≈ 'incredible'
Wie schnell! 'so fast'	*Wie schön!* 'so beautiful'	*Wow stark!* 'wow awesome'	*Wunderbar!* 'wonderful'		

The questionnaire was disseminated via the Viennese neighbourhood social media platform FragNebenan (www.fragnebenan.at). 83 German speaking participants (67 female, 16 male; age range: 23–76 years (mean 50.36; SD = 14.85 years)) completed the questionnaire. The participants were asked to judge how ironic given written utterances are. They had to indicate on a 9-point scale how they judge an utterance to be used. The scale went from 1 (only used with an ironic meaning) to 9 (only used in a literal sense). The participants were instructed to choose the value 5 whenever it only depends on the situation or context whether an utterance is used ironically or literally. In addition, the participants were asked for the frequency with which they use the utterances (equally to be indicated on a

9-point scale with the additional possibility to indicate that the item is never used by the participant).

2.2 Statistical analyses

To analyse the responses of the questionnaire, mainly descriptive statistics are used. In addition, one-sample t-tests are used to verify whether the mean rating of the manner of use differs significantly from a purely context dependent use (rating = 5). In order to analyse the data concerning a possible relationship between the two ratings, a Pearson's product moment correlation is calculated.

2.3 Results

The analyses concerning a possible bias of the items revealed that the minority of the items is predominantly used in an ironic manner. Only five of the items had a mean value of less than 5. The value 5 means that an ironic or literal interpretation of the item exclusively depends on the situation. A one sample t-test revealed that two of them differed significantly from 5 (*Na toll!* 'great' mean = 3.12; $t(82)=-9.132$; $p<0.001$; *Na schön!* 'well' mean = 4.36; $t(80)=-2.744$; $p=0.007$). In the other direction, most values were larger than 5, indicating a predominately use in the literal sense. The following items did not differ significantly from 5: *Ganz toll!* 'great' ($t(79)=-0.486$, $p=0.628$), *Sauber!* 'neat' ($t(75)=0.147$, $p=0.884$), *Sehr toll!* 'very good' ($t(80)=0.663$, $p=0.509$), *So früh!* 'so early?' ($t(79)=-0.506$, $p=0.615$) and *Wie schnell!* 'so fast' ($t(78)=-0.409$, $p=0.684$). The mean ratings are visualised in Figure 1.

Moreover, the participants were asked to rate the frequency of use of the items to determine the familiarity of the utterances to Austrian participants. The results concerning the rating of the frequency of use are shown in Figure 2. The thus obtained mean values are used as additional variables in the following analyses to determine an influence of the familiarity (or frequency of use) on the production and/or perception of the utterances (experiment 2 and experiment 3). Equally, the mean values concerning a bias toward one manner of use of the items will be included in the statistical analyses of the following two experiments.

A Pearson's product moment correlation test revealed a weak positive correlation between the manner of use and the frequency of use ($t(39)=2.218$, $p=0.032$, $r=0.335$) indicating that utterances which are used predominantly in an ironic manner are less frequently used (see Figure 3). However, the correlation seems to be a side-effect of the stimuli selection.

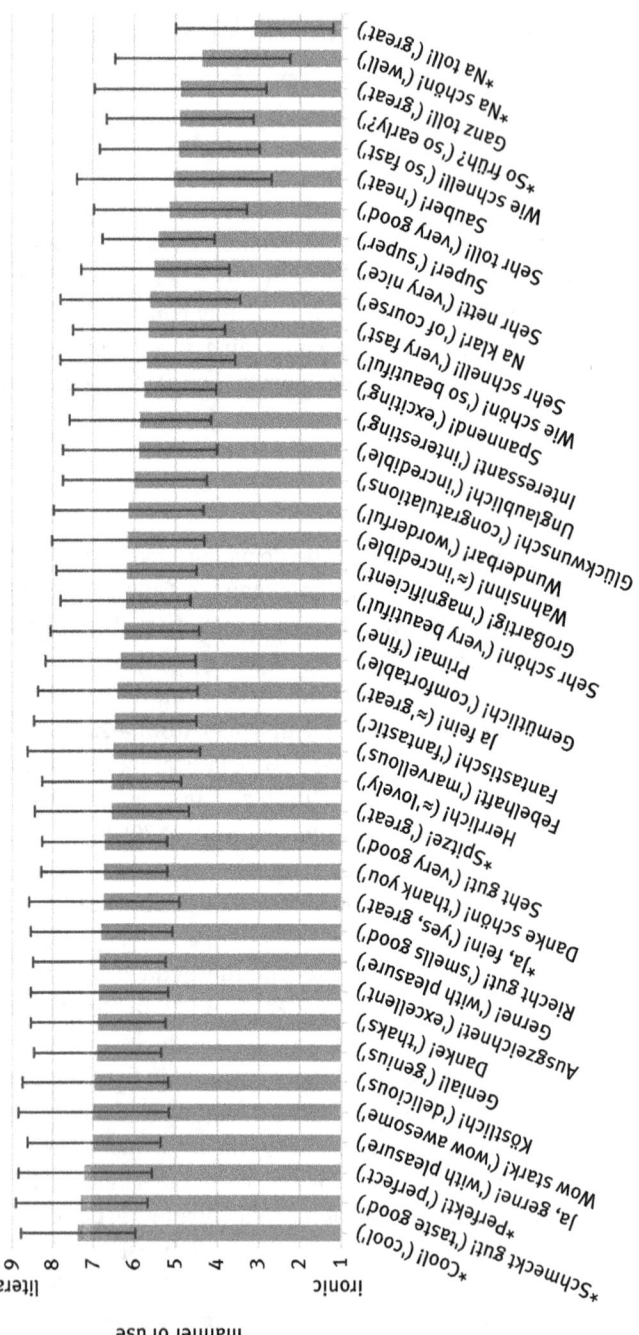

Figure 1: Results of the online pretest – manner of use (utterances not included in the production and perception part of the study are marked with an asterisk).

A pilot study on the diversity in irony production and irony perception — 287

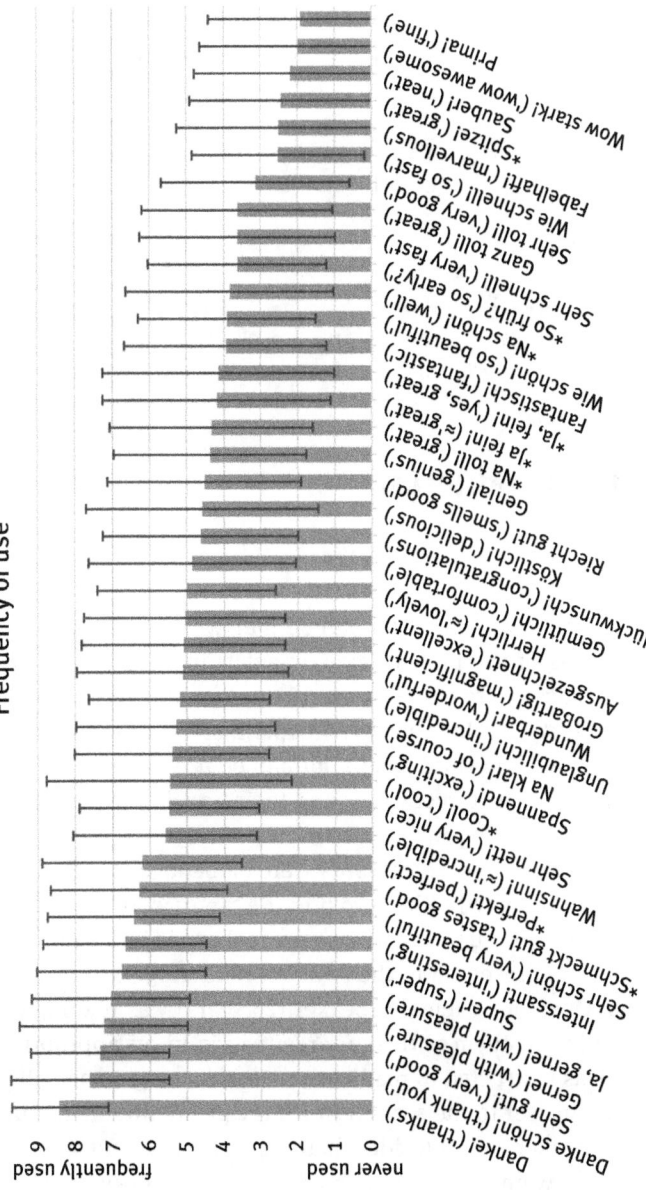

Figure 2: Results of the online pretest – frequency of use (utterances not included in the production and perception part of the study are marked with an asterisk).

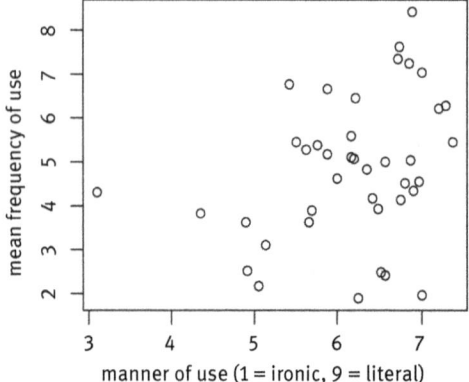

Figure 3: Correlation between frequency of use and manner of use.

3 Experiment 2: Production

3.1 Methods

One young female speaker of Standard Austrian German was asked to produce a subset of the utterances of the pretest (experiment 1) in an ironic or in a literal manner. All utterances were either two word utterances or multisyllabic words, since for the cochlear-implant listeners (experiment 3) it is more difficult to understand monosyllabic words (e.g., Dorman et al. 1989; Hey, Brademann, and Ambrosch 2016). The target words and their translations are listed in Table 2.

For the recording section, the target words were embedded in short scenarios (see the example (1) below) either evoking the target word in a literal manner or in an ironic manner. All target words were realised in both manners. In total, 66 scenarios were presented to the speaker, rendering 33 literal and 33 ironic expressions. One young female speaker (26 years) was reading the scenarios and responding to them with the target words in an appropriate manner. The speaker was instructed to read each scenario, imagine herself to be in the situation and answer to the scenario with the given utterance. After each target word, the speaker could decide whether she is confident with the realisation or whether she wants to redo it. In most cases, the speaker was confident with the first realisation. Seven utterances were realised several times by the speaker. From these utterances only the last realisation was analysed in the following sections. All utterances were audio and video recorded. The recordings were conducted in a sound-attenuating booth (Industrial Acoustics type IAC-1202A).

(1) Examples for scenarios eliciting *Na klar.* 'Of course.' in an ironic and a literal manner:

ironic	literal
Ein hoch verschuldeter Bekannter fragt:	*Ein sehr zuverlässiger Kollege fragt:*
-„Kannst du mir eben 250 € borgen, ich möchte dieses neue PC-Spiel kaufen."	*-„Kannst du mir kurz deinen Stift borgen, ich muss dieses Formular noch unterschreiben."*
-„Na klar."	*-„Na klar."*
A friend who is deep in debt asks you: "Can you just lend me 250 €, I want to buy this new computer game." "Of course."	A trustworthy colleague asks you: "Can you lend me your pen for a second, I just have to sign this form." "Of course."

Table 2: Target utterances.

Ausgezeichnet! 'excellent'	*Danke!* 'thanks'	*Danke schön!* 'thank you'	*Ganz toll!* 'great'	*Gemütlich!* 'comfortable'	*Genial!* 'genius'
Gerne! 'with pleasure'	*Glückwunsch!* 'congratulations'	*Großartig!* 'magnificent'	*Fabelhaft!* 'marvellous'	*Fantastisch!* 'fantastic'	*Herrlich!* ≈ 'lovely'
Interessant! 'interesting'	*Ja fein!* ≈ 'great'	*Ja, gerne!* 'with pleasure'	*Köstlich!* 'delicious'	*Na klar!* 'of course'	*Prima!* 'fine'
Riecht gut! 'smells good'	*Sauber!* 'neat'	*Sehr gut!* 'very good'	*Sehr nett!* 'very nice'	*Sehr schnell!* 'very fast'	*Sehr schön!* 'very beautiful'
Sehr toll! 'very good'	*Spannend!* 'exciting'	*Super!* 'super'	*Unglaublich!* 'incredible'	*Wahnsinn!* ≈ 'incredible'	*Wie schnell!* 'so fast'
Wie schön! 'so beautiful'	*Wow stark!* 'wow awesome'	*Wunderbar!* 'wonderful'			

The acoustic analyses were performed with the audio analysis software STx (Noll et al. 2007). The recordings were manually segmented and transcribed on an utterance level. Fine phonetic analysis includes the extraction of the following acoustic parameters: average fundamental frequency ($F0_{mean}$); standard deviation of F0 ($F0_{SD}$); minimal F0 value within each utterance ($F0_{min}$); maximal F0 value within each utterance ($F0_{max}$); F0 range (calculated by subtracting $F0_{min}$ from $F0_{max}$); the relative position of $F0_{max}$ within each utterance (in %); the utterance duration; and the mean utterance intensity. The stressed vowel of the target words was segmented manually to measure the Harmonic-to-Noise-Ratio (HNR) (see Teixeira, Oliveira, and Lopes 2013) as a parameter of voice quality. To obtain a high comparability, the parameters FO_{SD} and F0 range were converted to semitones (FO_{SD_ST}; FO_{range_ST}).

The facial expression was analysed manually by checking the video recording of the utterances for the presence (labelled as 1) or absence (labelled as 0) of the following cues: eyebrow raising, frown, and smiling.

3.2 Hypotheses

Concerning the production of ironic utterances by Standard Austrian German speakers, it is hypothesized that similar to speakers of German German (see Schmiedel 2017), speakers of Standard Austrian German will use F0 (mean F0 and SD of F0), intensity, durational cues, and voice quality to differentiate sarcastic irony from literal utterances. Ironic utterances are expected to be specified by (compared to literal utterances) a lower FO_{mean}, a smaller FO_{SD_ST}, a smaller FO_{range_ST}, a lower mean intensity, a longer duration, and a higher HNR.

3.3 Statistical analyses

The statistical analyses were conducted with R Studio (R Core Team 2015) by mainly, when applicable, fitting mixed-effects models and mixed effects logistic regression analyses (by using the lmer and glmer functions of the lme4 package) (Bates et al. 2015). Mixed-effects models have the advantage that random effects can be included in the analyses. The models were fitted using a forward approach: Effects were added one by one. Based on the p-value, it was decided to keep the variable or interaction in the model or to exclude it (threshold: $p=0.1$). Where necessary, Tukey post-hoc tests with p-value adjustment were carried out. For each dependant variable, a mixed effects model was fit with "utterance" as random factor.

3.4 Results

3.4.1 Acoustic analyses

A significant influence of the manner of realisation (ironic or literal) emerged for the word duration ($t(32)=7.14$, $p<0.001$), revealing longer durations of ironically produced utterances. Concerning the F0 a significant effect showed that the FO_{mean} is lower in ironic utterances ($t(62)=4.778$, $p<0.001$), but the FO_{SD_ST} did not differ with respect to the manner of realisation (t(62) = 1.196, p=0.236). Both, the smallest as well as the highest F0 value within an utterance were lower in the ironic realisations of the target words (F0$_{min}$: t(62)=2.607, p=0.011; F0$_{max}$: t(62)=4.072, p<0.001). The range between F0$_{min}$ and F0$_{max}$ within an utterance (F0$_{range\_ST}$) was equal for both types of realisation (t(62)=−0.136, p=0.893). In addition, the relative position of F0$_{max}$ within each utterance was calculated. The statistical analyses revealed that no significant differences between the two types of realisations emerged concerning the position of F0$_{max}$ (t(32)=−0.188, p=0.852). Concerning the intensity of the utterances, the analyses showed a significant effect for the mean word intensity with lower intensity values for ironic utterances compared to literal utterances (t(32)=6.265, p<0.001).

With respect to voice quality differences, the Harmonics-to-Noise Ratio (HNR) was measured. When comparing literal and ironic utterances, the HNR of ironic utterances was significantly higher (t(32)= −2.757, p=0.010) indicating more noise in literal utterances.

The mean values, the corresponding standard deviations (SD), and the results of the statistical analyses are summarised in Table 3.

Table 3: Results of the acoustic analyses (ST=semitones).

Parameter	ironic mean	ironic SD	literal mean	literal SD	significance
Word duration (in sec)	812.80	197.28	651.52	150.12	t(32)=7.14, p<0.001 ***
F0$_{mean}$ (in Hz)	188.46	27.05	224.84	34.62	t(62)=4.778, p<0.001 ***
F0$_{SD\_ST}$ (in ST)	4.27	1.83	4.81	1.75	t(62)=1.196, p=0.236 n.s.
F0$_{min}$ (in Hz)	102.72	42.10	131.64	46.54	t(62)=2.607, p=0.011 *
F0$_{max}$ (in Hz)	272.33	75.74	345.06	67.28	t(62)=4.072, p<0.001 ***
F0$_{range\_ST}$ (in ST)	23.27	5.76	23.08	4.86	t(62)=−0.136, p=0.893 n.s.
Relative position F0$_{max}$ (in %)	36.17	30.03	35.07	17.46	t(32)=−0.188, p=0.852 n.s.
Word intensity (in dB)	−36.54	2.80	−32.96	2.75	t(32)=6.265, p<0.001 ***
HNR (in dB)	12.00	4.99	9.55	4.07	t(32)= −2.757, p=0.010 **

3.4.2 Facial expression

The fitted generalised linear mixed-effects model showed that ironic utterances of the investigated speaker are characterised by less smiles (z=2.430, p=0.015) and more occurrences of eyebrow raisings ($z=-0.433$, $p=0.015$). For the presence of frowns a tendency for an effect ($z=-1.857$, $p=0.0632$) suggest more frowns while realising ironic utterances.

4 Experiment 3: Perception

4.1 Methods

In the perception experiment six normal-hearing (three male, three female) and two cochlear-implant listeners (one male, one female) participated. All participants were aged between 25 and 50 years (two normal-hearing listeners were 25–30 years old; four normal-hearing and both cochlear-implant listeners were between 40–50 years old). Prior to the perception experiment, the participants were asked for some listener-specific data (e.g. age, gender; for cochlear-implant listeners: age at hearing loss, age at implantation, time since implantation, use of telephone). Afterwards, all participants were familiarised with the subsequent perception task by hearing and seeing examples which were similar in design but not part of the perception experiment.

For the perception experiment, the stimuli were presented using the software PsychoPy (Peirce 2007). In order to study the contribution of auditory and visual (face expression) cues, the stimuli were presented in three conditions: auditory-only, visual-only, and auditory + visual. The stimuli were presented in random order in four blocks: A block consists of 20 utterances (once only 6 utterances) which were presented auditory, followed by 20 (once only 6) audio+video utterances, followed by 20 (once only 6) visual-only presentations of utterances. Afterwards, the next block followed. Between the blocks, the participants had the possibility to have a brief pause.

The auditory stimuli were played to the listeners via loudspeakers. The visual cues were presented on a computer screen. During the presentation of the auditory stimuli a loudspeaker symbol was shown on the screen. The listeners were instructed to categorise literal and ironical utterances in a two-alternative forced-choice test by pressing the appropriate button on a keyboard. Each listener did the perception test individually in a sound-attenuating booth to avoid disturbance from background noise. Each stimuli was presented to the listeners only once without an option to repeat it.

4.2 Hypotheses

It is expected that the listener groups will differ in their proficiency of detecting irony in the only auditory presented stimuli. Normal-hearing listeners will perform better than cochlear-implant listeners. Hereby, normal-hearing listeners will use F0 and intensity information for their judgments, whereas cochlear-implant listeners will mainly rely on intensity and durational aspects of the utterances.

Concerning the presentation modality, it is hypothesised that without visual cues cochlear-implant listeners perform worse than normal-hearing listeners, but visual cues help cochlear-implant listeners to better exploit auditory cues.

4.3 Statistical analyses

To analyse the influence of the acoustic and visual characteristics of the utterances on the correctness of the answers, logistic regression analyses were carried out using the glmer (generalised linear mixed-effects models) function in R (Bates et al. 2015). The variables "utterance" and "listener" were included in the models as random factors.

All models were fitted once including the cochlear-implant listeners once excluding them to avoid confounding influences of cochlear-implant-listener-specific hearing strategies and deficits. However, no relevant differences occurred when excluding the cochlear-implant listeners. Therefore, the perception data of the cochlear-implant listeners is included in all fitted models.

4.4 Results

In total, 82.29 % of the utterances were correctly identified by the participants. All listeners were better in recognizing literal utterances (86.26 %) compared to ironic utterances (74.58 %) ($p<0.001$). Concerning the presentation modality, the combined presentation of video+audio reached the highest recognition rates (87.02 %), followed by the solely auditory presented utterances (81.25 %). The lowest identification rate occurred for the video-only condition (78.84 %).

When having a closer look on the responses of the individual listeners (see Figure 4), it can be seen that for nearly all listeners the recognition rate is higher in both, the auditory only and the auditory+visual condition compared to the presentation of only the visual stimuli. However, one cochlear-implant listener (AJ) showed the best recognition rate in the video-only condition and was at

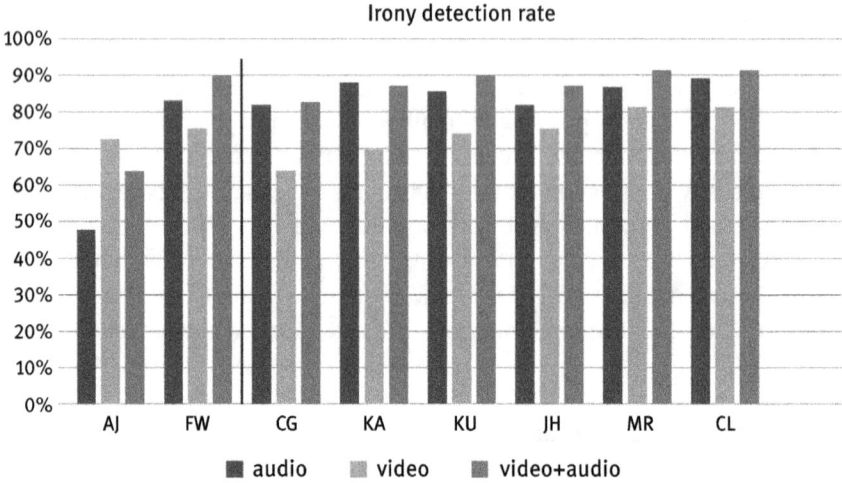

Figure 4: Irony detection rate by cochlear-implant listeners (AJ and FW) and normal-hearing-listeners (female listeners: AJ, JH, MR, CL; male listeners: FW, CG, KA, KU).

chance level for the audio-only presentation of the stimuli. The crucial difference between the two cochlear-implant listeners is that the listener AJ was severely hard of hearing from birth on, whereas listener FW was postlingually deafened. With respect to the other cochlear-implant-specific data (age at implantation, time since implantation, type of cochlear implant) both cochlear-implant listeners were similar.

4.4.1 Correctness of the responses

With respect to the correctness of the answers, logistic regression analyses were carried out. In the first fitted model the correctness of the responses of all listeners was investigated. Since the acoustic characteristics are identical for the audio-only and the audio+video presentation of the stimuli, the influence of the acoustic cues is investigated for the audio-only condition. When only the audio signal is played to the listeners, for the correctness of their judgement on ironically produced utterances significant effects of FO_{min} ($z=-2.213$, $p=0.027$), FO_{max} ($z=2.971$, $p=0.003$), FO_{range_ST} ($z=-2.651$, $p=0.008$), and the relative position of FO_{max} ($z=-2.519$, $p=0.012$) were found. More correct answers were given for ironic utterances with a lower FO_{min}, a higher FO_{max}, a lower FO_{range_ST} and an earlier position of FO_{max}. With respect to the correct identification of utterances produced in a literal manner, the analyses revealed significant effects of

HNR ($z=-2.770$, $p=0.006$) and of a bias toward a prevailing use of the utterances ($z=2.271$, $p=0.023$). For correctly identified literal utterances, the HNR was lower. Literal utterances with a lower scale in the pretest (= bias towards ironic use) were worse identified as being literal.

With respect to the joint presentation of the audio and video data, the statistical analyses revealed for the ironic stimuli significant effects for frequency of use ($z=-3.046$, $p=0.023$) and the relative position of FO_{max} ($z=-2.902$, $p=0.037$). Tendencies for an effect emerged for HNR ($z=1.666$, $p=0.096$) and for the occurrence of frown ($z=1.814$, $p=0.065$). Ironic utterances were better recognised when the frequency of use was lower, when the position of FO_{max} was earlier, when the HNR was higher and when the speaker frowned. The investigation of the recognition of literal utterances showed significant effects of the word intensity ($z=-2.200$, $p=0.028$), the irony-bias of the utterances ($z=2.523$, $p=0.011$), and the occurrence of smiles ($z=-2.152$, $p=0.031$), indicating that the recognition rate of literal utterances is higher when the word intensity is lower, when the speaker does not smile and when the items are categorised as being used more frequent in a literal manner.

The video-only presentation of ironic utterances leads to significant effect of raising of the brows ($z=-2.212$, $p=0.034$) and frowning ($z=3.488$, $p<0.001$) by the speaker. Correct recognised utterances are characterised by less raising of the eyebrows and by more occurrences of frowns. For literal utterances which were presented only visually, no significant effect of the investigated facial parameters were found.

4.4.2 Classification by the listeners

Regardless of the intended realisation, the participants rated auditory presented utterances as being ironic or literal depending of the following variables: word duration, word intensity, FO_{mean}, FO_{SD_ST} and HNR. Utterances were more likely to be categorised as being ironic when the word duration was longer ($z=3.730$, $p<0.001$), when word intensity was lower ($z=-4.000$, $p<0.001$), when the FO_{mean} was lower ($z=-3.974$, $p<0.001$), when its SD (FO_{SD_ST}) was lower ($z=-3.803$, $p<0.001$), and when the HNR was higher (=less noise) ($z=3.429$, $p<0.001$).

Concerning the audio+visual presented stimuli, significant effects of FO_{mean} ($z=-4.790$, $p<0.001$), FO_{SD_ST} ($z=-3.744$, $p<0.001$), HNR ($z=3.215$, $p=0.001$), word intensity ($z=-4.955$, $p<0.001$), smiles ($z=-2.061$, $p=0.034$), and frown ($z=2.524$, $p=0.012$) emerged. In addition, a tendency for an effect of word duration was found ($z=1.712$, $p=0.087$). The listeners rated utterances more frequent as being ironic when $F0_{mean}$, $F0_{SD\_ST}$ and word intensity were lower, when HNR was higher, when the speaker did not smile, when the speaker frowned and when the word duration was longer.

The auditory only presented stimuli received more ironic ratings when the speaker was not smiling ($z=-4.039$, $p<0.001$); when the speaker was frowning ($z=3.237$, $p=0.001$); and when the speaker raised her eyebrows ($z=2.956$, $p=0.003$).

4.4.3 Response times

The response time in the perception experiment was shorter when the listeners correctly identified the intended manner of realisation ($t(1319)=-4.353$, $p<0.001$). The response time for recognising ironic utterances did not differ from the response time for literal utterances ($t(1318)=0.906$, $p=0.365$). The response time was shorter when the video was presented (additionally and solely) compared to the presentation of only the acoustic signal (audio vs. video: $t(1258)=3.259$, $p=0.003$; audio vs. audio+video: $t(1263)=2.803$, $p=0.014$; video vs. audio+video: $t(1303)=-0.436$, $p=0.901$).

The detailed analysis of the response time was equally separated concerning the three presentation modalities. Concerning the stimuli which were only presented auditorily, the acoustic parameters of the signal were used as explanatory variables. For utterances which were produced by the speaker in a literal manner, a significant effect of the standard deviation of F0 ($F0_{SD\_ST}$) was observed ($t(29)=2.390$, $p=0.024$). For the minimal and the maximal F0 values tendencies for an effect occurred ($F0_{min}$: $t(29)=1.838$, $p=0.076$; $F0_{max}$: $t(29)=-1.978$, $p=0.058$). The response time was found to be higher for a larger $F0_{SD\_ST}$, a higher $F0_{min}$ and a lower $F0_{max}$. Ironically produced stimuli were found to influence the response time of the listeners when $F0_{SD\_ST}$ was higher (only tendency: $t(26=1.811$, $p=0.082$), when the word duration was longer ($t(26)=2.448$, $p=0.021$), when $F0_{max}$ was lower ($t(26)=-2.554$, $p=0.017$) and when the words were used less frequently ($t(26)=-2.771$, $p=0.010$).

Separating the acoustically presented items in terms of whether they were perceived as being literal or ironic, the response time analyses revealed for literal perceived items longer response times when $F0_{mean}$ was lower ($t(107)=-2.228$, $p=0.028$), when $F0_{SD\_ST}$ was higher ($t(88)=2.086$, $p=0.040$), when $F0_{range\_ST}$ was lower ($t(102)=-2.123$, $p=0.036$) and when the duration of the word was longer ($t(44)=2.893$, $p=0.006$). Utterances which the listeners classified as being ironic had longer response times when $F0_{SD\_ST}$ was higher ($t(34)=2.189$, $p=0.036$) and when $F0_{max}$ was lower ($t(49)=-2.212$, $p=0.032$).

With regard to the response times on items which were presented auditorily and visually simultaneously, the statistical analyses revealed for literal produced items significant effects of $F0_{mean}$ (t(187)=−4.351, $p<0.001$), $F0_{SD\_ST}$ (t(187)=−2.686, $p=0.008$), $F0_{range\_ST}$ (t(187)=3.853, $p<0.001$), and $F0_{min}$ (t(187)=4.316, $p<0.001$). The response times were longer when the mean F0 was lower, when $F0_{SD\_ST}$ was lower, when $F0_{range\_ST}$ was higher, and when the $F0_{min}$ value within the utterance was higher. For ironically produced items, the response time was longer when the word duration was longer (tendency: t(163)=1.666, $p=0.098$), when $F0_{min}$ was lower (t(163)=−2.807, $p=0.006$) and when the HNR was higher (t(163)=2.331, $p=0.021$).

Audio+visual presented utterances which were perceived as being literal had a longer response time when $F0_{mean}$ was lower (t(186)=−4.358, $p<0.001$), when $F0_{range\_ST}$ was higher (t(187)=3.092, $p=0.002$), when $F0_{SD\_ST}$ was lower (t(186)=−2.259, $p=0.025$) and when $F0_{min}$ was higher (t(187)=3.234, $p=0.001$). In contrast to the former results, for audio+visual presented stimuli which were categorised as being ironic, neither acoustic nor visual properties of the utterances significantly influenced the response times. However, a significant effect emerged for the frequency of use of the utterances (t(151)=2.078, $p=0.039$): The response times were longer for more frequently used items.

When the video-only presentations are under investigation, a significant influence on the response time was only found for utterances which were perceived by the participants as being ironic. When the speaker was frowning, the response time were shorter (t(175)=−3.464, $p<0.001$). In addition, response times were longer when the speaker was raising the eyebrows (t(175)=2.535 $p=0.012$) for ironically perceived utterances.

5 Summary and general discussion

With regard to the production of ironic and literal utterances, the hypotheses stated that ironic realisations of utterances are expected to have a lower mean F0, to be more monotonous (smaller SD of F0 and smaller F0 range), the intensity of the utterances was expected to be lower, as well as longer durations were predicted. Moreover, due to the results of studies on irony in German German (Schmiedel 2017) the HNR was expected to be higher in ironic utterances. With one speaker realising 33 utterances, once ironically, once literally, evidence for some of the hypotheses was found. The ironic realisation of the utterances differed from the literal realisations, as expected, by longer durations, a lower $F0_{mean}$, a lower word intensity, and a higher HNR. However, neither $F0_{SD\_ST}$ nor $F0_{range\_ST}$

differed between the two types of realisations of the investigated speaker. The lack of differences in these two parameters is either explainable by speaker specific strategies to mark irony or by language variety specific characteristics. By contrast with German German, the prosody of Standard Austrian German is different (Ulbrich 2002).

Regarding the facial expression, the presence of eyebrow raising and frown and the absence of smiling can be interpreted as visual cues for irony.

Not all words share the same "irony features"; some differ in one or more measurements from the obtained statistical significant results concerning global differences between literal and ironic utterances. Nevertheless, most of the characteristics are shared by most utterances.

With regard to the perception experiment, it was expected that on the one hand, normal-hearing listeners will be better at recognising verbal irony compared to cochlear-implant listeners. On the other hand, cochlear-implant listeners were expected to benefit more from an additional presentation of visual stimuli, as they show large audio-visual synergy effects (Winn et al. 2013). With the small group of listeners the first part of the hypothesis can partly be supported by the results: One of the cochlear-implant listeners performed worse than all normal-hearing listeners in the audio-only condition. Yet, the other cochlear-implant listener was able to recognise the irony as good as the group of normal-hearing listeners. With the restricted number of participants no evidence for audio-visual synergy effects was found. Equally, the hypothesis that cochlear-implant listeners mainly rely on intensity and durational aspects for their judgments, whereas normal-hearing listeners use F0 and intensity information of the utterances, could neither be proved nor rejected. Since only two cochlear-implant listeners participated in the perception experiment of this pilot study, the outcomes concerning cochlear-implant listeners are not yet interpretable. For all listeners, it seems that durational and intensity cues as well as mean F0 and the standard deviation of F0 are used for the decision whether an utterance is ironic or literal. Yet, the number of speakers and listeners is not large enough to draw conclusions.

So far, most results concerning the response time on the utterances are not conclusive. The fact that listeners were faster when their answer was correct is explainable by longer time of consideration for utterances with ambiguous acoustical and/or visual cues. Since no response time difference between ironic and literal utterances was found, the present results can be interpreted as support for theories which allow a direct processing of ironic meanings of utterances which are presented without any further context. However, due to the limited number of participants, differing results are possible when more speakers and more listeners are under investigation.

6 Conclusion and outlook

Due to the fact that only a pilot study with one speaker and eight listeners (only two of them cochlear-implant listeners) was conducted until now, the generalisability of the results is limited. Yet, the speaker uses quite prototypical acoustic features to mark her ironic utterances. A follow-up study with more speakers of Standard Austrian German revealed results which are highly similar to the results of the one speaker in the present study (Leykum 2019). The results of this first pilot study show that at least some cochlear-implant listeners are able to detect verbal irony at a level comparable to normal-hearing listeners. The analyses were not yet able to figure out which cues are used by cochlear-implant listeners to detect irony in auditory presented utterances. A fine-grained analysis of the facial cues characterising irony has still to be done.

On the one hand, the pilot study gives an insight to the relevant acoustic and visual cues present in verbal irony in Standard Austrian German and their contribution to the recognition of verbal irony by normal-hearing and cochlear-implant listeners. On the other hand, the pilot study shows the directions in which the larger project is currently proceeding and reveals several open questions of which at least some will be investigated within the project in the near future, hopefully contributing valuable findings on the large topic of the production and perception of irony and especially on the perception of irony by cochlear-implant listeners. After extending the study (20 speakers, 20 normal-hearing listeners, 20 cochlear-implant listener), results will not only provide information on irony production by speakers of Standard Austrian German, but will, most importantly, identify the cues and strategies cochlear-implant listeners use to detect verbal irony and thus give insights into the processing of non-verbal and paraverbal cues for the discrimination between literal and ironic utterances. Moreover, differences in the availability of the acoustic cues between the two groups of listeners and the probably greater reliance on facial cues by cochlear-implant listeners will give further insights in the multimodal perception of ironic utterances. The results of the extended study will provide information on whether cochlear-implant listeners only show audio-visual synergy effects for general speech understanding or whether they are also better at integrating the information of both modalities to recognise an ironic intent of utterances.

References

Alghamdi, Najwa, Steve Maddock, Guy J. Brown & Jon Barker. 2015. A comparison of audiovisual and auditory-only training on the perception of spectrally-distorted speech. *Proceedings of the 18th International Congress of Phonetic Sciences (ICPhS)*.

Ambert-Dahan, Emmanuèle. 2014. *Perception des émotions non verbales dans la musique, les voix et les visages chez les adultes implantés cochléaires présentant une surdité évolutive*. Lille: Université de Lille Dissertation.

Anolli, Luigi, Rita Ciceri & Maria G. Infantino. 2000. Irony as a Game of Implicitness: Acoustic Profiles of Ironic Communication. *Journal of Psycholinguistic Research* 29(3). 275–311.

Anolli, Luigi, Rita Ciceri & Maria G. Infantino. 2002. From "blame by praise" to "praise by blame": Analysis of vocal patterns in ironic communication. *International Journal of Psychology* 37(5). 266–276.

Attardo, Salvatore, Jodi Eisterhold, Jennifer Hay & Isabella Poggi. 2003. Multimodal markers of irony and sarcasm. *Humor – International Journal of Humor Research* 16(2). 243–260.

Averbeck, Joshua M. & Dale Hample. 2008. Ironic Message Production: How and Why We Produce Ironic Messages. *Communication Monographs* 75(4). 396–410.

Bates, Douglas, Martin Mächler, Ben Bolker & Steve Walker. 2015. Fitting Linear Mixed-Effects Models Using lme4. *Journal of Statistical Software* 67(1). 1–48.

Braun, Angelika & Christa M. Heilmann. 2012. *SynchronEmotion* (Hallesche Schriften zur Sprechwissenschaft und Phonetik 41), 1st edn. Frankfurt a.M: Peter Lang GmbH Internationaler Verlag der Wissenschaften.

Bryant, Gregory A. & Jean E. Fox Tree. 2002. Recognizing Verbal Irony in Spontaneous Speech. *Metaphor and Symbol* 17(2). 99–119.

Carlyon, Robert P. & John M. Deeks. 2015. Combined neural and behavioural measures of temporal pitch perception in cochlear implant users. *The Journal of the Acoustical Society of America* 138(5). 2885–2905.

Caucci, Gina M. & Roger J. Kreuz. 2012. Social and paralinguistic cues to sarcasm. *Humor* 25(1). 1–22.

Chatterjee, Monita, Danielle J. Zion, Mickael L. Deroche, Brooke A. Burianek, Charles J. Limb, Alison P. Goren, Aditya M. Kulkarni & Julie A. Christensen. 2015. Voice emotion recognition by cochlear-implanted children and their normally-hearing peers. *Hearing research* 322. 151–162.

Cheang, Henry S. & Marc D. Pell. 2008. The sound of sarcasm. *Speech Communication* 50(5). 366–381.

Cheang, Henry S. & Marc D. Pell. 2009. Acoustic markers of sarcasm in Cantonese and English. *The Journal of the Acoustical Society of America* 126(3). 1394–1405.

Chen, Aoju & Lou Boves. 2018. What's in a word: Sounding sarcastic in British English. *Journal of the International Phonetic Association* 48(01). 57–76.

Colston, Herbert L. (this volume). Eye-Rolling, Irony and Embodiment.

Colston, Herbert L. 2002. Contrast and assimilation in verbal irony. *Journal of Pragmatics* 34(2). 111–142.

Cutler, Anne. 1974. On saying what you mean without meaning what you say. *Chicago Linguistic Society: Papers from the Tenth Regional Meeting*. 117–127.

Deliens, Gaétane, Kyriakos Antoniou, Elise Clin, Ekaterina Ostashchenko & Mikhail Kissine. 2018. Context, facial expression and prosody in irony processing. *Journal of Memory and Language* 99. 35–48.

Dews, Shelly, Joan Kaplan & Ellen Winner. 1995. Why not say it directly?: The social functions of irony. *Discourse Processes* 19(3). 347–367.

Dews, Shelly & Ellen Winner. 1999. Obligatory processing of literal and nonliteral meanings in verbal irony. *Journal of Pragmatics* 31(12). 1579–1599.

Dorman, Michael F., Maureen T. Hannley, Korine Dankowski, Luke Smith & Geary McCandless. 1989. Word recognition by 50 patients fitted with the Symbion multicannel cochlear implant. *Ear and hearing* 10(1). 44–49.

Gfeller, Kate, Christopher Turner, Jacob Oleson, Xuyang Zhang, Bruce Gantz, Rebecca Froman & Carol Olszewski. 2007. Accuracy of cochlear implant recipients on pitch perception, melody recognition, and speech reception in noise. *Ear and hearing* 28(3). 412–423.

Gibbs, Raymond W. 1994. Figurative thought and figurative language. In Morton A. Gernsbacher (ed.), *Handbook of psycholinguistics*, 412–446. San Diego: Academic Press.

Gibbs, Raymond W. 2000. Irony in Talk Among Friends. *Metaphor and Symbol* 15(1–2). 5–27.

Gibbs, Raymond W. 2002. A new look at literal meaning in understanding what is said and implicated. *Journal of Pragmatics* 34(4). 457–486.

Gibbs, Raymond W. & Herbert L. Colston. 2002. The Risks and Rewards of Ironic Communication. In Luigi Anolli, Rita Ciceri & Giuseppe Riva (eds.), *Say not to say*: New perspectives on miscommunication (Emerging communication 3), 181–194. Amsterdam: IOS Press.

Giora, Rachel. 2002. Literal vs. figurative language: Different or equal? *Journal of Pragmatics* 34. 487–506.

González-Fuente, Santiago, Victoria Escandell-Vidal & Pilar Prieto. 2015. Gestural codas pave the way to the understanding of verbal irony. *Journal of Pragmatics* 90. 26–47.

González-Fuente, Santiago, Pilar Prieto & Ira Noveck. 2016. A fine-grained analysis of the acoustic cues involved in verbal irony recognition in French. *Speech Prosody*. 902–906.

Grice, Paul. 1989. *Studies in the Way of Words*. Cambridge, Massachusetts: Harvard University Press.

Hancock, Jeffrey T. 2004. Verbal Irony Use in Face-To-Face and Computer-Mediated Conversations. *Journal of Language and Social Psychology* 23(4). 447–463.

Hey, M., G. Brademann & P. Ambrosch. 2016. Der Freiburger Einsilbertest in der postoperativen CI-Diagnostik. *HNO* 64(8). 601–607.

Jorgensen, Julia. 1996. The functions of sarcastic irony in speech. *Journal of Pragmatics* 26(5). 613–634.

Khokhlova, Maria, Viviana Patti & Paolo Rosso. 2016. Distinguishing between irony and sarcasm in social media texts: Linguistic observations. *Proceedings of the International FRUCT Conference on Intelligence, Social Media and Web (ISMW FRUCT 2016)*.

Kreft, Heather A., Gail S. Donaldson & David A. Nelson. 2004. Effects of pulse rate and electrode array design on intensity discrimination in cochlear implant users. *The Journal of the Acoustical Society of America* 116(4 Pt 1). 2258–2268.

Kreuz, Roger J. & Gina M. Caucci. 2009. Social aspects of verbal irony use. In Hanna Pishwa (ed.), *Language and social cognition*: Expression of the social mind (Trends in linguistics Studies and monographs 206), 325–345. Berlin: Mouton De Gruyter.

Laval, Virginie & Alain Bert-Erboul. 2005. French-Speaking Children's Understanding of Sarcasm: The Role of Intonation and Context. *Journal of Speech, Language, and Hearing Research* 48. 610–620.

Leiner, Dominik J. 2014. *SoSci Survey*.

Leykum, Hannah. 2019. Acoustic Characteristics of Verbal Irony in Standard Austrian German. *Proceedings of the 19th International Congress of Phonetic Sciences (ICPhS)*. 3398–3402.

Lœvenbruck, Hélène, Mohamed Ameur Ben Jannet, Mariapaola D'Imperio, Mathilde Spini & Maud Champagne-Lavau. 2013. Prosodic cues of sarcastic speech in French: Slower, higher, wider. *Proceedings of the Annual Conference of the International Speech Communication Association, INTERSPEECH.* 3537–3541.

Loizou, Philipos C., Michael Dorman, Oguz Poroy & Tony Spahr. 2000. Speech recognition by normal-hearing and cochlear implant listeners as a function of intensity resolution. *The Journal of the Acoustical Society of America* 108(5). 2377.

Luo, Xin, Qian-Jie Fu & John J. Galvin. 2007. Vocal emotion recognition by normal-hearing listeners and cochlear implant users. *Trends in amplification* 11(4). 301–315.

Moore, Brian C. J. & Robert P. Carlyon. 2005. Perception of Pitch by People with Cochlear Hearing Loss and by Cochlear Implant Users. In Christopher J. Plack, Richard R. Fay, Andrew J. Oxenham & Arthur N. Popper (eds.), *Pitch: Neural Coding and Perception* (Springer Handbook of Auditory Research), 234–277. New York: Springer-Verlag.

Nauke, Astrid & Angelika Braun. 2011. The production and perception of irony in short context-free utterances. *Proceedings of the 17th International Congress of Phonetic Sciences (ICPhS).* 1450–1453.

Niebuhr, Oliver. 2014. "A little more ironic" – Voice quality and segmental reduction differences between sarcastic and neutral utterances. *7th International Conference of Speech Prosody.* 608–612.

Noll, Anton, Jonathan White, Peter Balazs & Werner Deutsch. 2007. *STx – Intelligent Sound Processing, Programmer's Reference.*

Nuolijärvi, Pirkko & Liisa Tiittula. 2011. Irony in political television debates. *Journal of Pragmatics* 43(2). 572–587.

Peirce, Jonathan W. 2007. PsychoPy--Psychophysics software in Python. *Journal of neuroscience methods* 162(1–2). 8–13.

Pexman, Penny M. & Kara M. Olineck. 2002. Does Sarcasm Always Sting?: Investigating the Impact of Ironic Insults and Ironic Compliments. *Discourse Processes* 33(3). 199–217.

R Core Team. 2015. *R: A Language and Environment for Statistical Computing.* Vienna, Austria.

Rockwell, Patricia. 2000. Lower, Slower, Louder: Vocal Cues of Sarcasm. *Journal of Psycholinguistic Research* 29(5). 483–495.

Rockwell, Patricia. 2001. Facial Expression and Sarcasm. *Perceptual and motor skills* 93. 47–50.

Rosenblum, Lawrence D. 2008. Speech Perception as a Multimodal Phenomenon. *Current directions in psychological science* 17(6). 405–409.

Scharrer, Lisa & Ursula Christmann. 2011. Voice Modulations in German Ironic Speech. *Language and Speech* 54(4). 435–465.

Schmiedel, Astrid. 2017. *Phonetik ironischer Sprechweise: Produktion und Perzeption sarkastisch ironischer und freundlich ironischer Äußerungen* (Schriften zur Sprechwissenschaft und Phonetik Band 8). Berlin: Frank & Timme.

Schwoebel, John, Shelly Dews, Ellen Winner & Kavitha Srinivas. 2000. Obligatory Processing of the Literal Meaning of Ironic Utterances: Further Evidence. *Metaphor and Symbol* 15(1–2). 47–61.

Tabacaru, Sabina. (this volume). Faces of sarcasm: Exploring raised eyebrows with sarcasm in French political debates.

Teixeira, João P., Carla Oliveira & Carla Lopes. 2013. Vocal Acoustic Analysis – Jitter, Shimmer and HNR Parameters. *Procedia Technology* 9. 1112–1122.

Ulbrich, Christiane. 2002. A Comparative Study of Intonation in Three Standard Varieties of German. *Speech Prosody.* 671–674.

Voyer, Daniel & Cheryl Techentin. 2010. Subjective Auditory Features of Sarcasm. *Metaphor and Symbol* 25(4). 227–242.

Williams, Jason A., Erin L. Burns & Elizabeth A. Harmon. 2009. Insincere utterances and gaze: eye contact during sarcastic statements. *Perceptual and motor skills* 108(2). 565–572.

Winn, Matthew B., Ariane E. Rhone, Monita Chatterjee & William J. Idsardi. 2013. The use of auditory and visual context in speech perception by listeners with normal hearing and listeners with cochlear implants. *Frontiers in psychology* 4: 824.

Zeng, Fan-Gang, Stephen Rebscher, William Harrison, Xiaoan Sun & Haihong Feng. 2008. Cochlear implants: system design, integration, and evaluation. *IEEE reviews in biomedical engineering* 1. 115–142.

Index

Acoustic analyses 281, 289, 291
Affect 15–61
– Affect-drivenness 29, 34, 35–37, 39, 59, 60
Affective attitude 135
Affectively framed value 35, 36, 38, 51, 60
Amazon Mechanical Turk 242, 243
Appeal 219–224, 230, 232
As a blood clot 7
Attenuation 17, 26, 29, 31, 32, 35–38, 49, 51–53, 55, 56, 59, 60
Attitude 18, 24, 39, 45, 46, 109, 112, 113, 117, 118, 120, 123, 124, 128, 129
ATT-Meta 17, 19, 32, 41–43, 45–51, 53–55, 57–59
Attributed 183

Benign violation 149, 155, 156
Benign violation theory of humor 137
Body politic 162, 169–172
Bystander 237, 250, 252

Cantonese-L1 162, 174
Cognitive processing 16
Common ground 258, 263, 264, 266, 268, 274
Compounding/compounds of figures 4, 40, 91, 92, 104.
Conceptual metaphor 137, 140, 156
Conceptual tool 134, 136, 137
Constructional parameters 78
Construction Grammar 81
Constructions 66–75
Context 115, 118, 125, 127
Contrast 25, 29, 59–61
Conventionalized 112, 114, 119
Corpus-based 68–71, 74, 75
Co-speech gesture 211, 214
Creativity 256

Default 66–75
– Defaultness Hypothesis 66–70, 74, 75
– interpretations 66–70, 74, 75
– nondefault 66–75

Demonstrativeness 219, 223
Detachment 213, 219, 220, 224, 233
Disapproval display 211–215, 220, 226, 231, 232
Discourse 108, 162, 164–167, 169, 177
Discourse context 108, 122, 125
Dissociative attitude 183, 194, 195, 200
Drama 20–28, 32, 34, 37–40, 49, 50, 53, 54, 57, 58, 60, 61
Dramatic irony 238, 239, 248

Echoing 183, 206
Ekman 260, 261, 270, 272, 273
Elliptical *if*-clauses 80
Embodied 135, 138, 154, 257
Embodied irony 219, 223
Embodiment 211, 213–233
Emotions 260–262, 273
Emphasis 91
Encrypted 137, 141
Encryption 137
English-L1 162, 164, 172, 174, 176, 177
Evaluative statement 237, 241, 242
Experiment 71
Eyebrow movement 257
Eye-roll/eye-rolling 211–233

Facial expression 18, 20, 24, 39, 256, 260–263, 272–274
Ficitvely-elaborating hyperbole 59
Fiction 41, 49, 57, 58
Fictively-elaborating hyperbole 25–29, 54
Focus 185, 188, 195, 201, 203–205
Focus fronting 188
FORCE 137, 154
Frame 256, 258, 272–273
Frame Semantics 81
Frequency of use 285, 287, 288, 295, 297
Frowning 264

Gestural triggers 256, 257, 260–261, 273
Gesture 211, 212, 214, 215, 222, 223, 263, 272, 274

Humor/Humour 1, 2, 133–137, 140–144, 146, 149–151, 154, 157–158, 164, 212, 256–258, 260–261, 272
Hyperbole 15–61, 91, 107, 109–111, 113, 114, 116, 117, 120–122, 124, 126–128
–*fictively-elaborating* hyperbole 19, 25–29, 54, 59
Hyperbolic irony 91
Hyperbolic metaphor 49, 53, 91
Hyperbolic tinges 99
Hyper-understanding 258, 261

Implicature 118, 119
Indirect relational tool 136
Intensification 27–30, 54, 55, 59, 184, 185, 191, 204, 206
Intention 257, 262, 273
Interaction 257, 260, 261, 274
Interpretations 66–70, 73–75
– default 66–70, 74, 75
– literal 68, 73
– nondefault 66, 68, 75
– sarcastic 68–70, 75
Interpretive effect 93
Intersubjectivity 243, 250
Intonation 18, 22, 30, 39
Ironic humor 134
Ironic metaphor 91
Irony 91, 123, 126, 162, 164, 166–171, 176, 177, 211–233, 257
– echoic irony 164, 167, 177
– pretense irony 164, 177
– self-irony 162, 169, 170, 177
Irony evocation 83
Irony/metaphor compounds 49, 57, 59
Irony signal 20, 30

Lack of control 219, 222–223
Layering 258
Layers 256, 258, 272

Mandarin L1 162, 174
Manner of use 285, 286
Mapping 17, 29–32, 43–49, 59
Meaning coordination 256
Mechanical Turk 245
Mental Space 238, 239, 249

Mental spaces theory 258
Metacommunicative *if*-clauses 83, 88
Metaphor 15–19, 41–48, 91
– hyperbolic metaphor 17, 59
Metaphor comprehension 162
Metaphor scenario 162, 168, 171, 177, 286, 288
Motivational complexity 224
Multifunctional 133, 141, 142, 144, 153, 157
Multifunctional relational tool 134
Multimodality 256–257

Nation 162, 163, 165, 170–177
Nationalism 163, 164, 170–172, 176, 177
Nonverbal behavior 211, 214, 225
Normative point 95

Opposition operator 28, 29
Optimality 213, 219, 223, 224, 233
Order of interpretation 91

Physical experience 219, 221, 222
Political debates 256, 257, 262
Pragmatic 258, 273
Pretence/Pretense 15–61, 218, 222, 223, 232
Pretense-as-drama approach 20
Pretense Theory 135
Processing 66
– in context 67, 68
– out of context 69
– speed 74
Production 66–75

Questionnaire 162, 163, 170, 172, 175–177

Raised eyebrows 256, 261, 263, 264, 266, 267, 269, 274
Relevance-theoretic account 135
Relevance Theory 183
Resonance (contextual) 70
– prior 70
– subsequent 70

Sarcasm 66–68, 70, 71, 74, 162, 164, 166–168, 177, 256–257, 259, 261, 262, 264, 266, 268, 272–274
–affirmative 68, 70
–negative 66, 74

Satires 20
Saving face 139, 141, 144, 146, 154, 156, 157
Sentiment analysis 251, 252
Situational irony 238, 248
Social cohesion 133, 134, 136, 146, 147, 149, 154–157
Standard Austrian German 280, 288, 290, 298, 299
Subject inversion 186, 188

Understatement 67

Verbal irony 79, 211, 214, 216–218, 220, 223, 225, 226, 232, 233
Verum focus 183, 185, 195, 202–203
View-of-a-viewpoint 236, 237, 239, 247, 251

Zoom-out configurations 236, 238, 247